Neo-Slavism and the Czechs
1898–1914

T0382440

SOVIET AND EAST EUROPEAN STUDIES

Neo-Slavism and the Czechs
1898–1914

PAUL VYŠNÝ

Lecturer in Modern History
University of St Andrews

CAMBRIDGE UNIVERSITY PRESS

CAMBRIDGE

LONDON · NEW YORK · MELBOURNE

CAMBRIDGE UNIVERSITY PRESS
Cambridge, New York, Melbourne, Madrid, Cape Town, Singapore,
São Paulo, Delhi, Dubai, Tokyo

Cambridge University Press
The Edinburgh Building, Cambridge CB2 8RU, UK

Published in the United States of America by Cambridge University Press, New York

www.cambridge.org
Information on this title: www.cambridge.org/9780521134453

First published 1977
This digitally printed version 2010

A catalogue record for this publication is available from the British Library

Library of Congress Cataloguing in Publication data
Vyšný, Paul, 1944–
Neo-Slavism and the Czechs, 1898–1914
(Soviet and East European studies)
Bibliography: p.
Includes index.
1. Bohemia–Intellectual life. 2. Panslavism.
I. Title. II. Series.
DB215.V95   943.7'02   76–4239

ISBN 978-0-521-21230-4 Hardback
ISBN 978-0-521-13445-3 Paperback

Contents

Bulgarians
Croats
Czechs
Great Russians
Lusatian Sorbs
Poles
Serbs
Slovaks
Slovenes
Ukrainians
White Russians

State boundaries
Internal boundaries
Ethnographic. boundaries

(Broken shading indicates areas including non-Slav peoples.)

Baltic Sea

W. Dvina

St Pet

Berlin

GERMANY

Elbe

Oder

Vistula

Warsaw

R   U   U

Ki

BOHEMIA
Prague

MORAVIA

GALICJA

Lvov

Danube

Vienna

Dniester

AUSTRIA — HUNGARY

Budapest

BUKOVINA

Drave

Po

Tisza

CROATIA-SLAVONIA
Sava

BOSNIA

Belgrade

RUMANIA

Bucharest

DALMATIA

HERZE-
GOVINA

SERBIA

Danube

ITALY

Adriatic Sea

BULGARIA

Sofia

MONTENEGRO

OTTOMAN

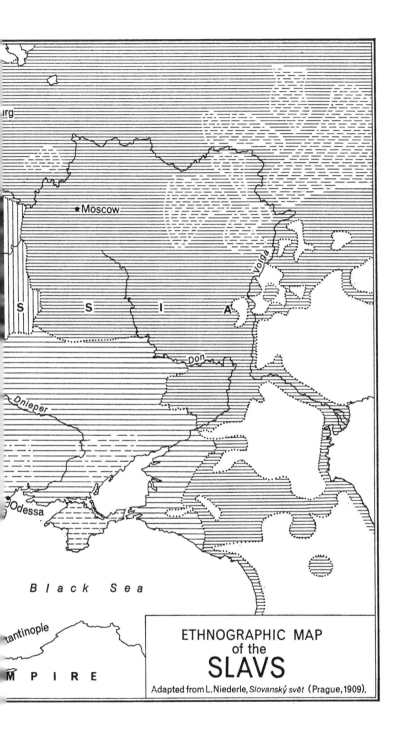

Moscow

Volga

S   S   I   A

Don

Dnieper

Odessa

B l a c k   S e a

tantinople

M P I R E

ETHNOGRAPHIC MAP
of the
SLAVS
Adapted from L. Niederle, *Slovanský svět* (Prague, 1909).

rg

Preface

The object of this study is to examine the extent and significance of a phenomenon known as the Neo-Slav movement, which flourished briefly in Eastern Europe during the decade immediately preceding the outbreak of the First World War. The movement was instigated, to a large extent, from within the Czech national leadership, with the principal aim of promoting greater understanding between the Slav peoples, thus making possible effective political co-operation amongst the Slavs of the Austro-Hungarian Empire. The founders of the Neo-Slav movement, who came largely from the Czech industrial and commercial middle class which provided the main political leadership of the nation at the time, were further motivated by the desire to improve relations between the Czech and Russian nations, with a view to increasing commercial contact.

In order to establish a background to the study of Neo-Slavism a brief analysis is also made of the differing attitudes adopted towards the Slav world in general, and Russia in particular, by various sections of the Czech and, to a lesser extent, also the Slovak nations, and of the responses these evoked from diverse circles in Russia and elsewhere.

Two valuable, though incomplete, works concerned specifically with the Neo-Slav movement have been published. E. Beneš devoted one chapter of his study of aspects of Slavism, *Úvahy o slovanství. Hlavní problémy slovanské politiky* (Prague, 1947), to the examination of Neo-Slavism. This work is essentially a critique of the movement through the eyes of a western orientated Czech political leader. The second publication, an article by K. Herman, 'Novoslovanství a česká buržoasie', which appeared in the symposium *Kapitoly z dějin vzájemných vztahů národů ČSR a SSSR* (Prague, 1958), provides a Marxist analysis of the subject. Further important sources of information on Neo-Slavism are the numerous writings of Karel Kramář, the Czech political leader who was responsible for founding the movement. The most significant of these are Kramář's reply to the criticism expressed by Beneš, *Na obranu slovanské politiky* (Prague, 1926), and a discussion of Czech foreign policy, *Pět přednášek o zahraniční politice* (Prague, 1922).

Unpublished primary sources consulted during the course of this study were the (now somewhat depleted) documents from the Austro-Hungarian Ministry of Foreign Affairs and various internal administrative bodies, in the Vienna Haus-, Hof- und Staatsarchiv, and the diplomatic and other reports in the Foreign Office files of the Public Record Office in London.[1] The material in the Vienna archives has been partly used in an unpublished doctoral dissertation for the University of Vienna by O. Heinz, 'Der Neoslawismus' (1963). Czech archival sources have been utilised by Herman – the Archive of the Czech National Council in the earlier mentioned study 'Novoslovanství a česká buržoasie'; and the few surviving relevant private papers of Kramář in K. Herman and Z. Sládek, 'Slovanská politika Karla Kramáře', *Rozpravy československé akadime věd: Řada společenských věd*, LXXXI, no. 2 (1971). A limited use of relevant unpublished Russian documents has been made in an article by J. Křížek, 'Česká buržoasní politika a "česká otázka" v letech 1900–1914', in *Československý časopis historický*, IV (1958). Collections of published documents from Czech, Russian, Austro-Hungarian, British and other sources have also been consulted. The voluminous published record of the treason trial conducted against Kramář by the Habsburg authorities during 1915 and 1916, *Proces dra. Kramáře a jeho přátel* (Prague, 1918), has been an invaluable source of information, as have the various official publications of the Neo-Slav movement, the records of congress proceedings, *Jednání I. přípravného slovanského sjezdu v Praze 1908* (Prague, 1910), and *Vtori podgotovitelen Slavyanski săbor v Sofiya* (Sofia, 1911), and reports on various projects prepared by special committees. Extensive use has also been made of reports and articles in contemporary Czech, Slovak, Russian, and other periodicals and newspapers. The Czech daily newspapers, *Národní listy* and *Čas*; the Russian newspapers *Novoe vremya* and *Rech'*; and the authoritative Czech periodical publication devoted to Slav affairs,

---

[1] Transcripts and translations of archival material appear by permission of the authorities of both institutions.

Slovanský přehled, have proved most useful in this category. These sources were supplemented by the memoirs and recollections of persons involved in, or observing, the events under study, such as the account of the Prague Congress of 1908 as recorded by the Russian delegate, Count V. A. Bobrinsky, *Prazhsky sezd. Chekhiya i Prikarpatskaya Rus'* (St Petersburg, 1909).

In recent years, Czechoslovak historians have devoted increased attention to the study of Czechoslovak–Russian relations and several general works concerned with this subject have been published. Typical of these publications are the book by I. Pfaff and V. Závodský, *Tradice česko-ruských vztahů v dějinách* (Prague, 1957), and the work edited by V. Čejchan, *Dějiny česko-ruských vztahů 1770–1917* (Prague, 1967; vol. 1 of *Dějiny československo-sovětských vztahů nové a nejnovější doby*). An earlier work of this nature is by J. Jirásek, *Rusko a my. Dějiny vztahů československo-ruských od nejstarších dob do roku 1914* (2nd edn, Prague, 1945). Concerned specifically with the role played by Imperial Russia in the formation of the independent Czechoslovak state is the book by J. Papoušek, *Carské Rusko a naše osvobození* (Prague, 1927). Other works have placed the interaction between the Czech and Slovak nations and Russia in the context of the wider relationship between the Slav peoples. A recent Czechoslovak publication in this category is the collection of essays entitled, *Slovanství v národním životě Čechů a Slováků* (Prague, 1968), edited by V. Šťastný and others. A comprehensive survey of the development of relations between the Slav community of nations is contained in H. Kohn's *Pan-Slavism: Its History and Ideology* (Notre Dame, 1953). The same subject is examined from the German point of view by A. Fischel in *Der Panslavismus bis zum Weltkrieg* (Stuttgart–Berlin, 1919).

Useful material on the general social and political history of the Czech and Slovak nations is contained in the relevant volumes of the following large works: Z. V. Tobolka, *Politické dějiny československého národa* (Prague, 1932–1936), and *Přehled československých dějin* (Prague, 1960), published by the Czechoslovak Academy of Sciences (*Československá akademie věd*). Two general books on Czechoslovak history are also available in the English language, R. W. Seton-Watson's *A History of the Czechs and Slovaks* (London, 1943), and S. H. Thomson's *Czechoslovakia in European History* (Princeton, 1953), though both are concerned only briefly with the 1898 to 1914 period. E. Wiskemann's *Czechs and Germans* (London, 1938), subtitled *A Study of the Struggle in the Historic Provinces of Bohemia and Moravia*, contains material on the domestic situation in the Czech lands relevant to the period under examination. A similar study of the racial strife in the Hungarian section of the Habsburg Empire, in which the Slovaks were involved, was made by R. W. Seton-Watson in *Racial Problems in Hungary* (London, 1908). Other works by this indefatigable writer on Slav affairs, concerned with a variety of related subjects, have also provided valuable information.

Of the multitude of books concerned with the examination of Russia, including the period preceding the First World War, most frequent use has been made of the two works by H. Seton-Watson, *The Decline of Imperial Russia, 1855–1914* (London, 1952), and *The Russian Empire, 1801–1917* (London, 1967). Both these books provide not only the Russian background to this study, but also outline the relationship between Russia and the other Slav nations. Further background material on Russia was obtained from M. T. Florinsky's *Russia: A History and an Interpretation* (2 vols., New York, 1960). Books on the Austro-Hungarian Empire are also plentiful. Most relevant, on account of the attention devoted to the component nationalities of the Dual Monarchy (including the Czechs and Slovaks), are the comprehensive two volume study by R. A. Kann, *The Multinational Empire: Nationalism and National Reform in the Habsburg Monarchy, 1848–1918* (New York, 1950) and the more analytical work by O. Jaszi, *The Dissolution of the Habsburg Monarchy* (2nd edn, Chicago, 1961). A valuable examination of the problems concerning the Czech nation in the nineteenth century and early years of the twentieth is provided by A. J. P. Taylor in *The Habsburg Monarchy, 1809–1918. A History of the Austrian Empire and Austria–Hungary* (2nd edn, London, 1948). Two other books of a general historical nature, A. J. May, *The Hapsburg Monarchy, 1867–1914* (Cambridge, Mass., 1951) and C. A. Macartney, *The Habsburg Empire, 1790–1918* (London, 1968), have also been used to establish the background to the narrative.

The principal works consulted for material on the wider field of European political history during the early years of the twentieth century, in which framework relations between the Czechs and Slovaks on the one hand and the Russians on the other have to be seen, were the multivolume survey by L. Albertini, *The Origins of the War of 1914* (Translated and edited by I. M. Massey, 3 vols., London, 1952–1957) and A. J. P. Taylor's *The Struggle for Mastery in Europe, 1848–1918* (Oxford, 1957). Amongst the detailed studies of specific occurrences in Europe during this period two are particularly important, as the events with which they are concerned had considerable repercussions on the Slav world and influenced the relations between the Czech and Slovak nations and Russia: these works are B. E. Schmitt's detailed analysis of the crisis precipitated by the Austro-Hungarian annexation of Bosnia and Herzegovina, *The Annexation of Bosnia, 1908–1909* (Cambridge, 1937), and the examination of the Balkan conflicts, which shortly preceded the First World War, by E. C. Helmreich, *The Diplomacy of the Balkan Wars, 1912–1913* (Harvard, 1938).

A significant problem in a study of this nature is that of circumscription. Natural boundaries, both spatial and chronological, are few, and consequently many of the delineations chosen are, to a certain extent, arbitrary. Most artificial are the boundaries of time. In this case the period under examination extends from 1898, approximately the time when the Czech political leadership became conscious of the importance of a 'foreign policy', to the outbreak of the First World War in 1914 when the objectives of the Neo-Slav movement lost their relevance. The War itself forms a period distinct from the one preceding it. The world conflict brought into question the continued existence of the Austro-Hungarian Empire, and Czechoslovak independence became, for the first time, a serious possibility. However, as historical information is not available in such convenient packages, these boundaries are inevitably on occasions transgressed. The geographical limits are equally arbitrary. The Czech lands and Slovakia were, at the time, components of the Habsburg Empire and it is, therefore, not possible to examine them in isolation. They have to be seen in the general context of Austria–Hungary, for which purpose it has been necessary to introduce a certain amount of material concerned with the Empire as a whole. Similarly, the Neo-Slav movement was only one aspect of the complex pattern of relationships between the Slav nations, and has to be seen in this wider Slav perspective.

The normal practice has been followed in transliterating names from languages using the Cyrillic script – Russian, Bulgarian, and

Serbian. Czech, Slovak, Polish, Slovene, Croatian, and German names appear unaltered. The exceptions are certain geographical names (such as Prague or Moscow) which have accepted English forms.

A further problem in any work concerned with pre-revolutionary Russia is that of dates, due to the fact that the Old style Julian calendar remained in use in Russia and elsewhere until 1918. In the main text dates are generally given according to the New Style Gregorian calendar in use in most of Europe. For the sake of clarity though, when dealing with events taking place in a country where the Julian calendar remained in use, the Old Style dates are also given in parentheses. In the footnote references however, the dating of sources is given in the form in which it appears on the original.

Finally, I would like to record my thanks to all those who provided assistance in the various stages of the production of this study, particularly to my wife, Helen, for her help throughout.

P. V.

St Andrews
September 1975

I

Introduction

At the beginning of the twentieth century, the map of Central and South-Eastern Europe was dominated by the vast form of the Habsburg Monarchy. This Empire, consisting of two separate units, Austria and Hungary,[1] both ruled by the House of Habsburg, extended over 600000 square kilometres, and contained within its boundaries close upon 45 million people of almost a dozen different nationalities. The dual structure of Austria–Hungary had been brought into being by the *Ausgleich* (or compromise), agreed between the Austrian Germans and the Magyars in 1867. Financial, foreign, and military affairs remained under joint control; for the purpose of internal administration, however, the Empire was divided into two equal and distinct parts.

Table 1. *Population statistics for the nationalities in the Austrian lands in 1900*[2]

Nationality	Total number	Percentage of total population
German	9170939	35.78
Czechs (including Slovaks)	5955397	23.24
Poles	4259152	16.62
Ukrainians	3375576	13.18
Slovenes	1192780	4.65
Italians	727102	2.83
Serbs and Croats	711380	2.77
Rumanians	230963	0.90
Magyars	9516	0.03

[1] Strictly speaking, Austria did not exist. Those parts of the Dual Monarchy which were ruled from Vienna were officially termed 'the Kingdoms and Lands represented in the Reichsrat'. The Hungarian part of the Empire was known as the Kingdom of Hungary.

[2] K.K. Statistiche Central-Commission, *Österreichisches Statistisches Handbuch, 1901* (Vienna, 1902), p. 5.

Table 2. *Population statistics for the nationalities
in Hungary in 1900*[3]

Nationality	Total number	Percentage of total population
Magyars	8 742 301	45.4
Rumanians	2 799 479	14.5
Germans	2 135 181	11.1
Slovaks	2 019 641	10.5
Croats	1 678 569	8.7
Serbs	1 052 180	5.5
Ukrainians	429 447	2.2
Others	397 761	2.1

The two components of the Dual Monarchy each followed
different paths of political development. At the turn of the century
the Austrian territories were controlled by the predominantly
German bureaucracy from Vienna, and Hungary was ruled by the
Magyar nobility from Budapest.

Within these lands, administered respectively by Germans and
Magyars, there lived, alongside the dominant national groups,
considerable numbers of people of other nationalities (see Tables
1, 2). In the Dual Monarchy as a whole, aligned against 12 million
Germans and 9 million Magyars, were 20 million Slavs and
4 million people of other nationalities.[4] It is hardly surprising,
therefore, that German–Magyar hegemony had to contend with
considerable opposition.

During the last half century of its existence – a period marked by
a great increase of national awareness in Central Europe which
followed the revolutionary upheavals of 1848[5] – the Habsburg
Empire became a cauldron of effervescent nationalism. Each
national group present in the Dual Monarchy began to assert its
nationality and to voice demands frequently conflicting, not only

---

[3] L'Office Central de Statistique du Royaume de Hongrie, *Annuaire statistique
hongrois, 1901* (Budapest, 1903), pp. 24–5.

[4] In practice, however, the nationalities did not form political groupings
exclusively along ethnic lines. The Poles, for example, showed little inclination
to form an alliance with the other Austrian Slavs, and loyally supported the
Habsburg authorities.

[5] The year 1848 marked the transition of Czech nationalism from an essentially
cultural and linguistic nature to a political and economic form

Introduction 3

with the interests of the state, but also with those of other nationalities, with whom they were often intermingled or living in close
proximity. Some nationalities, such as the Italians and the Serbs,
displayed irredentist tendencies, wishing to be united with their
compatriots outside Austria–Hungary. The majority, however,
including the Czechs, Germans, Poles, and Magyars, each wanted
the state to act in their own interest, which was frequently at the
expense of their national rivals. In the Austrian parts of the
Empire, no single nationality was sufficiently large, or sufficiently
powerful, entirely to subdue the others. In Hungary, on the other
hand, the Magyars, due to their numerical, economic, and cultural
superiority, were more successful in establishing and maintaining
their hegemony.

The territories of Austria–Hungary inhabited predominantly by
the Czechs and Slovaks, which constitute the present day Czechoslovakia, were, under the Habsburgs, divided between the two
components of the Monarchy. Bohemia, Moravia, and Silesia,
known as the Lands of the Crown of St Wenceslas, or Czech
Crownlands, were distinct constitutional territories, with separate
local legislative assemblies (Diets). These lands enjoyed a limited
measure of political and cultural autonomy within the Austrian

Table 3. *Statistics for the nationalities in
the Czech lands in 1900*[6]

	Nationality	Percentage of population
Bohemia	Czechs	62.68
	Germans	37.26
	Others	0.06
Moravia	Czechs	71.36
	Germans	27.90
	Poles	0.65
	Others	0.09
Silesia	Germans	44.69
	Poles	33.21
	Czechs	22.04
	Others	0.06

[6] K.K. Statistische Central-Commission, *Österreichisches Statistisches Handbuch*,
1901, p. 5. In Lower Austria there were 132 000 Czech inhabitants, more than
4 % of the population.

state. Slovakia, on the other hand, was an integral part of Hungary, with no autonomy whatsoever.

The above-mentioned areas were not, however, exclusively inhabited by Slavs. As in many other parts of Austria–Hungary, here also, the nationalities were inextricably intermingled, and many Czechs also lived in other parts of the Empire (see Table 3). In Hungary, within the twenty-one administrative areas which approximately constitute present day Slovakia, the Slovaks formed – according to official statistics – an absolute majority in eleven areas, and over a quarter of the population in a further four. The other nationality most strongly represented in the predominantly Slovak areas of northern Hungary were the Magyars, but Germans and Ukrainians were also present. Sizable Slovak colonies also existed elsewhere in Hungary outside the main Slovak region.[7]

Out of the multitude of national disputes which were causing serious disruption in the Habsburg Empire, two are of particular concern to this study. The first, and most important, was the virulent and clamorous conflict between the Czech and German inhabitants of the Czech Crownlands; and the second, the less evident, though no less acrimonious, struggle between the Slovaks and Magyars in northern Hungary.

The conflict between the Czechs and Germans,[8] because of its magnitude and protracted nature one of the most serious racial disputes within the Dual Monarchy, manifested itself during the latter half of the nineteenth century and the early years of the twentieth principally through the question of language, which had two main interlinked implications in the fields of education and administration. The Czechs, in common with other minority nationalities, objected to the predominance of the official German language, and demanded equal status for their own native tongue. They required that each Czech should receive a Czech education, and that the state administration should deal with each person in his national language. These demands were not made purely out

---

[7] L'Office Central de Statistique du Royaume de Hongrie, *Annuaire statistique hongrois, 1901*, pp. 22–5. In Southern Hungary in the county of Békés, Slovak inhabitants numbered 64000, constituting more than 23 % of the population; and in the adjacent county of Csanád, 17000 Slovaks accounted for over 12 % of the inhabitants.

[8] For details see E. Wiskemann, *Czechs and Germans: A Study of the Struggle in the Historic Provinces of Bohemia and Moravia* (London, 1938).

of a desire to satisfy national pride, for the consequences of such changes would be also of a political and economic nature. The spread of Czech education, in addition to increasing the national awareness and thus the cohesiveness of the nation, also strengthened it economically.[9] The introduction of bilingual administration would enable the Czechs to break the German monopoly in the civil service, and thus lead to greater opportunities for employment. Most educated Czechs spoke German, a world language, but few Germans were prepared to learn Czech, spoken only by the Czechs. The Bohemian Germans, in order to preserve their dominant position in areas where they were concentrated, resisted linguistic equality, but favoured the administrative division of the province into national areas. The Czechs, however, fiercely defended the indivisibility of Bohemia.[10]

The economic and accompanying social issues were significant aspects of the Czech–German dispute. Due largely to the fact that most of the financial resources of the Empire were in German hands, the economic development of Austria led to German ascendancy in the new industrial society. The initial growth of industry in Austria was not fostered by a middle-class coalition of the component nationalities, but by purely German enterprise. This uneven national distribution of industrial ownership was the cause of much additional friction between the nationalities. In Bohemia, a Czech middle-class grew up in opposition to the German bourgeoisie. They began to struggle for their own banking capital, and demanded autonomy in matters of taxation. This situation led to a remarkable degree of national unity. National antagonism cut across social stratifications, and most levels of Czech society were united in their struggle against the dominant German national group.

The basis of the dispute between the Slovaks and the Magyars was different from that in the neighbouring Czech lands. In Hungary, the Slovaks were fighting not so much for linguistic equality as for the survival, not only of their language, but of their

[9] Czech national consciousness was demonstrated by, amongst other methods, the insistence on purchasing only Czech made products from Czech owned shops. The Germans followed the same practice.
[10] The Czechs, basing their policies on the concept of Bohemian state rights (*Böhmisches Staatsrecht*), argued that the lands of the Crown of St Wenceslas, had, historically, formed a distinct political unit, and demanded autonomous status for the territories concerned.

very existence as a nation. Enforced Magyarisation was threatening
to eradicate all aspects of Slovak national character. The Magyar
endeavour to create a unitary Magyar national state led to the
ruthless persecution of the Slovak language and severe restrictions
being placed on Slovak education.[11] Unlike the Czechs, who,
although lacking a nobility, possessed a strong and nationally
conscious intelligentsia, the Slovak nation was not only devoid of
an aristocracy, but also had only a numerically very small intelligentsia.[12] Economically, the Slovaks, inhabiting the mountainous
areas in the north of Hungary, were also in an extremely weak
position. The limited industrialisation undergone by Hungary
towards the close of the nineteenth century brought little benefit
to the Slovaks, who remained almost entirely dependent on
agriculture.

Bordering on the Habsburg Monarchy in the north and east was
the Russian Empire – the largest and most powerful Slav country.
Not unnaturally, many of the smaller Slav nationalities living within Austria–Hungary who did not enjoy full independence at the
time looked towards their greater Russian brethren for inspiration
and assistance in overcoming the difficulties with which they were
confronted. The Czech and Slovak nations were no exception in
displaying this general Slav tendency to gravitate towards Russia.
In the case of the Czechs, however, their admiration of their
powerful relations was tempered with caution. Although conscious
of their ethnic link with the Slav community of nations, of which
the Russians were the undisputed leaders, the Czechs, due largely
to their geographical situation in the centre of Europe, became
familiar with European culture and ideas, and acquired a Western
outlook which caused them to be suspicious of the dark, autocratic side of Russia.[13] The Slovaks, on the other hand, because
of their relative isolation combined with a more desperate national
situation, in general turned less questioningly towards Russia.

It is significant that the idea of exploiting the close affinities
between the Slav nations originated, not from Russia, but from

[11] For details of the situation in Hungary see R. W. Seton-Watson (*Scotus Viator*), *Racial Problems in Hungary* (London, 1908).
[12] R. W. Seton-Watson in *The New Slovakia* (Prague, 1924), pp. 13–14, esti-mated that in 1918 the number of ' educated and nationally conscious Slovaks' was between 750 and 1000.
[13] Reservations about association with Russia were expressed by the Czech leaders, F. Palacký, K. Havlíček, and later, T. G. Masaryk.

Slovakia. The concept of Slav reciprocity was first formulated in the 1820s and 1830s by two Slovaks, J. Kollár and P. Šafařík. Kollár expressed his romantic vision of a great future for the united Slav race in a poem, *Slávy dcera* [Daughter of Slava], published in 1824. This was followed twelve years later by a famous treatise, written in German, *Über die Literarische Wechselseitigkeit zwischen den verschiedenen Stämmen und Mundarten der Slavischen Nation* [On the Literary Reciprocity between the Various Peoples and Dialects of the Slav Nation], in which the author asserted that the Slavs constituted one nation, speaking dialects of one language. In Kollár's view, however, the awareness of Slav unity did not entail a political union. He believed that cultural and literary co-operation between the Slav nations was possible within the existing political divisions of Europe. Although Kollár did admire Russia, he was largely ignorant of the object of his admiration, and remained, nevertheless, loyal to Austria. Šafařík, in his philological studies, started from the same supposition as did Kollár – the linguistic unity of the Slavs.

This romantic vision of a united Slav people was not the only one being portrayed at the time. The great Czech historian, F. Palacký, in his studies, linked the development of the Czech nation with Western Europe rather than with the Slav East. He saw the fifteenth-century Czech Hussite movement as being the precursor of Western European enlightenment.[14] In contemporary affairs, Palacký was opposed to Germany and Russia alike, believing that the small nations of Central Europe could preserve their independent identity only in a strong federal state, into which he wished to see the Habsburg Empire transformed. Palacký's views were shared by the prominent Czech journalist and poet, K. Havlíček, who, as a result of a period of residence in Russia, became familiar with that country's autocratic characteristics, and found them unworthy of admiration. These ideas, which acquired the name of Austro-Slavism, were to remain, in one form or another, the inspiration of mainstream Czech political activities up to the outbreak of the First World War.

The revolutionary year of 1848 resulted in the removal of the absolutist regime of Prince Metternich, and increased Czech hopes

---

[14] Palacký's principal historical work is the multivolume *Dějiny národu českého v Čechách a na Moravě* (5 vols., Prague, 1848–67). This also appeared in a German edition, *Geschichte von Böhmen* (5 vols., Prague, 1836–67).

for a brighter future in a reformed Austria. Many Germans, on the other hand, were dreaming of a united German nation, and wished to see Austria, including the Czech lands, become part of the German Empire. A Pan-German assembly (*Vorparlament*) met in Frankfurt for this purpose, and Palacký received an invitation to attend on behalf of the Czechs. He declined to be present, on the grounds that he was not a German but a 'Czech of Slav descent', and reiterated his belief in the continued existence of Austria, in the now famous words: 'Truly, if the Austrian Empire had not been in existence for a long time, it would be necessary in the interest of Europe and in the interest of humanity to create it.'[15]

As a counter-measure to the Frankfurt meeting, a Congress of Slav nations was staged in Prague during the summer of 1848.[16] Present were representatives of the Czechs, Slovaks, Poles, Ukrainians, Serbs, Croats, Slovenes, and one Russian – M. Bakunin. Despite much rhetoric, the Congress produced few concrete results and served only to indicate the magnitude of the dissensions dividing the Slav peoples. Nevertheless, in later years, the Prague gathering of 1848 was to provide inspiration to the Slavs, the Czechs in particular, and help to maintain the belief in the possibility of some form of united Slav action.

Meanwhile inside Russia, the emergence of the Slavophil movement resulted in an increased awareness of Russia's Slavonic character.[17] The Slavophils were a loosely connected group of intellectuals, reaching their greatest prominence in the 1850s and 1860s, who believed that Russia could only gain salvation through reverting to its Slavonic origins, and by rejecting what they considered to be the aberrations of Western civilisation. The Slavophils placed their faith in the Orthodox Church and the traditional wisdom of the Russian people. The non-Russian Catholic Slav

---

[15] F. Palacký (ed.), *Gedenkblätter* (Prague, 1874), p. 152. For an English translation see 'Letter sent by František Palacký to Frankfurt', *The Slavonic and East European Review*, xxvi (1948), pp. 303–8. Although Palacký made the words concerning the essentiality of Austria famous, they were not originally his. See C. A. Macartney, *The Habsburg Empire 1790–1918* (London, 1968), p. 353, n. 1.

[16] For details of the 1848 Slav Congress, see Z. V. Tobolka, *Slovanský sjezd v Praze r. 1848* (Prague, 1910).

[17] For details see N. V. Riasanovsky, *Russia and the West in the Teaching of the Slavophiles* (Cambridge, Mass., 1952), and F. Fadner, *Seventy Years of Pan-Slavism in Russia; Karazin to Danilevskii, 1800–1870* (Georgetown, 1962).

nations – with the exception of the Poles, who, in the eyes of the Slavophils, were traitors to their race – were regarded as allies, who had suffered Westernisation under duress, and a closer association between them and Russia was considered to be desirable. Subsequently, the Slavophil movement gradually shed its religious and philosophical overtones, acquired a more reactionary and imperial nature, and became increasingly Pan-Slav and even Pan-Russian in character. Russian scholars, such as M. P. Pogodin and V. I. Lamansky, rejected in their writings Kollár's original concept of equality amongst the Slav nations, substituting the idea of Russian hegemony. These views were most lucidly expressed in 1869 by N. Ya. Danilevsky, with the publication of his plans for a Russian dominated federal Pan-Slav empire, which was to contain all the Slav nations (and also the Greeks, Rumanians, and Magyars, in addition to the peoples of Asiatic Russia), extending in Europe from the Baltic to the Aegean, with Constantinople as the capital city.[18] Similar views were expressed by General R. A. Fadeyev, who also wished to see the Habsburg Monarchy deprived of its Slav territories, which were to be incorporated into a confederate Slav empire.[19] Although the ideas and policies of the Slavophils and later the Pan-Slavs were never officially adopted by the Russian government, which on occasion treated the movements with considerable suspicion, their activities were nevertheless utilised to further Russian imperial aims whenever appropriate.

Leading Slavophils were active in the foundation of the Slavonic Benevolent Society (*Slavyanskoe blagotvoritel'noe obshchestvo*) in Moscow in 1858, which together with the St Petersburg branch, created ten years later, became the principal unofficial agency for furthering Russian aims amongst the non-Russian Slavs.[20] The activities of the Slavonic Benevolent Societies reached their zenith during the period immediately preceding the Russo-Turkish War of 1877–8, when, in addition to financial assistance, volunteers were sent to aid the Serbian insurgents. This intense interest

[18] Danilevsky's views first appeared in 1869 as a series of articles in the periodical *Zarya*. These were later published in book form as *Rossiya i Evropa* (St Petersburg, 1871).
[19] Fadeyev expressed his ideas in *Mnenie o vostochnom voprose* (St Petersburg, 1869), which also appeared in an English translation, *Opinion on the Eastern Question* (trans. T. Mitchell, London, 1871).
[20] The organisations, originally termed Slavonic Benevolent Committees, were restyled as Societies in 1877. Two other branches were founded in Kiev and Odessa in 1869 and 1870 respectively.

demonstrated in the plight of the Balkan Slavs was indicative of the attention devoted by Pan-Slav circles in Russia to their Orthodox brethren. The Russian Pan-Slavs regarded the non-Orthodox Slavs with considerable suspicion and, in addition to totally rejecting the Poles, also distrusted the Westernised Czechs. The general Slav orientation of the Czechs contained correspondingly few elements of ardent Russophilism. Dreams of a glorious future for the Slavs under the leadership of Orthodox Russia, as proposed by the Pan-Slavs, were incompatible with Czech Austro-Slav aspirations. It required, what was from the Czech point of view the traumatic event of the creation of the dualistic structure of the Habsburg Empire to force them closer into the embrace of Russia. Czech reaction to the agreement between the Austrian Germans and the Magyars was extremely unfavourable, for the *Ausgleich* was regarded as the ruin of all hopes of achieving autonomy for the Czech lands, and in addition led to greater separation from the Slovaks.[21] In desperation, both the Czechs and Slovaks turned impulsively to Russia.

In May 1867, shortly after the conclusion of the compromise between Austria and Hungary, the Czechs took advantage of a Slavonic Ethnographic Exhibition being staged in Moscow, and sent a substantial delegation consisting of many leading Czech public figures, to demonstrate their solidarity with the other Slav nations, the Russians in particular.[22] Amongst the Czech visitors were Palacký; the leader of the Old Czech Party, L. Rieger; and the proprietor of the principal Czech nationalist newspaper *Národní listy*, J. Grégr. Representatives of most other Slav nations also attended the events in Moscow, with the notable exception of the Poles who declined to be present in protest against the Russian suppression of the 1863 Polish uprising. The Ethnographic Exhibition and accompanying festivities provided an opportunity for impassioned oration and dramatic gestures, but nevertheless proved an inauspicious demonstration of Slav solidarity. Spokesmen for the Czech delegation insisted on the right of each Slav nation to an independent existence, and included the Poles within this category, thus incurring the displeasure of their Russian

[21] The Czechs and Slovaks regarded the *Ausgleich* as a conspiracy between the Austrian Germans and the Magyars, designed to enable each group to dominate its respective part of the Empire.
[22] For details of the visit, see M. Prelog, *Pout' Slovanů do Moskvy roku 1867* (trans. M. Paulová, Prague, 1931).

hosts. Earlier, *en route* for Moscow, the Czech delegation together with other Slav guests visited St Petersburg, where they received an audience with the Tsar, Alexander II. Although the news of this official gesture of goodwill caused a considerable upsurge of Russophil and Pan-Slav feeling in the Czech lands, any political significance it may have had was completely negated when the Russian court subsequently apologised to Austria–Hungary for having accorded the Czechs this honour. The Russian authorities were not prepared to jeopardise relations with the Habsburg Empire for the sake of the Czechs and Slovaks. The visit of the Czech delegation to Russia achieved nothing whatsoever in concrete political terms, and succeeded only in antagonising the Poles and the Austro-Hungarian authorities. Nevertheless, despite this failure, a significant increase in Czech Russophilism can be traced from this demonstrative journey to Moscow in 1867.[23]

The general Czech preoccupation with Slav matters was also reflected in the political development of the nation. During the 1860s, the Czech nationalist movement began to split into two main factions, divided by various disagreements including the stand taken towards the Russo-Polish conflict. The more conservative elements among the nationalists supported the Russian government, whereas the younger and more radical section sympathised with the Polish cause. The former group became known as the Old Czechs, and their more youthful opponents as the Young Czechs. In 1874, the Young Czechs, wishing to play a more active role in the political life of the Austrian lands, broke away from the hereto united nationalist movement, which was pursuing a policy of passive opposition to the government, and formed an independent political organisation. The young Czech Party became the principal representative of Czech middle-class nationalist opinion. Despite the critical view taken of Russia over the suppression of the Polish uprising of 1863, the Young Czech movement retained a residue of Russophil sympathy, which acquired increased prominence in later years.[24]

[23] One consequence of the visit to Moscow was the intensification of the Russophil commitment of the influential Czech newspaper, *Národní listy*. The proprietor of the newspaper, J. Grégr, returned from Russia with greatly strengthened pro-Russian sympathies.

[24] During the first decade of the twentieth century, the Young Czechs devoted considerable attention to increasing contacts with Russia, and, with this aim in mind, were responsible for instigating the Neo-Slav movement.

With the exception of the Social Democratic Party formed in 1878,[25] which, though predictably antipathetic towards official Russia, displayed some interest in Russian opposition forces, further major Czech political organisations did not emerge until near the turn of the century. The most significant of these were the National Socialist Party, founded in 1898, strongly nationalistic and Russophil in character, which drew its support mainly from the Czech working class; and the Czech Agrarian Party formed a year later, which represented the sectional interests of the agricultural community, which though also nationalistic in attitude tended to regard Russia as an economic rival rather than an ally. The Czech Clerical Party, which was established in Moravia in 1896 and in Bohemia a year later, also exhibited little enthusiasm for Russia, largely for religious reasons. A fourth grouping, which appeared in 1900 was the numerically very small, though influential, Realist Party. The founder of this party, T. G. Masaryk, showed considerable interest in Russia, and as Palacký had done earlier, adopted a critical stand towards the Russian authorities and their imperial aspirations.[26] Although the formation of these and other political movements took place independently of the question of relations with Russia, the awareness of belonging to the Slav community of nations, and the association with Russia this implied, was ever present in Czech minds, and was reflected, to a greater or lesser extent, in the activities of these organisations.

In the case of the Slovaks, relations with Russia played an even more fundamental role in their political development. Slovak nationalism, existing in a different political climate from that of the Czechs tended, in general, to exhibit more pronounced Russophil characteristics. Indeed, it was from Slovakia that one of the first projects for a Pan-Slav empire, under Russian control, had emerged. In a book written during the 1850s, entitled *Slovanstvo a*

[25] Although the Austrian Social Democratic Party was founded in 1874, the Czech section, styled the Czechoslavonic Social Democratic Party, did not come into being until 1878.

[26] T. G. Masaryk made a detailed study of aspects of Russian history, philosophy, and literature, which was first published in German as *Russland und Europa. Studien über geistigen Strömungen in Russland* (2 vols., Jena, 1913). An English version appeared in 1918, entitled *The Spirit of Russia: Studies in History, Literature, and Philosophy* (trans. E. and C. Paul, 2 vols., London, 1919; 3rd vol., trans. R. Bass, London, 1967).

svet budúcnosti[27] [Slavdom and the World of the Future], the Slovak, L. Štúr, was highly critical of the Western nations and of plans to Slavicise the Austrian Empire, and argued that the Slavs would only have a future if they accepted the Orthodox faith together with the Russian language and united within a Russian state. Following the *Ausgleich* of 1867 the Slovaks, isolated from the Czechs and subjected to increasing persecution from the Magyar authorities, looked with growing eagerness to Russia for salvation. The chief exponent of these views was the so-called Martin group of nationalists,[28] later to form the Slovak National Party, whose members believed in devoting the highest priority to the development of Slovak language and literature and who hoped that political assistance would be forthcoming from Russia. Towards the end of the century, a younger generation of Slovak nationalists appeared on the scene who were opposed to the pro-Russian orientation of their elders and had little faith in Russian assistance, and believed that national independence could only be achieved through close co-operation with the Czechs. This group, known as the Hlasists,[29] was small but vociferous and influential, and maintained close links with the Realists in the Czech lands.

Despite the existence amongst both the Czechs and Slovaks of a feeling of general Slav consciousness, accompanied by an undercurrent of Russophilism, no significant developments in relations with Russia, or any other Slav nation, took place for a considerable period following the 1867 Moscow Exhibition. With the exception of the brief resurgence of Pan-Slav sentiment, which accompanied the Russo-Turkish War of 1877–8, the situation remained largely unaltered until the end of the nineteenth century. Although Czech and Slovak public figures did make private visits to Russia, contacts between them and their Russian counterparts were infrequent and lacked significance.[30] Official Russian circles remained, generally, uninterested in the fate of the culturally and religiously distinct

---

[27] Though written in German, Štúr's book first appeared in 1867 in Russian, translated by V. I. Lamansky, entitled *Slavyanstvo i mir budushchego. Poslanie Slavyanam s beregov Dunaya.*

[28] The Martin group was so termed because it endeavoured to make Turčiansky Sv. Martin the centre for its political activities. The organ of this group, *Narodnie noviny*, was published in the same town.

[29] The Hlasists acquired their name from their periodical *Hlas* [The Voice].

[30] T. G. Masaryk visited Russia in 1887 and 1888 in order to study conditions there. The leader of the Young Czech Party, K. Kramář, was a frequent visitor to Russia, having first travelled there in 1890.

Western Slavs.[31] During the closing years of the nineteenth century Russia had no outstanding territorial interests in Central Europe and was, in fact, intent on the preservation of the *status quo* in that area and in the Balkans, in order to concentrate efforts on expansion in the Far East. Similarly, Pan-Slavism did not exist as a coherent political force amongst the Czechs and Slovaks, although the general sense of ethnic association with Russia provided the Germans and Magyars with a convenient device to be used against the Slav nations. Czech flirtations with Russia were largely the consequence of frustration and despair with Austria. In the case of the Slovaks, Pan-Slavism served more to sustain morale than as a definite political programme.

Pan-Slavism as an intrument of Russian foreign policy did not exist, and was accurately described by S. H. Thomson as 'a phantom'.[32] The Czechs and Slovaks, in common with most other Slav nations, however, remained conscious of their ethnic links with Russia. Towards the end of the nineteenth century this feeling again intensified. The desire of certain sections of the Czech and Slovak nations to form closer relations with Russia and other Slavs increased, and culminated early in the twentieth century in the appearance of the Neo-Slav movement.

[31] The Austro-Hungarian ambassador in St Petersburg, Count (then Baron) Aehrenthal, reported to Vienna that he had observed 'a lack of interest – which could perhaps more accurately be termed apathy – prevailing at the present time in Russian society for everything Slav'. In his opinion, the active base for Pan-Slavism was to be found not in Russia, but amongst the Slav nationalities of the Dual Monarchy. In a subsequent dispatch, Aehrenthal drew attention to the fact that the Czechs, in particular, were of no interest to the Russians, on account of their association with German culture. Aehrenthal to Kalnoky, St Petersburg, 24 August 1891, 12 October 1893, and 19 September 1899, cited in E. Beneš. *Úvahy o slovanství. Hlavní problémy slovanské politiky* (2nd edn, Prague, 1947), pp. 115–27.

[32] S. H. Thomson, 'A century of a Phantom: Panslavism and the Western Slavs', *Journal of Central European Affairs*, XI (1951), pp. 57–77.

2

The re-emergence of an idea, 1898–1905

The closing years of the nineteenth century formed a period of great turbulence in the Czech lands of the Habsburg Empire, with the conflict between the Czech and German inhabitants reaching a new height of intensity and violence. The deterioration of the situation was caused by the introduction and subsequent withdrawal of measures designed to reorganise the administration of Bohemia and Moravia on a bilingual basis, giving equality to the Czech and German languages. The announced introduction of this scheme, known as the Badeni ordinances,[1] by the government of Count K. Badeni in 1897, gave rise to vehement opposition from the Bohemian Germans and their allies elsewhere in the Empire, who feared that their predominant position would be put at risk due to their lack of knowledge of the Czech language, and who also regarded the linguistic measures as a prelude to the federalisation of the Austrian parts of the Dual Monarchy. German obstruction of the Vienna Parliament, the Reichsrat, together with the serious rioting which occurred in the streets of Prague and many other Bohemian towns in protest against the proposed reforms, led to the dismissal of Count Badeni's government in November 1897, followed immediately by the suspension of the language ordinances and their eventual withdrawal in October 1899. These actions, in turn, led to renewed protests and outbreaks of violence, this time instigated from the Czech side. The determination of the Czechs to revenge what they considered to be a grave injustice also took the form of obstructing the business of the Vienna Reichsrat. The dispute between the Czechs and Germans, though centred essentially round conditions in the Czech lands, was, through the actions of both protagonists,

---

[1] The essence of the government's proposal was that Czech should also become the language of the 'inner service' of the administration throughout Bohemia and Moravia, alongside German. Communication between officials would take place in either language and each official would have to know both languages.

exerting a detrimental effect on the political life of the entire Austrian part of the Habsburg Empire, and its solution, or at least its alleviation, became the prime concern of successive Austrian administrations.

During 1900 E. Körber, a permanent civil servant, who saw as his most immediate task the reconciliation of the Czech and German inhabitants of Bohemia, was appointed to head the Austrian government. Without such a reconciliation Parliament could not function normally and the authorities had to resort to rule by emergency decree. A general election held early in 1901 did little to ease the situation or to change the composition of the Vienna Parliament.[2] The beginning of Körber's tenure of office also coincided with the initial stages of a period of economic depression in the Habsburg Empire. Government action to alleviate the widespread economic distress was used as an inducement to obtain a precarious truce between the warring Czech and German factions in Bohemia and Moravia. During the summer of 1901 the Austro-Hungarian government published plans for an extensive programme of public works, including the construction of railways and canals and improvements in the navigability of rivers, to be carried out throughout the Dual Monarchy to benefit the economic life of many of the Empire's nationalities, particularly the Czechs and Germans.

The period of relative calm was brief in duration, however, for the promised public works progressed very slowly and their extent satisfied few. Plans produced by the government to achieve a permanent reconciliation between Czechs and Germans in Bohemia failed to gain the support of either party. The proposed scheme envisaged the division of the province into three types of administrative areas: German, where the German language would predominate; Czech, where the Czech language would predominate; and mixed, bilingual areas. The Czechs, intolerant of any proposal to administratively divide Bohemia, demonstrated their opposition by again obstructing business in the Reichsrat, and the Vienna government once more had to restort to governing by emergency decree. The Germans, in turn, retaliated by obstructing business in the Bohemian Diet. Pressured from all sides, and unable to make any progress towards racial harmony, Körber was replaced by Baron Gautsch in December 1904. Throughout the remaining decade of the peace-time existence of the Habsburg Monarchy repeated attempts were made by various administrations to achieve a solution to the vexed questions of relations between the Czechs and Germans of Bohemia. Although some of the endeavours succeeded in obtaining a respite from the problem, no permanent settlement proved possible. One of the few positive developments of the period was the understanding achieved between the Czech and German inhabitants of Moravia during 1905, which indicated that coexistence between the warring nationalities was not beyond the bounds of possibility.[3]

During the period of sterile inter-racial strife which marked the turn of the century in the Czech lands an important new development took place in Czech political strategy. Following the abortive attempt to introduce bilingual administration into the provinces of Bohemia and Moravia, the failure of which was due predominantly to German nationalist pressure, the conviction grew amongst the Czech political leadership that allies had to be sought outside the boundaries of the Habsburg Empire. Only through the exertion of foreign influence, it was believed, could the Austrian authorities be induced to reform the Habsburg Monarchy in accordance with the wishes of the Czechs and other Slavs within the Empire. A determined attempt was therefore made to arouse international interest in what became known as the Bohemian, or Czech, question.[4]

[3] The agreement between Czechs and Germans in Moravia, known as the Moravian Compromise, divided the province into districts on ethnic lines, the administration of each district being carried out in the language of the majority. The representation of the nationalities in the Moravian Diet was fixed at 73 Czech deputies and 40 German. Each ethnic group voted for its own seats, electoral conflict between the nationalities thereby being avoided. Any significant legislation required the approval of a two thirds majority of at least 121 out of the 151 members of the Diet. The Germans could thus veto any measure by their absence. The Moravian Compromise was a remarkable step forward towards a solution of the nationalities disputes within the Austro-Hungarian Empire. It was, however, criticised by many Czechs in Bohemia as a capitulation to the Germans, and by others on account of the undemocratic nature of the electoral system. See J. Kolejka, 'Moravský pakt z roku 1905', *Československý časopis historický*, IV (1956), pp. 590–615.

[4] *Proces dra. Kramáře a jeho přátel*, ed. Z. V. Tobolka (5 vols., Prague, 1918–20) IV, part 2, pp. 15–16; J. Křížek, 'Česká buržoasní politika a "česká otázka" v letech 1900–1914', *Československý časopis historický*, VI (1958), p. 636.

K. Kramář, the leader of the Young Czech Party, which was the major Czech nationalist political organisation at the time, wrote two articles concerned with the problems confronting the Czech lands, and the Habsburg Empire in general, which appeared in prominent West European publications. The first was published in Paris in 1899 in *Revue de Paris*, and the second in 1902 in the London periodical *The National Review*.[5] The object of these articles, besides drawing attention to the existence of the Czechs and their problems, was to impress upon West European readers that the Czechs could be considered as potential allies in any struggle, peaceful or otherwise, against the growing power of Germany. In the first publication, he advocated the creation of an alliance between Austria–Hungary, France and Russia in order to counter what he considered the German menace.[6] In the latter article Kramář again stressed the importance of preserving a strong and independent Habsburg Empire as a barrier against German expansion, a role which, in his opinion, could only be performed by an Empire revitalised by reform on a federal basis, and one just to all its component peoples, irrespective of nationality. The Czech struggle against the Germans in Bohemia, together with the pressure exerted on the Habsburg authorities for alterations in the political structure of the Dual Monarchy, were thus linked with the wider European issue of the containment of the German Empire.[7] Although the Czech leader concluded one of the articles by stating that the Czechs did not require external

[5] The two articles were, 'L'Avenir de l'Autriche', *Revue de Paris*, VI, part 1 (January–February, 1899), pp. 577–600, and 'Europe and the Bohemian Question', *The National Review*, XL (September 1902–February 1903), pp. 183–205. The publication of the article in the *Revue de Paris* was arranged through the French politician L. Bourgeois, and the article in *The National Review* was written at the request of the periodical's proprietor L. Maxse. See K. Herman and Z. Sládek, 'Slovanská politika Karla Kramáře', *Rozpravy československé akademie věd: Řada společenských věd*, LXXXI, no. 2 (1971), p. 19, notes 70, 71.   [6] Kramář, 'L'Avenir de l'Autriche', pp. 591–600.
[7] Kramář wrote: 'The sole point [of the Bohemian question] now is, will the Czechs or will they not succeed in maintaining their position, and in gaining so much influence throughout Austria that they can work effectively in the direction of maintaining the old kingdom of the Habsburgs as a strong bulwark against all the aspirations of German Chauvinism, whether the latter strive for a greater Germany, extending from Hamburg to Trieste, or merely for an economic union based upon an alliance between Germany and Austria, and resting on constitutional guarantees, such as the more moderate members of the National-German party demand, as amounting practically to the same thing, but sounding less revolutionary?' Kramář, 'Europe and the Bohemian Question', p. 184.

assistance, he indicated that they did have 'one desire, namely, that non-German Europe also may at last show that it understands the meaning of the Bohemian question and how pregnant with fate it is, and may follow the struggles of the Czechs with that measure of sympathy which a good and righteous cause deserves.'[8]

In the years immediately following, the Czech political leadership continued to attach considerable importance to gaining external sympathy and support for the Czech point of view. With this aim in mind, the principal non-party political Czech national body, the Czech National Council (*Národní rada česká*) established, early in 1907, a Foreign Section. This subsidiary body, under the control of Kramář, was amongst other matters responsible for the publication of material, in German, English, French and Russian, intended to stimulate interest in the Czech question.[9]

As the publishing activities of the Foreign Section of the Czech National Council indicate, Czech attention was not directed exclusively towards the West; considerable emphasis was also placed upon gaining the support of Russia, traditionally regarded as the protector of the small Slav peoples under alien rule. Although it was the Western ties, those forged by Masaryk and E. Beneš, which at the end of the First World War proved more important, nevertheless, during the intervening years the majority of Czech and Slovak opinion directed its eyes predominantly towards the East, towards Russia.

After a prolonged period of inactivity following the visit of Czech leaders to Moscow in 1867, significant public contacts between Czechs and Russians were again revived in 1898, at the celebrations of the centenary of the birth of Palacký. The highlight of the festivities, held in Prague between 18 and 20 June of that year, was the laying of the foundation stone of the Palacký monument. Guests, mostly journalists and academics, from various Slav nationalities both inside and outside the Habsburg Empire were present in the Bohemian capital for the occasion. Some of these, including the Poles, M'. Zdziechowski, A. Doboszyński, M. Chyliński; the Slovene, I. Hribar; and the Russian, D. N. Vergun, were later actively involved in the Neo-Slav movement.[10]

---

[8] *Ibid.*, pp. 204–5. No responsible Austro-Hungarian political leader could openly advocate foreign interference in the internal affairs of the Dual Monarchy, even if such intervention were possible.
[9] *Proces dra. Kramáře*, III, part 1, pp. 51–2. The Czech National Council itself was founded in 1900.   [10] *Národní listy*, 18–21 June 1898.

In addition to the laying of the foundation stone itself, the Palacký festivities consisted of a commemorative gathering in the Pantheon of the Czech National Museum and the customary ceremonial banquets. At one of these banquets the speakers included Kramář, the leader of the Young Czech Party. In his address he thanked the Polish deputies in the Vienna Reichsrat for their support over the Badeni language ordinances but stressed that, despite this example of co-operation, there was little harmony in the Slav world. Repudiating any desire for political unity of the Slav peoples, he expressed regret that they were also far removed from the spiritual unity envisaged by Palacký. Almost as if foreshadowing the development of the Neo-Slav movement, the origins of which can be traced back to the Palacký celebrations of 1898, Kramář concluded by expressing the hope that the present events would not be mere festivities, but would give rise to a 'further step forward towards a great future' for the Slav peoples.[11]

A further opportunity for speech making arose the following day when a second banquet took place, this time in honour of the Slav journalists present in Prague. The speech which attracted the most attention at this gathering, and indeed at the entire Palacký celebrations, was delivered by one of the Russian guests, the publicist V. V. Komarov, a member of the executive of the St Petersburg Slavonic Benevolent Society. Komarov utilised the opportunity to deliver a virulent anti-German attack and appealed for Slav unity in order to defeat what he regarded as being the common German peril. The Russian visitor stated that the Czechs, who had always occupied a dangerous salient position on the western edge of the Slav world, were now, following the defeat of France in the Franco-Prussian War of 1870–1, once again in the front line against Germany. He assured the Czechs of Russian support in their struggle, adding that: 'We do not feel mere sympathy towards you...we regard your affairs as our own... only when we are confident that all is well here [in Bohemia] and that the German wave has been thrown far back to there from where it has come, then, and only then, will we be calm, contented and joyful...'[12]

---

[11] *Ibid.*, 19 June 1898.

[12] *Ibid.*, 21 June 1898. As an example of what the Slavs could achieve if united, Komarov recalled, somewhat inaccurately, that the combined forces of the Russians, Czechs and Poles had defeated the Teutonic Knights at Tannenberg (Grünnwald) in 1410.

Komarov's words did not please Austrian German opinion[13] or the Habsburg authorities and resulted in his expulsion from Prague.[14] The Austrian Germans were equally concerned about a telegram of greeting sent to the Czechs by the Russian Grand Duke Constantine, the President of the Imperial Russian Academy, in which reference was made to Palacký's contribution to the 'revival and strengthening of the independence of the Czech nation'.[15] The authorities in the Dual Monarchy also took objection to these remarks, which were regarded by the Austro-Hungarian ambassador in St Petersburg as 'inappropriate and unwarrantable' coming from a member of the Russian royal family. The matter was raised with the Russian authorities who expressed their regret over the incident.[16] An indication of the Russian government's repudiation of Komarov's views is given by the fact that, when he was elected chairman of the Slavonic Benevolent Society in St Petersburg during 1899, the authorities refused to ratify his appointment.[17]

A less sensational outcome of the Palacký festivities, though from the point of view of Slav unity potentially much more significant, was the formation, amongst the journalists present in Prague, of an association of Slav Journalists. This Association, formed on the instigation of the Czechs, consisted, at this stage, exclusively of journalists from the Slav nationalities of the Austro-Hungarian Empire, who gathered together to discuss problems confronting Slav journalism.[18] The meeting, known as the First Congress of Slav Journalists, took place on 19 June in the Prague Old Town Hall. The assembled journalists heard papers read on aspects of journalism in the Slav lands of the Habsburg Empire, and passed resolutions demanding, amongst other things, full civil liberties, freedom to use their own language, and a free press for the Slav peoples of Austria–Hungary. The establishment of a Slav news agency, which would provide 'objective' information on Slav

[13] *Neue Freie Presse*, 21, 22, 23 June 1898.

[14] E. Winter, *Der Panslawismus nach den Berichten der österreichisch-ungarischen Botschafter in St Petersburg* (Prague, 1944), p. 16.

[15] *Neue Freie Presse*, 21, 23 June 1898; *Národní listy*, 20 June 1898.

[16] Liechtenstein to Goluchowski, 64 A–C, St Petersburg, 28/16 June 1898, cited in Winter, *Panslawismus*, pp. 60–3. The Russian Minister of Finance, S. Yu. Witte, remarked to the Austro-Hungarian representative that the incident was 'regrettable' and that the Grand Duke had expressed only his own personal views.   [17] Winter, *Panslawismus*, p. 17.

[18] J. Hrubý, *Slovanská vzájemnost v časopisech* (Prague, 1910), pp. 1–3.

affairs, was considered essential.[19] The Prague gathering of journalists was followed by a series of congresses held at more or less regular intervals in various Slav towns up to 1911. Despite much discussion on a range of subjects, and despite frequent references to the need for establishing a Slav news agency, nothing concrete materialised from these meetings, though closer personal relations between the attending journalists were, no doubt, established.[20]

The Palacký celebrations were considered by Czech nationalist opinion to have been a considerable success. The leading Czech nationalist newspaper and organ of the Young Czech Party, *Národní listy*, drawing parallels from recent history, claimed that 'to the Slav Congress of 1848 and to the visit to the Moscow Ethnographic Exhibition in 1867 a further event, of equal significance for the Slav world, has been added'.[21] Expressing itself in more definite political terms, *Národní listy* also maintained that Prague had witnessed 'the renewal of the political union of the Austrian Slavs and the ceremonial proclamation of a Slav partnership to combat the German one'.[22] Despite the fact that *Národní listy* was prone to hyperbole, the events of the summer of 1898 were undoubtedly successful if measured in terms of the increased Czech interest in the Slav world. More attention began to be paid to the affairs of other Slav peoples including, of course, the Russians, and means of Slav co-operation began gradually to be explored. One concrete example of this stimulation of Czech interest in Slav affairs was the founding in Prague, during 1899, of a periodical devoted to the serious study of this subject, *Slovanský přehled* [Slavonic Review]. The founder and editor of this periodical was Adolf Černý, a distinguished Czech Slavist scholar. In its introductory editorial article, *Slovanský přehled* set itself the task of familiarising its readership with the life of other Slav peoples. It expressed the conviction that: 'Slav reciprocity, constructed on true mutual knowledge, will be a stronger structure than if based on unfounded nebulous enthusiasm.'[23] A further indication of the new upsurge of interest in the Slav world was provided, early in

[19] *Národní listy*, 20 June 1898.
[20] For further details of the activities of the Association of Slav Journalists, see below, pp. 180–2.   [21] *Národní listy*, 19 June 1898.
[22] *Ibid.*, 22 June 1898.
[23] 'Slovo úvodní', *Slovanský přehled* I (1899), p. 1.

1900, by the establishment of a Slavonic society in Prague, the *Slovanský klub*.[24]

The years immediately following the centenary celebrations of Palacký's birth in 1898 saw a gradual development of public contacts, mostly of a social and cultural nature, between individual Czechs and Russians. During the following year, in June (May) 1899, several prominent Czech persons, including J. Holeček and J. Hrubý (two journalists from *Národní listy*), and the leader of · the Sokol gymnastic association, J. Scheiner, were present in St Petersburg, amongst other foreign guests, at the celebrations of the centenary of the birth of Alexander Pushkin.[25] Scheiner, and another Czech visitor present at the festivities, V. Černý, were subsequently active in the Neo-Slav movement. Later that year, Czechs were present at a Russian archaeological congress in Kiev.[26] In 1901 a group of Czechs again visited Russia on the occasion of the St Petersburg première of the Czech opera *Dalibor*, when they were entertained by Komarov.[27] During the summer of 1903 it was again the turn of the Russians to be present in Prague, this time at the laying of the foundation stone of the Jan Hus memorial.[28] These events, though not themselves particularly important, provide an indication of the growing desire amongst at least some Czechs for closer relations with Russia.

The idea of increasing contacts between the Czechs and the other Slav peoples, particularly the Russians, received major encouragement a little earlier, at the Fourth Congress (*Slet*) of the Sokol gymnastic organisation which took place in Prague during 1901. The Sokol movement,[29] founded in 1862, and modelled on the German *Turnverein* gymnastic organisation, served as an important vehicle for the expression of Czech nationalistic sentiment. Although the organisation was devoted primarily to gymnastic training, this was essentially a means towards achieving a greater aim. Physical fitness and gymnastic exercise were utilised in order to train disciplined, alert and vigorous individuals, to

[24] *Slovanský přehled* II (1900), pp. 239–41.
[25] *Národní listy*, 9–14 June 1898; Winter, *Panslawismus*, pp. 17–18, and also enclosure in report 31B, St Petersburg, 14/2 June 1899, cited on pp. 65–7.
[26] *Slovanský přehled*, II (1900), pp. 23–6.
[27] *Národní listy*, 13–16 January 1901; *Slovanský přehled* III (1901), pp. 244–5.
[28] *Národní listy*, 4, 6 July 1903.
[29] For a contemporary Czech account of the Sokol movement see J. Scheiner, 'Sokolstvo', in *Slovanstvo. Obraz jeho minulosti a přítomnosti*, ed. J. Polívka and J. Bidlo (Prague, 1912), pp. 693–722.

instil in them an awareness of their nationality, and thus create a strong and conscious nation. The Sokol organisation performed this task very effectively and, despite periodic harassment by the Habsburg authorities, flourished throughout the Czech lands. The First Congress of the movement, at which mass gymnastic demonstrations were staged, was held in Prague during 1882, and further gatherings took place at irregular intervals.

Associated with the intense Czech nationalism of the Sokol movement was also a strong consciousness of belonging to the Slav family of nations, which manifested itself through the interest shown in the promotion of greater co-operation and unity between the Slavs. The orientation of the Sokols was not, however, exclusively Pan-Slav for, in addition to their contacts with the Slav nations, including Slav emigrants in the United States of America, close relations were also maintained with Western Europe, particularly with France. Considerable effort was expended by the Czechs in attempts to spread the Sokol movement outside the Czech lands, particularly amongst the Slav nationalities both inside and outside the Habsburg Empire. These endeavours were, in general, successful, and Sokol organisations gradually appeared amongst the South Slavs and the Poles.[30] Little progress was made, however, in spreading the Sokol idea to the major Slav power, Russia; a failure particularly irksome to the Czech leaders of the movement. Although much attention was devoted to rectifying this deficiency, virtually no headway was made until the first decade of the twentieth century, when the first Sokol units were established in Russia. After visiting St Petersburg in 1908 Kramář claimed that interest in the Sokol movement was increasing there, and expressed the hope that the organisation would become 'just such a national institution in Russia as it is with us in the Czech lands'.[31] Individual Russians were also anxious for the movement to spread to Russia, though the Russian authorities adopted an extremely cool attitude towards the Sokol idea.[32]

[30] These organisations came into being during the 1860s, 1870s and 1880s. The attitude of the Hungarian authorities prevented the formation of Sokol organisations amongst the Slovaks in Hungary.

[31] K. Kramář, 'Po petrohradských konferencích', Česká revue, II (1908–9), p. 578.

[32] See Památník šestého sletu všesokolského v Praze 1912 (Prague, 1912), pp. 402–12 (N. Manochyn, 'Ruské Sokolstvo'); V. A. Bobrinsky, Prazhsky sezd. Chekhiya i Prikarpatskaya Rus' (St Petersburg, 1909), p. 26. Writing after the Prague Neo-Slav Congress of 1908, Bobrinsky expressed regret that: 'In

Despite the lack of success in exporting the movement to Russia, guests from that country were usually present at Sokol congresses. The meeting held in Prague during 1901 was no exception. Between 28 June and 1 July of that year a series of festivities, including mass gymnastic displays, was staged in the city attended by 14000 members of the organisation and by visitors from several Slav nations, including Russia, and also visitors from France. Prominent amongst the Russians present at the Sokol gathering were General A. F. Rittikh of the St Petersburg Military Academy, who was also a leading member of the St Petersburg Slavonic Benevolent Society, and the journalists, V. P. Svatkovsky and Vergun.[33] Welcoming the Slav guests to Prague *Národní listy* asserted in characteristic prose:

Indeed we are not alone in our struggles, endeavours and hopes! Entire Austrian Slavdom looks to us with faith and love; golden Slavonic Prague is regarded by the Austrian Slavs as the glorious city of all their ideals. The remaining Slavs, primarily the Russians, are continually acquiring a greater understanding of our affairs, and interest in us [Czechs] is rapidly growing amongst them, as is evident from the great Russian newspapers, which sincerely defend the rightfulness of our Czech cause.[34]

Rittikh appeared to give support to this assertion when, at a social function held by the Prague Slavonic Society in honour of the guests attending the Sokol festivities in the Bohemian capital, he proposed a toast to the happy future of the Czech nation. He expressed the hope that the Czechs would continue to progress along the road to self-determination, asked them to retain in their hearts a love of Russia, and to extend contacts between the two nations through commercial ties, for which the possibilities were

Russia the Sokol movement is still in its infancy. It is to our shame that we [Russians], the greatest Slav nation, are so behind in an endeavour which has entered into the flesh and blood of our smaller brethren, and which has proved to be so beneficial to them. It will, of course, not be easy for us to cultivate this courageous and vigorous organisation, particularly as the Sokol movement absolutely excludes politics.'

[33] *IV. Slet všesokolský pořádaný v Praze*, ed. J. Scheiner (Prague, 1901), pp. 38–52, 181; *Národní listy*, 28, 29 June, 1, 2 July 1901.

[34] *Národní listy*, 28 June 1901. An indication that Czech public sentiment was not, however, exclusively Pan-Slav in character is provided by the fact that the French guests at the Sokol Congress received at least as much attention as did the Russians present. *IV. Slet všesokolský*, p. 50.

unlimited.[35] On his departure from Prague, Rittikh caused a sensation by writing the following letter, entitled 'A Greeting to the Czechs', for publication in *Národní listy*.

I came from the far Slav East, from the slumbering forests of the icy North, and from the boundless steppes of the Black Sea region. I came to bring you proof of our Russian love and to inform you that you can depend entirely upon the might of Russia. But I have to tell you something of even greater importance; you must study and become acquainted with this vast Russian-Slav country. In it you Czechs will find all that you seek, and that you hope for. Yes, you will find even more than you anticipate. You will find unexploited natural riches, products of the mind and the hand, economic and industrial progress; but you will also find strength and awareness – strength and awareness constantly growing and rooted in the conviction that all who belong to the nation must serve the nation. In our country everything is done for the people. Our autocratic Tsar is just as moved by a love of the people as a boyar, as any man, rich or poor. Our internal strength lies in our common united love of the people, and there where there exists internal strength, only an opportunity and a stimulus are required for this strength to appear externally also. It is not merely an invincible material strength, but also a moral strength, which sympathises with the weak and is ever ready to assist them. Until you have learned to know Russia, you Czechs will not realise the source of Slav strength. In this sign you will conquer!

It is my heartfelt wish that God may complete the regeneration of the Czech nation, enable the Czechs to enjoy true national liberty, enhance their consciousness, promote their culture and language, and grant them increased material wellbeing, which will be achieved when their commercial connections reach from the Adriatic Sea to the Pacific Ocean. Amen, amen I say unto you. Trust and believe in the God of Russia – He is great – for He created our Slavonic Russia.[36]

Rittikh's letter, predictably, caused a storm of protest from the Austrian Germans, who demanded to know in whose name the general had addressed his message to the Czech people.[37] The Habsburg authorities were also concerned about the tone of the message and were pleased to learn that, although the letter did echo the official propaganda of Imperial Russia, General Rittikh's stirring exhortation to the Czechs was an expression of his personal views and, as had been the case of General Komarov's utterances

---

[35] *IV. Slet všesokolský*, pp. 104–7; *Národní listy*, 1 July 1901.

[36] *Národní listy*, 3 July 1901; *IV. Slet všesokolský*, p. 205. See also *The Times*, 5 July 1901.

[37] *Neue Freie Presse*, 4 July 1901; *Národní listy*, 5, 7 July 1901.

three years earlier, did not reflect the attitude of the Russian government.[38]

The two above-mentioned incidents clearly indicate that, during the early years of the twentieth century, the governments of Russia and Austria–Hungary were anxious to avoid placing any strain on the cordial relations which existed between them. This harmonious atmosphere had been introduced into Austro-Russian relations in 1897, when an agreement was reached between the two powers to maintain the *status quo* in the Balkans.[39] The *entente* had come about largely due to the fact that Russia was primarily concerned with expanding its influence in the Far East, while Austria–Hungary was preoccupied with internal racial problems. A period of calm and stability in the Balkan Peninsula, an area of considerable strategic importance to Russia and the Dual Monarchy, was therefore desired by both parties.

Despite the agreement between the two great powers most closely concerned with the area, peace was not achieved in the Balkans. During 1903 a sizable insurrection against Turkish rule erupted in the province of Macedonia, which in turn led to brutal oppression by the Turkish authorities. The great powers, particularly Russia and Austria–Hungary, were anxious to contain the unrest, and with this aim in view proposed a programme of internal administrative reforms to be implemented by the Turks in Macedonia in order to pacify the discontented Slav population. The reform programme was drafted at a meeting between the Habsburg Emperor, Francis Joseph, and the Russian Tsar, Nicholas II, at Mürzsteg in Austria during October 1903. It was accepted by most of the other interested powers, including Turkey, and although never fully implemented, did alleviate somewhat the situation in Macedonia.

Inside the Dual Monarchy, the Czechs, together with most of the other Slav nationalities, followed the developments in relations between Austria–Hungary and Russia with considerable interest. The majority of Czech nationalist opinion, the Young Czechs in particular, enthusiastically supported the *entente* with Russia. The

---

[38] Winter, *Panslawismus*, pp. 21–2, and also Aehrenthal to Goluchowski, 39E, St Petersburg, 20/7 July 1901, cited on pp. 88–90.

[39] For the text of the treaty see A. F. Pribram, *The Secret Treaties of Austria–Hungary, 1879–1914*, English edition by A. C. Colridge (2 vols., Cambridge, Mass., 1920–1), I, pp. 184–95. Conflicting interpretations of this agreement were subsequently to cause difficulties between the two powers.

Austro-Russian accord was seen in Prague as an important step towards achieving the general objectives of their 'foreign policy'. At this juncture, as had been the case almost without exception since the revival of Czech political activity in the middle of the nineteenth century, Czech nationalism did not strive for complete political self-determination in the form of an independent Czech or Czechoslovak state. Those responsible for formulating the political objectives of the Czech nation were of the opinion that, in a region of Europe contested between the colossi of Russia and Germany, a small independent state would be unable to survive.[40] Beneš, in his study of Czech attitudes towards the Slav world, summarised the aims of Czech 'foreign policy' early in the twentieth century in the following words:

It is essential to create a barrier against the menacingly growing political, economic, military and cultural power of Germany. Directly or indirectly, Germany is attempting to acquire [control over] Central Europe, the Near East and Turkey, while Austria–Hungary remains a powerless pawn within the policy of the Triple Alliance. It is, therefore, essential to take positive steps towards achieving the gradual political and economic strengthening of the Slav element in Austria–Hungary, and thus bring about internal changes in the direction of federalism, which would place the Slavs in the majority and gain them ascendancy. It will then be possible to release Austria–Hungary from its ties with Germany, break up the Triple Alliance, and create in its place an *entente* between Austria–Hungary and Russia. This would act as a barrier against the eastward expansion of Germany, making it possible for even the Balkan Slavs to develop freely, assisted by the co-operation of Russia and Austria–Hungary.[41]

Although, at the turn of the century, following the withdrawal of the Badeni language ordinances, the likelihood of internal reform of the Monarchy had receded, the ultimate objective of achieving a major realignment of the European powers did still appear

[40] Kramář, stated during 1906 that: 'We [Czechs] are far stronger inside Austria, than we could be in any other state.' K. Kramář, 'Rakouská zahraniční politika v XIX. stol.', in *Česká politika*, ed. Z. V. Tobolka (5 vols., Prague, 1906–13), I, p. 180.

[41] Beneš, *Úvahy o slovanství*, p. 135. Z. V. Tobolka, in *Politické dějiny československého národa od r. 1848 až do dnešní doby* (3 vols., Prague, 1932–6), III part 2, p. 619, claims that although the Czech political leadership was 'unenthusiastic' about the Triple Alliance, its 'necessity' was accepted. The Czechs wished the Habsburg Empire to have greater freedom of action within the Alliance.

possible. The prospect of Austria–Hungary becoming the third partner in the existing alliance between Russia and France was, to the Czechs, much more attractive than the continued membership of the Triple Alliance with Germany and Italy. The chief proponent of this policy of seeking closer relations with Russia was the leader of the Young Czechs, Kramář.[42] His party, at the time the largest and most influential Czech political force in Bohemia, from its very first entry into the political arena had favoured a *rapprochement* between the Dual Monarchy and Russia. Kramář, a man of ebullient character, the son of a wealthy builder and manufacturer and himself a successful industrialist[43] besides being the leading figure on the Czech political stage during this period, was strongly Russophil in outlook and a staunch admirer, though with some qualifications, of the established autocratic order in Russia. This attitude is evident from his reaction to the revolutionary events taking place in Russia during 1905, when he voiced suspicion and even displeasure at the attempts being made there to introduce a more representative form of government.[44]

The Czech leader had first come to know and love Russia as a result of a six-months visit to that country in 1890.[45] Even at this early stage in his political career Kramář was conscious of the significance of inter-Slav relations in Czech political life. In a letter written in 1890 from Russia to a political associate, J. Kaizl, he stated: 'we must all assiduously cultivate Slavism – for in the end it is our *ultimum refugium*'.[46] In a further letter Kramář

[42] For his own statements of his foreign policy objectives see Kramář, 'Rakouská zahraniční politika v XIX. stol.', pp. 172–3; K. Kramář, *Poznámky o české politice* (Prague, 1906), pp. 54–60; K. Kramář, *Pět přednášek o zahraniční politice* (Prague, 1922), pp. 23–4.

[43] In 1915 Kramář's fortune allegedly amounted to three million crowns. He owned a brick factory in Semily and a textile mill in Libštát. *Proces dra. Kramáře*, III, part 2, p. 174.

[44] See K. Kramář, 'Ruské problémy', *Nová česká revue*, II (1904–5), pp. 241–54. These views are examined in greater detail on pp. 41–3 below.

[45] V. Sís, *Karel Kramář, Život a dílo* (Prague, 1930), pp. 39–43; M. Sísová, 'Život', in M. Sísová and others, *Karel Kramář. K padesátým narozeninám jeho* (Prague, 1910), p. 11. Kramář spent several weeks with a relation who managed an estate near the Volga belonging to a descendant of the prominent Slavophil, Yu. F. Samarin. The house contained Samarin's extensive library. Kramář later recalled that he had been greatly impressed by the endlessness of the Russian steppe and by the general 'Slav atmosphere'. *Paměti Dr. Karla Kramáře*, arranged K. Hoch (Prague, 1938), p. 208.

[46] J. Kaizl, *Z mého života*, arr. Z. V. Tobolka (3 vols., Prague, 1909–14), II, p. 599n, Kramář to Kaizl, 28 July 1890.

stressed the necessity for striving, together with the Croats and, if necessary, without the Poles, for an 'Austrian Slav policy'. Foreshadowing his later activities, he suggested that a programme for such a policy should be drawn up by the Czechs and communicated to the other Austrian Slavs. Further in the future, he envisaged gatherings of Slav representatives being held and perhaps a periodical being founded.[47] In a later letter to Kaizl, written shortly after his return to Austria, Kramář explained further the objectives underlying his thinking:

I do not wish to pursue an anti-Austrian policy, until it is absolutely necessary, but I would like to see a Slav policy in Austria. It will be pointed out that that is beyond our power; but that can be contended by arguing that it is both easier and more promising to pursue a wider, greater policy than a narrow, egotistic, purely Czech policy, which will fail to receive support from any quarter, even from the other Austrian Slavs. The strength of the Germans is founded on such a wide all-Austrian policy. We Slavs must imitate them. We must indicate that the realisation of our endeavours will not only be of benefit to Bohemia, but to all of Austria.[48]

Subsequently, Kramář commented on these suggestions: 'My visit to Russia, evidently, had a considerable effect on my political plans, though these were at the time rather fantastic, as no preparation whatsoever had been made for co-operation between the Austrian Slavs.'[49] However, despite the enthusiasm for greater Slav unity, which his first visit to Russia had generated, Kramář later observed with dismay that 'as regards Russian Slavism, which I naturally looked for most, I was very disappointed'. Russian liberals, Kramář complained, were totally disinterested in the Slavs, and traditional Russian Slavophilism, linked to the concepts of absolutism and orthodoxy, he found unpalatable, though it was amongst the adherents of this latter philosophy that some interest in the Czechs was shown.[50]

Nevertheless, despite these reservations, in a series of articles published on his return to Bohemia in the then weekly periodical *Čas*, Kramář stressed the desirability of deepening Czech knowledge of Russia and of the Slav world in general. He pointed out

---

[47] *Ibid.*, p. 603n, Kramář to Kaizl, 23 August 1890.
[48] *Ibid.*, p. 605n, Kramář to Kaizl, 2 October 1890.
[49] *Paměti Dr. Karla Kramáře*, p. 231.   [50] *Ibid.*, p. 237.

that, although the Czechs were familiar with social and political conditions in far flung parts of Western Europe, they remained largely ignorant of conditions inside Russia. Steeped as they were in West European culture, it was not easy for the Czechs to comprehend Russia, but if the Czechs wished to be true Slavs, Kramář argued, it was essential that they should familiarise themselves with all aspects of life in the Slav world – Russia included.[51]

The articles themselves, however, despite being entitled 'Impressions of Russia', were concerned almost exclusively with Russian Poland. Subsequently, in his memoirs, Kramář explained that he had lacked the courage to write about Russia, as the more he knew that country, the more enigmatic it became.[52] In the articles themselves the author came close to making the same admission. He stated modestly that he had intended 'getting to know Russia', but despite his extensive travels in the European parts of that country, he had 'no more than seen it'.[53]

Despite the limitations of his first visit to Russia Kramář, nevertheless, did manage to prepare the foundations for a deep and lasting relationship with that country. During this and frequent subsequent visits to Russia he became acquainted with many influential persons active in Russian cultural, political, and commercial life.[54] The Czech leader was later to attempt to utilise these extensive contacts with Russia in his determined attempt to achieve greater cohesion between the Slav nations, particularly between the Czechs and Russians, which he regarded as a prerequisite to achieving the desired reorientation of Austro-Hungarian foreign policy.

In addition to the political relationship Kramář also developed strong family ties with Russia. His wife, Nadezhda Nikolaevna Khludova-Abrikosova, whom he married in 1900, was the daughter of a successful Russian businessman and the divorced wife of a Russian industrialist. Through his wife Kramář obtained a villa, *Barbo*, near Livadia on the Crimea, where the couple spent a considerable amount of time each year. Even in Prague,

---

[51] K. Kramář, 'Dojmy z Ruska', *Čas*, v (1891), p. 6.
[52] *Paměti Dr. Karla Kramáře*, p. 235.   [53] Kramář, 'Dojmy z Ruska', p. 6.
[54] In his memoirs Kramář recalled that during his stay in Russia in 1890 he met, amongst others, the novelist, L. N. Tolstoy, the philosophers V. S. Solovev and S. N. Trubetskoy, the Slavists V. I. Lamansky and A. N. Pypin, and several prominent Russian economists and journalists. *Paměti Dr. Karla Kramáře*, pp. 234–5, 237.

however, thanks to the influence of his wife, the domestic environ-
ment in which he lived was strongly Russian in character.[55]
Czech Russophilism, however, was not restricted exclusively
to the Young Czech Party. The Czech National Socialist Party,
though at the time a less significant political force in Bohemia than
the Young Czechs, was at least as enthusiastic in its admiration of
Russia. The leader of this political organisation, Václav Klofáč
also actively pursued a policy of cultivating closer relations with
Russia and the Balkan Slavs though he lacked both the political
ability and popular support enjoyed by Kramář. Klofáč's journalistic activities made him a frequent visitor to the Balkans and to
Russia, where he worked as a war correspondent in the Far East
during the Russo-Japanese War of 1904–5.[56] Later, he was to
use the opportunities provided by his travel to pursue activities
inimical to the interests of the Habsburg Empire.
The numerically small Realist Party, centred round the influential figure of Masaryk, reflected the attitude adopted towards
Russia by its leader, and advocated a more cautious policy towards
that country, preferring to seek support for their plans to transform the Habsburg Empire into a federal state from amongst the
Austrian Slavs themselves, and in Western Europe and North
America. From his youth Masaryk had devoted much attention
to the study of Russia and its problems. He visited Russia on
several occasions and became familiar not only with existing conditions there, but also with the political and philosophical ideas of
that country.[57] Masaryk developed a considerable interest in
Russian culture and undertook a detailed examination of Russian
Slavophilism, particularly the ideas of I. V. Kireyevsky, one of the
instigators of the movement.[58] Subsequently, Masaryk remarked
to Karel Čapek about his visits to Russia that: 'On the whole
I left [the country] with the same feelings as Havlíček; love for

[55] Herman and Sládek, 'Slovanská politika Karla Kramáře', p. 12; K. Krofta,
Politická postava Karla Kramáře (Prague, 1930), p. 10. See also K. Kramář,
'Moje žena', *Dr. Karel Kramář. Život, dílo, práce vůdce národa*, ed. V. Sís
(2 vols., Prague, 1936–7), II, pp. 89–94.
[56] B. Šantrůček, *Václav Klofáč: (1868–1928) Pohledy do života a díla* (Prague,
1928), pp. 84–8, 123–6; *Obžalovací spis proti Václavu Klofáčovi a Rudolfu
Giuniovi*, ed. Z. V. Tobolka (Prague, 1919), pp. 14–15.
[57] K. Čapek, *Hovory s T.G. Masarykem* (London, 1941), pp. 99–103; J. Papoušek, 'Masaryk i slavyanstvo', *Volya Rossii*, VII (1930), pp. 277–80.
[58] See T. G. Masaryk 'Slavjanofilství Ivana Vasiljeviče Kirejevského', *Slovanské
studie*, I (1889).

the Russian people and dislike of the official policy and the ruling intelligentsia.'[59] In addition to the study of Russia itself, the Realist leader was interested in the associated question of relations between Russia and the smaller Slav peoples. His knowledge of Russia in general, and of the Slavophils in particular, led Masaryk to believe that the Russians were not particularly concerned with the fate of the Czechs. Although admitting that the awareness of belonging to the Slav community of nations did have a cultural significance, he resolutely opposed political Pan-Slavism, which he regarded as being tantamount to Pan-Russianism. Masaryk desired to see every national group within the Dual Monarchy, whether Slav or non-Slav, achieve full cultural independence and some form of political autonomy; a state of affairs which was manifestly not enjoyed even by the Slav national minorities within the Russian Empire.[60]

Ideas very similar to those expressed by Masaryk were also propounded by the Slavist scholar Adolf Černý in the periodical *Slovanský přehled*. Černý was strongly critical of traditional Czech Russophilism for its 'romantic interpretation of the Slav question' and for its idolatry of Russia.[61] Czech Russophils, he argued, 'had been, and still were, impressed by the external greatness of Russia, and it never occurred to them to inquire whether the foundations of the mighty Slav state were sound; on the contrary, they closed their eyes to all that was evil in Russia'.[62] In contrast with this attitude, Černý claimed that he and those who shared his outlook,

wish to love a free and therefore strong Russia, based on the principles of right and justice and no longer poised on a volcano of popular discontent. We wish to see Russia become the moral support of all Slavdom. This can, however, only be achieved by a Russia acting with complete justice towards its own Slavs (the Poles and Ukrainians) and also not open to accusations of injustice towards non-Slavs.[63]

On the far left of the Czech political spectrum, the Social Democrats, who were to become a considerable political force in the

[59] Čapek, *Hovory s T. G. Masarykem*, p. 100.
[60] *Ibid.*; T. G. Masaryk, *The Slavs among the Nations* (London, 1916), p. 16.
[61] A. Černý, 'O slovanské vzájemnosti v době přítomné', *Naše doba*, XIII (1906), pp. 651–3.
[62] A. Černý, 'Odpověd' na otevřený list L. Pantělějeva', *Slovanský přehled*, VIII (1906), p. 13.
[63] *Ibid.*, p. 15; A. Černý, 'O slovanské vzájemnosti', p. 809.

Czech lands during the final years of the existence of the Habsburg Empire, showed a relatively mild interest in Russia. Despite the internationalism of the socialist movement, Czech Social Democracy was basically national in outlook, as is evident from the strained relations between the Czech and Austrian German Social Democrats and the eventual rupture between them which occurred in 1911.[64] Paradoxically, it was precisely the national attitude of Czech Social Democrats which produced their interest in Russia and caused them to share the general but vague Russophilism of the nation as a whole. Although, predictably, they were opposed to the formation of ties with official Russia, the Czech socialists did maintain contacts with Russian Social Democracy, but these were not particularly close, even though the Russian Bolsheviks chose Prague as the venue for their Sixth Conference in January 1912.[65]

At about the same time that the *entente* between Russia and Austria–Hungary, generally welcomed by the Czechs, was being

[64] Although the various socialist organisations within the Austrian lands were united in the Austrian Social Democratic Party in 1889, the national groups within the party were frequently in conflict amongst themselves. The major differences occurred between Czech and German socialists. The Czech movement insisted on maintaining its own national identity, whereas the Austrian German socialists favoured a more centralised political organisation. Friction between the nationalities forced the Austrian Social Democratic Party, in 1899, to adopt a loose federal structure consisting of seven autonomous national sections. The differences between Czech and German socialists continued to increase, however, particularly after the introduction of full manhood suffrage into parliamentary elections in 1907. The national character of Czech Social Democracy led to the formation of a purely Czech trade union movement within the Czech lands, which further exacerbated relations with the German Socialists. In 1911, the majority of Czech Social Democrats severed relations with the Austrian Social Democratic Party by establishing a fully independent Czechoslavonic Social Democratic Party.

[65] The lack of understanding between Czech Social Democrats and the Russian Bolsheviks is evident from the exchanges which occurred at a joint meeting held in Prague after the conclusion of the Bolshevik Party conference. The Czech socialist leadership evidently treated its Russian brethren with considerable condescension. The chairman of the Czech party, Antonín Němec, expressed his bewilderment at the divisions within the ranks of Russian Social Democracy and held out the united Czech Social Democrats as an example to be emulated. At this point the Bolshevik leader, V. I. Lenin, is reported to have turned towards G. K. Ordzhonikidze, one of his closest followers, and remarked, 'the fool'. Lenin also visited Prague during 1900 and 1901, although little is known about his activities there. M. Janda, 'Několik poznámek ke stykům V. I. Lenina s Československou stranou sociálně demokratickou', *Z bojů za svobodu a socialismus*, ed. J. Vávra (Prague, 1961), pp. 124–5.

reinforced by the Mürzsteg agreement concerning Macedonia, the seeds of future discord between the two powers were being sown in another part of the Balkan peninsula. In June 1903 a palace revolution occurred in Serbia which removed the Obrenovich dynasty from power by the assassination of King Alexander and his consort. The insurgents recalled to the throne the Kara-georgevich family, in the figure of King Peter. The political changes which accompanied this dynastic transition, the intro-duction of a more democratic form of government, were to have far-reaching consequences on Balkan developments. Although towards the end of the reign of Alexander Serbia was no friend of Austria–Hungary, the new rulers of the county, more responsive to public opinion and therefore intent on creating a Greater Serbia which would include the South Slav lands of the Habsburg Empire, began to look even more to Russia for support. This development caused considerable displeasure in Vienna, and relations between Austria–Hungary and the small South Slav state steadily deterio-rated. The alienation turned to enmity, which after 1906 manifested itself in the form of a tariff war between Serbia and the Dual Monarchy. The Habsburg authorities placed severe restrictions on Serbian exports, and Serbia retaliated by boycotting Austro-Hungarian goods. On account of the fact that exports from Serbia consisted overwhelmingly of agricultural produce, mainly pigs, the conflict became known as the 'Pig War'. The dispute was damaging to both parties, though Serbia did find alternative out-lets in Europe for its produce. Although normal trading relations between the two countries were restored in 1908, the atmosphere of suspicion and hostility remained.[66]

The dispute between Serbia and the Habsburg Empire, as was to be expected, did not pass unnoticed in the Czech lands. The Czech national leadership showed considerable consternation at the developments in the Balkans. This was partly due to the fact that it was painful for the Czechs to see their own state, Austria–Hungary, in conflict with the Serbs, whom they regarded as being a friendly and related Slav people and with whose aims and ob-jectives they felt considerable sympathy.[67] The tension between

---

[66] See W. S. Vucinich, *Serbia between East and West: The Events of 1903–1908* (Stanford, 1954).
[67] Kramář was highly critical of the Austro-Hungarian tariff policy towards Serbia. Kramář, 'Rakouská zahraniční politika v XIX. stol.', pp. 173–4.

the Dual Monarchy and Serbia also led to an objection of a much more practical nature on account of the damage which the 'Pig War' was inflicting on the economic life of the Czech lands. Czech owned industry and commerce, which had developed in the Czech lands in direct competition with Austro-German undertakings, reached a high state of development during the first decade of the twentieth century, particularly in the fields of banking, engineering, textiles and chemicals,[68] but suffered from the disadvantage of having a relatively restricted market. Austro-German industry, allied to that of the German Empire, dominated much of the Dual Monarchy, forcing Czech industrialists and businessmen to become export orientated. Even in this respect, however, life was not easy for the Czechs who, lacking their own exporting agencies, were dependent on the goodwill of Austro-German financial institutions. Relatively little headway was, therefore, made in exporting to Western Europe and though some progress was made in the direction of Russia, the greatest trading successes were achieved in the Balkan area, particularly with Serbia. The Serbian boycott of all goods manufactured in the Habsburg Empire, introduced as retaliation to Austro-Hungarian restrictive measures against Serbia, did not discriminate between the products of Czech owned industry and that under German and other ownership. Consequently, Czech exports suffered a serious decline. This state of affairs was particularly displeasing to the Czech industrial middle class, organised mostly in the Young Czech Party, who observed with considerable anguish that the German Empire was acquiring much of the trade lost by the Dual Monarchy.[69] Czech anxiety to increase trading links with the Slav world was an important factor in stimulating interest in the subject of inter-Slav relations, particularly in relations with Russia, where the commercial opportunities were greatest. The general Czech endeavour to draw the Habsburg Empire and Russia

[68] The Czech lands constituted one of the most highly developed industrial regions of the Dual Monarchy, with the industry divided between Czech and German ownership. It is difficult to establish the exact size of the Czech owned sector, though it is generally estimated that between 20% and 33% of the industrial potential of Austria–Hungary was in Czech hands at this time. For a detailed account of the economic situation in Bohemia and Moravia prior to the First World War, see *Foreign Office Peace Handbooks*, vol. 1, *Austria–Hungary*, part 1, no. 2, 'Bohemia and Moravia', pp. 42–101.

[69] Kramář, 'Rakouská zahraniční politika v XIX. stol.', p. 171. The following statistics on Serbian imports from Austria–Hungary and Germany are cited

into closer contact was motivated, at least partially, by the same consideration.

Czech opinion, however, was not unanimous in its opposition to the anti-Serbian policies of the Vienna government. The Czech Agrarian Party which, together with the Social Democrats, was to achieve increasing prominence in the political life of the nation during the early years of the twentieth century, raised no objections to the restrictive measures introduced by the Habsburg authorities against Serbia. Favouring a policy of greater protection for agriculture within the Dual Monarchy the Czech Agrarians welcomed the tariff war with Serbia, with whose agricultural exports to the Habsburg Empire they were in direct competition.[70] Indeed, throughout the period under study, the Czech Agrarians responded unenthusiastically to the endeavours of the majority of Czech nationalist opinion, led by the Young Czechs, to obtain greater co-operation between the Slav peoples. The Agrarians had little interest in the formation of closer ties, particularly commercial ones, with Russia and the Balkan Slavs, whose economies were predominantly agrarian in character and whom they therefore regarded as potential rivals. This general disinterest in Slav affairs was also shared by the Czech Clerical Party, though the reasons for its attitude were religious rather than economic.

Further significant demonstrations of Czech feelings towards the Slav world, this time towards Russia, occurred during the Russo-Japanese War and the subsequent Revolution of 1905. The war between Russia and Japan was followed with considerable interest throughout the Slav world, the Czech lands being no exception. The Russophil majority of the Czech nation, under the leadership of the Young Czechs, strongly supported the Russian

in *Naše doba*, xx (1913), p. 375:

Year	Total value of Serbian imports in thousands of francs	Imported from Austria–Hungary		Imported from Germany	
		Value in thousands of francs	(%)	Value in thousands of francs	(%)
1905	55601	33414	60.11	6263	11.57
1906	44329	22228	50.16	9733	21.96
1907	70583	26650	36.34	20320	28.79

[70] K. Kramář, *Na obranu slovanské politiky* (Prague, 1926), p. 75.

military campaigns in the Far East.[71] A foreign loan floated in Europe by the Russian government to help finance the war was enthusiastically subscribed to in the Czech lands where a third of the entire Austro-Hungarian contribution was raised.[72] In February 1904, shortly after the war had broken out, representatives of the Prague municipality, including the Mayor and other dignitaries, attended a service in the Russian Orthodox church in the city to pray for the victory of Russian arms. A further indication of popular feeling was given by the frequent demonstrations which occurred in the streets of the Bohemian capital, and other towns, in support of Russia. Public sentiment, however, was not entirely Pan-Slav in character, as is evident from the fact that gratitude was also expressed to France – Russia's ally. In contrast, the other major powers became targets of abuse. Attempts were made to stage demonstrations outside the British, German, and United States consulates in Prague, protesting against the sympathetic attitude these states were believed to have adopted towards Japan. The Czech pro-Russian demonstrations produced a reaction amongst the Bohemian Germans, particularly amongst German students in Prague, whose counter-demonstrations led to clashes between the two nationalities, which had to be subdued by the army.[73]

The Bohemian Germans were not alone, however, in wishing for the defeat of Russia. A minority of Czech opinion, consisting principally of Social Democrats and Realists, believed that a Japanese victory would exert a beneficial effect on the Russian Empire, by precipitating long overdue political reforms which would replace the autocracy by a constitutional government and lead to the introduction of greater civil liberties. During February 1904 the Czech Social Democrats countered the Russophilism of the Young Czechs and their supporters by organising demonstrations protesting against the war in the Far East and the policies of Imperial Russia in general.[74] The Realist attitude was outlined by A. Černý who, during 1905, after the battle of Tsushima at which

---

[71] *Národní listy* expressed considerable concern about the alignment of the other European powers in the Russo-Japanese conflict. In its opinion, the question of which side to support was inapplicable to the Czechs, as 'our sympathies can only be with Russia'. *Národní listy*, 11 February 1904.
[72] *Ibid.*, 13 January 1905.
[73] *Ibid.*, 22, 23, 29 February, 7 March 1904.
[74] *Právo lidu*, 29 February, 1 March 1904; *Národní listy*, 29 February 1904.

the Japanese navy inflicted a decisive defeat on the recently reinforced Russian naval forces, commented with evident satisfaction that: 'The battle of Tsushima has tipped the balance in
favour of the Russian nation and the other peoples of Russia.
The [old] system of government suffered a humiliating defeat –
and the Russian peoples are claiming a victory.'[75]

The hopes of those Czechs who were opposed to Russian
absolutism soon began to be realised. By the time the war with
Japan was concluded, Russia was in chaos. The military failures in
the Far East acted as a crushing psychological blow and the
ensuing hardship and demoralisation contributed directly to the
Revolution of 1905. For the first time, the Russian autocracy
showed signs of crumbling. Widespread civil unrest forced the
introduction of a measure of constitutional government with the
creation of a representative assembly, the Duma.

In addition to the revolutionary unrest and the ensuing internal
reforms, the outcome of the war against Japan also caused changes
in the foreign policy of the Russian Empire. Traditionally, Russia
had two main fields of action available. The Russian government
either devoted its attention to the Balkans, under the convenient
guise of assisting the Balkan Slavs to independence, or it concentrated on imperial expansion in Asia. After 1905 Russia, effectively
checked in the Far East, began to show increasing interest in
European affairs, particularly in those of the Balkans and the Near
East. This withdrawal to Europe was further underlined in 1907,
when agreement was reached between Russia and Great Britain
on the division of spheres of influence in Persia and other disputed
Asian territories. In the same year, and again in 1910, Russia and
Japan settled their remaining differences. The new European
phase in Russian foreign policy was initiated in May 1906, when
A. P. Izvolsky replaced Count V. N. Lamsdorf as Minister of
Foreign Affairs. There were several compelling reasons why
Russian attention should be focused on the Near East. German
expansion into the Balkans, Turkey and Persia was steadily grow-
ing and becoming increasingly a direct threat to Russia. The
Russian authorities were also aware of the probable coming disintegration of the Ottoman Empire and wished to stake a claim for
some of Turkey's European possessions. In addition, Izvolsky

---

[75] A. Černý, 'Na prahu velké doby. K současnýmudálostem v Rusku', *Slovanský
přehled*, VII (1905), p. 434.

was determined to realise Russia's historic ambition of opening the Straits of the Bosphorus and the Dardanelles to enable the free passage of Russian warships to and from the Black Sea, restricted by the convention of 1841. Finally, Russia's renewed interest in the Balkans was also partly due to the increased pressure exerted under the new political system by an, albeit limited, public opinion, which was nationalistic in character and keenly interested in the welfare of the Orthodox Balkan Slavs.

This new orientation of Russian foreign policy inevitably produced far-reaching consequences on the relations between Russia and the Austro-Hungarian Empire. The external interests of Russia and those of the Habsburg Empire, allied to Germany, were now geographically in close proximity and conflict became more probable, more especially after 1906, when control of Austro-Hungarian foreign policy came into the hands of Count A. Aehrenthal. Aiming to enhance the international standing of the Habsburg Empire, he pursued an expansionist policy in the Balkans which culminated in the annexation of Bosnia and Herzegovina in the autumn of 1908. From that point onwards, relations between Russia and the Dual Monarchy, which had been cordial during most of the last decade, steadily deteriorated. This estrangement took place despite attempts on both sides to draw the two Empires and Germany together and to re-create the League of Three Emperors, in order to preserve the principles of strong monarchical rule.

Most of the smaller Slav nations of Central and South-Eastern Europe welcomed the change in Russian foreign policy, and the Czechs and Slovaks were no exception. Between 1878 (the end of the Russo-Turkish War) and 1905, due to a combination of domestic problems and concentration on expansion in Asia, the Russian government had paid little attention to the Slavs.[76] *Národní listy* lost no time in pointing out in an editorial article on the Treaty of Portsmouth, which concluded the Russo-Japanese War, that Russia was now able to return to Europe:

The most significant consequence of the Peace of Portsmouth for the entire Slav world would be if the Russians, instead of concentrating on the most distant parts of the Far East, where they met with such great

[76] Beneš, in *Úvahy o slovanství*, pp. 130, 137, restricts the period from 1900 to 1904.

disaster, now turned their attention back to their western and southern borders in Europe and provided a moral and diplomatic defence for their Slav brethren, who are exposed to mortal danger from a ferocious alien tide which is eroding further and further the shores of Slavdom and endangering the very heart of European Russia.[77]

The reorientation of Russian foreign policy was also welcomed by Kramář. He argued at the time that the Habsburg Empire had no cause to fear increased Russian involvement in European affairs for the two countries, in his opinion, shared a common interest – that of restricting the expansion of Germany. Kramář also hastened to indicate that, due to its economic underdevelopment, Russia would not become a serious economic rival of Austria–Hungary in the Balkans for some time to come.[78]

Also, the political changes taking place within the Russian Empire as a consequence of the 1905 Revolution did not pass unnoticed in Austria–Hungary, and exerted a significant influence on relations between Czechs and Russians. The constitutional reforms, which followed the turbulent events of that year, had the effect of stimulating general Czech interest in Russia as the Russian autocracy, in the eyes of many Czechs one of the principal obstacles in the way of closer relations between them and the Russians, appeared to have been significantly weakened.[79] Kramář (the leading Czech Russophil) did not, however, realise this fact at the time, though he was to show awareness of it two years later. He expressed his reactions to the 1905 Revolution in an important article, entitled 'Russian problems', published in the periodical *Nová česká revue* during 1905.[80] Although the article is essentially an analysis of the issues raised by the revolutionary events which had recently taken place in Russia, it also provides a revealing insight into the general attitude which Kramář held towards that country at the time.

He accepted the premise, upon which the Slavophils had based their theories, that Russia differed fundamentally from the West. As evidence of this the author pointed to the enormous contradiction in Russian life – contrasting the sophistication of the intelligentsia, Western in its attitude and outlook, with the

[77] *Národní listy*, 3 September 1905.
[78] Kramář, 'Rakouská zahraniční politika v XIX. stol.', pp. 170, 172.
[79] A. Černý, 'O slovanské vzájemnosti', pp. 739–40, 807.
[80] Kramář, 'Ruské problémy', pp. 241–54. For the Czech leader's views concerning the events of early 1905 in Russia see also *Le Temps*, 23 February 1905.

primitive Russian peasant: 'Everywhere [in Russia] there exist, side by side, without organic links and without the benefit of historical development, which reconciles and removes the sharp edges, two worlds – the new, even hyper-modern, and the old, which is unbelievably ancient.'[81] The problems produced by this dichotomy, Kramář maintained, could not be solved by the superimposition of a Western-style constitution and the introduction of a legislative assembly.[82] Though conceding the necessity for reform, he believed that this should be directed towards reconciling the differences which had arisen between the intelligentsia and the state. Conditions needed to be created in which the great potential of the intelligentsia could be utilised to the benefit of the entire nation.[83] He favoured the retention of the autocracy, not because of its inherent virtues, but because he considered it to be the governmental system most suited to the needs of Russia. He also forecast that, if introduced in Russia, parliamentary rule would be no more than an autocracy with the trappings of a parliament.[84]

When making a diagnosis of Russia's revolutionary troubles, Kramář attributed the prime responsibility for the dissatisfaction and unrest to the bureaucracy and not the autocracy. He explained that, in his opinion, 'the main reason behind the evil in Russia is a lack of faith amongst the ruling circles in the absolute necessity of the autocracy in the existing conditions'. This lack of faith was caused by the bureaucracy, which had created the oppressive regime, not in order to defend the autocracy, but solely to protect itself.[85] It had now become evident that if the autocracy was to survive, the bureaucracy had to be radically transformed, its methods modernised, and the intelligentsia had to be drawn into the government service.[86] Relations between the state administration and the public required to be improved and increased, but, in the author's view, this could not be achieved through a parliamentary system, for Russia was not yet prepared for the 'sovereignty of the people'. Therefore, Kramář argued:

Russia must seek its own special method of enabling the intelligentsia to participate in government; such a method would reconcile the just

[81] Kramář, 'Ruské problémy', pp. 241–2.   [82] *Ibid.*, p. 242.
[83] *Ibid.*, pp. 243–4.   [84] *Ibid.*, p. 244.
[85] *Ibid.*, p. 246. Kramář asserted that: 'In absolutist Russia *L'etat c'est moi* did not apply, but *L'etat c'est la bureaucratie* did.'   [86] *Ibid.*, pp. 247–8.

demands of the socially and culturally developed upper classes of society not to be kept in humiliating subservience, with the preservation of the autocracy which is regarded as a sacred institution by the simple Russian people.[87]

Such a solution could only be achieved by the creation of a consultative assembly, which would not inhibit the freedom of action of the Crown, but would exercise a controlling influence over the bureaucracy.[88] His lack of enthusiasm for a full parliamentary system in Russia, Kramář explained, was 'mainly due to the fact that the ground had not been prepared for it there...neither amongst the intelligentsia, nor amongst the masses'.[89] Limited reforms, along the lines indicated were, however, in his opinion essential and required to be carried out 'in the interest of the autocracy'. Kramář concluded the article as follows:

Every sincere friend of Russia will joyfully welcome the day when the great Slav Empire will awaken to a new and better life in which the incompetent and ailing bureaucracy, which demonstrated only the worst aspect of Russia, will no longer be its main representative. The Tsarist autocracy will no longer have any cause to fear that which is the very best Russia has to offer – its intelligentsia, longing for freedom, for civil liberties, and for the opportunity to work for the benefit of the entire nation. On the contrary, the autocracy will, with complete confidence, invite the intelligentsia to participate in the governing of the state, will no longer be subjected to attacks from both inside and outside Russia and, without fear, with faith in the future, and no longer suspicious of each move towards liberty, will fully enter an era of extensive cultural and economic reforms. These are essential if Russia's political role in the world is not to be severely and irreparably damaged.[90]

Kramář's conservative attitude towards the 1905 Russian Revolution, though reflecting the general opinion within the Young Czech Party[91] was not, however, shared by all Czechs, and was later

[87] *Ibid.*, p. 249. [88] *Ibid.*, pp. 249–50. [89] *Ibid.*, p. 253. [90] *Ibid.*, p. 254.
[91] *Národní listy* was extremely dismayed by the Revolutionary events inside Russia. In its reaction to the 'Bloody Sunday' shootings the paper attributed responsibility for the incident, in equal measures, to both the demonstrators and the authorities. *Ibid.*, 23 February 1905. At the height of the intensified unrest in Russia, which occurred during October 1905, the Young Czech organ, aware of the critical nature of the situation, expressed the hope that 'at the last moment the terrible, catastrophic tragedy would be averted in holy Russia'. *Ibid.*, 29 October 1905. After the proclamation of the October Manifesto, promising the introduction of a constitution in Russia, *Národní listy* somewhat reluctantly welcomed the development, hoping that 'the

to become an embarrassment to him.[92] Prominent amongst those who welcomed the developments in Russia during 1905 were, predictably, the Social Democrats. Czech socialists not only expressed their support for the Russian Revolution in words, at public meetings and in the press, but also organised monetary collections in aid of the revolutionaries.[93] The Realist Party also adopted a positive attitude towards the changes taking place inside Russia. Masaryk, the Realist leader, subsequently wrote that: 'Judged as a whole, the Revolution of 1905–1906 was advantageous to the development of Russia.'[94] And it was not only Russia which was affected by the events of those years, for as Masaryk also stated: 'The Russian Revolution had a favourable repercussion on Europe. In Austria, for example, manhood suffrage was introduced as an outcome of the pressure exercised by the Russian Revolution.'[95]

During the course of 1905, a wave of civil and industrial unrest spread through many parts of the Dual Monarchy in response, partially at least, to the revolutionary events in Russia. The Czech lands, being amongst the industrially most highly developed areas of the Habsburg Empire, experienced a large number of strikes, some caused by purely economic grievances but many also political in character.[96] These political strikes accompanied by public demonstrations, led mostly by the Social Democrats, were part of a campaign for the introduction of universal manhood suffrage, which had been gaining momentum for some time in the Austrian lands. The achievements of the Russian Revolution, the promise

constitution would enable...Russia to grow as strong internally, as the autocracy had enabled Russia to became powerful externally'. This, however, was not expected to be an easy task. *Ibid.*, 1 November 1905.

[92] When, during 1908, prior to launching the Neo-Slav movement, Kramář, accompanied by two other prominent Austrian Slavs, made an exploratory visit to St Petersburg (see below, pp. 69–90), the editor of the periodical *Slovanský přehled*, A. Černý, commented that the Czech leader's opposition to constitutionalism in Russia did not provide him with the best qualifications for his mission. A. Černý, 'Po slovanských dnech v Petrohradě a ve Varšavě', *Slovanský přehled*, x (1908), p. 439.

[93] Lists of contributors to a Russian Benevolent Fund appeared in the Social Democratic newspaper *Právo lidu* throughout the early part of 1905.

[94] Masaryk, *The Spirit of Russia*, II, p. 347.

[95] *Ibid.*, p. 565.

[96] See J. Doležal and J. Beránek, *Ohlas první ruské revoluce v českých zemích* (Prague, 1954); *Rok 1905. Prameny k revolučnímu hnutí a ohlasu první ruské revoluce v českých zemích v letech 1905–1907*, ed. O. Kodedová and others (Prague, 1957).

of a constitution and the creation of the Duma, provided an additional stimulus to the movement for electoral reform and a near revolutionary situation occurred in parts of the Dual Monarchy. The Czech lands were no exception, and Social Democrats there threatened to follow the example set in Russia and were determined to 'speak Russian' to the Habsburg authorities.[97] The campaign culminated on 28 November 1905 when a one day general strike, accompanied by mass demonstrations, took place in many towns and cities throughout the Austrian lands, including Prague and Brno, in support of the demand for extending the franchise. Meanwhile, the Vienna government had given way to the mounting pressure and announced its intention to introduce the desired electoral changes.[98] Although the campaign for extending the suffrage had been initiated by the Social Democrats in various parts of the Austrian territories, the success of the movement was contributed to by the virtually united action of the entire Czech nation. All the major Czech political parties added their voices to the demands for electoral reform, though in some cases with varying degrees of reluctance.[99] The Young Czechs, who had been unenthusiastic in their attitude towards widening the franchise in recent years, came out strongly in support of the reforms.[100] Kramář, who amongst others had been responsible for formally proposing in the Austrian Parliament the extension of the suffrage,[101] subsequently explained that he had been directly motivated by events in Russia. He stated that: 'My personal experience of the Russian Revolution, being in a train attacked by revolutionaries, inevitably made me consider the possible

---

[97] J. Hejret, *Češi a Slovanstvo* (London, 1943), p. 56; I. Pfaff and V. Závodský, *Tradice česko-ruských vztahů v dějinách. Projevy a doklady* (Prague, 1957), p. 255.
[98] W. A. Jenks, *The Austrian Electoral Reform of 1907* (New York, 1950), pp. 40–4.
[99] J. F. N. Bradley, 'Czech Nationalism and Socialism in 1905', *The Slavic Review*, XIX (1960), pp. 80–1, 83–4.
[100] K. Kramář, 'Za vedení národní strany svobodomyslné', in *Česká politika*, ed. Z. V. Tobolka, III, pp. 714–17; S. B. Winters, 'The Young Czech Party (1874–1914): An Appraisal', *The Slavic Review*, XXVIII (1969), pp. 436–7. The Young Czech Party had advocated the introduction of universal manhood suffrage at its inception in 1874, though it subsequently lost interest in the reform. The demand was not revived until 1905. T. G. Masaryk, *Politická situace. Poznámky ku poznámkám* (Prague, 1906), pp. 39–40.
[101] *Stenographische Protokolle über die Sitzungen des Hauses der Abgeordneten des österreichische Reichsrates, XVII. Session* (Vienna, 1905), XXXV, p. 31446.

consequences. I saw that it was politically expedient to introduce
changes voluntarily, while we remained strong enough to resist the
pressure, rather than be forced into action later.'[102]
The Russian Revolution was not, however, the only factor which
contributed to reforming the franchise in Austria. One contemporary observer described the introduction of full manhood
suffrage as 'in a sense...an accident',[103] resulting from the
conflict between the two sections of the Empire which arose in
1905 over Hungarian agitation for greater independence. The
Emperor Francis Joseph forced the Magyar nationalists, who had
recently gained control of the Hungarian Parliament, to give up
demands for greater independence, principally in the form of a
separate army, by threatening to extend the franchise in Hungarian parliamentary elections. This measure would have considerably altered the composition of the Budapest Parliament and
weakened the grip of the Magyar ruling class. The political forces
in the Austrian part of the Monarchy, who were demanding the
introduction of universal manhood suffrage, took full advantage
of this situation. It was obviously difficult for the Emperor to
refuse to carry out in Austria the very same reforms proposed for
Hungary.[104] The third, and perhaps most significant reason for
the changes was the necessity, felt by many Austrian political
leaders, to steer Austrian politics away from the sterile atmosphere
of national rivalries and introduce, instead, politics based on socio-
economic groupings cutting across purely ethnic divisions.[105]

[102] *Proces dra. Kramáře*, II, pp. 329–30.
[103] H. W. Steed, *Through Thirty Years, 1892–1922: A Personal Narrative* (2 vols., London, 1924), I, p. 261.
[104] Jenks, *Austrian Electoral Reform*, pp. 27–30. The proposed electoral reform in the Hungarian part of the Dual Monarchy never materialised and the non-Magyar nationalities remained largely disenfranchised. Despite this handicap, the national minorities were relatively successful in the elections of 1906. The non-Magyar grouping in the Budapest Parliament rose from ten to twenty-five members, the Slovaks increasing their representation from two seats to seven. The united stand adopted by the two Slovak political organisations, the National Party and the People's Party (founded in 1905), undoubtedly contributed to this success. These modest electoral achievements of the non-Magyar nationalities, however, provoked the Hungarian authorities into taking repressive measures, including the arrest and imprisonment of many newly elected deputies. Tobolka, *Politické dějiny československého národa*, III, part 2, pp. 368–75.
[105] R. A. Kann, *The Multinational Empire: Nationalism and National Reform in the Habsburg Monarchy, 1848–1918* (2 vols., New York, 1950), II, pp. 220–2; Tobolka, *Politické dějiny československého národa*, III, part 2, pp. 388, 444–5.

The first elections under the reformed electoral system took place in May 1907. The electoral contest was purely political and was not fought between the various nationalities of the Austrian lands as the national distribution of parliamentary seats had been determined in advance, roughly in proportion to the size of each ethnic group. [106] After the elections the main object of the reforms seemed to have been attained. The representation of the extreme nationalist parties in the Vienna Parliament was reduced, and the Social Democrats together with the Christian Socialists emerged as victors. The Social Democrats, who had previously held eleven seats, now won eighty-seven out of five hundred and sixteen, and were only prevented from being the largest single parliamentary group by the partial amalgamation of the Christian Socialists with the German Clericals.[107]

In common with most other nationalist parties, the Young Czechs, who had up to then constituted the major Czech political force, suffered a substantial reverse; their parliamentary representation being significantly reduced. In the elections of 1901, the Young Czechs, in alliance with the Old Czechs and other groupings, obtained fifty-three seats. In the 1907 elections, standing on their own, the Young Czechs won only fifteen seats. Their former allies, the Old Czechs, obtained five seats. The results of the first election held under full manhood suffrage indicated that the Czech nation had cast its votes along socio-economic lines. The Czecho-slavonic Social Democratic Party and the Czech Agrarian Party

[106] The national distribution of seats was as follows.

Nationality	Number of seats	Percentage of seats	Percentage of total population
Germans	233	45.16	35.78
Czechs	107	20.74	23.24
Poles	82	15.89	16.62
Ukrainians	33	6.40	13.18
Slovenes	24	4.65	4.65
Italians	19	3.68	2.83
Serbs and Croats	13	2.52	2.77
Rumanians	5	0.97	0.90
	516		

Column 1 from Jenks, *Austrian Electoral Reform*, p. 164, and column 3 from the census of 1900, see above p. 1, Table 1.

[107] Jenks, *Austrian Electoral Reform*, p. 215.

gained votes, at the expense of the Young Czechs, from the industrial workers and the agricultural community respectively. The Czech Social Democrats increased their representation from two seats to twenty-four, and the Agrarians from five to twenty-seven. Gains were also recorded by the Czech Clerical Party, which obtained seventeen seats in place of two held previously, and by the National Socialists who increased their parliamentary representation from four seats to six, with their allies, the Progressive State-Rights Party, obtaining a further three seats. In terms of percentages, the Young Czechs succeeded in receiving only 7.31 per cent of the total votes cast for the Czech parties in the first, and more representative, of the two ballots. This compared unfavourably with 36.25 per cent secured by the Social Democrats, 19.22 per cent by the Agrarians, and 16.97 per cent by the Clericals. Of the major Czech parties, only the National Socialists, excluding their allies, performed worse, obtaining 6.98 per cent of the vote.[108] The most significant outcome of the new political situation, as far as the Young Czechs were concerned, was that they could no longer maintain their claim to the leadership of the entire nation. Their role was clearly reduced to what it had in fact been from the party's formation in 1874 – the political organisation of the Czech middle class.[109]

Although he anticipated the election results[110] Kramář was, predictably, extremely disappointed by the performance of his

[108] Figures adapted from K. K. Statistische Central-Commission, *Österreichische Statistik*, VIII, part I, 'Die Ergebnisse der Reichratswahlen in Jahre 1911' (Vienna, 1912), pp. 6, 10–11; Bosl, ed., *Handbuch der Geschichte der böhmischen Länder*, pp. 460–1; and Jenks, *Austrian Electoral Reform*, p. 215. The number of votes cast in the first ballot for the five major Czech parties were as follows: Social Democrats, 389960; Agrarians, 206784; Clericals, 182500; Young Czechs, 78679; National Socialists, 75101.

[109] Winters, 'The Young Czech Party', pp. 429–30, 434.

[110] Kramář was aware of the fact that the Young Czechs were steadily losing ground to other political parties, particularly to the Agrarians and the Social Democrats, even before the introduction of the electoral reform. In his book, *Poznámky o české politice* [Notes on Czech Politics], published during 1906, which was essentially a justification of past and present Young Czech policies, Kramář conceded the inevitability of the appearance and growth of parties based on social groupings, but he maintained that it was 'absurd' that each party should pursue its own national policies. The Young Czech leader warned that: 'Should it become evident that the wave of sectional interests, on the one hand, and unenlightened radicalism, on the other, are stronger than the organisation of our party, naturally weakened by time, the consequences will not only be felt by the party but by the entire nation.' Kramář, *Poznámky o české politice*, pp. 78, 82.

party, which was underlined by the fact that he himself only gained his seat in the Vienna Parliament on the second ballot.[111] Later, he wrote with some bitterness: 'It was the end of Young Czech leadership in Czech politics. Nothing more remained of the former greatness than the habit of holding the Young Czech deputies responsible for all that took place in Vienna. The dream of an influential Czech policy in Vienna had also evaporated'.[112] Kramář realised that it would, in future, be difficult for him to play the role of a leading Czech political figure as in Parliament he would be no more than a leader of a minor party. Therefore, largely out of a desire not to be edged out of the mainstream of Czech politics, and sensing a growing Russophil tendency and a heightened Slav awareness in the Czech lands and an increasing interest within post-revolutionary Russia towards the smaller Slav nations, he launched a campaign aimed at promoting closer ties between the Slav peoples.[113] The new movement, in order to distinguish it from the Pan-Slavism of the past, acquired the name of Neo-Slavism.[114] The appearance of this movement was not, however, an entirely new departure. It was rather the culmination of the gradual re-emergence of what the Czechs termed the 'Slav idea' – that is an awareness of belonging to the Slav community of

[111] *Národní listy*, 16, 24 May 1907. Failing to win a clear majority in the first ballot, Kramář had to fight a second round contest against a Social Democratic candidate in the Německý Brod constituency. He won the run-off ballot by 5439 votes to 3098 votes.
[112] Kramář, 'Za vedení národní strany svobodomyslné', p. 772.
[113] The view that Kramář was motivated largely by opportunism in his decision to promote the Neo-Slav movement is substantiated by the fact that, although a hint of his forthcoming change of attitude towards Russia is contained in his book *Poznámky o české politice*, published in 1906, relations with the Slav world do not feature prominently in it. He did express the expectation that, as a consequence of the 1905 Revolution, Russian officialdom, in the form of the bureaucracy and the Orthodox Church, and the Polish hatred of Russia would both disappear. He believed that, in the long term, these changes would exert a beneficial effect on relations between all the Slav peoples. Kramář, *Poznámky o české politice*, p. 56. At the treason trial conducted against Kramář in Vienna during 1915 and 1916, the accused denied being the instigator of the Neo-Slav movement. *Proces dra. Kramáře*, IV, part 2, p. 16. This is strictly true. The concept did not originate from him but from the editorial board of the periodical *Máj* and from the Czech National Council. See below pp. 56–7. Nevertheless, although the original idea was not Kramář's, without his enthusiastic support the movement might never have achieved prominence.
[114] The term Neo-Slavism had first been used by the Russian publicist, M. M. Fedorov. Tobolka, *Politické dějiny československého národa*, III, part 2, p. 611.

nations and a desire for increased contact and co-operation between the Slav peoples – which had commenced at the Palacký
centenary celebrations in Prague during 1898.
Recent developments in the Dual Monarchy had given inter-
Slav relations a new political significance. The belief in the possibility of united Slav action within that country had been greatly
reinforced by the agreement reached, towards the end of 1905,
between Serbs and Croats in the South Slav territories of the Dual
Monarchy.[115] The electoral reform of 1907 encouraged further
effort in the development of this ideal.

In the new Austrian Reichsrat, elected by full manhood suffrage,
the Slavs – that is the Czechs, Poles, Ukrainians, Serbs, Croats and
Slovenes – could, for the first time, if combined, constitute a vir-
tual parliamentary majority.[116] Slav unity within the lands had
thus acquired an increased importance, of which the instigators
of the Neo-Slav movement were fully aware. Kramář himself
wrote:

For reasons of practical politics the primary concern had to be to ensure
that the Slavs, united in a stable Slav block, would form the firm foundation of every parliamentary majority and thus become an even greater
obstacle to Austrian anti-Slav policies in both domestic and external
affairs, particularly in the case of those policies directed against Russia
and Serbia.[117]

He believed that if the Slavs, hitherto divided on many issues,
could be brought together and persuaded to vote in unison in the
legislature, then their position within Austria–Hungary could be
improved and the Empire's foreign policy changed to their advantage. The long term Czech objective of turning the Dual Monarchy
away from its alliance with Germany and drawing it closer

[115] On October 1905 Croat representatives from Croatia and Dalmatia met in
Rijeka (Fiume) and adopted resolutions demanding, among other things,
greater national freedom and the reunion of Dalmatia with Croatia. Shortly
afterwards representatives of the Serbs from Croatia met in Zadar (Zara) and
associated themselves with the same programme. The following month, in
the same city, representatives of the Serbs and Croats in Dalmatia did likewise,
and declared that their two peoples formed one nation. See R. W. Seton-
Watson, *The Southern Slav Question and the Habsburg Monarchy* (London,
1911), pp. 146–50.
[116] Theoretically, the Slav nationalities controlled 259 seats against 257 controlled by the German and Latin peoples: see above p. 47, n. 106. In the
election, however, the Slavs obtained only 256 seats; three seats assigned to the
Slavs, in Galicia and Bukovina were unexpectedly won by Jewish candidates.
[117] Kramář, *Na obranu*, p. 16.

towards Russia could then be attained.[118] Subsequently, Kramář claimed that:

At the time this was not a utopia, for the Austrian Minister of Foreign Affairs was Count Aehrenthal, whom I knew well from the days of my first visit to Russia, where he was [at the time] ambassador...and with whom I had detailed political conversations each time he returned to Austria from St Petersburg. From these discussions I learned that he was in favour of a *rapprochement* with Russia in order to weaken the dependency on Germany.[119]

The second most numerous Slav group in the Austrian Parliament, after the Czechs, was formed by the Poles. Their cooperation was, therefore, essential if Kramář's strategy was to succeed. The leaders of the Austrian Poles, however, were unlikely to join any Slav coalition while their compatriots in Russian Poland remained the victims of Russian oppression. Kramář fully realised that the necessary first step towards Slav unity, both inside and outside the Habsburg Empire, was to improve the position of the Poles under Russian rule and thus attempt to end the protracted dispute between the two nations.[120] The Russo-Polish conflict, morbidly described by A. Černý as 'an ever suppurating and bleeding ulcer on the Slav body', [121] was widely regarded as the principal obstruction in the way of greater Slav unity.[122] The changes that had taken place in Russia following the 1905 Revolution, held out improved prospects of an understanding between the Russians and Poles being achieved. Voices began to be raised in Russia favouring a *rapprochement* with the Poles based on respect of their separate nationality.[123] A further product of the more tolerant atmosphere which followed the revolutionary events of 1905, was an unofficial conference of representatives of Russian and

---

[118] Kramář, *Pět přednášek*, pp. 28–9.
[119] Kramář, *Na obranu*, p. 18. Aehrenthal, on becoming Austro-Hungarian Minister of Foreign Affairs in 1906, did desire to make the Dual Monarchy more independent of Germany. During his period of office, however, he achieved the opposite.
[120] Kramář, *Na obranu*, p. 16; Kramář, *Pět přednášek*, pp. 28–9.
[121] A. Černý, 'Otázka autonomie království polského', *Slovanský přehled*, VIII (1906), p. 117.
[122] Beneš, *Úvahy o slovanství*, pp. 136–7; A. Černý, 'O slovanské vzájemnosti', p. 651.
[123] A. Černý, 'Nejnovější úvahy o slovanské politice', *Slovanský přehled*, X (1908), pp. 257–61, 300–7.

Polish liberals which took place in Moscow in April of that year. The question of autonomy within the Russian Empire for the Kingdom of Poland was not only openly discussed, but a resolution passed demanding its introduction. A similar demand was also expressed at an all-Russian congress of rural and urban local government representatives which met later that year.[124] Although nothing concrete emerged from these and other discussions of the Polish question many Czech observers, including Kramář, regarded these developments as most encouraging.[125]

The main factor of the Polish situation was that, at the turn of the century, there was no independent Polish state; the Polish nation, after the third partition in 1795, being divided between Austria, Germany and Russia. Only the Austrian Poles enjoyed some measure of political autonomy. Galicia, the Austrian part of Poland, gradually acquired, during the nineteenth century, a limited amount of self-government in return for which the Polish ruling classes became firm supporters of the Habsburg government in Vienna. The Poles living within the Russian and German Empires were in a less fortunate position, and had to contend with considerable oppression from their respective colonisers. It was, in particular, the harsh treatment meted out by the Russians to the Polish inhabitants of Russian Poland that helped to maintain the close ties between the Austrian Poles and the Habsburg Authorities. Although the Russian oppression was political, economic and cultural, hardest to bear were the measures directed against Polish culture and education in an attempt to Russify the Polish population. With the exception of the period from 1905 to 1907, when the establishment of private schools in which teaching took place in the Polish language was permitted, the use of Polish was strictly limited.[126]

The Russo-Polish conflict had earlier attracted the attention of

---

[124] A. Černý, 'Na prahu velké doby', pp. 438–40; A. Černý, 'Otázka autonomie království Polského', pp. 102, 104. The Russo-Polish conference was held on 21 and 22 (8 and 9) April 1905. Amongst the one hundred or so participants were journalists, academics and local government representatives. *Novoe vremya*, 12 (25) April 1905; *Slovanský přehled*, VII (1905), p. 421. See also E. Chmielewski, *The Polish Question in the Russian State Duma* (Knoxville, 1970), pp. 27–9.
[125] Kramář, *Poznámky o české politice*, p. 56; A. Černý, 'Na prahu velké doby', p. 445.
[126] W. F. Reddaway and others (eds.), *The Cambridge History of Poland* (2 vols., London, 1941–50), II, pp. 387–460.

Kramář during his journey to Russia in 1890, which had included a visit to Russian Poland. In the previously mentioned series of articles inspired by his travels, published early the following year in the periodical *Čas*, the author devoted considerable attention to Russo-Polish relations, thereby instituting a lengthy polemic on the subject.[127] Although he attributed responsibility for the existing antagonism between the two Slav nations to both parties, he expressed the view that the first steps towards an improvement in relations would have to come from the Russian side, by granting cultural, religious, and linguistic rights to the Polish nation. These measures would encourage the development of the Polish peasantry and reduce the power of the aristocracy which, in Kramář's opinion, was responsible for much of the tension between Russians and Poles. Full autonomy for the Polish nation, he maintained, was out of the question as the Poles 'were not yet ripe for it.'[128] Even at this early stage, he was aware of the potential beneficial effect that a *rapprochement* between the Russians and the Poles could exert on inter-Slav relations in general, and on those between the Slavs of the Austrian lands in particular. He believed that if a solution could be found to the problem, it would not only enable the Poles to play a full and active part in the affairs of the Slav community of nations, but would also remove a barrier to Slav co-operation within the Dual Monarchy.[129] The years to come were to show how crucial Russo-Polish relations were to the wider issue of Slav unity.

Kramář's patronage of the Neo-Slav movement, dedicated to improving inter-Slav relations, an essential component of which were relations with Russia, implied the adoption of a very different attitude towards that country from that which he had expressed a few years earlier during the height of the 1905 Revolution. Despite the fact that he had performed a *volte-face* and was to attempt, with characteristic vigour and determination, to involve the more liberal sections of Russian society in Neo-Slavism by stressing the movement's democratic nature, his earlier expressed conservative views increased the difficulty of this self-imposed task and caused many people of liberal outlook to avoid association with it. The

[127] Kramář, 'Dojmy z Ruska', pp. 5–6, 22–4, 52–5, 69–72, 84–5. See also V. Šťastný, 'Polemika v Čase roku 1891 o polsko-ruské otázce', *Slovanské historické studie*, v (1963), pp. 85–116.
[128] Kramář, 'Dojmy z Ruska', p. 84.   [129] *Ibid.*, p. 85.

credibility of his change of heart was not enhanced by the fact
that at about the very time that he was placing his political hopes
on post-revolutionary Russia, the newly acquired democratic
institutions in that country were being significantly weakened.[130]
   In an article written towards the end of 1907, only a few months
prior to Kramář's launching of the Neo-Slav movement, A. Černý
regretted that the forces of reaction were re-asserting themselves
in Russia. These developments – together with the collapse of
Russo-Polish negotiations, rising tension between the Poles and
Ukrainians in Galicia, and renewed dissent amongst the South
Slavs – in his words, were 'casting a cloud' on relations between
the Slav peoples, though he did remain optimistic about the long
term prospects.[131] This optimism, however, was tempered with
caution. In an earlier article on the subject of inter-Slav relations,
the eminent Czech Slavist itemised the internal problems bedevilling the Slav world. In addition to the Russo-Polish conflict,
which attracted the most attention, Černý distinguished four other
protracted disputes between members of the Slav family of
nations. These conflicts were between Ukrainians and Russians;
Ukrainians and Poles; Serbs and Croats; and Bulgarians and
Serbs. To this total the author added a further item – the recently
emerged dispute between Czechs and Poles in Silesia. This
catalogue of discord caused him to comment, with evident
disenchantment, that 'wherever two Slav nations lived alongside,
they came into conflict'.[132] The Neo-Slavs, desiring to establish
harmony in the relations between the Slav peoples, evidently had
set themselves a task of Herculean proportions.

[130] The First and Second Dumas, elected by a wide franchise, were dissolved
by the government in July 1906 and June 1907 respectively. Elections to the
Third Duma, later in 1907, were held under a considerably less democratic
electoral system.
[131] A. Černý, 'Nejnovější úvahy o slovanské otázce', pp. 113–14.
[132] A. Černý, 'O slovanské vzájemnosti', pp. 736–7.

3
The rise of the Neo-Slav movement, 1905–1908

The first seeds, out of which grew the Neo-Slav movement, had been sown early in 1906. In a series of articles entitled 'The Slav Union' a Russian journalist in Vienna, Svatkovsky, indicated that the only effective answer to the increasing danger from the eastwards expansion of Germany was in a united Slav approach. This Slav unity should, however, not be based on the old principles of Pan-Slavism, that is, Russian domination, but on the basis of equality of all the Slav nations. Before such a union could be achieved the Russians and the Poles would have to become reconciled and relations between Russia and Austria–Hungary improved, thus enabling the Slavs of both Empires to draw closer together. Svatkovsky believed that the Slavs could initiate closer ties among themselves by organising social events such as visits, exchanges, and congresses, and by increasing commercial contacts. In addition, he proposed the formation of a customs union between Russia and the Habsburg Empire, also including the Balkans.[1] Shortly after the publication of these views Svatkovsky founded in Russia a Slavonic Society, the aim of which was to implement the ideas for Slav co-operation, as outlined by himself. This organisation did not, however, remain in existence for very long.[2]

Later that year, during the first few meetings of the newly formed Russian Duma, the liberal academic M. M. Kovalevsky suggested to the Duma that it should express its sympathy for the small Slav nations and urge the need for greater inter-Slav co-operation. Kovalevsky spoke of the duty of Russian democracy 'to protect all the Slav nationalities...to maintain their cultural individuality...and secure opportunities for their further development'. He rejected Pushkin's poetic formula for the 'Slav streams to converge in the Russian sea', preferring instead to see

[1] Beneš, *Úvahy o slovanství*, p. 138. Svatkovsky's articles, 'L'union slave', appeared under the pseudonym Nestor in *Revue Slave*.
[2] V. Švihovský, 'Slovanské sjezdy', *Naše doba*, XVI (1909), pp. 27–8.

them 'flow side by side along different courses, but in the same
direction towards the wider world...'[3] However, due perhaps to
the struggle which the young Russian parliament was waging for
its own survival, Kovalevsky's suggestion was not implemented.
Simultaneously, the Czechs were also showing an increased
interest in promoting closer relations between the Slav nations.
During 1906 the Czech literary journal, Máj, conducted a survey
of opinion with the object of ascertaining to what aims future Slav
policy would be directed. A number of prominent Slavs from the
Dual Monarchy were asked whether they believed that a united
Slav movement, within the boundaries of the Austro-Hungarian
Empire, was possible; and, if it was, how they imagined this unity
could be brought about.[4] Over thirty answers were received and
published in subsequent editions of the journal.[5]
   One of the most interesting responses came from the Slovene
deputy in the Vienna Reichsrat, Hribar, who was later to figure
prominently amongst the founders of the Neo-Slav movement.
Hribar believed that the boundaries for concerted Slav action, set
by the editorial board of Máj, were too restrictive. He argued that
it was a mistake to regard the frontiers of Austria–Hungary as
barriers to Slav partnership. Large numbers of Slavs lived outside
the Dual Monarchy, and they also should be included in any future
plans. The Slovene leader envisaged this co-operation taking place
in three distinct fields – those of politics, economics, and culture.
Political co-operation, he believed, was possible only between the
Slavs of the Austrian half of the Empire. It should be based on a
united Slav parliamentary organisation in the Vienna Reichsrat.
Economic co-operation, on the other hand, could cover a wider
area and involve the Slavs of both halves of the Dual Monarchy.
A union of Slav financial institutions would help to promote this
aim. Co-operation in the third field, that of cultural relations,
could be wider still and include all the Slav nations, both inside
and outside the Austro-Hungarian Empire. Cultural links could be
strengthened by the concerted action of organisations endeavouring

[3]   *Gosudarstvennaya duma, stenograficheskie otchety, sessiya 1* (2 vols., St Petersburg, 1906), I, p. 108. Pushkin's words are from his poem *Klevetnikam Rossii*
[To the Slanderers of Russia] written in 1831 in response to West European
protests over the suppression, by the Russians, of the Polish uprising of that
year.   [4] 'Slovanský postup', *Máj*, IV (1905–6), pp. 414, 433.
[5]   *Ibid.*, IV (The answers appeared at intervals throughout 1906). K. Kramář did
not participate in the survey.

to increase the national awareness of their particular nation.[6] These views were shared by another correspondent, J. Hrubý, of the editorial staff of *Národní listy*. He also stressed that the interests of the Austro-Hungarian Slavs could not be separated from those of the Slavs outside the Dual Monarchy; Austro-Slavism only divided and weakened the entire Slav world.[7]

As a result of this survey of opinion the editorial board of *Máj* called on the Czech National Council to organise a congress of Slav nations in commemoration of the sixtieth anniversary of the first Slav Congress, held in Prague in 1848.[8]

The Czech National Council discussed this proposal at a meeting on 1 June 1907, when a decision was taken to hold further consultations with prominent Czech political figures and other interested persons.[9] A second confidential meeting on this subject took place on 13 October. Present were parliamentarians from most Czech political parties, eminent Slavist scholars, and representatives of the arts and sciences. J. Herold, the leader of the Czech National Council, was in the chair. The plan to call a Slav congress was accepted in principle, and a special committee was established to continue the preparations. This committee was also delegated the task of making further soundings of opinion amongst other Slavs, both within the Dual Monarchy and elsewhere. In November 1907 a circular was sent to all the Slav nations outlining the proposals for the congress. Enclosed with this was a summary of the replies received in the *Máj* survey.[10]

The growing enthusiasm for calling a Slav congress was further reinforced by the congress of the Sokol gymnastic organisation,

---

[6] I. Hribar, 'Slovanský postup', *Máj*, IX (1911), pp. 617–19, 629–30. Although written in response to the survey carried out in 1906 Hribar's views were not published until 1911 as they had arrived too late for inclusion with ꞏthe other replies.   [7] 'Slovanský postup', pp. 497–9.

[8] *Jednání 1. přípravného slovanského sjezdu v Praze 1908* (Prague, 1910; hereafter cited as *Jednání sjezdu 1908*), p. 1 (unnumbered). (This is an abbreviated version of the transcript of the Congress proceedings.) The communication was sent to the Czech National Council on 29 May 1907.

[9] *Ibid.*, p. 1 (unnumbered).

[10] *Ibid.* At his trial in 1916 the prosecution alleged that Kramář, together with the Russophil Ukrainian leader, Markov, was responsible for replacing the original proposal, made by the editorial board of *Máj*, to hold a congress of Slavs from Austria–Hungary only, with a plan for a congress to be attended by all the Slav nations. In his defence, Kramář claimed that the decision to include Slavs from outside the Dual Monarchy was taken by the Czech National Council. *Proces dra. Kramáře*, I, pp. 19, 21; IV, part 2, p. 7.

which was held in Prague during the summer of 1907. The gathering, known as the Fifth Sokol Congress, took place between 28 June and 1 July, when mass gymnastic displays and other events were staged in the Bohemian capital before large numbers of foreign visitors from both Slav and non-Slav countries. Several Russian guests attended the festivities, amongst them V. M. Volodimirov and N. N. Azarev representing the city of St Petersburg; a representative of the Russian Ministry of Defence, A. P. Skugarevsky; the author K. A. Borisov-Korzhenevsky; and several journalists including Vergun and V. Prokofev from *Novoe vremya*, a leading conservative newspaper. The numerous representatives of other Slav peoples included the Slovene Hribar and the Russophil Ukrainian M. Glebovitsky,[11] both of whom were to feature prominently in the Neo-Slav movement. The only Slavs who declined to be present were the Poles, who chose to hold their own gymnastic display in Lvov, to coincide with the events in Prague.[12] Prominent amongst the guests attending the Sokol Congress was a non-Slav group, a delegation from the city of Paris accompanied by several representatives of the French press.[13]

Despite the presence of the French visitors, most Czechs regarded the Sokol Congress as an important demonstration of their Slav consciousness. In a leading article, published shortly before the events, *Národní listy* noted with satisfaction that: 'The idea of Slav reciprocity is making victorious progress, despite the shadows which are cast over it, and despite the consequences of disturbing situations. During precious moments of deep awareness of common aims it fills both our hearts and minds.' The writer added, with foresight: 'Political unity [of the Slavs] is not, for the time being, our main objective; our minds are working towards such a form of reciprocity, in which each Slav nation would preserve its freedom and independence.'[14] After the conclusion of the Sokol celebrations, however, *Národní listy* was somewhat less enthusiastic. Considerable disappointment was caused by the fact

[11] *Pátý slet všesokolský v Praze ve dnech 28.–30. června a 1. července 1907*, ed. J. Scheiner (Prague, 1907), pp. 117–34, 226; *Národní listy*, 26, 28, 29, 30 June and 1, 2 July 1907; *Novoe vremya*, 17 (30) June 1908.
[12] *Národní listy*, 1 June, 12 July 1907. Although the Poles officially boycotted the Prague Sokol festivities, one representative was present from the German division of Poland. *Pátý slet všesokolský*, p. 227.
[13] *Pátý slet všesokolský*, p. 127.
[14] *Národní listy*, 27 June 1907 ('Před sokolskými dny').

that the liberal political forces in Russia, the Kadets (the Constitutional Democratic Party) in particular, failed to show great interest in the Sokol festivities, or in the wider pursuit of Slav understanding.[15]

For many of the Russian guests, the visit to Prague had also not come up to their expectations. One commentator, the publicist Vergun, reported that, in comparison with the past, 'the citizens of Prague... had weakened in their demonstration of Slav feeling'. He also complained that the atmosphere at the banquets had been 'somewhat faint' and that references to politics were avoided in order not to inhibit Czech co-operation with the Habsburg authorities.[16] Others were left with the impression that the Czechs had not treated them with the respect they deserved, and felt particularly slighted by what they considered to be the preferential treatment given to the French representatives.[17] One of the Russian guests who had been present at the Sokol Congress, on returning to St Petersburg, explained in a newspaper article that the Russians themselves were responsible for the lack of attention they received. He argued that this was due to the fact that in the past they had shown little interest in the Slavs in general, and the Czechs in particular. The writer regretted that most of the Russian visitors in Prague had attended as private individuals, and pointed out that the only official Russian guests were two representatives of the St Petersburg municipality and three representatives of the press.[18] Azarev, one of the delegates of the city of St Petersburg, voiced similar regrets when speaking at a banquet held during the Prague Sokol festivities. He excused Russia's lack of concern for the Slavs by referring to the fact that Russia had only recently awakened from a deep slumber. Azarev expressed the conviction that the new Russia would firmly espouse the Slav cause, and foresaw the spread of the Sokol movement throughout Russia.[19]

The other representative of St Petersburg at the Sokol Congress was General Volodimirov, who was later to play a prominent role in the founding of the Neo-Slav movement. Volodimirov was not an eminent person, being a little known retired professor from the Russian Military Academy and an alderman of the city of St

[15] *Ibid.*, 10 July 1907.   [16] *Novoe vremya*, 22 June (5 July) 1907.
[17] Kramář, *Pět přednášek*, p. 27.
[18] *Národní listy*, 12 July 1907 (report of an article by N. N. Maksimov in the Russian newspaper *Svet*.).
[19] *Pátý slet všesokolský*, pp. 226–7; *Národní listy*, 1 July 1907.

Petersburg. Although not previously concerned with Slav affairs, largely because of their reactionary associations, Volodimirov's sojourn in the Bohemian capital, during which he had met leading Czech political figures including Kramář, aroused his interest in the subject. The enthusiastic welcome accorded in Prague to the French guests made him determined to see relations between Russia and the other Slavs strengthened by placing them on a new footing of mutual understanding and respect.[20] In addition to visiting Prague, Volodimirov travelled to Vienna and Budapest, returning to Russia via Serbia and Bulgaria, where he further examined various aspects of relations between the Slav peoples.[21] On arrival back in St Petersburg he began actively to promote greater interest in the non-Russian Slav nations.[22]

In Russia, during this time, the idea of calling a Slav congress was also gaining popularity. The impetus to the scheme was given by Professor A. A. Borzenko of Odessa University, a politically and publicly insignificant figure, who, during July 1907, announced his intention of donating 100 000 roubles to finance a Slav congress, with the aim of promoting the union of the Slav peoples.[23] Borzenko had become interested in the future of the Slavs after reading the views of the German economist W. Sombart, who had seen a correlation between the cultural predominance of a race and its numerical strength. Sombart substantiated his theory by pointing out that, a century previously, the Latin race had not only been the most numerous in Europe but also, culturally, the best developed. During the nineteenth century, this dominant position had been held by the Germanic nations. Statistics indicated that the Slav population was now becoming the largest in Europe and a period of Slav predominance, Sombart believed, was therefore bound to follow. Under the influence of these ideas, the unknown professor from Odessa decided to encourage the growth of Slav unity.[24]

[20] Švihovský, 'Slovanské sjezdy', p. 98; Kramář, *Pět přednášek*, p. 27; *Proces dra. Kramáře*, II, pp. 38–9; IV, part 1, p. 16. Subsequently the Austro-Hungarian authorities became convinced that Volodimirov was a dangerous 'Pan-Slav agitator', and a special file was kept on his activities. Haus-, Hof- und Staatsarchiv (H.H.St.A), Politisches Archiv (PA), XL 219, *Panslav Bewegung* [section] 6, 'General Wolodimiroff 1908–1910'.   [21] *Den* 24 January 1908.
[22] Švihovský, 'Slovanské sjezdy', p. 99.
[23] *Novoe vremya*, 17 (30) December 1907.
[24] *Národní listy*, 28 July 1907, 5 September 1911; *Proces dra. Kramáře*, V, part 1, pp. 45–8.

Borzenko had announced his intention of donating the large sum of money to the Slav cause in an open letter to the Russian Prime Minister, P. A. Stolypin, in which he requested that the Russian government take the initiative in bringing the Slav community of nations closer together. After some delay, Stolypin made a guarded reply stating that, although the government would be prepared to accept the financial gift to be used as specified by Borzenko, the actual task of convening a Slav meeting should be left to the various Russian Slavonic societies. In addition, the Russian Prime Minister stressed that the aim of such a Slav assembly could only be to promote closer cultural contacts, and he firmly ruled out any form of political co-operation.[25]

Meanwhile, Borzenko had also written to several Russian public and private bodies, indicating the need for Slav unity and informing them of his proposed gift. Among these was the Association of Public Figures (*Klub obshchestvennykh deyateley*), a multi-party grouping recently formed in St Petersburg, consisting mostly of Duma representatives and local dignitaries. The Association, after discussing the proposals, accepted in principle the idea of calling a Slav congress and suggested, as a preliminary step, that a meeting of representatives of all the Slav nations should be held in St Petersburg in order to make preparations for a major congress equal in significance to that held in Moscow in 1867. The Association of public figures then turned to Borzenko for the promised sum of money, but received nothing more than an evasive answer.[26] The hundred thousand roubles never materialised.

In addition to publicising his ideas in Russia, Borzenko also communicated with the Slavs in Austria–Hungary. In a letter addressed to Kramář and to two other prominent Slav deputies in the Vienna Parliament, the Slovene, Hribar, and Russophil Ukrainian, D. A. Markov, he informed them of his intended

[25] *Novoe vremya*, 17 (30) December 1907, 8 (21) March 1908; *Národní listy*, 28 July 1907, 5 September 1911; *Proces dra. Kramáře*, v, part 1, pp. 45–8.

[26] *Novoe vremya*, 17 (30) December 1907, 8 (21) March 1908; *Národní listy*, 25 March 1908; *Čas*, 3 April 1908; Švihovský, 'Slovanské sjezdy', p. 100. Later, Borzenko informed B. Pavlů that the chairman of the Association of Public Figures, Krasovsky, who replied to Borzenko's letter, while himself in sympathy with the idea of raising the issue of Slav unity on the floor of the Duma, was far from certain that conditions were right for this. Krasovsky feared that discussion of the subject might lead to serious disputes, which could result in the dissolution of the Duma. *Národní listy*, 5 September 1911; *Proces dra. Kramáře*, v, part 1, p. 47.

donation and called upon them to organise the congress.[27] On the instigation of Markov, a meeting of interested Slav members of the Reichsrat took place in Vienna, on 27 November 1907, to discuss the proposals received. The gathering was attended by representatives of most of the Slav peoples in the Austrian lands, except the Poles. Amongst those present were the Czechs, Kramář and Klofáč; the Russophil Ukrainians, Markov and Glebovitsky; and the Slovene, Hribar.[28] Kramář later stated that he had attended very reluctantly, claiming that he was exhausted after the prolonged struggle for the reform of the suffrage.[29] At the meeting he nevertheless outlined his views on the future relations between the Slav nations, stressing that any co-operation would have to be of an exclusively non-political nature. He also maintained that any new Slav movement would have to reject the Pan-Slav principles of 'Orthodoxy, autocracy, and nationality', as proclaimed by Count Uvarov in the previous century,[30] and replace these by the democratic principles of 'freedom, equality and, brotherhood'. In addition, Kramář warned that no progress could be made towards greater Slav understanding before the Russian and Polish nations became reconciled.[31] These ideas were to become the basic tenets upon which the Neo-Slav movement was later to be founded. The Vienna meeting agreed in principle that a congress of all the Slav

[27] Kramář, *Pět přednášek*, p. 27; *Proces dra. Kramáře*, I, p. 20; v, part 1, p. 42. At his trial in 1916, Kramář stated that: 'Borzenko was a rather comic figure. He was unknown, and the 100000 roubles which he proposed to donate were never seen by anyone. I took no notice of his letter, as was the case with many others; only...Dr Markov, who presumably had more free time at his disposal, was of the opinion that a reply had to be given and he, therefore, called several Slav deputies to a meeting' (II, p. 31). Kramář also claimed that he informed Borzenko in no uncertain terms, through Glebovitsky, that the Neo-Slav organisers 'wished to have nothing to do with his roubles' (IV, part 1, p. 8).

[28] *Jednání sjezdu 1908*, p. II (unnumbered); *Novoe vremya*, 8 (21) August 1908; *Proces dra. Kramáře*, II, p. 38; I. Hribar, *Moji spomini* (4 vols., Ljubljana, 1928–33), I, pp. 231–2.

[29] Kramář, *Pět přednášek*, p. 27. Herman, in 'Novoslovanství a česká buržoasie', in *Kapitoly z dějin vzájemných vztahů národů ČSR a SSSR* (Prague 1958), p. 273, indicates that this was unlikely, as the elections had been held more than six months previously.

[30] Count S. S. Uvarov, an influential conservative Minister of Education from 1833 to 1849, insisted that Russian education should be based on the formula of 'Orthodody, autocracy, and nationality'. These principles were incorporated into the Pan-Slav programmes of the various Russian Slavonic agencies.

[31] Kramář, *Pět přednášek*, p. 27; *Proces dra. Kramáře*, II, p. 38; IV, part 2, pp. 8–9.

peoples, to be concerned primarily with matters of a cultural nature, should be held in Russia in the near future. A four-man committee, under the chairmanship of Kramář, and consisting also of Klofáč, Hribar, and the Russophil Ukrainian deputy, Glebovitsky, was elected to examine the suggestion further and to enter into exploratory talks with representatives of other Slav nations.[32] After consultation with leaders of the Austrian Poles, their representatives attended a further gathering of Slav members of the Austrian Reichsrat on 14 April 1908. This meeting confirmed the task set for the executive committee at the earlier gathering.[33]

Shortly before the second meeting took place, a letter from one of the participants, the Croat A. A. Tresić-Pavičić, was published in *Novoe vremya*. In this, Tresić-Pavičić argued that the convocation of a Slav congress, preferably in St Petersburg, was desirable in order to stimulate Russian interest in the Western Slavs and to indicate to the world that, despite the recent Russo-Japanese War, the Slavs remained strong. He envisaged that the congress would be concerned with cultural matters and stressed that politics would have to be excluded from the agenda.[34]

In Russia the resurgence of Slav feeling continued. The Sokol Congress recently held in Prague had helped to stimulate interest in the small Slav nations. The Russian press, which at this time enjoyed a not inconsiderable amount of freedom, devoted more attention to Slav affairs and sent out correspondents to the Slav countries.[35] The reaction of *Novoe vremya* to the question of establishing a Russian consulate in Prague, which had been raised a few days previously in the Austrian Delegation by Kramář, was indicative of this new attitude. He had pointed out that the majority of the trade carried out between Austria–Hungary and Russia was transacted *via* Prague, yet Russia had no official representation there.[36] In an editorial article on this subject, which the newspaper described as being 'a sore spot in Czech–Russian relations', *Novoe vremya* was at a loss to understand why the Russian government was so uninterested in this issue. It was the Russian authorities,

[32] *Den*, 22 January 1908 (V. M. Volodimirov, 'Komu přísluší právo svolat všeslovanský sjezd?'); *Jednání sjezdu 1908*, p. 11 (unnumbered).
[33] *Novoe vremya*, 8 (21) August 1908. See also Hribar, *Moji spomini*, 1, pp. 232–4.
[34] *Novoe vremya*, 30 March (12 April) 1908.
[35] *Národní listy*, 28 July 1907; *Čas*, 4 April 1908; Svihovský, 'Slovanské sjezdy', p. 31; *Novoe vremya*, 18 February (2 March) 1908.
[36] *Národní listy*, 1 February 1908.

and not those of the Dual Monarchy, who were preventing the
establishment of official Russian representation in the Bohemian
capital. The usual explanation given in Russia for the non-existence
of a consulate in Prague was that the authorities in St Petersburg
wished to maintain 'correct' relations with the Habsburg Empire.
Novoe vremya failed to comprehend how the presence of a representative of the Russian government in Prague could endanger this
'correct' relationship, as relations between Russia and Austria–
Hungary had been cordial for some considerable time.[37]
   The increasing attention paid to Slav affairs was also manifested
in other respects. Early in 1908, the Russian Academy of Sciences, a semi-official body, honoured the memory of the Slavophil
thinker, A. S. Khomyakov,[38] who, together with I. V. Kireyevsky,
had been responsible for the formation of the Slavophil philosophy in the 1840s. The Slavonic Benevolent Societies, which
had been inactive during the last few years, also began to show
signs of revival.[39] Public interest was further demonstrated by the
formation of several new societies and associations concerned with
Slav matters. The most significant of these were the Society for
Slav Scholarship (*Obshchestvo slavyanskoy nauky*), established in
St Petersburg during April 1908, and two societies founded in
Moscow at about the same time, the Society for Slav Culture
(*Obshchestvo slavyanskoy kultury*) and the Aksakov Society
(*Obshchestvo imeni Aksakova*), named after the prominent Slavophil. These organisations declared themselves to be non-political
in nature, and were predominantly interested in encouraging
cultural and economic co-operation amongst the Slav community
of nations. They were to become the leading spirits of the new
Slav movement in Russia. The membership of the St Petersburg
based society, led by the Octobrist Yu. N. Milyutin, contained
many figures active in the forefront of Russian public life,
belonging mainly to the centre of the political spectrum,
the Kadet and Octobrist parties. The Society's membership included the Kadet leaders P. B. Struve, P. N. Milyukov, and V. A.
Maklakov; the prominent Octobrists A. I. Guchov and N. A.
Khomyakov; the Progressists N. N. Lvov, M. A. Stakhovich, and
M. M. Fedorov; and other individuals with moderate liberal views

[37] *Novoe vremya*, 21 January (3 February) 1908.
[38] *Národní listy*, 9 January 1908.
[39] *Čas*, 5 April 1908 (V. Švihovský, 'U generála V. M. Volodimirova').

such as Professor Kovalevsky. The two Moscow societies, the Society for Slav Culture and the Aksakov Society were headed by, respectively, the eminent academic F. E. Korsh and the publicist S. F. Sharapov.[40] Many of these persons were later to be active, alongside Kramář and other representatives of the non-Russian Slavs, in the Neo-Slav movement. Others, much to Kramář's chagrin, chose to avoid any association with Neo-Slavism, largely because of suspicions of its reactionary nature. The attitude of this section of moderate Russian opinion was indicated early in 1908, when a group of persons, including Struve, Milyukov, A. I. Guchkov, M. A. Stakhovich, and Kovalevsky, declared themselves publicly against the idea of calling a Slav congress in the near future. They were of the opinion that the time was not yet right for this, as they wished to avoid any connection between the new movement and the old ideas of Pan-Slavism.[41] A similar point of view was expressed by Khomyakov, the President of the Duma. Although he envisaged a Slav congress being called to mark the culmination of the unification of the Slav nations, he did not regard such a meeting as being the most suitable first step in that direction.[42]

Another Russian who opposed the idea of calling a Slav congress at that time was the publicist Sharapov. In an open letter to Borzenko he agreed with the necessity of uniting the Slav nations against what he considered to be the German threat, but stressed that unity could not be achieved before the Russians and the Poles became reconciled. Sharapov suggested, therefore, that a Russo-Polish conference should precede any wider Slav meeting.[43]

Despite these dissenting voices, a considerable amount of attention in Russia was focused on the suggestion of calling a Slav congress. One of the first problems to be resolved, before any

[40] *Novoe vremya*, 29 April (12 May) 1908; Švihovský, 'Slovanské sjezdy', pp. 102–3; A. Fischel, *Der Panslawismus bis zum Weltkrieg* (Stuttgart–Berlin, 1919), pp. 516–17. *Čas*, the organ of the Czech Realists, commented with relief that 'this time [the control of] Slav affairs has fallen into clean hands'. *Čas*, 3 April 1908.
[41] *Národní listy*, 26 April 1908 (These views were outlined in an article by S. A. Kotlyarevsky in the St Petersburg *Slovo.*). None of the persons mentioned attended the 1908 Prague Congress, though Guchkov did attend the Sofia Congress in 1910.   [42] *Čas*, 27 May 1908.
[43] A. Černý, 'Nejnovější úvahy o slovanské otázce', pp. 304–5; *Proces dra. Kramáře*, II, p. 32. Sharapov's letter, entitled 'Vozmozhen-li slavyansky sezd?' appeared in the periodical *Svidyatel'*, II, no. 7 (January, 1908), pp. 5–35.

progress could be made in that direction, was that of deciding which organisation would be responsible for making the necessary preparations. There were several contenders for this honour. The Slavonic Benevolent Societies considered it their prerogative to assume responsibility for preparing the grounds for a meeting of the Slavs. An alternative proposal was that the matter should be placed in the hands of the Russian Academy of Sciences. Many supporters of the new Slav movement in Russia were, however, unhappy about both these suggestions, for the bodies mentioned were considered to be too closely associated with officialdom and reaction. They believed that the multi-party Association of Public Figures would be the most suitable organisation to undertake the preparatory work for a Slav congress. On the suggestion of Volo-dimirov, the Association accepted this task and thus became, from the organisational point of view, the chief promoter of the Neo-Slav movement in Russia.[44]

At a meeting held on 19 (6) March 1908, the Association of Public Figures debated at length the subject of convening a Slav congress. The proceedings were opened by Vergun who outlined the history of previous Slav gatherings and drew attention to their marked lack of success but who, nevertheless, was of the opinion that circumstances had changed and that the time was right to call a further meeting of the Slav nations. This view was supported by Kovalevsky who stressed, however, that the congress should be concerned only with cultural matters. Fedorov also spoke in favour of the idea but warned that the proposed congress would require very careful preparation, if it were not to result in exacerbating the existing disputes between the Slav nations. He maintained that the Russians and the Poles would have to reach an understanding before such a meeting could take place. As the financial support promised by Borzenko appeared not to be forth-coming Vergun suggested that a committee be established, con-sisting of representatives of the Duma and the State Council, which would have the task of raising the required capital and of organising the congress in conjunction with the committee, previously established in Vienna, consisting of Kramář, Hribar,

[44] *Den*, 22, 23 January 1908 (Volodimirov, 'Komu přísluší právo svolat všeslo-vanský sjezd?'). The suggestion that the Russian Academy of Sciences should organise the proposed congress was made by A. Sobolevsky in *Novoe vremya*, 31 December 1907 (13 January 1908).

Glebovitsky, and Klofáč. Two speakers, Milyutin and A. A. Bash-makov objected to this proposal on the grounds that it was the privilege of the St Petersburg Slavonic Benevolent Society to call the congress. Bashmakov, one of the leaders of the Slavonic Benevolent Society, spoke out in defence of the old Slavophils and their ideas, and criticised the Neo-Slavs for having nothing new to offer. Volodimirov countered with the suggestion that the initiative to convene a Slav congress be left with the Austrian Slavs. The 'compromised' Slavonic Benevolent Society, and similar reactionary organisations, were, in his opinion, not suit-able bodies for this purpose, because he considered it wrong to associate the Congress with the discredited Pan-Russian ideas of the Slavophils. Volodimirov also advocated the establishment, in Russia, of a Neo-Slav society, in direct competition with the traditional Slav organisations. This society, for which he suggested the name All-Slav League, Volodimirov envisaged as a wide grouping of all democratic Slav elements, both individuals and organisations, who desired to solve the problems of Slav relations by 'progressive methods'. The meeting of the Association of Public Figures was inconclusive, no definite decision having been taken about the proposed Slav congress. Volodimirov, who was shortly again to visit Prague bearing a gift from the city of St Peters-burg, was, however, empowered by the Association to ascertain, during his journey, the attitude of the Austro-Hungarian Slavs on this subject.[45]

Later, in an interview with a Czech journalist, Volodimirov outlined the reasons for his opposition to the proposed Slav congress being associated with the Slavonic Benevolent Society. He explained that:

Perhaps once, under Aksakov and Khomyakov, these Societies had worked for the Slav cause. Now, however, they are refuges for de-mented sixty year old ladies, and people who think only of the auto-cratic Tsar and aim to convert everyone to Orthodoxy. Nothing of significance is discussed at their infrequent, boring meetings; anyone who has the courage to express progressive ideas is shouted down... Their feebleness and incapacity are indicated by the fact that during the last four years, when life [in Russia] came to the boil, they

[45] *Novoe vremya*, 8 (21), 9 (22) March, 31 March (13 April) 1908; *Národní listy*, 25–28 March 1908; *Čas*, 3, 5 April 1908; Švihovský, 'Slovanské sjezdy', pp. 100–1.

completely ceased their activities, and did nothing – absolutely nothing. The Societies came to life again only when the reactionary forces regained the initiative. They are the nests of all reaction, the greatest enemies of the Slav idea.[46]

Volodimirov arrived in Prague for his second visit early in April 1908. As instructed by the Association of Public Figures he held discussions in the Bohemian capital and in other centres with leaders of the Austrian Slavs about the question of increasing co-operation between the Slav nations. During his stay in Prague Volodimirov stressed the importance of calling a Slav congress in the near future. He stated that although, ideally, he would like to see this take place in Russia, if that were not possible Cracow or Prague would be acceptable alternatives. As regards the programme of the proposed congress, Volodimirov offered no definite suggestions. In his view, the preparation of the agenda could be left to the Western Slavs. He indicated, however, that he believed it unlikely that the congress proceedings could be kept within the narrow limits of being purely cultural in character and totally excluding politics, laid down by P. A. Stolypin in his reply to Borzenko. Before returning to Russia Volodimirov held further consultations with Slav leaders in Vienna (where he met representatives of Slav members of the Reichsrat), and in Cracow, and Warsaw. He was reported to have been overjoyed by the positive response with which his proposals were received, and to have found the attitude of the Poles particularly encouraging.[47]

When asked, while in Prague, for his views on how Czech–Russian relations could be improved, Volodimirov replied that both nations had to learn more about the other. A Russian library and reading room was needed in Prague in order to increase the availability of Russian books and periodicals. Personal contacts between Czechs and Russians also required encouragement. Russian students should be invited to study at the Czech university, and an effort made to advertise Bohemia in Russian publications. Volodimirov believed that events taking place in the Czech lands passed unnoticed in Russia, because no attempt was made to inform the Russian public.[48]

[46] Čas, 5 April, 1908 (Švihovský, 'U generála V. M. Volodimirova').
[47] Čas, 4, 7 April, 28 May 1908; Jednání sjezdu 1908, pp. II–III (unnumbered); Švihovský, 'Slovanské sjezdy', p. 102.
[48] Čas, 10 April 1908 (V. Švihovský, 'V. M. Volodimirov o česko-ruských stycích'). While in Prague, Volodimirov was very favourably impressed by the

In this connection, it was decided during the discussions in Prague that, in order to familiarise the Russian public with Neo-Slav ideas, some journalistic preparation was essential. In a series of articles, published on his return to Russia in the newspaper *Birzhovye vedomosti*, Volodimirov outlined the basic aims of the new movement, 'ceremonially renounced the old Pan-Slavism', and repeated the proposals he had previously put forward at the meeting of the Association of Public Figures in St Petersburg.[49] In addition, Volodimirov published a translation of an article by Kramář in which the Czech leader recorded with satisfaction that, at last, the 'new Russia' was demanding a hearing. Kramář welcomed the fact that the Slav conscience of Russia was being reborn out of the humiliation suffered on the Far Eastern battlefield:

The heavy trials of a lost war and a revolution have taught [Russia] to view, seriously, existing realities. They have brought about the realisation that no longer is it possible to treat with contempt the sympathy offered by the [other] Slav nations. Russia has learned that, on the contrary, their support is essential in order to avoid isolation in a sea of enemies.

Kramář also stressed the importance of respecting the separate identities of the various Slav nations, and pointed out that no one had reason to fear the new Slav movement. He claimed that 'the Slavs...do not wish to set at variance the two largest Slav domains, Russia and Austria; on the contrary, they are endeavouring to make it possible for the two states to live in peace and jointly defend themselves against a common enemy'.[50] The enemy, by implication, was, of course, Germany.

Before his departure from Austria–Hungary Volodimirov had extended an invitation to leaders of the Austrian Slavs to visit St Petersburg where talks on the subject of Slav co-operation could be continued.[51] In response to this invitation, a deputation

periodical devoted to Slav affairs, *Slovanský přehled*, published by A. Černý. The Russian visitor made it known that, on his return to St Petersburg, he would attempt to make arrangements for the periodical to be published also in Russia. *Čas*, 7 April 1908 (Švihovský, 'U generála V. M. Volodimirova'). The Russian edition, however, never appeared.

[49] *Proces dra. Kramáře*, II, pp. 39–40.
[50] *Den*, 24 January 1908 (K. Kramář, 'Komu přísluší právo svolat všeslovanský sjezd?'). This is the original form of the article published in translation by Volodimirov in *Birzhovye vedomosti*. *Proces dra. Kramáře*, II, p. 40.
[51] *Proces dra. Kramáře*, II, p. 39; Švihovský, 'Slovanské sjezdy', p. 102.

of Slavs from the Habsburg Empire, consisting of Kramář, Hribar, and Glebovitsky, all members of the Austrian Parliament, left for the Russian capital on 22 May 1908.[52] The purpose of the visit was to hold consultations with interested parties in Russia, in order to establish whether conditions were right for calling a Slav congress which would lay the foundations for cultural and economic co-operation between all the Slav peoples. Political co-operation outside of Austria–Hungary was considered to be out of the question.[53]

The visit of the Austrian Slav delegation to St Petersburg was undertaken with the knowledge and approval of both the Austro-Hungarian Prime Minister, Baron Beck, and of Count Aehrenthal, the Minister of Foreign Affairs.[54] Kramář himself stated that he had spoken 'very openly' with Aehrenthal before going to Russia, adding that: 'Aehrenthal, as I expected, assured me specifically that it was his wish to see my attempt to institute closer ties with St Petersburg succeed.'[55]

Relations between the two Empires had been disturbed, rather suddenly, earlier in the year. On 27 January 1908 Aehrenthal had, unexpectedly, announced in a speech to the Hungarian Delegation, the Austro-Hungarian intention of constructing a railway through the Sandjak of Novi Bazar. This projected link, between Uvac in Bosnia and Mitrovica in Turkish Macedonia, would connect the railway network of the Dual Monarchy with Salonica, and thus open a new direct route to the East, bypassing Serbian territory. The consent of the Turkish government had been obtained largely thanks to German pressure. In Russia the government and the press reacted very unfavourably to the proposal. It was considered in St Petersburg that the Sandjak Railway would alter the *status quo* in the Balkans and would therefore be a breach of the agreements signed between Russia and Austria–Hungary in 1897 and 1903. The Austro-Hungarian government, however, did not accept this view, claiming that the proposed railway link was no more than a commercial development. Relations between the two countries rapidly deteriorated. Izvolsky, the Russian Foreign Minister, proposed that military action be taken to defend Russia's interest in the Balkans. The Prime Minister, P. A. Stolypin, aware

[52] *Národní listy*, 22 May 1908.
[53] Kramář, *Pět přednášek*, p. 27; *Národní listy*, 22 May 1908.
[54] Kramář, *Pět přednášek*, p. 29; *Proces dra. Kramáře*, II, pp. 40–1.
[55] Kramář, *Na obranu*, p. 18.

of the fact that the country was unprepared for war decided, however, that Russia had no alternative but to resort to diplomacy. Izvolsky, therefore, had to content himself by giving his support to the previously proposed Serbian scheme for a railway connecting the Danube with the Adriatic, through Rumania, Serbia, and Montenegro, thus avoiding territory under Austro-Hungarian control.[56] Although Russia's conciliatory attitude defused what was a potentially dangerous situation, the Sandjak Railway dispute was a precursor of more serious crises to follow in the relations between Russia and Austria–Hungary.

At the time of the crisis, Kramář had shown a considerable interest in the Balkan Railway scheme. During a foreign policy debate in the Delegation, which took place shortly after the announcement of the Sandjak Railway project, the Czech leader launched a strong attack against the proposals and implored the Austro-Hungarian Minister of Foreign Affairs to remain faithful to the Austro-Russian *entente*. Although he did not consider the railway project to be an act of aggression, it could nevertheless, in his view, have two serious consequences. Good relations between the Habsburg Empire and Russia could be endangered, and the implementation of the urgently required reforms in Turkish controlled Macedonia, which had been agreed between the major powers, jeopardised. Kramář was of the opinion that the country likely to benefit most from the proposed railway was Germany.[57] *Národní listy* reacted similarly to the Austro-Hungarian project, pointing out that, if implemented: 'Russian influence would be completely excluded from the Balkans and the Slav lands there would be left to the mercy of Austro-German ascendancy.'[58]

In his Delegation speech Kramář had also reaffirmed his faith in the accord between Austria–Hungary and Russia, which he considered to be the best guarantee of peaceful development in the Balkans.[59] The Czech leader intended to use his visit to Russia to promote this understanding, and informed the Austro-Hungarian

[56] For details see A. J. May, 'The Novibazar Railway Project', *The Journal of Modern History*, x (1938), pp. 496–527. Neither of the projected railways was constructed during the period under study. Following the annexation of Bosnia and Herzegovina later that year, Austria–Hungary evacuated the Sandjak of Novi Bazar and abandoned the projected scheme.
[57] *Stenographische Sitzungs-Protokolle der Delegation des Reichsrates, 42. Session* (Vienna, 1908), pp. 126–34.
[58] *Národní listy*, 8 February 1908.
[59] *Stenographische Protokolle der Delegation, 42. Session*, p. 134.

Minister of Foreign Affairs of his intentions. Count Aehrenthal raised no objections.[60]

In a letter to Count Berchtold, the Austro-Hungarian ambassador to Russia, dated 14 June 1908, Aehrenthal confirmed that he welcomed Kramář's attempt to widen contacts between the Austrian Slavs and the Russians. Aehrenthal wrote:

I am also of the opinion that the attempt to unite the Slavs – of course, only in the fields of culture and peaceful co-operation – could favourably affect relations between Austria–Hungary and Russia...Our eastern neighbours must be brought to realise that a strong Austria in which the various Slav nationalities will naturally, with time, attain greater influence, is more important to Russia than the fantastic aspirations of Serbia or Montenegro.[61]

Although Aehrenthal evidently did not disapprove of Kramář's visit to St Petersburg he was, nevertheless, not entirely convinced that the Neo-Slav movement would benefit the Habsburg Empire. As a form of insurance he relied on the support of the Galician Poles. In the same dispatch, the Foreign Minister stated that the Austrian Poles did not support Kramář's campaign. Although they were prepared to go through the motions of co-operating with the Neo-Slav movement, they were far from certain that a Slavicised Austria–Hungary was in their interest. Aehrenthal continued: 'According to one...theory, it is not impossible that Neo-Slavism could benefit our aims in the Balkans; if, however, another theory were to be realised we would have to ensure, in good time, that strong barriers were available against the anti-cultural stormy waves – barriers which, thank God, we already have.'[62]

The sympathy which the leaders of the Austrian Poles felt for the Austro-Hungarian authorities was confirmed in a conversation between Sir A. Nicolson, the British ambassador in St Petersburg, and an unnamed Pole. The ambassador was informed that: 'The Austrian Poles were under great obligations to the Emperor Francis Joseph and would not associate themselves with their brother Slavs in any course which would be unwelcome to his Majesty.'[63] The oppression of the Polish inhabitants of the Russian

[60] *Proces dra. Kramáře*, II, p. 41.
[61] Aehrenthal to Berchtold, Vienna, 14 June 1908, cited in Beneš, *Úvahy o slovanství*, pp. 184–5.   [62] *Ibid.*
[63] Public Record Office (PRO), Foreign Office (FO), 371/519, Nicolson to Grey, 42551, St Petersburg, 26 November 1908.

division of Poland helped to maintain and strengthen the ties between the Austrian Poles and the Habsburg authorities. Thus the situation in Russian Poland, which produced the bitter Russo-Polish dispute, appeared to form the key to the future of the Slav movement. In a leading article on the preparations for a Slav Congress, *Národní listy* wrote: 'Until this [Russo-Polish] dispute is solved there is no likelihood of a Slav congress succeeding, or of the foundations of Pan-Slav reciprocity being laid.'[64]

The recently changed conditions in Russia, however, gave rise to the hope that a solution to the Russo-Polish problem was, at last, within the bounds of possibility. It was widely believed, by the Czechs in particular, that the chief instigators of Russian anti-Polish, and thus anti-Slav, policies were the St Petersburg court circles whose policy, in the words of *Národní listy*, 'was directed from Berlin'.[65] Undoubtedly, there were, at the time, a not inconsiderable number of persons in important positions who exerted a strong pro-German influence on the policies of the Russian authorities. In a report on conditions in Russia during 1906 Nicolson stated that 'German influence is today predominant both at the Court and in Government circles', and he described relations between the Russian and German authorities as being 'intimate and cordial'.[66] He was, however, careful to add that this feeling was by no means universal within Russia. Outside the court, government, and military circles, many considered Germany partially responsible for encouraging Russia to initiate the disastrous policies in the Far East. This belief was particularly strong among a section of the press and within the commercial and industrial community.[67] A further report from the British embassy in St Petersburg, made in 1908, refers again to this situation and also indicates the recent changes:

The Germans, thanks to their superior culture and force of character, have been for nearly two centuries, and still continue to be, a powerful

---

[64] *Národní listy*, 22 May 1908.   [65] *Ibid.*
[66] *British Documents on the Origins of the War 1898–1914*, ed. G. P. Gooch and H. Temperley (11 vols., London, 1926–38), IV, pp. 256–8, no. 243, 'Extract from Annual Report for Russia for the Year 1906'. In the ambassador's opinion: 'If the Emperor and the Russian Government were free from any other political ties they would gladly form an intimate alliance with Germany who represents, in their view, the stoutest bulwark of monarchical principle combined with the strongest military force on the continent.'
[67] *Ibid.*

factor at the Court and in the Administration; but they have remained an element distinct from, and profoundly antagonistic to, the Slavs. With the greater facilities for the expression of popular opinion which have come with the last few years, this antagonism of the Slav to the German has naturally tended to display itself more plainly than before.[68]

As a consequence of the altered circumstances, brought about by the 1905 Revolution, the court circles, which had been at least partially responsible for the persecution of the Russian Poles, were no longer the only effective political force in the country. Kramář and his supporters certainly believed that the dominant role of the allegedly Germanophil court would soon be at an end.[69] Although Russia had not become a democracy, nevertheless, the power base had been widened, and the voice of the new representative assembly was audible. This was a development of considerable significance. Although the Third and Fourth Dumas were less democratic than their two predecessors, the various groups represented in them, including a section of the middle class, were united mainly by their nationalism which manifested itself in a desire to pay increased attention to the Slav world. The government could not afford totally to ignore these voices.[70]

Inside the Duma, those who were most interested in improving relations with all the Slav nations and, in particular, in making peace with the Poles, were the deputies of the centre parties, the Kadets and the Octobrists. Many of their leading figures featured prominently in the new liberal Slav organisations, and several were later active in the Neo-Slav movement. The liberal section of the Russian press, in general, also welcomed the new initiative towards promoting closer relations between the Slav nations.[71]

Both the extremes of the Russian political spectrum, left and right, were either opposed to or uninterested in the newly formed Slav movement. A spokesman for the Socialist Revolutionary party explained that: 'Although we are Slavs, we are unable to concern ourselves with the Slav question. We have no time for it. Other, more urgent, matters demand our attention. The Russian peasant requires, in the first place, land; and he would not understand the

[68] PRO, FO, 371/517, O'Beirne to Grey, 19622, St Petersburg, 2 June 1908.
[69] Kramář, *Poznámky o české politice*, p. 56.
[70] H. Seton-Watson, *The Decline of Imperial Russia, 1855–1914* (London, 1952), pp. 317–18.
[71] Kramář, *Na obranu*, p. 46; A. Černý, 'Po slovanských dnech', pp. 442–3; *Národní listy*, 26 June 1908.

issue if we were to include Slav affairs in our programme.'[72] The attitude of the Social Democrats was, predictably, even more negative. Their policies were based on the principles of proletarian internationalism, and any exclusively Slav organisation was regarded with suspicion, especially one which was being promoted by the liberal bourgeoisie.[73] At the opposite extreme, on the far right, among such organisations as the Union of the Russian People (*Soyuz russkogo naroda*), there was also a lack of enthusiasm for the new Slav cause.[74] Previously, when the Slav movement had been used to further the political and territorial aims of the Russian Empire the conservative forces had actively supported it, and they continued to show considerable interest in the Orthodox South Slavs and the Russophil Ukrainians in Eastern Galicia. This support was, however, not extended to the new movement which professed to be liberal in spirit, based on the principle of equality of all the Slav nations and, therefore, anathema to the right.[75]

A significant statement of the views of Russian liberals is contained in an article by a leading member of the Kadet Party, Struve, entitled 'A Great Russia', which appeared in 1908.[76] In this article, Struve attributed Russia's economic and political weakness, at least partially, to the problems of the national minorities living within the Russian Empire. One of the most important of these was the question of Poland. The fact that Poland was an integral part of the Russian Empire, politically and economically linked with Russia could and should, Struve believed, be used to Russia's advantage in improving relations with the non-Russian Slavs. He declared that:

Our Polish policy should serve to draw us nearer to Austria, which is now principally a Slavonic power. A liberal Polish policy will enormously raise our prestige in the Slavonic world and psychologically will quite naturally create for the first time in history a moral tie between us and Austria as a state. Economically, we shall ever be in competition in the

[72] *Čas*, 3 April 1908.
[73] *Ibid.* The correspondent complained that the Russian Social Democrats had evidently taken to heart K. Marx's assertion about the reactionary nature of the Slav peoples.
[74] A. Černý, 'Po slovanských dnech', p. 443; *Čas*, 3 April 1908.
[75] *Čas*, 3 April 1908.
[76] P. B. Struve, 'Velikaya Rossiya', *Russkaya mysl'*, XXIX, no. 1 (1908), pp. 143–57. For an abbreviated English translation, see 'A Great Russia', *The Russian Review*, II, no. 4 (1913), pp. 11–30.

Near East; but this will be softened and smoothed if there is between us a moral and political solidarity.[77]

Until a solution was found to the Polish problem, the author argued, Russia would remain at the mercy of Germany and its ally, Austria-Hungary.

So long as we have no real Slavonic policy and treat Poland as a subject people and shirk our historic mission on the Black Sea, where is to be found the natural economic basis of a Great Russia; Austria–Hungary, even as a Slavonic power, or rather, just because she is one, is bound to try to grow larger at our expense.[78]

The problem of Poland, and of the other nationalities, had to be solved before Russia could become great, as greatness could only be achieved if the government enjoyed popular support. This, in Struve's opinion, was only possible in a free society.[79]

Although Struve's assessment of the strength of Slav influence in Austria–Hungary, which was at the time shared by many Slavs inside the Habsburg Empire, was later shown to be incorrect, the general tone of the article was indicative of the thinking of liberal Russians at the time when Kramář and his two compatriots arrived in St Petersburg.[80] Indeed, it was precisely with this section of Russian political opinion that Kramář wished to associate both himself and the emergent Neo-Slav movement.[81] This was evident from the fact that, during their visit to Russia, the Austrian Slav trio pointedly attempted to avoid contact with the right wing Pan-Slav circles of the Slavonic Benevolent Society. This prompted *Národní listy* to report, with some dismay, that the visit of the Austrian Slav delegation was directed against the traditional Slav forces in Russia.[82] Kramář later explained that:

[77] Struve, 'A Great Russia', p. 22.   [78] *Ibid.*, p. 25.
[79] *Ibid.*, pp. 27–8.
[80] Similar pleas for justice for the Polish nation were made in the periodical *Moskovsky ezhenedelnik* early in 1908 by Prince G. N. Trubetskoy and A. L. Pogodin. A. Černý, 'Nejnovější úvahy o slovanské otázce', pp. 260–1, 303.
[81] Kramář, *Pět přednášek*, pp. 27–8.
[82] *Národní listy*, 26 June 1908. Later, however, the paper was able to report, with relief, that: 'there are no basic ideological differences between the old Slavophilism and the new [movement]'. *Národní listy*, 5 July 1908 (P. Grégr, Nový slavismus', 1). During this period *Národní listy*, though remaining in sympathy with the ideals of the Young Czech Party, was strongly critical of the conciliatory policies towards the Austro-Hungarian authorities pursued by Kramář. This rift had arisen largely due to the failure of the Young Czech Party in the general election of 1907. During the course of that year Kramář

[Russian] Slav policy was directed semi-officially by the Slavonic Benevolent Society, which was completely controlled by reactionary elements who, in the field of Russian domestic affairs, defended the Russification of Poland and of the Baltic Provinces...This factor influenced us when we arrived in St Petersburg in 1908 and, consequently, we rather obviously pushed the Slavonic Benevolent Society to one side...There was between us a basic disagreement in that the circles of the Slavonic Benevolent Society, and the political views with which they were closely associated, considered the Russo-Polish question to be a purely Russian affair, whereas we considered it to be of interest to all Slavdom.[83]

Despite their endeavours to do so, Kramář and his colleagues were unable totally to avoid coming into contact with the Slavonic Benevolent Society. Much to his dismay, the St Petersburg branch of the Society gave a dinner in honour of the Slav guests, an event which he described in a letter to his wife as being 'rather unpleasant'.[84] The Austrian Slav visitors evidently found it impossible not to attend this function, though Kramář excused himself and departed early.[85] It appears that at least one member of the Slavonic Benevolent Society was equally suspicious of Kramář and his colleagues. Bashmakov, a prominent figure in the St Petersburg branch of the Society, described the delegation of Austrian Slavs as the 'standard bearers of red, revolutionary Neo-Slavism'.[86]

The three representatives of the Austrian Slavs, Kramář, Hribar, and Glebovitsky, received an enthusiastic welcome on their arrival in St Petersburg on 25 (12) May 1908. The entire visit attracted a considerable amount of attention and the opportunity was taken to stage a 'Slav Week' in the Russian capital. Banquets and speeches were plentiful and a reception given by the city of St Petersburg in honour of their Slav guests on 27 (14) May 1908, was attended by several members of the government including the Prime Minister, P. A. Stolypin; the Minister of Finance, V. N.

established a rival organ, *Den*, which was under his own personal control. Early in 1910, the Young Czech Party leadership purchased *Národní listy*, thus regaining editorial control of the newspaper. K. Tůma, 'Padesát let boje a práce', in *Půl století Národních Listů. Almanach 1860–1910* (Prague, 1910), pp. 34–5.

[83] Kramář, *Na obranu*, p. 46.
[84] Archiv Národního Musea, Prague, Kramář papers, 2/2/2423, cited in Herman and Sládek, 'Slovanská politika Karla Kramáře', p. 29, n. 109.
[85] *Novoe vremya*, 14 (27) May 1908.
[86] A. Černý, 'Po slovanských dnech', p. 444.

Kokovtsov; and the Minister of Education, A. N. Schwarz.[87] At the occasion, according to Kramář, Stolypin spoke 'in tune with our endeavours'.[88] Amongst the many other prominent figures present at the reception was the President of the Duma, Khomyakov.[89] Earlier, Kramář and his colleagues had paid a visit to the Duma, where they observed a debate in progress on the question of Finland.[90]

Although the main purpose of the journey of the Austrian Slav delegation to St Petersburg was to hold detailed discussions with the Association of Public Figures and with other organisations interested in Slav affairs about the feasibility of staging a Slav congress in the near future, Kramář also used the opportunity for consulting directly with prominent figures in the Russian government. The general object of these discussions, held with the Prime Minister, Stolypin, and the Minister of Foreign Affairs, Izvolsky, was to pave the way for a better understanding between Russia and Austria–Hungary. With the approval of the highest authorities in the Habsburg Empire Kramář aimed to reassure the Russian government about Austro-Hungarian intentions in the Balkans and to explain the lack of consultation prior to the announcement of the intention to construct the Sandjak Railway. He informed his hosts that Count Aehrenthal had revealed the plans for the Balkan railway in such an unexpected fashion in Budapest, purely out of a desire to create a sensation, and that the announcement was not intended as a snub to Russia. Kramář believed that he achieved the objectives of this self-imposed task and regarded the subsequent short-lived improvement in relations between the two Empires, culminating at the meeting between Aehrenthal and Izvolsky at Buchlau in Moravia during September 1908, as evidence of his success.[91]

During the conversations with members of the Russian government, Kramář also introduced the subject of the Russo-Polish

[87] H.H.St.A., PA, XL 219, *Panslav Bewegung* 2, Berchtold to Aehrenthal, 27B, St Petersburg, 2 June/20 May 1908; *Novoe vremya*, 13 (26) – 19 May (1 June) 1908.
[88] Kramář, *Na obranu*, p. 15; Kramář, *Pět přednášek*, p. 28. The Czech leader claimed that Stolypin took a considerable risk in attending the reception against police advice, for in the crowded hall he was very exposed to a possible assassination attempt.   [89] *Novoe vremya*, 15 (28) May 1908.
[90] *Ibid.*, 13 (26) May 1908.
[91] Kramář, *Na obranu*, p. 15; Kramář, *Pět přednášek*, p. 30; *Proces dra. Kramáře*, II, p. 42.

dispute. Here again, the Russian reaction seemed encouraging. Kramář claimed that the Prime Minister, Stolypin, had agreed to satisfy the Polish demands, though not immediately. He promised to grant urban local government and zemstvo administration (elected provincial and district assemblies) to Russian Poland, and it was understood that these local authorities would have the right to establish Polish schools.[92] In his later writings, Kramář also referred to a letter which he received from Stolypin in reply to an appeal to speed up the introduction of the promised measures in Poland. In this letter, according to the Czech leader:

[The Russian Prime Minister] complained of heavy obstacles which were being placed in his path, but again formally promised that the Poles would be granted zemstvo administration. This would also include [their own] schools. But he implored me to believe him, and not to regard the inability to fulfil his promises immediately as a wish to depart from them.[93]

These undertakings, if ever given in as precise terms as Kramář claimed, were never kept. A more accurate indication of the attitude of the Russian authorities was given in the semi-official government newspaper, *Rossiya*, which, at the time of the Austrian Slav visit, published an article strongly hostile to the Poles. *Rossiya* did not even consider the Polish nation to be part of the Slav race: 'Because, except for their language, they have nothing in common with the other Slavs... They are Slav speaking foreigners... In the interests of Slavdom the Poles must remain at the mercy of Russia, and anything that Russia does with them in her own interests will be advantageous to [all] Slavdom.'[94]

Kramář, also, had not omitted to include the South Slavs in his plans for Slav co-operation. During his discussions with Russian officials, he explained that Serbia would be one of the principal beneficiaries of the Slavicisation of Austria–Hungary, which the Neo-Slav movement was designed to promote. A more sympathetic government in Vienna, he argued, would not commit hostile acts against the small South Slav state such as the closure of the Austro-Hungarian borders to the import of Serbian live-stock, and improved relations between the Dual Monarchy and Serbia would

[92] *Proces dra. Kramáře*, II, p. 42.
[93] Kramář, *Na obranu*, p. 15. Kramář gave no indication of when the letter was written and claimed that it was destroyed after his arrest in 1915.
[94] A. Černý, 'Po slovanských dnech', p. 444, cited from *Rossiya*.

bring greater stability to the Balkan Peninsula and thus be of benefit also to Russia.[95] In a dispatch from the Austro-Hungarian Foreign Minister to the ambassador in St Petersburg it was reported, however, that Kramář, on his return to Vienna, had informed Count Aehrenthal that Izvolsky displayed 'little understanding' of the arguments that Russia should assist this development by co-operating with the Habsburg Empire in the Balkans. The Russian Deputy Minister of Foreign Affairs, N. V. Charykov, however, was said to have listened with greater interest.[96]

Commenting later on the attitude of the Russian government towards the talks conducted between the Austrian Slavs and their Russian hosts (the Association of Public Figures) about increasing Slav co-operation, Kramář claimed that the Russian authorities participated with enthusiasm and that Stolypin himself 'followed the negotiations with the greatest of interest'.[97] The Czech leader's assessment of the situation was, however, coloured by his optimism. Some members of the Russian government had little sympathy for the Neo-Slav plans. The Austro-Hungarian ambassador in St Petersburg, Count Berchtold, had earlier reported to the Foreign Ministry in Vienna a conversation with the Russian Minister of Foreign Affairs, Izvolsky, during which the Russian Minister had expressed the hope that the proposed Slav congress would never materialise.[98] This was, presumably, due to Izvolsky's desire not to antagonise the Austro-Hungarian government, as he was hoping to negotiate an agreement with the Habsburg Empire for the opening of the Black Sea Straits to the passage of Russian warships. In the opinion of uncommitted observers the Russian authorities appeared to adopt a somewhat reserved, though not totally unsympathetic, attitude towards Kramář and his compatriots and, by implication, towards their ideas for increasing co-operation between the Slav nations. The St Petersburg correspondent of *The Times* reported that: 'The Russian government, while preserving a strictly neutral position towards the Slav meetings, has shown a benevolent disposition towards the visit of Dr Kramarz and his associates.'[99]

[95] *Proces dra. Kramáře*, ii, p. 332.
[96] Aehrenthal to Berchtold, Vienna, 14 June 1908, cited in Beneš, *Úvahy o slovanství*, pp. 184–5.   [97] Kramář, *Na obranu*, p. 15.
[98] Berchtold to Aehrenthal, 45C, St Petersburg, 28 December 1907, cited in Beneš, *Úvahy o slovanství*, p. 179.   [99] *The Times*, 30 May 1908.

The Austrian Slav delegation received a much more enthusiastic response, as was to be expected, from the recently formed organisations interested in increasing contacts between Russia and other parts of the Slav world. Prominent amongst these was the Association of Public Figures at whose invitation Kramář and his colleagues travelled to Russia and under whose auspices a series of exploratory talks took place concerning the proposals which the Austrian Slav trio brought with them, for drawing the Slav community of nations into closer contact.[100] Those involved in the discussions on the Russian side came mostly from the ranks of the moderate conservative section of Russian political opinion, though some representatives of the liberal centre were also present. In addition to Volodimirov, who had been instrumental in bringing about the Austrian Slav visit to the Russian capital, prominent in the discussions were: M. V. Krasovsky, the chairman of the Association of Public Figures; and the journalists Vergun and Svatkovsky. The Kadet leader Milyukov and the Progressists M. A. Stakhovich and Fedorov also participated. The Poles from Russian Poland most actively involved in the deliberations were R. Dmowski, the leader of the National Democratic Party (the largest and most important Polish political party), and Count J. Olizar.[101] The subjects discussed at the St Petersburg meetings were all to receive further, more detailed, airing at the Prague Neo-Slav Congress and at subsequent gatherings of adherents to the movement. In addition to arranging details of the forthcoming Congress itself, and to enunciating the basic tenets of the Neo-Slav movement, various practical suggestions for increasing inter-Slav co-operation were also discussed. The Neo-Slav movement was to be based on the principles of equality of all the Slav peoples and their right to administrative autonomy whilst retaining their loyalties to the state of which they were citizens. The major practical topics considered were the establishment of a Slav bank and the staging of a Slav industrial exhibition. The Slav bank, which was to be modelled on the official German *Deutsche Bank*, was envisaged by its proposer, Hribar, to be principally responsible for promoting trade and industrial development in the Slav world. The idea of

---

[100] The meetings between the Austrian Slav delegation and their Russian hosts were held in private. Information was released to the press through a special committee headed by Kramář. *Novoe vremya*, 14 (27) May 1908.
[101] *Novoe vremya*, 14 (27) – 17 (30) May 1908; *Rech'*, 14 (27) – 18 (31) May 1908.

a Slav exhibition to be staged in Moscow in 1911, put forward by Prince N. N. Trubetskoy, was enthusiastically welcomed by Kramář. He stressed the need for the exhibition not to concentrate on cultural matters, but also to be concerned with encouraging the development of inter-Slav trade. Aspects of cultural co-operation and measures for promoting increased social contact between the Slav peoples were also discussed. These proposals included increased co-operation between Slav educational societies, greater exchange of literature between the Slav peoples, and improvements in the dissemination of information by the creation of Slav journalistic agencies. The formation of Sokol gymnastic organisations throughout the Slav world were to be encouraged, as were visits for agricultural training of peasants from the less developed Slav countries to those Slav lands where agricultural methods were more highly developed.[102]

These ideas for promoting greater unity within the Slav world, which were to be further discussed at the forthcoming Prague Neo-Slav Congress, met with a generally favourable response in the Russian capital. *Novoe vremya* devoted a considerable amount of attention to reporting the events of the 'Slav Week', and expressed approval of the practical steps proposed by the Austrian Slav visitors for increasing inter-Slav co-operation. Although the newspaper foresaw certain financial problems concerning the Slav exhibition, it reacted favourably to the suggested creation of a Slav bank and other proposals.[103] The more liberal section of the Russian press was on the whole enthusiastic about the emergent Neo-Slav movement, but the extreme right remained hostile. The attitude of the liberals was particularly important, for it was with this Russian political group that Kramář and his associates

[102] H.H.St.A., PA, XL 219, *Panslav Bewegung* 2, Berchtold to Aehrenthal, 27B, St Petersburg, 2 June/20 May 1908; *Novoe vremya*, 17 (30) May 1908; *Národní listy*, 5 June 1908. O. Heinz in 'Der Neoslawismus' (unpublished doctoral dissertation for the University of Vienna, 1963), pp. 41–2, citing H.H.St.A., PA, XLV [*sic*] 219, extract from Berchtold to the Ministry of the Interior, 5 July 1908, in addition to enumerating most of these points of the Neo-Slav programme adds a further one – the establishment of a Russian consulate in Prague. Although the Czech Neo-Slavs strongly advocated such a measure, and Kramář did in fact raise the subject during the St Petersburg discussions (*Novoe vremya*, 17 (30) May 1908), this demand never became part of the official Neo-Slav programme.

[103] *Novoe vremya*, 9 (22) June 1908. In his memoirs I. Hribar recalled that his plan for a Slav bank met with a favourable response. Hribar, *Moji spomini*, II, p. 63.

were most anxious to co-operate. The organ of the liberal Kadet Party, *Rech'*, in an editorial article, expressed general satisfaction with the outcome of the visit of the Austrian Slav delegation, but also betrayed certain apprehensions. *Rech'* was relieved that the 'fears that the Slav visit would reveal our internal dissensions and destroy the newly begun work of Slav *rapprochement*...were unfounded', and added that the visit 'appears to mark...a turning point in our public attitude towards the Slav question'. This positive response to the approaches of the Austrian Slav delegation was somewhat diluted in a further editorial article published the following day. In this second, more cautious, assessment *Rech'* reserved its judgement as far as the Neo-Slav movement was concerned stating that 'only the results of the conference [in Prague] will provide an indication of the nature of the enterprise'.[104] This second article provided an indication of the reserved attitude which was to be adopted towards the Neo-Slav movement by most Russian liberals. For the moment, however, this fact did not attract very much attention. The British observer of the Russian scene, B. Pares, commenting on the visit of the Austrian Slav delegation to St Petersburg, stated that 'practically all parties were unanimous in taking up the idea of a resumption of Russia's Slavonic policy'.[105] The St Petersburg correspondent of *The Times* echoed this view, stating: 'Most of the political parties in Russia seem to support, or at least do not oppose, the new movement, the exception being the extreme right. The organ of this group, *Znamya*, denounced the Neo-Slav movement as a "Jewish plot".'[106] The hostility of the right wing, however, was not unanimous. As Pares indicated: 'Kramář made it quite clear in his speeches that the movement was anti-German, but even the Right continued to try to get their share of entertaining him'.[107]

Although, almost by definition, any movement designed to unite and strengthen the Slav nations could be construed as being anti-German, the Slav representatives went to considerable lengths to indicate that their plans did not, in any way, threaten the Dual Monarchy. In speeches made during his stay in Russia, and

[104] *Rech'*, 17 (30), 18 (31) May 1908.
[105] PRO, FO, 371/512, 30910, B. Pares, 'Memorandum on the Third Duma', p. 19.   [106] *The Times*, 2 June 1908.
[107] PRO, FO, 371/512, 30910, B. Pares, 'Memorandum on the Third Duma' p. 19.

subsequently on his return to Prague, Kramář constantly reiterated this assurance.[108] The Austrian Slav delegation further demonstrated their loyalty to the Habsburg Empire by making a symbolic visit to the Austro-Hungarian embassy in St Petersburg. When it became known in the embassy that this visit was to take place it gave rise to some consternation, and advice was sought from Vienna about how to behave towards the uninvited callers.[109] In addition, Kramář pointedly avoided being presented to the Tsarina-mother, Maria Fedorovna, who was known for her strong antipathy to Austria–Hungary.[110]

Undoubtedly, the most remarkable achievement of the exploratory visit by the Austrian Slavs to St Petersburg was the fact that Kramář and his colleagues secured the support of the leadership of the Russian Poles for the Neo-Slav movement. The Polish representatives in the Duma constituted the Polish Circle (*Koło Polskie*) under the direction of Dmowski. Although, obviously, he had no alternative but to accept the existing political divisions of Poland, he firmly believed in the indivisibility of the Poles as a nation, in the cultural and linguistic sense. In the opinion of the Polish leader, the main danger threatening the existence of the Polish nation came from Germany and not Russia. The increasing severity of the persecution of the Polish inhabitants of the German division of Poland convinced Dmowski and his followers that it was in the interest of the Poles to select the lesser of the two evils, and to co-operate with Russia against Germany. The Polish leader believed that a united Poland could never be achieved while Germany dominated the Central European scene. For these reasons, he and the members of the Polish Circle in the Russian

[108] *Novoe vremya*, 15 (28), 16 (29), 17 (30) May 1908; *Národní listy*, 20 June 1908.

[109] Fürstenberg to Aehrenthal, 25, St Petersburg, 12 May (29 April) 1908, cited in Beneš, *Úvahy o slovanství*, pp. 181–3. Kramář later stated that the reception which he received at the embassy was 'most cordial'. *Proces dra. Kramáře*, II, p. 42.

[110] V. M. Volodimirov des cribed to an acquaintance (J. K. Pojezdný) how he had attempted to present the Austrian Slav delegates at the Court on the occasion of a memorial service for the fallen at the Battle of Tsushima. Kramář objected to participating in the religious ceremonies and resolutely refused to kneel. Later, when Volodimirov led the guests towards the Dowager-Empress, Kramář and Glebovitsky remained deliberately behind, and only Hribar was presented. *Lidové noviny*, 5 October 1910. In *Proces dra. Kramáře*, III, part 2, p. 152, this incident is erroneously reported to have taken place during a subsequent visit to Russia in 1910.

Duma did not oppose measures taken to strengthen the Russian Empire. In return, Dmowski hoped that, with the aid of the liberal forces awakening in Russia, he would be able to extract from the Russian authorities concessions for the Polish nation.[111] There was also a further reason for the attachment of the Russian Poles to Russia – that of economics. Just as the Czech Neo-Slavs were, partially at least, motivated by economic considerations, so were the leaders of the Russian Poles. Whereas the Czech industrialists were anxious to gain entry to the markets of Russia, the Polish industrialists wished to maintain their already considerable trading activity in that direction. The Polish National Democrats in particular, representing the industrial middle-class, were aware of the economic dependence of Russian Poland on the Russian state, and thus had an interest in preserving the existing political framework. Within that framework, however, they desired greater freedom, particularly for the cultural development of their nation.[112] The adhesion of the St Petersburg Polish Circle to the emergent Neo-Slav movement was consistent with these aspirations.

The announcement that the Russian Poles were prepared to join the Neo-Slav movement was made by Dmowski at a meeting between the Austrian Slav delegation and their Russian sympathisers. In his statement the Polish leader declared that the Russian Empire, including Russian Poland, weakened by the war in the Far East, was now endangered by Germany. Although all attempts to Russify Poland had failed, not a single Pole having been transformed into a Russian, the new threat confronting the Poles was considerably more serious. Dmowski believed that German culture and efficiency were as dangerous as was German imperial power. Polish culture could only compete with that of Germany if allowed free and unhindered development. In the Austrian and German divisions of Poland, Polish culture was developing successfully; only in Russian Poland had little or no progress been made. Poland's role in the contemporary world, Dmowski maintained, was to act as a barrier to the eastwards expansion of Germany, and he continued:

---

[111] Dmowski's ideas are contained in his book *Niemcy, Rosya i kwestya polska* (Lvov, 1908). This work also appeared in French translation as *La question polonaise* (Paris, 1909). See also S. Kozicky, 'Roman Dmowski, 1864–1939', *The Slavonic and East European Review*, xviii (1939), pp. 118–28.
[112] L. Levine, 'Pan-Slavism and European Politics', *Political Science Quarterly*, xxix (1914), p. 676.

Poland will only be able to fulfil this task if her cultural forces are rapidly developed. The Polish nation considers its work in this field as its chief aim, together with the struggle throughout the Polish territories for the right political conditions to enable this task to be undertaken. The reversal of the position of Poland and her historic role...rests on the fact that Poland's main battle will now be waged in the west, against the German tide...Our natural allies in this campaign are the Slav nations, who have long since been struggling against Germanism, and who are as endangered by it as we are. Their task is also our task. I therefore find incomprehensible the question – 'Under what conditions will the Poles participate in the Slav movement?' For us, I repeat, a Slav task is our task; without conditions, without reservations. Today we are fighters in the struggle for the future of Slavdom, and we place no obstacles in the path of Slav unity.[113]

Although Dmowski made this declaration unconditionally, the terms were, nevertheless, implicit. The stipulation was free cultural development for the Polish nation.[114]

The Austrian Slav visitors received Dmowski's statement with great satisfaction, Kramář expressed his favourable reaction in a speech, delivered in St Petersburg, in which he declared:

The Poles feel they are Slavs and wish to be Slavs. The renewal of an independent Poland is out of the question, and the Poles can only be strong when united with other Slavs. We were informed of this by the leader of the Poles in the Russian Duma, Dmowski, and we are convinced that these are not just empty words, but the logical conclusions deduced from the conditions in which the Poles see themselves situated.[115]

This belief in Dmowski's sincerity was later shown to have been unduly optimistic. In 1916, Dmowski informed Beneš that he had not been drawn towards the Neo-Slavs because of their particular Slav policies, but simply in order 'to extract something or other for Poland from all this'.[116] This revelation vindicated the incredulity registered by the British chargé d'affaires in St Petersburg who, at the time of the visit of the Austrian Slav representatives, reported that the Polish attitude was 'somewhat unexpected'. Referring to Dmowski's statement, he continued: 'It is, however,

[113] A. Černý, 'Po slovanských dnech', p. 440; PRO, FO, 371/517, Bayley to Nicolson, Warsaw, 9 June 1908, enclosed in O'Beirne to Grey, 21291, St Petersburg, 13 June 1908.
[114] A. Černý, 'Po slovanských dnech', p. 440.
[115] *Národní listy*, 19 June 1908.
[116] Beneš, *Úvahy o slovanství*, pp. 154–5, 217.

difficult to believe that this utterance reflects the true view of the Polish party and that the latter would really be prepared to waive their national claims in return for the shadowy advantages of a Pan-Slav union.'[117] Dmowski and his associates had not for one moment renounced their national demands, they were merely prepared to employ different tactics in order to achieve these. It was hoped that the other non-Russian Slav nations, in combination with the liberal elements inside Russia, could exert sufficient pressure on the Russian government to ease the situation in Russian Poland.

Opinion in the Russian division of Poland was, however, by no means unanimously in favour of involvement with the Neo-Slav movement. Before returning to Austria–Hungary, the Austrian Slav delegation, accompanied by Volodimirov; I. P. Filevich, a Russian academic at Warsaw University; and a Pole, L. Dymsza; travelled to Warsaw where further discussions were held with Polish representatives on the subject of Slav unity.[118] The decisions taken in St Petersburg were endorsed by the Poles, but with reservations.[119] Reporting the events, the British consul in Warsaw stated that:

An informal Conference...took place with leaders of the principal parties, excluding the socialistic element, and...a tentative programme was drawn up for adoption by all Pan-Slavonic Societies...Some conflicting sentiments were expressed respecting M. Dmowski's speech at the Congress [in St Petersburg] as committing the National Democratic party to a policy which is too pacific and is not sufficiently strong in the variety of its demands for political reforms in Russian Poland.[120]

The more radical sections of Dmowski's own party remained unconvinced by his arguments, and were opposed to the attempts to foster greater Slav co-operation.[121] Indeed, the attitude of most Russian Poles to the Neo-Slav ideas was rather guarded, as is evident from the British consul's observations. He continued thus:

[117] PRO, FO, 371/513, O'Beirne to Grey, 19625, St Petersburg, 4 June 1908.
[118] H.H.St.A., PA, XL 219, *Panslav Bewegung* 3, Ugron to Aehrenthal, (telegram) 9713, Warsaw, 31 May 1908, and Ugron to Aehrenthal, 13, Warsaw, 2 June 1908; PRO, FO, 371/517, Bayley to Nicolson, Warsaw, 9 June 1908, enclosed in O'Beirne to Grey, 21291, St Petersburg, 13 June 1908.
[119] *Novoe vremya*, 19 May (1 June), 26 May (8 June) 1908; *Národní listy*, 5 June 1908.
[120] PRO, FO, 371/517, Bayley to Nicolson, Warsaw, 9 June 1908, enclosed in O'Beirne to Grey, 21291, St Petersburg, 13 June 1908.
[121] *Novoe vremya*, 26 May (8 June) 1908; A. Černý, 'Po slovanských dnech', p. 443.

In general it may be said that, except for the most optimistic of the National Democrats, nobody takes the programme very seriously, as experience has made them sceptical, many such movements, though begun under excellent auspices, having only provided copy for the newspapers and topics for long-winded speeches, and then been consigned to oblivion.[122]

This scepticism which was not only expressed from the Polish side[123] did not, however, dampen the enthusiasm of the Neo-Slavs. Kramář, who had felt considerable apprehension about his exploratory visit to Russia,[124] later described the time spent in St Petersburg, in the spring of 1908, as being amongst 'the brightest days of Slavdom'.[125] The satisfaction of the Neo-Slav envoys was not totally unjustified. In general, Russia had appeared very receptive to the ideas for a new approach to the recurrent theme of inter-Slav relations, and the attitude of the Polish representatives was also encouraging.[126] It remained to be seen, however, how sincere or how influential the Russian followers of Neo-Slavism were. Nevertheless, during the visit to St Petersburg, Kramář and his colleagues, together with their Russian sympathisers and representatives of the Russian Poles, had succeeded in formulating the guiding principles of the new Slav movement. These stressed the equal status of all the Slav peoples, the right of each to unhindered cultural and economic development, and detailed several fields in which inter-Slav co-operation could most beneficially take place. It was also agreed that a congress of representatives from all the Slav nations should meet in Prague, in July of the same year, with the purpose of further defining the aims of the Neo-Slav movement, the preparation of a programme, and of providing the new movement with the impetus required to achieve the aspired goals.[127]

On his return to Prague, Kramář gave a public explanation of the motivation behind the new course in inter-Slav relations. He

[122] PRO, FO, 371/517, Bayley to Nicolson, Warsaw, 9 June 1908, enclosed in O'Beirne to Grey, 21291, St Petersburg, 13 June 1908.
[123] *Čas*, 14 June 1908 (Lidlin, 'Slovanský týden v Petrohradě', 11). The author reported that many foreign newspapers were of the opinion that the glowing speeches about Slav solidarity had been made 'under the expansive influence of sparkling champagne'.
[124] *Novoe vremya*, 16 (29) May 1908; *Proces dra. Kramáře*, 11, p. 41.
[125] Kramář, *Na obranu*, p. 15.
[126] Kramář claimed this to be the case in *Pět přednášek*, pp. 27–8.
[127] *Jednání sjezdu 1908*, p. 111 (unnumbered).

stressed the changes which Russia had recently undergone, the autocracy being replaced by what was believed to be a more representative form of government, more responsive to public opinion. The traditional Pan-Slav ideas based on the three principles of Orthodoxy, autocracy, and nationality had, the Czech leader claimed, disappeared together with the old Russia. Pan-Slavism had its place in history, and had played a useful role in its time, but circumstances were now altered. All future relations between the Slav nations would be based on new enlightened principles, those of liberty, equality, and brotherhood. Turning to the political aspects of the Neo-Slav movement, Kramář stated that Russia was becoming increasingly concerned with German expansion in the Balkans, and towards Constantinople and Asia Minor. He continued:

But, as is the case with us in Austria, Russia does not seek a conflict with Germany. We Slavs do not desire a policy of abrupt changes. However, it is essential at this time to erect, against the cultural and economic organisation of Germany, an equally strong and conscious Slav cultural and economic organisation which would vigorously defend every inch of Slav ground and every single Slav soul.

For the benefit of the Germans and of the Habsburg authorities, Kramář indicated the pacific nature of the new movement, claiming that: 'Our Slavism endangers no one in the whole world. We do not desire to destroy any states. Our modern Slavism is loyal to the states to which we belong; but there where we make our stand, we make it resolutely, we demand the right to live and the right to free material development.'[128]

Earlier, Kramář and his two colleagues had reported on their Russian visit at a gathering of Slav representatives in the Vienna Reichsrat. This meeting, held on 17 June 1908, approved the plans for the projected Slav congress.[129] He also reported back to the Austro-Hungarian Prime Minister, Baron Beck, and to the Foreign Minister, Count Aehrenthal, who raised no objections to a Slav congress being held in the Bohemian capital.[130]

A considered judgement of these latest developments in relations

[128] *Národní listy*, 20 June 1908. Text of a speech given by Kramář on 19 June. See also report of this in H.H.St.A., PA, XL 219, *Panslav Bewegung* 3, copy of police report no. 13 242 pp, Prague, 20 June 1908.
[129] *Novoe vremya*, 8 (21) August 1908.
[130] *Proces dra. Kramáře*, II, pp. 42–3.

between the Slav nations was provided by the A. Černý. His words, representative of moderate Czech and Slovak opinion, indicated the importance attached to inter-Slav relations and also the hope derived from recent changes in Russia that, in the future, these relations would be more harmonious. Summarising the situation following the visit to St Petersburg of the Austrian Slav delegation Černý commented in characteristically measured tones: 'I am of the opinion that, although there is no reason for jubilation, there is also no need for despondency. In Russia sympathetic forces are rising to the surface, and need to be utilised in the interest of the cause which is very dear to us – which is the life question of us all.'[131]

[131] A. Černý, 'Po slovanských dnech', p. 446.

4
The 1908 Prague Neo-Slav Congress

In Prague, preparations for the Neo-Slav Congress were initiated immediately on the return of the Austrian Slav delegation from their visit to Russia. The task of organisation was assigned to the Slav Committee of the Czech National Council, which had recently come under the direct control of Kramář. Herold, the chairman of both the Czech National Council and of the Council's Slav Committee died, unexpectedly, early in May and Kramář was elected as his successor on the Slav Committee.[1] A special Congress office was established in the City Hall and, under the direction of Kramář and the Mayor of Prague, K. Groš, a series of consultations held with interested individuals and organisations.[2] A detailed programme was prepared and a list of delegates to be invited drawn up. The Prague gathering was, Kramář explained, termed only a Preparatory Congress 'out of caution',[3] and the invitations restricted to persons active in the fields of politics and cultural affairs.[4] Financial support for the Congress was received from Czech merchant banks and various Czech municipalities.[5]

[1] *Jednání sjezdu 1908*, p. III (unnumbered). J. Čelakovský succeeded Herold as chairman of the Czech National Council.

[2] *Ibid.*

[3] Kramář, *Na obranu*, p. 15.

[4] *Jednání sjezdu 1908*, p. III (unnumbered). The Neo-Slav organisers originally intended the Prague gathering to be a meeting of Slav parliamentarians. At a later stage in the preparations, the composition of the delegations was widened to include persons from other walks of life. J. Rozvoda, 'Přípravný slovanský sjezd v Praze', *Česká revue*, I (1907–8), p. 645.

[5] Archive of the Czech National Council, minutes of a meeting of the sub-committee of the Slav Committee, 18 January 1909, cited in Herman, 'Novoslovanství a česká buržoasie', p. 277; Willy, 'S slavyanskogo sezda v Prage', appendix to V. N. Korablev, *Slavyansky sezd v Prage 1908 goda* (St Petersburg 1908), p. 35. J. F. N. Bradley, in 'Czech Pan-Slavism Before the First World War', *The Slavonic and East European Review*, XL (1961–2), p. 200, referring to H.H.St.A., Aehrenthal to Berchtold, 445/4/I.B., 2 March 1908, states that the Neo-Slav cause received financial support from Britain. No further corroboration of this report has, however, been found and it is therefore

Although the Congress was acclaimed as a meeting of all the Slavs, this was far from the case. The composition of the various delegations, and especially the notable absence of representatives of entire nationalities and of certain sections of others, were a revealing indication of the existing state of affairs in the Slav world. Absent were the Slovaks, the Lusatian Sorbs, the White Russians, the majority of the Ukrainians, and the Poles from the German division of Poland.[6] The Poles from German Poland, together with the Lusatian Sorbs, were prevented from being present in Prague by the German government.[7] The Czech delegation undertook to represent the Lusatian Sorbs and also the Slovaks.[8] The latter had not been invited to the Congress, in order to avoid alarming the Hungarian government which was only too ready to regard any expression of Slav sentiment, however vague, as a dire Pan-Slav threat to the Magyar nation.[9] During the consultations held over the preparation of a Congress programme it was suggested that the question of the oppression of the Slovaks in Hungary and that of the Poles in Germany should be included on the agenda. These proposals were, however, rejected by Kramář on the grounds that: 'There would be difficulties with governments, states and political parties. It would be a mistake to incite the Germans and the Magyars against Slavism. The Congress must not be directed against anyone.'[10]

The majority of the Ukrainians, although invited to the Congress, refused to attend. Their leaders in Galicia and the Russian Ukraine sent a declaration to the Congress in which they stated that they were unable to be present as the Ukrainian question had been

---

probable that the unlikely provision of British monetary assistance existed purely in the imagination of the Habsburg authorities.

[6] Details of the membership of the participant delegations are given in *Jednání sjezdu 1908*, pp. III–VI (unnumbered).

[7] Tobolka, *Politické dějiny československého národa*, III, part 2, p. 613. Although most observers agree that no German Poles were present at the Congress, nevertheless, two Polish journalists from Poznań were listed in the official record of delegates.

[8] *Jednání sjezdu 1908*, p. 62. Despite the fact that no Slovaks from Slovakia attended the Congress, the Czech delegation did contain a Slovak resident in Prague, B. Pavlů. *Ibid.*, p. IV (unnumbered).

[9] For details of the attitude of the Hungarian government towards the non-Magyar nationalities see R. W. Seton-Watson, *Racial Problems in Hungary*.

[10] Archive of the Czech National Council, minutes of a meeting of the Slav Congress Committee, 10 July 1908, cited in Herman, 'Novoslovanství a česká buržoasie', p. 278.

excluded from the agenda.[11] This omission was due to the fact that most Neo-Slavs denied the existence of a Ukrainian nation, and simply regarded all Ukrainians as Russians; others, at best, favoured the adoption of a position of non-interference in the dispute between the Ukrainians and the Russians over the recognition of the former as a separate Slav nation.[12]

At the turn of the century the Ukrainian nation was divided between Russia and Austria–Hungary. In neither of these two Empires was it in a particularly happy situation. The Ukrainians inhabiting the Russian Ukraine were subjected to persistent Russification, which was the general policy of the Russian government towards all national minorities, though the 1905 Revolution had brought temporary relief. Those living within the Austro-Hungarian Empire had to contend with oppression from the Poles, who enjoyed a privileged position in Galicia not unlike that of the Magyars in Hungary. The electoral reforms carried out in the Austrian part of the Habsburg Empire in 1907 did improve somewhat the political situation for the Ukrainians and helped to strengthen their nationalist mqvement which was anti-Polish, but divided in its attitude towards Russia.[13] Only the pro-Russian faction of the Ukrainian movement, the so-called Old Ruthenian Party, was represented in Prague. These delegates can hardly be regarded as true representatives of the Ukrainians as they denied the existence of their own nation, claiming to be Great Russians.[14]

During the course of the Congress when a Polish delegate did raise the issue of Ukrainian national existence, despite the fact that it did not appear on the agenda, the Russian, Count V. A. Bobrinsky, insisted that there were no Ukrainians and that eastern Galicia, Bukovina and northern Hungary were inhabited by the 'united' Russian nation.[15] The Czech Neo-Slavs held a similar view.

[11] *Novoe vremya*, 7 (20) July 1908; A. Černý, 'Slovanské sjezdy r. 1908', *Slovanský přehled*, XI (1909), p. 65.

[12] Rozvoda, 'Přípravný slovanský sjezd v Praze', p. 644. The official published record of the Congress proceedings, *Jednání sjezdu 1908*, p. v (unnumbered), refers to the Ukranian delegation as 'Galician Russians'. At the Congress Kramář addressed the Ukrainians in the same way. *Národní listy*, 14 July 1908.

[13] M. Hrushevsky, *A History of Ukraine* (New Haven, 1941), pp. 508–13; W. E. D. Allen, *The Ukraine: A History* (Cambridge, 1940), p. 255. An important concession was made to the Ukrainians in Russia early in 1906 when the Russian Academy of Sciences reached the decision that Ukrainian was not a Russian dialect but a separate language.

[14] A. Černý, 'Slovanské sjezdy r. 1908', p. 65.

[15] Willy, 'S slavyanskogo sezda v Prage', p. 39.

Several years later, in an interview with a correspondent of the Russian newspaper *Novoe vremya*, Kramář stated that: 'The Ukrainian movement is basically unnatural, anti-Russian and therefore anti-Slav.'[16] The fact that the Congress organisers had not even considered inviting the White Russians was not surprising because they too were generally regarded, not as a separate nationality, but as an integral part of the Russian nation. Indeed, at the beginning of the century, White Russian nationalism was itself only just awakening.[17]

Further absences from the Congress were of a purely political nature. No social Democrats from any of the Slav nations were present in Prague.[18] The concept of exclusive Slav co-operation conflicted with the wider internationalism of the socialist movement. The Polish Social Democrats, in particular, treated the Neo-Slavs with considerable derision.[19] A similar attitude was initially adopted by the Czech Social Democrats. Subsequently, however, at least some had second thoughts about the usefulness of the Neo-Slav movement.[20]

The Czechs, as the organisers, had numerically the strongest representation at the Congress. The entire Czech delegation, including substitutes, consisted of twenty-four members. The overwhelming majority of these, fifteen, were politicians; either members of the Vienna Reichsrat or of one of the provincial Diets. The remaining Czech delegates consisted of the Mayor of Prague, Groš; the leader of the Sokol gymnastic organisation, Scheiner; the chairman of the Czech National Council, J. Čelakovský; one financier several journalists and an academic.[21]

Of the Czech political parties, most numerously represented were the Young Czechs with eight members in the delegation including, of course, their leader, Kramář. The Agrarian Party sent four delegates to the Congress, amongst them J. Dürrich, a member of the Austrian Parliament. Also represented were the

---

[16] Cited in H. Boczkowski, 'Dr. Kramář proti Ukrajincům', *Slovanský přehled*, XIV (1912), p. 134.

[17] N. P. Vakar, *Belorussia: The Making of a Nation* (Cambridge, Mass., 1956), pp. 73–4, 87–92; A. Černý, 'Běloruské snahy národní a literární v l. 1909–1910', *Slovanský přehled*, XIII (1911), p. 416.

[18] *Národní listy*, 11 July 1908.

[19] PRO, FO, 371/517, Bayley to Nicolson, Warsaw, 9 June 1908, p. 1, enclosed in O'Beirne to Grey, 21291, St Petersburg, 13 June 1908.

[20] See below, pp. 113–14.

[21] *Jednání sjezdu 1908*, pp. III–IV (unnumbered); *Národní listy*, 14 July 1908.

National Socialists, by their leader Klofáč, and the Realists but, as mentioned previously, not the Social Democrats.

Although Masaryk's name appeared on the official list of delegates he did not actively participate in the Congress, his place as a representative of the Realist Party being taken by a substitute member, P. Šámal.[22] The reasons for Masaryk's decision not to attend the Congress, made presumably at a fairly late stage, are not absolutely clear. A few years later, in an interview with a Polish journalist, he explained that he had not wished to become involved with the Neo-Slav movement because it had been initiated by the Young Czechs and that, besides, he held different views on the subject. He believed that Neo-Slavism, in the form in which it appeared, would never achieve what was expected of it. Masaryk continued:

Slav reciprocity has, unfortunately, up to the present been based on complete mutual ignorance of conditions. It was not possible to work with people who had come from Russia not knowing each other, and who were unfamiliar with Polish and Czech conditions and with the complex Polish-Ukrainian relationship. Such work was unrealistic and I, as you know, am a realist. With such people it was only possible to attend banquets.

Masaryk claimed that he had intended speaking about the Russo-Polish dispute, which he considered to be the most serious problem facing the Slavs, but was told that this question would not be discussed at the Congress. The organisers had also informed him that, although no political issues could be raised, the discussion of economic problems was permissible. Masaryk, however, failed to see how the two subjects could be divorced.[23]

Also conspicuous by his absence from the Prague Congress was A. Černý, the eminent Czech Slavist and editor of the admirable periodical concerned with Slav affairs, *Slovanský přehled*. Despite its considerable size, as A. Černý pointed out, the Czech delegation contained only one Slavist scholar of any standing, Professor J. Polívka of the Czech University of Prague.[24]

The very evident bias in the composition of the Czech delegation towards political figures, and the predominance of Young Czech

[22] *Jednání sjezdu 1908*, p. 19: Kramář, *Na obranu*, p. 24.
[23] *Čas*, 12 April 1910 ('Prof. Masaryk o neoslavismu'). Report of an interview between Masaryk and a correspondent of the *Kurjer Warszawski*.
[24] A. Černý, 'Slovanské sjezdy r. 1908', p. 11.

Party supporters among these, gave rise to criticism of the selection. The Realist organ *Čas*, for instance, demanded to know why the various fields of the arts and the sciences were not represented: 'We cannot regard the Congress as cultural when no representatives of our culture are present, and we deplore the Young Czech misuse of the idea of Slav reciprocity in such an unpleasant manner for their own unfriendly, non-Slav, petty party-political ends.'[25]

The second most numerous presence at the Congress was that of the Russian delegation headed by Krasovsky, a prominent member of the conservative majority in the State Council, the upper house of the Russian legislature. A substantial proportion of the persons comprising the twenty-two man delegation were, like the Czechs, political figures; six were members of the Duma and four were members of the State Council. The others were representatives of the business community, journalists, and academics.[26] The choice of the Russian delegation was subsequently criticised in Russia, and elsewhere, on the grounds that only five of its members, Filevich, V. A. Francev, Vergun, Svatkovsky, and V. N. Korablev, were at all familiar with Slav affairs, the remaining Russian representatives being largely ignorant of the subject.[27]

The majority of the delegation came from right of centre of the Russian political spectrum, though the forces on the extreme right were not represented. Prominent among the delegates with liberal views were the Kadets Maklakov and A. A. Stakhovich.[28] Milyukov, the eminent liberal and a leader of the Kadet Party, declined an invitation to attend the Congress.[29] Other liberals, such

[25] *Čas*, 13 July, 1908.
[26] H.H.St.A., PA, XL 219, *Panslav Bewegung* 3, Berchtold to Aehrenthal, 30M St Petersburg, 21 June/4 July 1908; *Jednání sjezdu 1908*, p. v (unnumbered).
[27] *Národní listy*, 25 August 1908, report of an article in the Russian newspaper *Rossiya*; Willy, 'S slavyanskogo sezda v Prage', p. 37; J. Polívka, 'Rusko a lux ex Oriente', *Česká revue*, XII (1918–19), p. 333.
[28] A. Černý, 'Slovanské sjezdy r. 1908', p. 12.
[29] P. N. Milyukov, *Vospominaniya, 1859–1917* (2 vols., New York, 1955), II, p. 46. Confusing the sequence of events, Milyukov stated that 'sensing hypocrisy...I did not attend the congress in Sofia or the following one in Prague'. Herman, 'Novoslovanství a česká buržoasie', p. 278 and J. Křížek, *T. G. Masaryk a naše dělnická třída* (Prague, 1955), p. 80, both see a connection between Milyukov's and Masaryk's absences at the Congress. Both these men were acquainted with the American millionaire Charles Crane, and it is suggested that he might have instructed them to boycott the Prague Congress and to avoid involvement in the Neo-Slav movement. No evidence is provided, however, to substantiate this assertion.

as D. N. Shipov, M. A. Stakhovich, and Kovalevsky, also refused to attend, protesting that the Russian delegation had fallen into the hands of right wing elements.[30] With the exception of a few members, such as Lvov, I. Kh. Ozerov, I. S. Klyuzhev, Svatkovsky, and Volodimirov, who held moderate political views, the remainder of the delegates were mostly old-style Slavophils.[31] The more notable among these were Korablev, the secretary of the St Petersburg Slavonic Benevolent Society; Count Bobrinsky of the Moderate Right Party; the journalists G. V. Komarov and Vergun; and Professor Filevich. Also present was the neuropathologist V. M. Bekhterev.[32] A. A. Stolypin, a member of the editorial staff of *Novoe vremya*, and the brother of the Russian Prime Minister, joined the Russian delegation during the course of the Congress.[33]

The Poles also sent a substantial delegation to Prague, the majority of which (eleven) came from the Russian division of Poland. The Austrian Poles were represented by six delegates but, as mentioned previously, no Poles from the German division were present.[34] It appears that Kramář had some difficulty in persuading the Austrian Poles to participate in the Neo-Slav gathering. Their leader in the Vienna Reichsrat, Count Dzieduszycki, who was not present at the Congress, was reluctant to lend his support to Kramář and is reported to have told him frankly: 'I know that you are endeavouring to become the leader of the Austrian Slavs, but I also would like to fulfil this role.'[35] In order, presumably, to avoid causing offence to the Austro-Hungarian authorities, none of the Galician Poles selected to attend the Prague gathering were, at the time, members of the Vienna Parliament.[36]

Politicians again constituted the largest section of the Polish delegation, the remainder consisting of journalists, lawyers, and academics, including Professor Zdziechowski of the University of

---

[30] A. Černý, 'Slovanské sjezdy r. 1908', p. 12.   [31] *Ibid.*
[32] *Jednání sjezdu 1908*, p. v (unnumbered); A. Černý, 'Slovanské sjezdy r. 1908', p. 12; G. V. Komarov was the son of V. V. Komarov, whose activities in Prague during the Palacký festivities of 1898 have been mentioned above, pp. 20–1.
[33] PRO, FO, 371/519, Nicolson to Grey, 33395, St Petersburg, 19 September 1908.
[34] *Jednání sjezdu 1908*, pp. iv–v (unnumbered); *Národní listy*, 14 July 1908.
[35] Kramář, *Na obranu*, p. 17.
[36] Kramář, 'Po petrohradských konferencích', p. 579.

Cracow, and eminent Slavist and editor of the periodical on Slav affairs, *Słowianski Swiat* [The Slav World].[37] Most numerously represented was the National Democratic Party which was in existence in all three divisions of Poland and whose aim was, eventually, to reunite the Polish nation. The National Democrats from Russian Poland included Dmowski and J. Stecki. The Galician section of the party was represented by, among others, Doboszyński and S. Grabski, both former members of the Vienna Reichsrat. The Polish Realists from the Russian division were represented by H. Potocki and L. Straszewicz, and the Progressives by V. Łypacewicz. M. Grek attended the Congress on behalf of the Galician Populists. The Polish Conservatives had only one member in the delegation, Chyliński, chairman of the Union of Slav Journalists in Cracow.[38]

The remaining Slav nations sent considerably smaller delegations to Prague. The Russophil Ukrainians from Galicia were represented at the Congress by four delegates, all deputies in the Austrian Reichsrat. Among these was Glebovitsky, who had accompanied Kramář on the journey to St Petersburg a few months previously.[39] During the course of the Congress the Ukrainian representatives amalgamated with the Russians to form one delegation.[40] The Bulgarians sent a three-man delegation headed by S. S. Bobchev, an academic and president of the Sofia Slavonic Benevolent Society.[41] The Croatian delegation consisted of five persons, all active politicians, three of whom also had considerable reputations as authors: the leader of the Agrarian Party, S. Radić, L. Babić-Gjalski and Tresić-Pavičić.[42] The four Slovenes present at the Congress were led by Hribar, the third member of the Austrian Slav expedition to St Petersburg. All but one were politicians, and they represented only one political organisation, the Liberal Party. Invitations had been sent to I. Šušteršič and I. Krek, the leaders of the largest Slovene political party, the Clericals, but they refused to attend because the Liberal leader, Hribar, their political rival, was involved with the Congress

[37] *Jednáni sjezdu 1908*, p. iv–v (unnumbered); Rozvoda, 'Přípravný slovanský sjezd v Praze', p. 645.
[38] *Jednáni sjezdu 1908*, iv–v (unnumbered); *Národni listy*, 14 July 1908.
[39] *Jednáni sjezdu 1908*, p. v (unnumbered); *Národni listy*, 14 July 1908.
[40] *Proces dra. Kramáře*, iv, part 1, p. 26.
[41] *Jednáni sjezdu 1908*, p. iii (unnumbered).
[42] *Ibid.*, p. iv (unnumbered).

organisation.[43] The six-man Serbian delegation contained four representatives from the Kingdom of Serbia, of whom two were former government ministers and the other two academics.[44] The Austro-Hungarian ambassador in Belgrade, surprised by the lack of interest shown in Serbia in the activities of the Neo-Slavs, reported to Vienna that:

At the last moment, probably in response to an insistent invitation from the Prague committee, a small delegation of politicians and representatives of other bodies was selected and sent to Prague. The only personality in the delegation is the State Councillor, G. Gershich,...a university professor and former minister, a quiet old man.[45]

The two delegates representing the Serbs living within the Habsburg Empire were both political figures.[46]

The selection of the representatives invited to attend the Prague Congress, made by the organising committee under Kramář's direction, was subjected to general criticism for two main reasons. It was pointed out that, although the organisers claimed that the Congress would be concerned only with cultural and economic aspects of Slav life – indeed it was specifically stated that political issues would be excluded from the discussions – nevertheless, the majority of the delegates were politicians. Persons attending the Congress who were active in the fields of Slav culture were few in number.[47] The second point of criticism was the right-wing orientation of most of the delegations.[48] Although the extreme right was not strongly represented, there were comparatively few delegates present with pronounced liberal views. Most obvious was the absence of many prominent liberal Russians, who might have been expected to support the Neo-Slav movement. It appears that at least some of the responsibility for the right wing bias in the Russian delegation rested with the leader of the Czech National Socialists, Klofáč. Although Kramář wished the movement to be associated exclusively with the more liberal section of Russian political opinion, represented by persons such as Milyukov and

[43] *Ibid.*, p. VI (unnumbered), 60–61; A. Černý, 'Slovanské sjezdy r. 1908', p. 67.   [44] *Jednání sjezdu 1908*, p. VI (unnumbered).
[45] Forgach to Aehrenthal, C39, Belgrade, 16 July 1908, cited in Beneš, *Úvahy o slovanství*, p. 187.   [46] *Jednání sjezdu 1908*, p. VI (unnumbered).
[47] A. Černý, 'Slovanské sjezdy r. 1908', p. 11; Rozvoda, 'Přípravný slovanský sjezd v Praze', p. 645.
[48] A. Černý, 'Slovanské sjezdy r. 1908', p. 68.

his associates, Klofáč, together with some South Slavs present during the preliminary negotiations, insisted that representatives of Russian conservative forces were also invited to the Congress.[49] The decision of the organisers not to admit journalists to the Congress but to establish a so-called Press Commission consisting entirely of journalists sympathetic to the movement, which would be exclusively responsible for reporting the Congress proceedings, met with predictable criticism from other sections of the press.[50] This ruling, an obvious attempt at censorship, was eventually relaxed and journalists were permitted to attend the Congress sessions, providing that their presence was approved by their respective national delegations. Kramář declared that he expected the journalists present to be loyal to the Congress and to respect the confidential nature of proceedings whenever this was appropriate.[51] After the conclusion of the Congress it was alleged that an objective and accurate account of the proceedings had not been released and that Kramář himself had been responsible for the censorship.[52]

The Neo-Slav Congress, held in the Council Chamber of the Prague Old Town Hall, was opened on 13 July 1908. After hearing a few words of welcome from the Mayor of Prague, Groš, the eighty or so delegates present were addressed by Kramář. The Czech leader took advantage of this unique opportunity to demonstrate his linguistic abilities and during the course of his speech addressed each delegation in turn in their own tongue, using the Czech, Slovene, Serbo-Croat, Bulgarian, Polish and Russian languages.[53] Kramář recalled the last Slav Congress, held in Prague sixty years previously, and stressed that the principles of liberty, equality and brotherhood for all the Slavs, first voiced at the 1848 Congress, were once again emerging as the leading ideas of the Slav movement. Absent friends were remembered and 'sincere greetings' sent to the German Poles, the Slovaks and the Lusatian Sorbs. To the Poles present Kramář expressed the hope that the principles of Neo-Slavism would enable a solution to be found to the protracted dispute between the Polish and Russian nations.

---

[49] Willy, 'S slavyanskogo sezda v Prage', pp. 33–4.
[50] *Čas*, 13 July 1908.
[51] *Jednání sjezdu 1908*, p. 15; *Čas*, 15 July 1908.
[52] *Národní listy*, 25 August 1908, report of an article in the Russian newspaper *Rossiya*; Willy, 'S slavyanskogo sezda v Prage', p. 36.
[53] *Jednání sjezdu 1908*, pp. 1–2; *Národní listy*, 14 July 1908.

In his words addressed to the Russian delegates Kramář pointed
out, rather hopefully, that: 'You have come with a love of freedom
for all the Slav nations, not only on your lips but also in your
hearts,...you carry an [olive] branch of peace to all the Slav
nations'.[54] Krasovsky, the leader of the Russian delegation, responded in the same spirit: 'Russia has no designs against any
other Slav nation; she is aware of her size and her greatness, but
does not wish to force her cultural order or any administrative
restrictions on anyone...Russia stands for the free existence,
progress, and development of every Slav nation.'[55] Replying on
behalf of the Poles, Dmowski reiterated the hope expressed by
Kramář, that the Russo-Polish dispute would soon be settled.[56]

The following day, at the first working session of the Congress,
Kramář was predictably elected as chairman, other officers were
chosen, and the standing orders discussed and approved. He again
took the opportunity to stress that unless a satisfactory solution
could be found to the Russo-Polish dispute, it would not be
possible to make any progress towards Slav unity.[57]

The three days during which the Congress held working sessions
were occupied by the discussion of a variety of subjects, all concerned with the promotion of Slav co-operation and unity in the
fields of culture and economics. The two most significant items on
the agenda were concerned with purely economic matters.[58] The
desire to further economic co-operation between the Slav nations
was one of the predominant characteristics of Neo-Slavism, and
partially explains why the movement came into existence. The
Czech industrial middle class, whose representatives were largely
responsible for instigating the Neo-Slav movement, owned some
of the most highly developed and fastest growing industries within
the Austro-Hungarian Empire. This Czech owned section of
industry, however, had to contend with strong competition from
industry under German control and its opportunities for further
expansion within the Dual Monarchy were limited. New outlets
for industrial produce had to be found, and the relatively under-
developed Balkan Slav States, together with the vast Russian
Empire, offered almost unlimited possibilities. Hence the intense
interest shown by the Czech Neo-Slavs in two projects of

[54] *Národní listy*, 14 July 1908.   [55] *Jednání sjezdu 1908*, p. 5.
[56] *Ibid.*, p. 7; *Národní listy*, 14 July 1908.   [57] *Jednání sjezdu 1908*, pp. 14–15.
[58] For details of the Congress agenda see *Národní listy*, 14 July 1908.

an economic nature; the Slav bank and the Slav industrial exhibition.

The most important issue raised at the Prague Congress, in the opinion of the Czech Neo-Slavs and others, was the proposal for the establishment of a Slav bank.[59] J. Preiss, a director of the largest Czech bank, the *Živnostenská banka*, initiated the debate by delivering a detailed report on the project.[60] He proposed that the bank be established as a joint-stock company, modelled on the official German commercial bank, the *Deutsche Bank*. It would have a working capital of 100 million crowns, approximately 40 million roubles, and the shareholders would be both existing banks and private individuals.[61] The similarity to the *Deutsche Bank* would be in form only, for it was tacitly understood that no German capital would be accepted by the Slav bank. The head office of the bank would be situated in Moscow, with subsidiaries in other Slav lands and elsewhere in the world.[62]

The Slav bank, as envisaged by Preiss, was to have three basic aims. Firstly, it would be responsible for the development of banking in all Slav countries and act as an agency for furthering economic links between them. It would also assist in raising state loans for Slav countries. The bank's second main activity would be to promote the growth of Slav owned industries by making investments in this field. This was, however, envisaged as a long term function, the investment activities would have to be limited as the provision of loans was considered to be of greater importance. The loans, in turn, would be restricted and granted mainly for improvement purposes.[63] Particular emphasis would be placed on

[59] Preiss described the Slav bank proposal as the 'greatest of all' the issues debated at the Congress. See Archive of the Czech National Council, transcript of Congress proceedings, p. 203, cited in Herman 'Novoslovanství a česká buržoasie', p. 286. A. Černý, the eminent Czech Slavist, who was not a Neo-Slav and was otherwise critical of the movement, also shared this view. See his 'Slovanské sjezdy r. 1908', p. 9. The British consul in Warsaw, C. Bayley, also regarded the Congress decision in favour of founding a Slav bank as 'the most important of the resolutions' passed. PRO, FO, 371/512, Bayley to O'Beirne, 28438, Warsaw, 25 July 1908.

[60] Preiss' report on the proposed Slav bank is missing from the published transcript of the proceedings, *Jednání sjezdu 1908*. Herman, in 'Novoslovanství a česká buržoasie', p. 285, states that a large part of the report is also missing from the record of the Congress proceedings in the Archive of the Czech National Council. A report of Preiss' speech was given in *Národní listy*, 16 July 1908, and also in Korablev, *Slavyansky sezd v Prage*, pp. 13–17.

[61] *Proces dra. Kramáře*, III, part 1, pp. 77–8.   [62] *Jednání sjezdu 1908*, p. 36.

[63] *Národní listy*, 16 July 1908; Korablev, *Slavyansky sezd v Prage*, pp. 15–16.

municipal loans, a type of credit unknown in Russia, because the promotion of municipal improvements, such as the improvement of communications, the introduction of electric power, the installation of water mains and similar public works, were calculated to result in an increase in trade between Russia and Austria–Hungary from which the Czech owned section of industry would reap the benefits.[64] The third aim of the Slav bank would be to encourage and promote trade, not only between the Slav countries, but also between the Slav lands and Western Europe. For this purpose it was proposed to establish branch offices of the bank in Paris and London. Periodically, the bank would issue information about the economic state of the Slav nations and would ensure that this information was available in Western Europe.[65] Preiss concluded his statement on a note of caution by drawing attention to the fact that the establishment of a Slav bank would not be an easy task and that some considerable time would elapse before it achieved a standing comparable with that of the *Deutsche Bank*.[66] Subsequent events were to prove this caution to be well founded.

The Congress also heard an alternative plan for a Slav bank put forward by Hribar, who had first raised the matter during the recent visit of the Austrian Slav delegation to St Petersburg. Hribar proposed the establishment of a larger financial institution with an initial working capital of 50 million roubles, to be doubled after two years. Though it would be desirable for the majority of the shares to remain in Slav hands, British and French capital would not be excluded. German capital, by implication, would be unacceptable. Hribar envisaged that the share capital would be divided as follows: 35 per cent from Russia, 25 per cent from the other Slav lands, and the remaining 40 per cent from elsewhere. The bank, headed by a Russian director, would be under the control of the Russian government, but representatives of the other Slav nations would participate in the commercial management. St Petersburg was proposed as the location of the bank's head office, on the grounds that it had to be situated close to the controlling government. A subsidiary would be established in Vienna. In addition, branch offices would be set up in Paris, London,

[64] *Proces dra. Kramáře*, III, part 1, p. 77.
[65] *Národní listy*, 16 July 1908; Korablev, *Slavyansky sezd v Prage*, pp. 14, 17.
[66] *Jednání sjezdu 1908*, pp. 37–8.

Hamburg, Constantinople and possibly also in Alexandria and Cairo.[67]
A third plan for a Slav bank had been prepared by J. Lošt'ák, the director of the Bohemian Land Bank, who was not a delegate at the Congress. This proposal was for the creation of a bank concentrating exclusively on promotive activities – establishing new joint-stock companies.[68]
The Russian delegates responded to these proposals with a marked lack of enthusiasm. While accepting in principle the idea of a Slav bank, Krasovsky suggested that the best approach would be to establish the bank initially in Prague with a view to transferring it to St Petersburg at a later stage. St Petersburg was favoured as the eventual seat of the bank because it was the financial capital of Russia, whereas Moscow, the location preferred by Preiss, was only the industrial centre.[69] Krasovsky warned that, although in Russia no political obstacles would be placed in the way of the proposals, nevertheless, the fact that Russian financial legislation differed considerably from that in Austria–Hungary and elsewhere would give rise to substantial difficulties.[70] Similar objections were raised by other Russian delegates, the economist, Professor Ozerov and F. Ya. Gey. Ozerov also spoke out against the plan to introduce municipal loans in Russia.[71]
The general disinterest of the Russian delegates in the Slav bank project prompted one Czech observer to comment that the bank, as envisaged by Preiss, was 'for the time being a pure fantasy'.[72] The Congress, nevertheless, decided in favour of the proposals outlined by Preiss[73] and elected two committees which were given the task of preparing more detailed plans. The system

[67] *Ibid.*, p. 35; Korablev, *Slavyansky sezd v Prage*, p. 17.
[68] *Proces dra. Kramáře*, III, part 1, p. 77.
[69] *Jednání sjezdu 1908*, p. 36. The proposal of the Czech Neo-Slavs to situate the head office of the Slav bank away from St Petersburg is, in itself, interesting. Moscow was presumably chosen as the proposed location because of its more central geographical position and also precisely because it was the industrial capital of Russia. The same city was also selected as the site of the projected Slav exhibition.   [70] *Ibid.*, p. 37.
[71] Korablev, *Slavyansky sezd v Prage*, p. 17; *Proces dra. Kramáře*, III, part 1, p. 78.
[72] J. Pátek, 'Okolo Slovanské banky', *Pokroková revue*, IV (1907–8), p. 593. Pátek accepted that a Slav bank was desirable and believed that it might come about in a decade. Meanwhile, he suggested, a modest, purely Czech, venture should be started, in order to keep the idea alive.
[73] *Proces dra. Kramáře*, III, part 1, p. 78.

of two committees was chosen for convenience. Minor issues were to be settled by a small inner committee, thus avoiding the time wasting procedure of frequently convening the full general committee.[74] The larger committee was composed of twelve members; three representatives each from the Czechs, Poles, Russians, and South Slavs. Its meetings were to be held in Warsaw. The inner committee consisted of three persons; Preiss, Hribar, and Šámal.[75]

The other economic subject discussed at the Prague Congress was the project for a Slav exhibition, the proposal for which was also outlined by Preiss.[76] He explained that the idea of a Slav exhibition was not new. The original plan, first produced in 1901,[77] had been to hold an ethnographic and artistic exhibition in St Petersburg. The project was subsequently widened, and the exhibition was to include all aspects of Slav life.[78] The Russian government had participated in the preparations and a site, the Taurida Palace, had been selected. Due to the Russo-Japanese War, however, the exhibition had never taken place. The subject had again been raised at the discussions held during the visit of the Austrian Slav delegation to St Peterburg earlier in 1908. Preiss believed that the time was opportune for reviving the scheme, and proposed that the exhibition should be held in Moscow within the next few years.[79] He later explained that the decision to stage the proposed exhibition in Russia had been taken 'not only because [it was desirable] to locate the project in the largest Slav state, but also because it was intended that the exhibition would promote the spread of Slav ideas and Slav awareness throughout Russia'.[80]

The Czech Neo-Slavs envisaged an exhibition consisting of two main sections: one concerned with cultural, the other with

[74] *Jednání sjezdu 1908*, p. 38.
[75] V. Černý, 'Sestavení návrhů a resolucí přijatých při přípravném sjezdu v Praze' (hereafter cited as 'Sestavení resolucí sjezdu'), cited in *Proces dra. Kramáře*, v, part 1, p. 66. The larger general, Slav Bank Committee consisted of: K. Mattuš, J. Preiss, and P. Šámal (Czechs); A. Doboszyński, J. Montwiłł, and J. Swieźyński (Poles); F. Ya. Gey, I. Kh. Ozerov, and V. Dudykevich (the two former Russians, the last a Ukrainian); M. Drashkovich (Serb); I. Hribar (Slovene); A. Lyudskanov (Bulgarian).
[76] *Jednání sjezdu 1908*, pp. 15–16. The Russian V. N. Korablev considered this to be the main item of the agenda. Korablev, *Slavyansky sezd v Prage*, p. 8.
[77] J. Preiss, 'Anketa o slovanské výstavě v Praze r. 1913', *Máj*, ix (1911), p. 1.
[78] *Jednání sjezdu 1908*, p. 15.
[79] *Ibid.*, p. 16; Korablev, *Slavyansky sezd v Prage*, p. 11.
[80] Preiss, 'Anketa o slovanské výstavě', p. 1.

economic affairs.[81] The economic section would provide an opportunity for staging a display of Czech industrial products, thus performing the valuable function of introducing these products into the, otherwise rather inaccessible, Russian market. In addition Preiss suggested that after the exhibition had closed a Slav museum should be founded in Moscow, where the best exhibits from the exhibition would remain on permanent display.[82]

This time it was the Poles who were less than enthusiastic about the plan. Straszewicz indicated to the Congress the difficulties in the way of Polish participation in both the economic and cultural sections of the proposed exhibition. Financial reasons would restrict Polish presence in the first section, and the widely differing cultural conditions under which the Polish nation lived in Galicia and Russian Poland would make participation difficult in the cultural section. Nevertheless, Straszewicz concluded that the exhibition could be held sometime before 1915. The leader of the Bulgarian delegation, Bobchev, recognised the problems confronting the Poles and stressed that the project could not materialise before a settlement was reached in the protracted Russo-Polish dispute.[83]

The immediate response of the Russians present at the Congress was not unfavourable. The economist, Ozerov, was in favour of the exhibition being held in 1911 or, at the latest, in 1915, but indicated that in order to make the venture worth while the exhibition would have to have some economic significance and not be staged for 'entertainment' purposes only.[84] Later, in an interview with the press, Ozerov expressed the opinion that the exhibition would help to pave the way towards the creation of a Slav bank. He was confident that the Russian government would, in its own interest, support the plan.[85] Another Russian, Vergun, envisaged the aims of the exhibition as being: 'To familiarise us with Slav [industrial] production, and enable us to discover in which fields successful competition was possible with German, English, and even, up to a point, with American products.'[86]

A counter-proposal made by the Croatian delegate, Radić, that the Slav exhibition should be located in either Cracow or Warsaw, was rejected by both Preiss and Vergun.[87] From the point of view

[81] *Jednání sjezdu 1908*, p. 16.   [82] *Ibid.*, p. 20.   [83] *Ibid.*, p. 20.
[84] *Ibid.*, p. 19.   [85] *Národní listy*, 23 July 1908.
[86] *Jednání sjezdu 1908*, p. 21.   [87] *Ibid.*, pp. 20–1.

of the Czechs, if the exhibition was to serve the purpose for which it was intended, it was essential that it took place in Russia proper, and in Moscow rather than St Petersburg. The Russians for their part, largely for nationalistic reasons, did not wish to see the exhibition staged on Polish territory, neither inside nor outside the Russian Empire. The Congress delegates accepted the proposal to hold a Slav exhibition in Moscow between 1911 and 1915, and a committee was elected to prepare detailed plans.[88] The Exhibition Committee, in turn, proposed the establishment of a wider general committee consisting of forty-two members.[89]

The other issues discussed at the Neo-Slav Congress were mostly concerned with cultural and educational co-operation, the exchange of scientific and technical information, and the arrangement of visits and exchanges of both individuals and groups, between the Slav nations. The majority of these schemes were approved by the Congress.[90]

Čelakovský, the chairman of the Czech National Council, read a paper on Slav cultural co-operation and proposed that a special organisation be established to promote this.[91] A Slovene delegate, A. Gabršček, spoke about the desirability of increasing the exchange of books and other printed matter between the Slav lands.[92] Other speakers stressed the need for scientific and technical co-operation, for the free exchange of ideas, and for some co-ordination of courses in universities and other institutes of higher education to enable students to spend some time studying in other Slav countries.[93] The Congress proclaimed cultural activities to be of paramount importance in spreading the ideas of Slav reciprocity.[94]

[88] V. Černý, 'Sestavení resolucí sjezdu', cited in *Proces dra. Kramáře*, v, part 1, p. 65. The Exhibition Committee consisted of I. Kh. Ozerov, E. M. Dementev, and V. M. Bekhterev (Russians); L. Straszewicz, L. Rydygier, and J. Swieżyński (Poles); M. Drashkovich and D. Baljak (Serbs); B. Vinković, and I. Lorković (Croats); I. Hribar and A. Gabršček (Slovenes); A. Lyudskanov and G. Kalinkov (Bulgarians); J. Scheiner, J. Dürich and J. Preiss (Czechs).

[89] *Jednání sjezdu 1908*, p. 62. The wider committee was to comprise fourteen Russians, eight Poles, eight Czechs (who would also represent the Slovaks and the Lusatian Sorbs), four Serbs, three Bulgarians, two Slovenes, and three Croats.

[90] For details see, V. Černý, 'Sestavení resolucí sjezdu', cited in *Proces dra. Kramáře*, v, part 1, pp. 63–74.   [91] *Jednání sjezdu 1908*, pp. 24, 38–43.

[92] *Ibid.*, pp. 43, 56–7.   [93] *Ibid.*, p. 31.

[94] V. Černý, 'Sestavení resolucí sjezdu', cited in *Proces dra. Kramáře*, v, part 1, p. 69.

The role of the press was also not forgotten. Kramář proposed the formation of an organisation of Slav journalists and also of a Slav telegraphic agency, which would have the aim of informing Slav public opinion by providing objective reports on Slav and other affairs.[95] Attempts had been made a few years previously to establish a Slav press-agency within the Habsburg Empire but these failed, largely due to the lack of both enthusiasm and financial support.[96] It was agreed that the Congress of Slav Journalists from Austria–Hungary due to be held later that year in the Slovene capital, Ljubljana, would be widened to include representatives of journalists from all the Slav nations.[97]

A report on Slav tourism presented by V. Černý included proposals for the establishment of a Slav tourist organisation to be responsible for encouraging the growth of tourist traffic between the Slav nations. The speaker's suggestion that the Czech Tourist Club should be approached with the request to form the Slav organisation was accepted by the Congress.[98]

A representative of the Czech Agrarian Party, K. Viškovský, stressed the economic importance of agriculture to the Slav nations and proposed that peasant farmers and agricultural students should be encouraged to visit other Slav areas in order to become familiar with different farming techniques. He also wished to see steps taken to further the exchange of agricultural scientific information. Both these and other proposed measures were aimed at assisting the growth of agricultural production in those areas of the Slav world where agriculture was under-developed.[99]

Scheiner, the head of the Czech Sokol gymnastic organisation, which had spread from Bohemia to most other Slav nations, reported on the state of the organisation and outlined ideas about how its growth could be further encouraged. The movement was extremely successful in the Czech lands and was also flourishing among the South Slavs and among the Poles in Galicia and German Poland but regrettably, in the speaker's view, there were no Sokol organisations in Russian Poland. In Russia itself, Scheiner complained, it had taken a considerable time for the movement to

[95] *Ibid.*, pp. 64–5; *Jednání sjezdu 1908*, p. 33.   [96] See below, pp. 181–2.
[97] *Jednání sjezdu 1908*, p. 34.
[98] *Ibid.*, pp. 16–17, 26–8; V. Černý, 'Sestavení resolucí sjezdu', cited in *Proces dra. Kramáře*, v, part 1, p. 65.
[99] *Jednání sjezdu 1908*, pp. 43–5; V. Černý, 'Sestavení resolucí sjezdu', cited in *Proces dra. Kramáře*, v, part 1, pp. 66–9.

become accepted but, even there, recent events had indicated that the Sokol idea was gaining recognition and, with it, popularity.[100] A Polish spokesman pointed out that the Russian government had forbidden the formation of Sokol organisations in the Russian division of Poland. Other delegates expressed their gratitude to the Czechs for spreading the Sokol idea, and it was agreed to further encourage the establishment of Sokol organisations in all Slav lands.[101]

Regarding the future organisation of the Neo-Slav movement the Congress approved a proposal, made by Kramář, to elect an Executive Committee whose responsibility it would be to arrange further Congresses and to ensure that the decisions taken at the Prague Congress were carried out. The Executive Committee would also be responsible for promoting the formation of Committees of Slav Reciprocity throughout the Slav world. The Committees of Slav Reciprocity were envisaged as consisting of five sections; cultural, economic, touristic, Sokol, and journalistic. Each section would have the task of implementing those resolutions passed by the Congress which were relevant to its own particular field. Kramář was elected chairman of the Executive Committee and the other members chosen were the Russians, Bobrinsky and Krasovsky; the Russophil Ukrainian, Glebovitsky; the Poles, Doboszyński, Zdziechowski and Dmowski; the Czech, V. Černý; and Tresić-Pavičić, K. Kumanudi, Hribar, and Bobchev, represented, respectively, the Croats, Serbs, Slovenes and Bulgarians.[102] The decision was also taken that, should it wish to do so, the Ukrainian nation could at any time also be represented on the Neo-Slav Executive Committee.[103] Despite the dampening words pronounced by the Russian delegate, Korablev, that, 'being a sceptic, I have my doubts whether it will be possible to build a Slav organisation with such ease; particularly before Russia regains her economic strength',[104] Kramář's proposal, to hold a further Preparatory Slav Congress in St Petersburg the following year, was approved.[105]

[100] *Jednání sjezdu 1908*, pp. 28–30.
[101] *Ibid.*, pp. 55–6; V. Černý, 'Sestavení resolucí sjezdu', cited in *Proces dra. Kramáře*, v, part 1, p. 66.
[102] *Jednání sjezdu 1908*, pp. 33, 60, 63; V. Černý, 'Sestavení resolucí sjezdu', cited in *Proces dra. Kramáře*, v, part 1, p. 64.
[103] *Jednání sjezdu 1908*, p. 58.   [104] *Ibid.*, p. 63.
[105] *Ibid.*, p. 64. A full Slav Congress did not take place in 1909, but a meeting of the Neo-Slav Executive Committee was held in the Russian capital.

In his closing address Kramář stressed the 'beautiful and harmonious' nature of the Congress proceedings, and expressed the
hope that a new era had dawned for Slavdom, an era of 'true
brotherhood and love'. Providing that each Slav nation received
the right of unhindered national, cultural, and economic development, he saw no reason why they should not 'fall into each others
embraces'.[106]

Equally optimistic and divorced from reality was the following
resolution, proposed by Krasovsky for the Russian delegation, and
unanimously approved by the Congress.[107]

The Preparatory Congress of Slav Delegates recognises the concept of
Slav understanding as a viable proposition, capable of achieving positive
results, and proclaims that the conditions, which are an essential prerequisite to the ending of misunderstanding between the Slav nations,
can only be achieved by the universal recognition and realisation of the
principle of equality and unhindered development of the national and
cultural life of each nation.[108]

Dmowski, on behalf of the Poles, expressed satisfaction with the
declaration, stating: 'We completely concur with the resolution
proposed by the Russian spokesman, for this resolution represents
a significant step by the Russian delegates towards a *rapprochement*
with us.'[109]

On the surface, the Prague Congress appeared to have succeeded
in bringing about peace, or at least a truce, between the Russians
and the Poles present. In response to a dramatic appeal by
Bobchev, addressed to the two largest Slav nations, to set an example of peace and harmony to their smaller brethren, Krasovsky
and Dmowski marked what was hoped to be the reconciliation of
their nations by symbolically shaking hands.[110] Theatrical performances of this nature accompanied by fine words of freedom
and equality, impressive though they were on the occasion, were

---

[106] *Jednání sjezdu 1908*, p. 64.   [107] *Ibid.*, p. 66.   [108] *Ibid.*, p. 65.
[109] *Ibid.*
[110] V. A. Bobrinsky, *Prazhsky sezd*, pp. 21–2. Kramář, *Na obranu*, p. 21. One
observer recorded that the Congress proceedings were not as harmonious as
was implied in the official publications. It was alleged that during the meetings
there was considerable tension between the Russian and Polish delegates, but
that this fact was suppressed by Kramář's personal censorship of press reports
and Congress publications. Willy, 'S slavyanskogo sezda v Prage', pp. 36,
38–9.

not an adequate foundation for the construction of a lasting understanding between the Russians and the Poles. In reality as
A. Černý, the Czech Slavist, indicated at the time, the Prague
Congress had made little or no progress towards the solution of
the Russo-Polish dispute. During previous conferences between
the Russians and the Poles held in 1905, the subject of Polish
autonomy had been seriously discussed. At the Neo-Slav Congress
there was no mention of this, nor of any other concrete proposal
for improving the situation of the Poles in the Russian division.[111]
Similarly the other symbolic demonstration of Slav solidarity, the
formal coalescing during the course of the Congress of the four
groups of South Slav delegates, the Serbs, Croats, Slovenes, and
Bulgarians, into one united South Slav delegation,[112] was little
more than an empty, though well intended, gesture. The various
disagreements between the South Slavs, such as the Serbo-
Bulgarian dispute over Macedonia, or the bitter hostility between
the Serbs and the Croats, had not even been discussed at the Prague
Congress, let alone satisfactorily resolved. Nevertheless, it appeared that some progress had been made towards improving inter-
Slav relations. The formal repudiation of the old principles of
Pan-Slavism based on Russian supremacy, gave rise to hopes of
a brighter future.[113] The majority of the delegates present at the
Prague meetings did not, however, represent governments and
had, therefore, little direct control over future policies. It remained
to be seen how much attention would be paid to the newly proclaimed principles by those who possessed the power to take
action.

The Neo-Slav Congress was concluded on 18 July 1908. The
final words addressed by Kramář to the assembled delegates exhorted them to work diligently for the realisation of their aims.[114]
For the time being, however, little thought was given to the task
ahead. The Neo-Slavs, in particular the Czechs, were in a jubilant
mood. The dramatic reconciliations which had taken place at the
Congress gave rise to the conviction that a new promising

[111] A. Černý, 'Slovanské sjezdy r. 1908', p. 10.
[112] *Jednání sjezdu 1908*, pp. 19, 67; Kramář, *Na obranu*, p. 25; Rozvoda,
'Přípravný slovanský sjezd v Praze', p. 644.
[113] Rozvoda, in 'Přípravný slovanský sjezd v Praze', p. 642, considered the
repudiation of Pan-Slavism to have been the 'most significant' result of the
Congress.
[114] *Jednání sjezdu 1908*, p. 70.

beginning had been made in the long search for Slav unity.[115] It was believed that, with Russia's assistance, the expansion of Germany would be contained and that the Austro-Hungarian Slavs would be able to democratise, and thus Slavicise, the Habsburg Empire and enable it to play a fully independent role in Europe. A similar development was forecast for Russia, leading to some form of autonomy for the Poles.

Predictably, *Den*, the Young Czech organ under Kramář's direct editorial control, was extremely enthusiastic about the outcome of the Congress.[116] *Národní listy*, editorially independent of the Young Czech Party leadership, was somewhat more reserved in its judgement. It noted with satisfaction both the uniting of the South Slav representatives into one delegation and the Russo-Polish understanding reached at the Congress, but cautiously pointed out that: 'The breaking of the ice between the Russians and the Poles which has taken place in Prague is, at present, far from a Russo-Polish peace but could, nevertheless, easily lead to it.'[117] The editorial article further expressed the hope that, when the representatives of the Russian and Polish people reached a complete understanding between themselves, the Russian government would fully support the arrangement. Even *Čas*, the organ of the Czech Realist Party, regarded the Neo-Slav Congress as a success.[118]

The Czech National Socialist Party, despite having previously denounced the 'colourless' Neo-Slav movement as the 'negation' of Slav co-operation, and having reaffirmed its belief in the old Pan-Slav ideas,[119] nevertheless participated actively in the Congress.[120] Later, the party organ, *České slovo*, expressed satisfaction with the outcome of the Slav gathering, in particular with the Russo-Polish *rapprochement*.[121] During the course of the Prague proceedings Klofáč was responsible for a rather curious adjunct to

[115] Rozvoda, 'Přípravný slovanský sjezd v Praze', p. 645. In an otherwise not uncritical assessment of the Prague Congress, Rozvoda, stressing the importance of the role that the Czech nation could play in the future, wrote that: 'Prague, if it were fully aware of the unique position it occupied in the Slav world, could truly become the Athens of the Slavs'.
[116] *Den*, 19, 20, 21 July 1908.
[117] *Národní listy*, 20 July 1908.   [118] *Čas*, 19 July 1908.
[119] *České slovo*, 12, 16 July 1908.
[120] Klofáč, the leader of the National Socialist Party, was not only present at the Congress, but also participated in the preparatory discussions.
[121] *České slovo*, 17 July 1908.

the Congress. A public meeting was held under the slogan 'Democracy and Slavism', with the object of promoting the National Socialist interpretation of Slav co-operation. In his address to the meeting, Klofáč expressed the hope that the idea of Slav reciprocity would receive the wide support of the masses, and that in practical terms it would make possible the free movement of labour from one Slav country to another. Other speakers at the meeting were the leader of the Russian delegation, Krasovsky, and two other Russian representatives, Lvov and Bekhterev. Several other Congress delegates were present.[122] Amongst these was Vergun, with whom Klofáč had been in correspondence earlier in the year, entreating him to attend the Prague gathering and to support 'Slav socialism' against the ideas of Kramář.[123] This unofficial, and rather half-hearted, attempt in search of a popular base for the Neo-Slav movement met with little success and nothing more was heard of it. The remarkable amount of interest shown in Klofáč and his party, which the Russian Neo-Slav delegates demonstrated by their presence at the National Socialist meeting, did, however, reappear at a later stage. The following year, after Kramář had given his qualified support to the Austro-Hungarian annexation of Bosnia and Herzegovina, an attempt was made in Russia to replace Kramář by the more intransigent Klofáč as the leader of the Neo-Slavs.[124]

Although, officially, the Czech Social Democratic Party did not adopt an attitude towards the Neo-Slav movement, on the grounds that it was of no relevence to their policies,[125] some Social Democrats, who had up until the Congress regarded Neo-Slavism as being of little consequence and tended, therefore, to ignore it, began to have second thoughts about the movement. The Social Democratic writer and journalist, F. V. Krejčí, argued, in an article in a socialist journal,[126] that it would be an error if the working class permitted the bourgeois political leaders to act as spokesmen for the entire nation on the issue of inter-Slav relations. The aim of achieving closer ties between the Slav nations, in his opinion, deserved the support of the Social Democrats because all forms of

[122] *České slovo*, 19 July 1908; *Novoe vremya*, 12 (25) July 1908; Šantrůček *Václav Klofáč*, pp. 120–1.
[123] Křížek, 'Česká buržoasní politika a "česká otázka"', p. 655.
[124] See below, pp. 161–2.
[125] *Právo lidu*, 8 June 1909 (J. Hudec, 'Kramář a Daszyński').
[126] F. V. Krejčí, 'Nové slovanství', *Akademie*, XII (1908), pp. 439–45.

international co-operation were of benefit to the Socialist cause. Krejčí stressed that socialists must remain faithful to their internationalist ideas but claimed, nevertheless, that: 'Slav solidarity, based on the similarities of language and culture, would be regarded differently from the general international solidarity of the proletariat; it would be firmer and more active than, for example, the [relationship] between a Czech workman and his French or English counterpart.'[127] Similar attitudes were expressed the following year by two other prominent Czech Social Democrats, J. Hudec and F. Tomášek, both deputies in the Vienna Reichsrat.[128] These views were, however, subjected to sharp attacks from other Austrian Social Democrats including the leading theoretician, O. Bauer.[129]

In Russia, reaction to the Congress was mixed. Approval came mostly from the centre right, whereas the far right and the centre and extreme left of the political spectrum disapproved of, or were disinterested in, the activities of the Neo-Slavs. Perhaps the most perspicacious assessment of the movement was made in the Kadet newspaper *Rech'* which, though showing interest in the Prague events, was far from enthusiastic about their outcome. In a detailed analysis of the Congress, that newspaper's special correspondent in Prague exposed the principal weakness of the Neo-Slav movement. He pointed out that within the movement, and particularly within the Russian branch of it, there were two antipathetic streams of thought. On the one hand there were the traditional Slavophils believing in the hegemony of Russia, who argued that

[127] *Ibid.*, p. 444.
[128] *Právo lidu*, 8 June 1909 (Hudec, 'Kramář a Daszyński'), 17 June 1909.
[129] Bauer objected to the Neo-Slav movement 'in the interests of European revolution'. He appealed to Czech Social Democrats to remain faithful to the traditions of the International and to oppose, what he believed were, the attempts of the Russian liberal bourgeoisie to gain greater power at the expense of the subject peoples of the Russian Empire. The Russo-Polish *rapprochement*, for which Bauer held the Neo-Slav movement responsible was, he maintained, 'a union of treacherous Polish liberalism with treacherous Russian liberalism directed against the political and social revolution of the proletariat and against the national revolutions in the Ukraine, Latvia, and White Russia'. *Ibid.*, 18 June 1909 (O. Bauer, 'Panslavismus'). Bauer's strictures induced, in turn, a response from F. V. Krejčí, who drew attention to the 'deeply rooted Slav awareness among...the masses of the [Czech] people'. Krejčí also stated that the Slav world was the only direction in which the Czechs could expand their cultural and economic influence. 'The liberal-bourgeois Slav idea' would, he believed, in due course lead to 'socialist' Slav co-operation. *Ibid.*, 19 June 1909 (F. V. Krejčí, 'K otázce neoslavismu').

Neo-Slavism was merely a restatement of their own philosophy in twentieth century terms. On the other hand there were the liberals who saw inter-Slav co-operation as a means towards the national and cultural development of the individual Slav peoples. Some of these liberals, such as Maklakov and Lvov and also many of the Polish delegates, suggested that Slavophilism had undergone a transformation, that it had become liberalised. The correspondent of *Rech'*, however, was sceptical and considered this assertion to be unproven. He subscribed to the view, shared also by sceptics amongst the Czechs, that the Neo-Slav movement could not achieve its declared aims until it rid itself of the reactionary elements so strongly represented within it.[130]

The organ of the Octobrists, *Golos Moskvy*, under the direction of A. I. Guchkov, was more directly critical of the Neo-Slavs, though for different reasons. The newspaper complained that the Congress, which had ostensibly been convened to deal exclusively with cultural matters, had in fact been used for political and financial purposes. The proposals for the creation of a Slav bank were subjected to particularly virulent criticism. The *Golos Moskvy* wrote, with mocking sarcasm, that:

We Czechs are so small and Russia is so large and so good! Therefore, let Russia contribute 35 per cent of the foundation capital and we other Slavs 15 per cent. But in our financial enthusiasm we omitted the idea! Which is, that in order to frighten the Germans, the traditional enemies of Slavdom, we shall refuse to accept a single pfennig [of German capital], and instead, offer our friends, England and France, the opportunity to provide 50 per cent [of the capital]...Taking risks, however, is a hazardous business, and we shall, therefore, allow the Russian government the right of nominating the bank's director and the 'great honour' of having influence over banking matters. In other words; under the protection of Russian foreign credit, unshaken by adversity, a disproportionately weaker Slav credit will ostentatiously flourish.[131]

The Octobrist organ added, authoritatively: 'We are of the opinion that it can now be stated with certainty that this masterly banking scheme was still-born.' Elsewhere, *Golos Moskvy* accused

[130] *Rech'*, 11 (24) July 1908.
[131] A. Černý, 'Slovanské sjezdy r. 1908', p. 13 (cited from *Golos Moskvy*, no. 161).

Kramář and the Poles of attempting to turn Russia against Germany and Austria–Hungary.[132]

Of the conservative press, only *Svet* and *Novoe vremya* were reasonably satisfied with the results of the Prague gathering.[133] One of the Russian participants at the Congress, Filevich, reported on it with considerable enthusiasm in the columns of *Novoe vremya*. 'The success of the Slav Congress', he declared, 'exceeded all expectations.'[134] Another Russian present in Prague, Vergun, also wrote a generally favourable assessment of the Congress, although he did give expression to a criticism voiced by an unnamed colleague that the Congress organisers had given preferential treatment to the Poles at the expense of the Russians. On the positive side, however, he remarked that the fear of many Russians, that they would have to 'stand trial' in Prague on the Russo-Polish issue, proved to be unfounded. Vergun also expressed the hope that the Prague events 'would not resemble the "straw fire" which had ignited amongst the Slavs on more than one fraternal occasion, but died down as rapidly as it flared up.'[135]

Other comment in the conservative press, however, was less favourable. P. N. Durnovo, who had held the post of Minister of the Interior in the Russian government for a short period in 1905 and 1906, stressed, in his comments on the Neo-Slav movement in *Sankt-Peterburgskie vedomosti*, the necessity of maintaining friendly relations between Russia and Germany. In his opinion, Russia should not be concerned with the Western Catholic Slavs but only with those who were of the Orthodox faith. He regarded 'the union of Western and Eastern Slavs as a utopia', and added: 'Why should we force the various nations and races of the Russian Empire to spill their blood for the benefit of the Poles, Czechs, Croats, Slovaks, and our dear little brothers, the Bulgarians?' If the Western Slavs were left to fall under the German sphere of influence there would, Durnovo claimed, be no danger of a clash with Germany.[136] Other Germanophil Russians linked the Prague Neo-Slav Congress with the recent visits of the British Monarch, Edward VII, and the French President, Fallières, to Nicholas II at Reval, and presented these events as a concerted attempt aimed

[132] *Ibid.*
[133] *Národní listy*, 5 August 1908.
[134] *Novoe vremya*, 10 (23) July 1908.
[135] *Ibid.*, 18 (31) July 1908.
[136] *Národní listy*, 7 August 1908; A. Černý, 'Slovanské sjezdy r. 1908', p. 14.

at isolating and surrounding Germany.[137] The extreme right wing of the Russian political spectrum maintained its critical attitude towards Neo-Slavism and was, in particular, opposed to all attempts made in search of some form of cultural autonomy for the Poles in the Russian division. *Kolokol*, the organ of the extreme right, wrote: 'In the Russian state there can be none other than Russian culture, that culture which was formed, and for centuries defended, by the Russian nation.'[138]

With great interest and, no doubt, some trepidation, the Neo-Slavs, the Czechs and Poles in particular, awaited the Russian government's verdict on the Congress. After an extended silence on the subject, of almost a month, *Rossiya*, the semi-official government organ controlled by the Prime Minister, P. A. Stolypin, published what *Národní listy* considered to be a 'favourable, though tactful and reserved' comment on the Prague deliberations.[139] It recognised the legitimate desire of the Slav nations for cultural and economic co-operation, but indicated that this understanding could only be fully realised after a considerable period of time. Addressing itself to disquietened German opinion, *Rossiya* stressed that the intentions of the Neo-Slav movement were entirely peaceful and that it was directed against no one.[140] It is probable that the apparently favourable, though cautious, reaction of the Russian government to the Prague Congress was connected with Russian foreign policy in the Balkans and the Near East. During the summer months of 1908, the Russian government intensified its attempt to reach an agreement with Austria–Hungary on the Balkans with a view to opening the Black Sea Straits to Russian warships. Presumably it was felt in St Petersburg that the support of the Austrian Slavs would be of considerable advantage in negotiations with the Habsburg Empire which lay ahead.[141] The correspondent of *Rossiya* reporting on the Congress also commented, as did Vergun in *Novoe vremya*, that the Poles enjoyed preferential treatment in Prague, accurately attributing this to the fact that the Czechs were hoping to win the co-operation of the Poles in the Vienna Reichsrat.[142]

[137] *Národní listy*, 7 August 1908. Edward VII visited Reval on 9 and 10 June (27 and 28 May) and was followed by President Fallières on 27 (14) July.
[138] *Národní listy*, 24 July 1908.   [139] *Ibid.*, 25 August 1908.
[140] *Ibid.*, 7 August 1908.
[141] The meeting between Count Aehrenthal and Izvolsky took place at Buchlau on 15 and 16 September 1908.   [142] *Národní listy*, 25 August 1908.

The Polish response to the Prague Congress was also mixed. The Russian Poles were divided in their reaction to Neo-Slavism and the attitude of the Poles from Austria–Hungary remained sceptical. Even within Dmowski's own National Democratic Party there was disagreement about the usefulness of the movement. Most of the Poles who had been present in Prague shared the general Neo-Slav optimistic view of the future; those who had been opposed to Neo-Slavism maintained their doubts.[143] In an interview with a correspondent of *Rech'*, Dmowski expressed general satisfaction with the outcome of the Prague Congress. Although conscious of the fact that the Russian delegation contained individuals hostile to the Polish cause, the Polish leader considered their silence as evidence that the 'spirit of the Congress was against them'. In general, Dmowski believed that the Prague gathering had taken an important step towards placing inter-Slav relations on a new basis, though he was sufficiently realistic to admit that few changes would occur in the foreseeable future.[144] Other Poles were a little more precise in their hopes. Nicolson, the British ambassador in St Petersburg, reported to the Foreign Office a meeting with an unnamed Pole, who had attended the Congress and was 'much gratified with the results'. During the course of the conversation the ambassador enquired about the likely results of the proceedings, and subsequently reported as follows:

I was informed that it was hoped, so far as Poland was concerned, that a more generous policy would be followed by Russia towards her Polish subjects. It was observed to me that the brother of the Russian Prime Minister was one of the delegates and that some of the leading members of the [Kadet, Octobrist, and other] political parties...were also delegates. It was, therefore, expected that the effect of this fraternisation would be shown during the approaching session of the Duma.

Nicolson himself, however, was not as optimistic, adding that 'Personally I should doubt if any such desirable results will be manifest for the present.'[145] His assessment of the situation was shortly to be proved correct.

The Balkan Slavs, also, disagreed amongst themselves about the

[143] A. Černý, 'Slovanské sjezdy r. 1908', pp. 62–4.
[144] *Rech'*, 10 (23) July 1908.
[145] PRO, FO, 371/519, Nicolson to Grey, 33395, St Petersburg, 19 September 1908.

usefulness of the Neo-Slav movement. In general, the movement was supported only by those sections of the South Slav nationalities within the Dual Monarchy – the Slovenes, Croats, and Serbs – who, like the Czechs, favoured a federalist reconstruction of Austria–Hungary. Of the independent (or soon to be independent[146]) Balkan Slavs, the Bulgarians were most enthusiastic about the Prague Congress though their government, like that of Russia, adopted a cautious attitude. The leader of the Bulgarian delegation to the Neo-Slav gathering, Bobchev, described the Prague Congress as 'the most significant event...in the history of the Slavs'. He justified this assertion by claiming that, unlike the Prague Slav Congress of 1848 and the Slav gathering in Moscow in 1867, the Neo-Slav Congress of 1908 had been fully representative of the Slav world.[147] The Austro-Hungarian ambassador in Belgrade reported that in Serbia little significance was attached to Neo-Slavism and pointed out that: 'The Czechs, the organisers of the Prague Congress, are not regarded with great favour here because Czech [Roman] Catholic officials in Bosnia are considered as being a particularly Austrian element, dangerous to Serbia.'[148] Those Serbs, both in Serbia and in the Habsburg Empire, who advocated the union of all the territories inhabited by their nation into a Greater Serbia, were unable to combine their aims with those of the Neo-Slavs. Similarly, those Croats who were dreaming of a Greater Croatia, either as an independent state or as the third composite part of a reconstructed Habsburg Empire, had little sympathy for the Neo-Slav movement.

The Prague Congress had paid little attention to the many contentious issues outstanding in the Balkan Peninsula. This omission, justified on the grounds that the Balkan problems were of a political nature and, therefore, outside the terms of reference of the Congress, was in fact due largely to a significant clash of interests. From the point of view of the Czech, Russian, and Polish Neo-Slavs, agreement between Russia and Austria–Hungary, which would, of necessity, concern the Balkans, was not only desirable but essential for the fulfilment of their aims. This was not so

[146] Bulgaria, at the time subject to the nominal suzerainty of the Ottoman Empire, declared full independence on 5 October 1908.
[147] S. S. Bobchev, 'Za slavyanskiya săbor v Praga', *Bălgarska sbirka*, xv (1908), p. 557.
[148] Forgach to Aehrenthal, 39C, Belgrade, 16 July 1908, cited in Beneš, *Úvahy o slovanství*, p. 187.

in the case of the South Slavs, who were likely to become pawns in any settlement between the two great powers with the consequence that their problems would never be solved and their aspirations never realised.

The general tendency amongst those uncommitted to the Slav cause was to regard the Prague Neo-Slav gathering as being relatively unimportant and its achievements insignificant. This certainly was the view taken by the Habsburg authorities, who showed little interest in the proceedings and no signs of alarm at the dramatic demonstrations of Slav solidarity. It was believed in the Austrian capital that the existing dissensions between the Slav nations made any form of lasting unity very unlikely.[149] Nevertheless, Kramář attempted to allay any fears the Austrian Germans might have had by publishing an article on the Slav Congress in the Vienna periodical *Österreichische Rundschau*. In this he stressed that Neo-Slavism had 'no direct political aims' and was 'loyal to existing states'. Kramář added, however, that it was desirable that Vienna should pursue in the Balkans a policy less dependent on Berlin and of more benefit to the Slavs.[150] This last point was not far removed from the views held at the time by the Austro-Hungarian Minister of Foreign Affairs, Count Aehrenthal, though he was more concerned with obtaining greater freedom of action for the Habsburg Empire than with the well-being of the Slavs. In Hungary, after some initial agitation over the Congress, Magyar opinion also quietened when it was learned that no representatives of the Slovaks were present in Prague.[151] An uninvolved observer, the British diplomatic representative in Vienna, sharing the widespread scepticism about the Neo-Slav movement expressed the opinion that the Congress had achieved 'very little' but had been 'nevertheless, a great theatrical exhibition of Slav solidarity'.[152]

In a critique of the Neo-Slav movement, written twenty years after the events, Beneš, although generally in agreement with the above expressed sentiment, nevertheless, conceded that:

[149] There are no indications of official consternation in the reports on the Prague Congress in the Vienna archives. H.H.St.A., PA, XL 219, *Panslav Bewegung* 3, 'Allslavische Kongress in Prag, Juli 1908' (reports from Staathalterie in Prague).

[150] K. Kramář, 'Die Slawenkonferenz im Prag', *Österreichische Rundschau*, XVI (July–September 1908), pp. 215–16.   [151] *Národní listy*, 24 July 1908.

[152] PRO, FO, 371/399, Carnegie to Grey, 26022, Vienna, 23 July 1908.

The Congress itself was a considerable improvement on all that had previously been attempted within the Slav world in this field. The need for positive inter-Slav co-operation in everyday economic and cultural life, which had been felt for decades, was seriously examined and, for the first time, a real attempt was made to progress from words to deeds.[153]

Undoubtedly an attempt had been made, but it was an attempt destined to failure and the positive results were few.

Only one item of lasting value was to emerge from the multitude of words pronounced at the Prague Congress, and this had no direct connection with any of the main issues discussed. During the course of the proceedings, the Russian and Polish delegates collected amongst themselves the sum of 3600 crowns, which they presented to the Congress organisers, specifying that it was to be used to finance the publication of a popular booklet on the history and contemporary affairs of the Slav world, which would also explain the principles of the Neo-Slav movement. The book, entitled *Slovanstvo. Obraz jeho minulosti a přítomnosti*[154] [Slavdom. A Record of its Past and Present], was published in Prague in 1912. The wishes of those who assisted in financing its publication were not fully implemented. In place of a popular booklet there appeared a large volume comprising a collection of articles by eminent Czech Slavists. Kramář contributed the introduction.[155] The work though not free from imperfections, was on the whole an objective and scholarly survey and made a valuable contribution to the field of Slavonic studies.[156]

The factors responsible for the failure of the Prague Congress to achieve any noteworthy results, other than in words, were many; and the most significant of these were beyond the control of both the organisers and the participants.[157] The Congress did, however, suffer from one deficiency, the remedy of which appeared, at first

[153] Beneš, *Úvahy o slovanství*, p. 147. Beneš first made public these views in a series of articles in *Slovanský přehled* during 1925 and 1926. They were subsequently published in book form as *Úvahy o slovanství*.
[154] J. Bidlo and J. Polívka eds., *Slovanstvo., Obraz jeho minulosti a přítomnosti* (Prague, 1912). Other contributors were:, A. Boháč, V. Černý, V. Dvorský B. Franta, J. Guth, J. Hejret, A. Jirák, K. Kadlec, J. Máchal, Z. Nejedlý, B. Prusík, F. J. Rambousek, J. Scheiner, and F. Táborský.
[155] K. Kramář, 'Předmluva', *Slovanstvo*, pp. v–xv.
[156] For a critical review of the book see A. Černý, 'Nová kniha o slovanstvě', *Slovanský přehled*, XIV (1912), pp. 226–30, 276–9.
[157] These factors are examined in the following chapter.

sight, to be within the power of the Neo-Slavs. The entire Neo-Slav movement in general, and the Congress in particular, totally lacked a definite political programme. During the course of the Prague deliberations, matters of a political nature were referred to only in the most general terms. The broad outlines of Slav political aims were sketched – the need for defence against German political and economic expansion was advocated and the ideas of Slav equality and unity were stressed – but no concrete political programme was produced. Even if the Neo-Slavs had been able to agree amongst themselves on a detailed manifesto, the international political situation would have prevented its public proclamation. Beneš explained that:

As an expression of a new practical Neo-Slav movement the Congress was...politically and internationally a badly thought out and unfinished venture. Forced by existing conditions to demonstrate visibly its loyalty to both Empires, [the Congress] was unwilling and unable to formulate thoroughly, in political terms, the problems and demands of the Slav nations.[158]

The Congress organisers were, of course, aware of the fact that in order not to disturb the extremely delicate balance between Russia and Austria–Hungary, on which the very existence of the Neo-Slav movement depended, the discussion of issues of international politics was not possible, and the formulation of a Slav political programme out of the question. Although the Neo-Slavs repeatedly stressed that the Congress would not consider political matters, nevertheless, the Prague gathering was, unavoidably, concerned with politics. These political topics were, however, carefully selected. Certain issues of internal politics were raised; principally, the question of relations between the Russian and Polish nations within the Russian Empire and, to a much lesser extent and against the wishes of the Congress organisers, also the Russo-Ukrainian and Polish–Ukrainian disputes. All problems involving international politics, in the sense of relations between states such as those of the Balkans, were prudently avoided.

Critics of the Neo-Slav movement pointed out at the time, with justification, that the Prague Congress had not concerned itself with many, if any, of the burning issues in the Slav world. Comparing the Slav Congress of 1848 with that of 1908 A. Černý wrote, shortly after the conclusion of the Neo-Slav gathering that: 'The previous Congress had on its agenda questions of vital importance to the Slav nations, even though these were restricted to the Austro-Hungarian Empire only. This year's Congress, *a priori*, carefully avoided these issues, which was a fundamental mistake.'[159] The criticism was fair – few significant Slav problems were thoroughly debated at the Prague Congress. Many of these important issues were, however, either partially or entirely connected with wider questions of international politics and, therefore, could not be raised. This was due to no fault of the Neo-Slavs, but forced by external circumstances. The Austro-Hungarian authorities, though tolerant of Neo-Slavism, were suspicious of it and the mere mention of a more concrete programme of action would likely have resulted in the movement being proscribed. Similarly, the attitude of the Russian government, cautious though it was, would have been even less encouraging had political demands of an international nature been voiced.

Nevertheless, the Neo-Slav Congress did mark an important stage in the relations between the Czech and Russian nations. The organisers, mostly Czechs, through the medium of the Congress made a determined attempt to broaden and improve relations between themselves and the Russians. Conditions existing at the time were responsible for this attempt taking place within a wider scheme of drawing Russia and Austria–Hungary closer together. This was consistent with contemporary mainstream Czech political thinking, for independence was considered to be out of the question, and a federal reconstruction of the Habsburg Empire regarded as the only satisfactory solution to the nation's problems. It was also significant that several prominent Russian public figures, amongst them Maklakov, were prepared to be publicly associated with this move. Subsequently, however, it became evident that the Russian Neo-Slavs were either unwilling or unable to make a more definite contribution towards improving relations with the Western Slavs.

Despite the fact that, in the course of time, the Prague Congress was shown to have achieved very little in concrete terms, the Neo-Slav gathering did achieve all that it could reasonably have been

---

[159] A. Černý, 'Slovanské sjezdy r. 1908', p. 9. Černý was particularly critical of the fact that although the existence of the Russo-Polish dispute was admitted no practical steps were taken towards finding a solution and, also, that the very existence of the Ukrainian nation was denied by the Congress organisers. *Ibid.*, pp. 9–11.

expected to. It was again Beneš who indicated that, although the majority of important Slav questions were simply avoided, some positive political results were, nevertheless, achieved. These were 'the agreement reached on further steps to be taken towards achieving definite advances in Slav cultural and economic matters, the spirit of conciliation, and the public display of willingness to end all inter-Slav disputes.'[160]

The Neo-Slav organisers were not entirely unjustified in feeling elated at the outcome of, what they termed, the First Preparatory Congress. This satisfaction was, however, to be brief in duration; for in the poetic words of Kramář: 'No sooner had Neo-Slavism come into bloom, than it was beset by the frost.'[161]

[160] Beneš, *Úvahy o slovanství*, pp. 155–6.
[161] Kramář, 'Za vedení národní strany svobodomyslné', p. 794.

5
Neo-Slavism in decline, 1908–1910

The sense of achievement and the mood of optimism, which the apparently successful Prague Congress had evoked in the ranks of the Neo-Slavs and their supporters, was short-lived. The dramatic reconciliations which had taken place in Prague, the fraternisation of the Russian and Polish delegates and the amalgamation of the South Slav representatives into one delegation, were destined to become little more than cherished memories of what could have been the beginning of a promising chapter in Slav relations. Within a matter of weeks following the Congress, two events took place which were responsible for the death of the Neo-Slav movement. Significantly, these events were instigated by the governments of Russia and Austria–Hungary respectively, and served to indicate how divorced from reality the Neo-Slavs were and how totally they lacked power and influence over their respective governments. The more momentous of these traumatic events was the Austro-Hungarian annexation of Bosnia and Herzegovina but no less important was the renewed repression, by the Russian authorities, of the Polish inhabitants of Russian Poland. These two events removed, what were at the time, the essential pre-conditions for any form of meaningful Slav co-operation; the sympathy of both Russian and Austro-Hungarian governments, and the accord between them. The Neo-Slav movement was entirely dependent on the continuation of the *entente* between Russia and Austria–Hungary, and its failure was inevitable as soon as it had become evident, during and after the annexation crisis, that relations between the two Empires had deteriorated beyond immediate repair.

The unhappy situation in which the majority of the Polish nation found itself during most of the nineteenth century did not significantly improve until the early years of the new century. With the exception of Galicia, the Austrian division of Poland, which enjoyed limited autonomy, the other sections of partitioned

Poland, under the control of Russia and Germany respectively, were in a very unenviable position. In Russian Poland, particularly after the abortive Polish uprising of 1863, the Russian rulers, with varying degrees of intensity, attempted to Russify the Polish nation, though without much success. This state of affairs remained largely unaltered until 1905 when the Poles, together with other subject nationalities within the Russian Empire, extracted concessions from a government weakened by military defeat and revolution. The most significant gains made in Russian Poland were in the fields of culture and education. The Russian authorities granted permission for the foundation of private schools where most of the teaching was permitted to take place in the Polish language, and the Polish Schools Association (*Macierz Szkolna*), which promoted the establishment of such schools, came into being. The creation of the Duma, in which the Poles gained a not inconsiderable representation, further raised the hopes for a better future.[1] This, however, was not to be realised and in the Second and Third Dumas, which rapidly succeeded the First, the Polish representation was considerably reduced. The new electoral law, introduced in 1907 before the election of the third Duma, was directed not only against the political left, but also against the non-Russian nationalities. As the forces of reaction began to reassert themselves in Russia it became evident that the promised further improvements would not materialise and the limited concessions, recently granted, were gradually removed. In December 1907 the Russian government again struck out against Polish education by suppressing the recently formed Polish Schools Association.[2]

In the German division, life for the Poles was no easier. There, also, their language and national identity had been under severe attack for an extended period. During 1908 the persecution was intensified by further restrictive legislation and provisions enabling the compulsory expropriation of Polish owned land.[3]

The increasing oppression of the Poles in German Poland served

[1] The Poles sent fifty-one deputies to the first Duma, where they formed the Polish Circle (*Koło Polskie*). Due largely to the fact that the Socialists did not participate in the election, the majority of the deputies elected belonged to the National Democratic Party.

[2] Reddaway and others eds., *The Cambridge History of Poland*, II, pp. 389–404; H. Seton-Watson, *The Russian Empire, 1801–1917* (London, 1967), pp. 487–9, 607, 622, 628.

[3] O. Halecki, *A History of Poland* (London, 1955), p. 267; Reddaway and others ed., *The Cambridge History of Poland*, II, pp. 426–7.

to encourage the attempts being made towards unifying the Austrian Slavs in face of what they considered to be the common danger: Germanism. A British diplomatic dispatch from Vienna records that the introduction of the Polish Expropriation Bill in the Prussian Diet, 'as was to be expected, ignited the inflammable passions of the Slav element in this country'. Referring to the strong speeches made in the Austrian Parliament, the report continued:

An idea of the solidarity of feeling upon this question animating an otherwise heterogeneous collection of parties may be gathered from the fact that among the...speakers [critical of Germany]...were the President of the Polish Club, a Slovene deputy, a Russo-Phil Ruthene, a Polish Socialist, a Radical Czech, a nationalist Jew, a representative of the Polish People's Party, a Clerical South Slav, an Italian and a Ruthenian Social Democrat.[4]

It was in this gloomy atmosphere of fading Polish hopes and growing disillusionment that Kramář launched the Neo-Slav movement, openly declaring that a settlement between the Russian and Polish nations was essential before any progress could be made towards Slav unity. Faced with the unpromising outlook for Russian Poland, but nevertheless persisting in his belief that Russia was the lesser of the two evils confronting the Polish nation, Dmowski decided to lend his support to the movement even though, as he subsequently asserted, he was never in sympathy with the Neo-Slav aims. Unable to turn to any major power for outside assistance, Dmowski calculated that the smaller Slav nations might be able to exert sufficient pressure on the Russian government to ease the situation in its division of Poland. The assurance that concessions would be granted to the Polish nation, which Kramář claimed he received during his visit to Russia in 1908 from P. A. Stolypin personally, and the apparently promising discussion of the Russo-Polish dispute at the Neo-Slav Congress both came to nothing. Within weeks of the conclusion of the hopeful debates in Prague, reports were coming in of intensified oppression of the Polish inhabitants of Russian Poland. Polish schools were again being closed, the use of the Polish language restricted,[5] and worse was to follow. The normally Russophil *Národní listy* commented bitterly that:

[4] PRO, FO, 120/841, Carnegie to Grey, 202, Vienna, 30 November 1907.
[5] A. Černý, 'Slovanské sjezdy r. 1908', p. 14; *Národní listy*, 6 November 1908.

The Russian government has indicated by its action that it does not intend to comply with the principles pronounced at the Slav Congress, that it does not intend to encourage and support Russo-Polish reconciliation, and that it will continue to carry out its policy of persecuting the Polish nation. By choosing this anti-Slav, uncivilised course of action the Russian government is accepting a serious responsibility; because in the grave situation in which Russia and all Slavdom find themselves today, it is neither tactical nor sensible to widen the gulf between the Polish and Russian peoples.[6]

The insistence of the Russian government in continuing in its policy of repression in Russian Poland made evident the fact that the Russian Neo-Slavs, assuming that at least some were sincere in their professed desire for a reconciliation with the Poles,[7] were completely uninfluential within their own country. The only motive likely to make the Russian authorities alter their attitude towards the Poles would have been an attempt to win the support of the Austro-Hungarian Slavs against the expansive Balkan policies of the Vienna government. It was, perhaps, with this in mind that Stolypin had promised Kramář that the situation in Russian Poland would be eased. The Russian government's cautious approval of the outcome of the Prague Congress can also be explained in the same light. However, any hopes that the Russian authorities might have had, about the willingness or ability of the Slavs in the Habsburg Empire to restrain Aehrenthal's adventurous policies, were shattered by the Austro-Hungarian annexation of Bosnia and Herzegovina and the subsequent muted protests from Slav political leaders within the Dual Monarchy. From the nationalistic and centralistic point of view of the Russian government, there remained little reason for altering their attitude towards the Polish nation.

Bosnia and Herzegovina, previously the two most north-westerly territories of the Ottoman Empire, had been since 1878 occupied and administered by Austria–Hungary under the terms of the Treaty of Berlin, though officially remaining Turkish provinces. It soon became apparent, however, that, in the long term at least, the Habsburg Empire was intent on annexing this area.

[6] *Národní listy*, 20 October 1908.
[7] Some of the Polish and Russian participants in the Prague Congress met for further consultations on Russo-Polish problems after their return to St Petersburg. *Národní listy*, 6, 7 November 1908.

The first definite steps in that direction were not taken until 1908 when Count Aehrenthal met his Russian counterpart, Izvolsky, at Buchlau, in Moravia, on 15 and 16 September. A remarkable aspect of the Buchlau meeting was the fact that, although the two sides did reach an agreement, nothing was recorded on paper and both parties were soon to disagree about what had been agreed. As far as the ensuing events are concerned, the actual Buchlau agreement is less significant than the conflicting interpretations subsequently given to it by either side. Izvolsky believed, or claimed to believe, that in exchange for an assurance that Russia would not oppose the Austro-Hungarian annexation of Bosnia and Herzegovina, Aehrenthal had agreed to support Russia's claim for the opening of the Straits, and that it was understood by both sides that no action would be taken until the arrangements had been sanctioned by the other signatories of the Treaty of Berlin. Aehrenthal, on the other hand, maintained that the Russian Foreign Minister had consented to the annexation of the occupied provinces in return for Austro-Hungarian support for a revision of the Straits Convention, and that the agreement was not conditional on obtaining the approval of the other powers.

Developments in Turkey forced Austria–Hungary to resort to speedy action over Bosnia and Herzegovina. The Turkish revolution of July 1908 brought into power the Young Turks, a party favouring democratic reforms and aiming to transform the Ottoman Empire into a constitutional monarchy. The Austro-Hungarian government realised that the appearance of a reformed Turkey could lead to the withdrawal of the mandate, granted by the Treaty of Berlin, to control and administer Bosnia and Herzegovina, which were of considerable economic and strategic importance to the Dual Monarchy. On 5 October 1908 Bulgaria (since 1878 an autonomous principality under Turkish control) declared independence, and the following day the Austro-Hungarian government officially announced the annexation of Bosnia and Herzegovina.

This unexpected action of the Austro-Hungarian government met with a critical response from most of the other interested powers with the exception of Germany, which wholeheartedly backed Aehrenthal's move. In Russia the annexation crisis gave rise to intense hostility against Austria–Hungary and Germany and led to an upsurge of Pan-Slav feeling. Russian reaction was, in its intensity, second only to the feeling expressed in Serbia, where demands for war against Austria–Hungary or for suitable territorial compensation were voiced. The vehemence of the Serbian reaction was understandable, as the incorporation of Bosnia and Herzegovina into the Habsburg Empire made permanent the separation of Serbia from Croatia and Dalmatia, reduced the chances of Serbia gaining access to the Adriatic, and put an end to the dream of a Greater Serbia. As a result, tension mounted between Serbia and the Habsburg Monarchy, and early in 1909 both sides made preparations for war. In Russia, both the government and the press continued to protest loudly against what they claimed to be an injustice perpetrated by Austria–Hungary against the South Slavs, but in spite of the gesture of concentrating troops on the frontier Russia was still unprepared for war and there was little that could be done to aid Serbia. Eventually, as a direct result of strong German pressure on the Russian government Serbia was forced to submit to Austro-Hungarian demands, renouncing its claims for compensation and, together with Russia, recognising the annexation. Aehrenthal, thanks to the support of Berlin, had scored a diplomatic triumph; Russia had been utterly humiliated. The Austro-Hungarian victory was, however, a costly one. Not only had the Habsburg Monarchy intensified the hostility of Russia and Serbia, and further antagonised its own South Slav subjects, but it had also greatly increased its dependence on Germany.[8]

Predictably, the annexation crisis also had far-reaching repercussions amongst the Slav population of the Habsburg Empire. The Czech lands were no exception. Most affected there by the sudden rupture between Russia and Austria–Hungary were the Neo-Slavs. Almost without warning the Czech leaders of the movement were placed in the most uncomfortable dilemma of having to choose sides in a dispute between their Slav allies in Russia and Serbia on the one hand, and their own state Austria–Hungary and Germany, the traditional enemy of the Slavs, on the other.

The unexpected news of the annexation of Bosnia and Herzegovina reached Kramář while travelling from his villa in the Crimea to attend a meeting of the Delegations in Budapest. Immediately on arrival, he hurried off to Aehrenthal for further

---

[8] For details of the annexation crisis see B. E. Schmitt, *The Annexation of Bosnia 1908–1909* (Cambridge, 1937); A. J. May, *The Hapsburg Monarchy, 1867–1914* (Cambridge, Mass., 1951), pp. 410–24.

information on the situation and to enquire about the attitude adopted by Russia.[9] Aehrenthal assured the Czech leader that Izvolsky had approved the annexation plans at the Buchlau meeting and, as evidence of Russia's consent, produced a letter from the Russian ambassador in Vienna, Prince Orlov, which stated that while in Italy the Russian Foreign Minister had prepared the ground for the implementation of the Buchlau agreement. Kramář did not learn of Izvolsky's version of events until some time later.[10]

A meeting of the Slav members of the Delegations was immediately convened under Kramář's chairmanship, where he explained 'the necessity of providing unconditional support for the annexation, in order that no sign of dissension within the monarchy be visible to the outside world on this issue'.[11] The assembled Slav deputies agreed to follow this advice and during the ensuing foreign policy debates in the Delegations, loyally supported the recent activities of their government. Kramář later justified this action on the grounds that he was following a policy of being 'first a Czech and then a Slav'.[12] In other words he placed the interests of the Czech nation, believing these to be the preservation and strengthening of the Empire and the maintenance of some, however limited, influence in Vienna, before those of the Slavs in general. Failure to support the annexation would have ended all hopes of closer co-operation with the Habsburg authorities and of achieving some satisfaction of Czech demands for a considerable time ahead.

In an address to the Foreign Policy Committee of the Austrian Delegation Kramář indicated that the annexation of Bosnia and Herzegovina was a unilateral breach of an international treaty and no justification could be found for it in terms of international law. Nevertheless, in his opinion the annexation was justified, and it was up to the Austro-Hungarian government to earn a retrospective moral right for its action by carrying out the mandate it had received at the Congress of Berlin to grant a free and just administration to the annexed South Slav provinces. Kramář also urged the Austro-Hungarian government to adopt a more conciliatory attitude towards Serbia, and advised the Serbs to abandon their idea of a Greater Serbia.[13] These sentiments were shared by other Czech deputies and were reiterated by Kramář in a later

[9] *Proces dra. Kramáře*, II, p. 61.   [10] Kramář, *Na obranu*, p. 26.
[11] *Proces dra. Kramáře*, I, p. 31; II, p. 61.   [12] Kramář, *Na obranu*, p. 26.
[13] *Národní listy*, 10 October 1908.

speech to the entire Austrian Delegation.[14] Similar views were also held by Masaryk who, in a speech made in 1910, stated that he had never denied Austria–Hungary's right to annex the occupied provinces of Bosnia and Herzegovina, but that he had disapproved of the manner in which the annexation had been carried out.[15] The radical Czech politician Klofáč, however, was highly critical of the Austro-Hungarian action, and demanded a referendum to determine the future of the annexed territories.[16]

Although not entirely happy about the method used by the Austro-Hungarian government to incorporate the two Balkan provinces into the Habsburg Empire, most Czech political leaders saw no reason for opposing the move, especially as they then believed that it had taken place with Russia's consent. It was assumed that in the agreement reached between Russia and Austria–Hungary the interests of Serbia had been safeguarded.[17] The *status quo* in the Balkans had not been significantly altered by Aehrenthal's action. Bosnia and Herzegovina had previously been under the control of the Dual Monarchy; only the method of exercising this control had changed. Furthermore, from the point of view of Kramář and his associates, the annexation did have a significant advantage. The incorporation of the two Balkan provinces, inhabited predominantly by Serbs and Croats, increased the Slav population of the Habsburg Empire by over one million, thus bringing the aim of Slavicising the Empire a little nearer to realisation.[18]

Not all the Czechs, however, shared this view. A contemporary observer recorded that: 'In Bohemia the measure [i.e. the annexation] was intensely unpopular. The people – rightly as events have proved – believed that the Empire would become yet more subservient to Germany.'[19] The more extreme sections of Czech

[14] *Stenographische Protokolle der Delegation, 43. Session* (Vienna, 1908), pp. 134–41.
[15] T. G. Masaryk, *Rakouská zahraniční politika a diplomacie* (Prague, 1911), p. 38.
[16] *Stenographische Protokolle der Delegation, 43. Session*, pp. 27–38; Šantrůček, *Václav Klofáč*, pp. 99–103.
[17] Kramář, *Na obranu*, p. 26.
[18] *Proces dra. Kramáře*, II, p. 113. Kramář explained this point of view at a meeting of the Czech National Council and also in a letter to Krasovsky. *Ibid.*, II, p. 63. At the 1910 census the Slav population of Bosnia and Herzegovina was approximately 1 250 000. The great majority of the remaining 650 000 Mohammedans were also of Slav origin.
[19] F. Lützow, *Bohemia: An Historical Sketch* (London, 1910), p. 350.

nationalist opinion condemned, in vigorous terms, the action of the Austro-Hungarian government. *České slovo*, the organ of Klofáč's National Socialist Party, was strongly critical of the annexation.[20] A group of Czech deputies in the Bohemian Diet issued a statement protesting against the annexation of Bosnia and Herzegovina, declaring that a plebiscite should have been held to determine the wish of the population of the occupied provinces before any action was taken.[21]

The expression of Czech disapproval of the Austro-Hungarian action in the Balkans was not restricted to words only. The annexation increased tension between the Czechs and Germans in Bohemia, and from mid-October to mid-December many serious disturbances occurred throughout the province, the immediate cause of which was the suspension of the Bohemian Diet due to German obstruction of business. When troops were called in to prevent further clashes taking place between Czech and German youths in Prague, they were welcomed from the Czech side by cries of: 'Murderers! Down with Austria! Death to Beck! Long live Serbia!'[22] Martial law was in force in Prague from 2 to 14 December.[23] Although the unrest in the Bohemian capital was marked by a strong expression of sympathy for Serbia it did not have an exclusively Pan-Slav character, as can be seen from the following British diplomatic report from Vienna.

On November 30th matters reached a head and scenes of almost revolutionary character occurred in Prague in the course of which a hostile demonstration was made by a Czech mob against the house of Baron D'Aehrenthal's brother, the Radetzky monument was pelted with stones and the Austrian flag thrown in the Moldau. The mob then raised the cry of 'Long live Serbia' and cheers were given for England and the Union Jack was paraded round the town.[24]

These expressions of popular disapproval, however, had little or no effect on the cautious acquiescent attitude adopted by leading Czech politicians. This 'official' Czech reaction to the annexation of the occupied provinces was received with considerable disappointment in Russia. Early in November *Národní listy* commented

[20] *České slovo*, 10 October 1908.
[21] *Národní listy*, 16 October 1908.
[22] *Ibid.*, 19 October 1908.
[23] *Ibid.*, 2 December (afternoon edition), 15 December 1908.
[24] PRO, FO, 120/853, Carnegie to Grey, 311, Vienna, 4 December 1908.

that: 'After the strong upsurge of Russian sympathy for [the plight of] the Slavs during recent months, the last few days have shown a weakening of this feeling; or rather, that doubts are creeping in, not all along the line, but in certain quarters. The reason for this is that some Russians do not trust the Slavs, particularly those from Austria.'[25]

While still in Budapest for the meeting of the Delegations, Kramář did his utmost to calm Russian fears. He explained to Bobrinsky, who happened to be in the Hungarian capital at the time, why outright opposition by the Austrian Slavs against the actions of their government was both impossible and undesirable.[26] Bobrinsky subsequently responded with a reasoned letter, in which he explained to Kramář that Russian recognition of the annexation was an 'organic impossibility'. He maintained that this view was shared in Russia by both those who favoured closer Slav ties and those who opposed this aim; in fact, by all shades of Russian opinion. The letter continued: 'We fully appreciate the difficult situation in which you find yourself, and do not wish to see differences of opinion over the Bosnian question obstruct the course of Slav unification.' Concluding on a hopeful note, Bobrinsky stated:

We realise that the final word on the annexation will be pronounced in your Parliament and not in the Delegations, and impatiently await this pronouncement. You may, with every justification, rely on both the Russian government and the Russian people for a definite policy; but do not forget that Russia is still an invalid and, although satisfactory progress is being made towards recovery, she is not yet in good health.[27]

When the annexation was subsequently debated in the Vienna Reichsrat early in December, Kramář did express his disapproval of the incorporation of the Balkan provinces in somewhat stronger terms than previously.[28] By then, however, it was too late for his words to have any effect on the situation though it is doubtful if they could ever have either influenced or seriously disturbed the Austro-Hungarian government.

The initial semi-official approach to Kramář from the Russian

[25] *Národní listy*, 8 November 1908.   [26] *Proces dra. Kramáře*, II, p. 62.
[27] H.H.St.A., *Polizei Direktion Wien*, Pr.Z. 21636K/52, 23 March 1916; *Proces dra. Kramáře*, I, pp. 32–4; II, p. 69. (Letter dated St Petersburg [?], 12 (25) November 1908.)
[28] *Stenographische Protokolle des Hauses der Abgeordneten*, XVIII. *Session* (Vienna, 1909), IX, pp. 7785–90; *Proces dra. Kramáře*, IV, part 1, p. 40.

government was also made in moderate terms. Within days of the annexation Svatkovsky sent Kramář a letter by courier from St Petersburg, in which he appealed to the Czech leader, in the name of the Russian Deputy Minister of Foreign Affairs, to defend the interests of the Slav population of the annexed provinces. Svatkovsky wrote:

Bosnia and Herzegovina must not be allowed to be placed in a situation in which they would be of no benefit to the Austro-Hungarian Slavs. Nikolai Valerianovich Charykov has asked me to inform you that such are our hopes and expectations. In his opinion we must both [Russians and Czechs] raise our voices and make every effort to ensure that Bosnia and Herzegovina do not become territories with a second class population, bearing all the responsibilities but not sharing the rights to participate in the common political life of the state...Nikolai Valerianovich is of the opinion that it would be of some consolation to the Serbs to know that Bosnia and Herzegovina were playing an appropriate role among the Austrian Slavs and that they would not remain locked in a separate cage.[29]

There was very little that Kramář could do in response to these appeals, and the Czech leader attempted to explain to his Russian associates the difficulties of the situation in which he was placed. At a meeting of the Czech National Council held in Prague on 21 November 1908, Kramář stated: 'The annexation of Bosnia and Herzegovina is very damaging to our cause. But that is purely temporary. I have recently sent Mr Krasovsky in Russia a letter [in which I explained] that it was out of the question for us to conduct a policy against the state.[30]

When it became evident that the Czech political leaders were unwilling to take any action against the Austro-Hungarian government, stronger feelings began to be expressed in Russia. The Russian Neo-Slavs were particularly offended by the pro-Austrian attitude adopted by the Czechs and launched a bitter campaign of recrimination directed largely at Kramář personally.

Filevich, who had been present at the Prague Congress, was highly critical of the Austrian Slav leaders, particularly of Kramář and the Pole S. Glombiński, for giving their approval to the annexation of Bosnia and Herzegovina. In an article in *Novoe*

---

[29] H.H.St.A., *Polizei Direktion Wien*, Pr.Z. 21636K/52, 23 March 1916; *Proces dra. Kramáře*, I, pp. 34–5; II, pp. 71–2. (Letter dated St Petersburg, 25 September (8 October) 1908.)   [30] *Proces dra. Kramáře*, I, p. 31.

vremya, Filevich singled out the Czech leader attacking him in the following words: 'Mr Kramář, who recently proclaimed with such fire and eloquence that a blow aimed at any part of Slavdom was a blow directed at all the Slavs, now calmly and confidently gives the annexation his "moral" sanction.'[31] A similar charge was made by Vergun, another Russian who had attended the Neo-Slav Congress. In an article, also in *Novoe vremya* and entitled 'Militant Austroslavism', he made a general attack on the Austrian Slavs, and on what he considered to be their unrealistic dream of Slavicising the Habsburg Empire. Kramář was singled out for particular criticism because of his assertion that the first interest of the Czech nation was the maintenance of a strong and powerful Austro-Hungarian state. Other prominent Slavs inside and outside the Dual Monarchy, including the Croat Radić and the Serb J. Cvijich, also did not escape censure, and the Austrian Poles were considered to be unworthy even of a detailed critical attack.[32] In effect, Vergun issued a warning to the Slavs of the Dual Monarchy that they would have to look after their own affairs, without the assistance of Russia, if they considered closer relation with Russia to be rather uncomfortable.

In a letter sent to Kramář from St Petersburg early in 1908, Volodimirov referred to the disillusionment felt by the supporters of the Neo-Slav movement and to the bitterly critical campaign, directed against Kramář, conducted by Vergun in the pages of *Novoe vremya*.[33] Apportioning responsibility for the recent events, Volodimirov wrote:

> With regret I have to repeat that you, Karel Petrovich, bear a significant part of the blame. In my opinion it was your duty, as soon as the first indications of the impending annexation appeared, to call a meeting of the Pan-Slav Committee, for this was not formed just for show. Had you called a meeting of the Committee you, Karel Petrovich, would have avoided many accusations and would have left behind a mark [of your views] even if the course of events had not been altered.

Referring to Kramář's more outspoken pronouncement, made during a debate in the Vienna Parliament, Volodimirov added:

[31] *Novoe vremya*, 1 (14) October 1908. See also *ibid.*, 10 (23) October 1908.
[32] *Ibid.*, 20 October (2 November) 1908 (D. N. Vergun, 'Voenstvuyuschy Avstroslavizm').
[33] H.H.St.A., *Polizei Direktion Wien*, Pr.Z. 21636K/55, 28 March 1916; *Proces dra. Kramáře*, III, part 2, p. 133. (Letter dated St Petersburg, 28 January (10 February) 1909.)

'The recent opposition speech made by Karel Petrovich struck a new refreshing note, but would it not have been better to begin with opposition [to the annexation] rather than end with it?'[34] Further indications of the attitude adopted by the Russian Neo-Slavs towards the annexation were given at a meeting of the Association of Public Figures, held in St Petersburg during October 1908. The principal speaker, Vergun, after giving an account of the Prague Neo-Slav Congress, turned his attention to the annexation of Bosnia and Herzegovina and to the discord this event had produced amongst the Slav peoples. He was again critical of the attitude adopted by Kramář but, hinting at a future line of approach, pointed out that there were many political leaders amongst the Western Slavs who did not share the Czech leader's attitude towards the annexation. For that reason, Vergun argued, it would be erroneous to abandon the task commenced at the Prague Congress and despite extremely unfavourable conditions it was essential to persevere with it. Other speakers critical of the annexation included Bobrinsky, Filevich, Maklakov and Krasovsky, all participants at the recent Prague Neo-Slav Congress. The last mentioned speaker, Krasovsky, stated that, although the Neo-Slavs did not wish to see Russia going to war with Germany and Austria–Hungary over Bosnia and Herzegovina, they were equally opposed to Russia appearing as an accomplice of Austria–Hungary in such an 'illegal and high-handed' action. Krasovsky, in the name of the Russian Neo-Slavs, advised Serbia and Montenegro to await the results of a congress of European powers, at which Russia would represent their interest and those of the annexed territories.[35]

The annexation crisis, and the attitude adopted towards it by the majority of the Czech and other Austrian Slav leaders, did little to enhance the popularity of the Czechs or to promote the growth of Neo-Slavism in Russia. An optimistic report, carried in *Národní listy* about the considerable upsurge in Slav feeling inside Russia among the intellectual and professional classes[36] was misleading. Strong feeling was being expressed for the plight of the Balkan Slavs, but little sympathy was wasted on the nations

---

[34] *Proces dra. Kramáře*, I, p. 32. Volodimirov was presumably referring to the Neo-Slav Executive Committee established at the Prague Congress.
[35] *Novoe vremya*, 17 (30) October 1908; *Národní listy*, 19 November 1908.
[36] *Národní listy*, 19 November 1908.

belonging to the Western branch of the Slav race. An indication of general Russian disinterest in the Czechs in particular was demonstrated during the celebration of the centenary of the birth of the Russian author, N. V. Gogol, held in Moscow during May 1909. The Czechs attending this event complained bitterly that they, together with other non-Russian Slavs present, received little attention from their Russian hosts.[37]

Neo-Slavism itself fared little better. In some quarters it was this Czech inspired movement which was held responsible for precipitating the recent international events. As Krasovsky explained in a letter to Kramář, perhaps exaggerating the situation by attributing his particular views to opinion in general; 'A strong anti-Neo-Slav sentiment prevails in wide circles. It is being said that the Prague Congress was responsible for the humiliation of Russia, since it forced Germany and Austria–Hungary to come out against Slavism.' It was being alleged by many, Krasovsky maintained, that the annexation was a direct result of the Prague Congress. Austria–Hungary and Germany had become afraid of the Neo-Slav movement, and resorted to the annexation of Bosnia and Herzegovina in order to ensure that the plans for Slav unity would lead to nothing.[38] A similar attitude was adopted by the St Petersburg Slavonic Benevolent Society.[39]

The Czech Neo-Slavs, however, remained undaunted by the adverse reaction from Russia. Early in 1909, Kramář, in his capacity as chairman of the Neo-Slav Executive Committee, contacted the Russian members of the movement suggesting that a meeting of the Committee be held in St Petersburg during May. This request came up for discussion at a meeting of the Russian Neo-Slav organisation, the Society for Slav Reciprocity (*Obshchestvo slavyanskoy vzaimnosti*).[40] This association was founded in St Petersburg following the Prague Neo-Slav Congress by the Russians who had participated in it.[41] Present at the meeting of the Society was Z. Reimann, a Czech resident in St Petersburg, who reported back to Kramář that two significant voices were raised against holding a meeting

---

[37] H.H.St.A., PA, xl 219, *Panslav Bewegung* 4, Szilassy to Aehrenthal, 18B, St Petersburg, 21/8 May; *Proces dra. Kramáře*, iv, part 2, p. 26; *Slovanský přehled*, xi (1909), pp. 446–7.
[38] H.H.St.A., *Polizei Direktion Wien*, Pr.Z. 21636K/74, 19 April 1916; *Proces dra. Kramáře*, iii, part 2, p. 192; iv, part 1, p. 48; iv, part 2, p. 26. (Letter dated 24 March (6 April) 1909.)   [39] *Proces dra. Kramáře*, ii, p. 63.
[40] *Ibid.*, i, pp. 35–6.   [41] *Slovanský přehled*, xi (1909), p. 136.

of the Executive Committee; the voices of Krasovsky and Maklakov. Replying during the debate to Krasovsky's undefined objections, Reimann, in the words of his letter, pointed out that a meeting was required in order to 'show Germanism that we are alive and that Slav solidarity is not an empty phrase'. The correspondent added in parentheses: 'Unfortunately, that is the case.' More significant, in Reinann's opinion, were the objections raised by Maklakov who claimed that after his government's recognition of the annexation of Bosnia and Herzegovina he would be ashamed to appear as a Russian before the Serbs and other Slavs. Nevertheless, in spite of these reservations, the Russian Neo-Slav organisation accepted the proposal to hold a meeting of the Executive Committee.[42]

The decision to call the meeting met with the approval of Dmowski. In a letter to Kramář, commenting on the annexation crisis, he wrote:

So, we are defeated – for I share your view that the solution of the Balkan crisis is a significant German victory. I am unable to find any solace in gloating over the fact that the Russian government, while resisting our ideas, has suffered an even more humiliating defeat, for it in no way improves our situation. You have acted correctly in convening the Executive Committee. In my opinion this question must be put in a very clear form, for the purpose of which a large meeting would not be suitable.[43]

The annexation crisis had placed the Poles in a dilemma similar to that of the Czechs, but one that was further complicated by the territorial division of the nation, part of which owed allegiance to Russia and part to Austria–Hungary and Germany. The leaders of the Galician Poles, in common with many Czechs and other Austrian Slavs, did not oppose the forcible incorporation of the Balkan provinces into the Dual Monarchy. A prominent Polish conservative politician stated in the press that the annexation in no way altered the political situation and warned against capital being made out of the crisis for the Pan-Slav cause.[44] During the foreign policy debate in the Austrian Delegation the leader of the Austrian Poles, Count Dzieduszycki, actually welcomed the action taken by the Austro-Hungarian government in Bosnia and

[42] H.H.St.A., *Polizei Direktion Wien*, Pr.Z. 21636K/55, 28 March 1916; *Proces dra. Kramáře*, 1, p. 36. (Letter dated 27 March (9 April) 1909.)
[43] *Proces dra. Kramáře*, 1, p. 37. (Letter dated 23 April (6 May) 1909.)
[44] *Národní listy*, 10 October 1908.

Herzegovina.[45] It also appears that at least some Poles living within
the Habsburg Empire were not dismayed by the prospect of armed
conflict between Russia and Serbia, on the one hand, and Austria–
Hungary and Germany, on the other. In a private report to his
newspaper in London, made on 3 April 1909, the Vienna correspondent of *The Times*, H. W. Steed, stated that: 'The leading
Austrian Poles seem to have been influenced by the hope of an
Austro-Hungarian occupation of Russian Poland. Even Dzieduszycki...seemed to think that the *coup* was worth risking; and
I have since gathered from other prominent Poles that they are
disappointed at the maintenance of peace.'[46]

The attitude of the Austrian Poles was confirmed in a dispatch
from the British embassy in St Petersburg which reported a
meeting between Nicolson and a 'Polish friend', who was known
to be 'in relations with many Austrians in high positions'. Nicolson wrote that: '[The Pole] pointed out to me that the recent
action of Austria–Hungary had, for the moment at any rate,
nullified the results of the Slav Congress at Prague so far as the
Austrian Slav subjects were concerned, and that it would check
the union of the Slavs within the Austrian dominions with their
brethren outside the Austrian frontiers.' After outlining the
historical reasons for the loyalty of the Galician Poles to the
Austro-Hungarian government, the unnamed Pole was reported
to have expressed the view that: 'In the matter of the annexation,
all Austrian Poles were...supporters of Baron d'Aehrenthal, and
he doubted whether the Poles in Russia would be disposed to
be enthusiastically in favour of the standpoint of the Russian
government.'[47]

Dmowski, though perhaps not enthusiastic about the policies of
the Russian government, did not exactly express his pleasure at
the attitude adopted by the Austrian Poles. Bobrinsky reported,
in a letter to Kramář, that Dmowski was extremely angry with the
Galician Poles because of their unqualified support for the Austro-
Hungarian government and that the Russian Pole had made his
views known to his fellow nationals in Austria.[48] Writing directly

[45] *Stenographische Protokolle der Delegation, 43. Session*, pp. 52–6.
[46] Steed, *Through Thirty Years*, I, p. 300.
[47] PRO, FO, 371/519, Nicolson to Grey, 42551, St Petersburg, 26 November 1908.
[48] *Proces dra. Kramáře*, I, p. 33; IV, part 1, p. 39. (Letter dated 12 (25) November 1908.)

to Kramář, Dmowski explained: 'Although I appreciate the difficulties facing my countrymen in Austria, I am, nevertheless, of the opinion that they have gone a little too far.' Referring to those Austrian Poles who hoped that a war between Russia and the Habsburg Empire would result in the Austro-Hungarian occupation of Russian Poland and thus, possibly, lead towards reuniting the Polish nation, he maintained that: 'The Poles would gain nothing from a conflict between Russia and Austria. On the contrary, they would suffer considerable losses, for such a conflict would result in weakening both states and in increasing German influence on their policies.' In Dmowski's opinion it was most unlikely, even in the event of war, that Austria–Hungary would be permitted by the other powers to acquire the territory of Russian Poland.[49]

The disagreement with the Austrian Poles over the annexation of Bosnia and Herzegovina was not Dmowski's only problem. His policy of co-operation with the Russian government was not producing any significant results and consequently lost support both among the population in general and within his own National Democratic Party. In February 1909 he resigned his seat in the Duma.[50] The British consul in Warsaw reported to his ambassador a conversation between himself and Dmowski, during which:

[The Pole had] tacitly acknowledged that ill-health was only an excuse to vacate a position which he found was hopeless. He stated that he clearly recognised the fact that none of the Polish demands were likely to be conceded by the present regime, and that any endeavours to obtain them were only a waste of time and energy. It is, however, stated that he found his position as leader of the National Democrats quite untenable, as he had little sympathy with the more radical section which forms the majority of the party.[51]

Dmowski's growing disillusionment with the Russian authorities was to have far-reaching effects on the entire Neo-Slav movement. The opportunistic adherence of the Russian Poles to the Neo-Slav movement had been undertaken largely on the instigation of Dmowski. His withdrawal from the political leadership in Russian Poland, and the circumstances which made him do so, resulted in

[49] *Ibid.*, II, pp. 69–70. (Letter dated 23 April (6 May) 1909.)
[50] Kozicki, 'Roman Dmowski', p. 123.
[51] PRO, FO, 371/728, Bayley to Nicolson, 19875, Warsaw, 25 May 1909.

the Poles, from Russia and elsewhere, ceasing to play an active role in the Neo-Slav movement.

The divisions within the Slav world, which the Neo-Slav movement aimed at healing, remained as pronounced as ever. The Poles, both in Austria–Hungary and in Russia, whose co-operation was regarded from the outset by the Czech instigators of the movement as being essential for its success, soon lost interest in Neo-Slavism. The Galician Poles who had never espoused the principles of Neo-Slavism with any warmth now had greater hopes in a war with Russia than in inter-Slav co-operation. The Poles from the Russian division, unable to see any sign whatever of progress towards greater national autonomy, lost confidence in the movement and withdrew their support from Dmowski and his associates. Relations between the Polish and Czech nations within the Habsburg Empire, which in the period immediately following the Prague Congress showed signs of improvement, deteriorated again the following year due largely to the resurgence of a bitter dispute over linguistic aspects of primary education in Silesia.[52] The behaviour of many of the leading figures of the Neo-Slav movement during the annexation crisis did nothing to enhance the attraction of their cause in the eyes of the Serbs and other South Slavs outside Austria–Hungary.[53] Some South Slavs from within the Habsburg Empire, however, welcomed the annexation and looked upon the newly acquired territories as forming a nucleus of a third South Slav component of the Empire, thus transforming the Dual Monarchy into one consisting of three equal parts. Amongst those who advocated such a development was the leader of the Slovene Clerical Party, Šusteršič.[54] The Russian government, which had never been enthusiastic about Neo-Slavism, showed even less interest in the movement after the annexation crisis and concentrated more intensely than in the recent past on the Balkans, cultivating relations with Serbia and Bulgaria in an attempt to form an alliance directed against Austria–Hungary. This was a policy very much to the liking of those who supported traditional Russian Pan-Slavism.

In Russia, not only was influential opinion turning against the

[52] *Slovanský přehled*, x (1908), pp. 77–80, and xi (1909), p. 272.
[53] *Národní listy*, 18 October 1908.
[54] *Ibid.*, 10 October 1908. For Šusteršič's Delegation speech on the annexation see *Stenographische Protokolle der Delegation, 43. Session*, pp. 142–3.

Neo-Slavs but rifts began to appear within the movement itself. These dissensions were not entirely new, they were inherent in the composition of the Russian movement, but did not come fully out in the open until the spring of 1909. During 19 (6) to 24 (11) April of that year a meeting of representatives from various Russian Slavonic societies was held in St Petersburg,[55] with the aim of ascertaining whether a common policy could be agreed on. The conference was attended by representatives of thirteen Slavonic organisations spanning a variety of opinions ranging from the traditional Moscow branch of the Slavonic Benevolent Society to the liberal Society for Slav Culture, also based in Moscow. In party-political terms the delegates present ranged from members of the moderate Kadet Party to the right-wing Union of the Russian People. The original intention was to divide the proceedings of the conference into five sections; the first four dealing respectively with political, educational, philanthropic, and cultural matters, and the fifth concerned with future Slav congresses and Slav exhibitions. During the course of the conference the educational, philanthropic and cultural sections were fused into one, and by far the most attention appears to have been paid to the discussion of political matters. The main political item which came up for discussion was the perennial question of Russo-Polish relations, which gave rise to clashes between representatives of the right and left wings of the Russian Neo-Slav movement. Balkan issues were also discussed, but these were less contentious.

The controversy concerning Russo-Polish relations was initiated by Sharapov, who represented the Moscow based Aksakov Society, although some members of this group subsequently disassociated themselves from the views expressed. In his address on the subject of 'Germany and Slavdom', Sharapov reiterated his stand in favour of Polish autonomy. He argued that the suspicions which the Slavs of the Habsburg Empire harboured towards Russia, fearing the danger of Russification if closer ties were developed, could only be overcome by a just solution of the problem of Poland along the lines he advocated. Only by encouraging the development of Austro-Slavism which, Sharapov believed, would be achieved by granting the Poles autonomy, would it be possible to detach the Habsburg Empire from its association with Germany

---

[55] *Novoe vremya*, 7 (20), 8 (21), 10 (23), 12 (25), April 1909; *Rech'*, 7 (20) – 11 (24) April 1909; *Slovanský přehled*, XI (1909), pp. 440–1.

and draw it into an alliance with Russia, Britain and France, and possibly even Italy. This view was opposed by Krasovsky, representing the Society for Slav Reciprocity, who stressed that Russo-Polish relations were an internal Russian matter and, therefore, should not be included amongst the major issues concerning the Slav peoples in general. It was further pointed out by, amongst others, Filevich and P. A. Kulakovsky, a prominent member of the St Petersburg Slavonic Benevolent Society, that the creation of an autonomous Poland would result in weakening the power of Russia and thus be detrimental to Slav interests.

The ideas outlined by Stakhovich did, however, find support amongst representatives of the Society for Slav Culture. One of their number, the Kadet leader Milyukov, tabled a resolution advocating the granting of full autonomous status to Russian Poland. This resolution was rejected and an alternative one, formulated by Vergun and Milyutin, was approved by the conference after considerable debate. Despite energetic attempts by Milyukov and Sharapov to alter the wording of the resolution the delegates present voted in favour of a cautious policy accepting only the need for a revision of Russo-Polish relations on the basis of 'the speedy granting of urban and rural autonomy [i.e., local government] to the Polish nation within the ethnographic boundaries of the Kingdom of Poland, together with guarantees for the rights of the Russian populations also inhabiting this territory'. A further resolution advocated the 'ending of discord between the Slav peoples on the basis of the recognition of the cultural and national rights of each and every Slav nation as an equal member of the Slav family.' This platitudinous principle was to be applied, in particular, in the field of Russo-Polish relations. Balkan problems, however, proved to be much less controversial and Milyukov's proposed resolution, expressing the conviction that the annexation of Bosnia and Herzegovina did not represent the 'final solution of the Serbian question', and also the need for the Slav world to make every effort to obtain 'full autonomy' for the territories concerned, met with approval. The other sections of the conference approved resolutions urging the establishment of a Slav chamber of commerce, the staging of a Slav exhibition in Russia 'as soon as possible', and the 'frequent' convention of Slav congresses.[56]

[56] *Novoe vremya*, 10 (23), 12 (25) April 1909; *Rech'*, 10 (23), 11 (24), April 1909.

More important than the resolutions themselves, however, was the emergent evidence of the rift existing within the Russian Neo-Slav movement reflecting differing political outlooks. One of the participants at the conference, Kulakovsky, indicated the attitude adopted by right wing representatives, here towards one of the more moderate Slavonic societies, in the following comment: 'It became evident [at the conference] that only the Moscow Society for Slav Culture stood apart from the others, and indeed that it hardly had the right to the title "Slav", for it came out as the only supporter of the Polish and "Ukrainian" standpoints.'[57] This point of view was shared by Filevich who, in an article in *Novoe vremya*, critical of what he termed to be Austro-Slavism, castigated the Society for Slav Culture particularly for its support of the Ukrainians and suggested that it should change its designation to an 'Austro-Slav society'.[58]

The proceedings of the conference of Russian Slavonic societies, and reactions of some of the participants, provided an indication of the changes taking place within the Russian Neo-Slav movement. Although Neo-Slavism was originally envisaged as being liberal in character, recognising the equal rights of all Slav nations, the right wing forces, which had always been present in the Russian movement, gradually exerted greater influence and gave it a more reactionary tinge.[59] The isolation of the moderate Society for Slav Culture was indicative of this tendency.

Despite these developments, the Neo-Slav Executive Committee met in St Peterburg between 25 (12) and 29 (16) May 1909. The meeting was held, as Kramář explained in a letter to members of the Committee, 'for the purpose of ascertaining whether, after the [recent] fateful events, it is reasonable to expect that further efforts made in the spirit of the Prague decisions are likely to be successful'.[60] Subsequently, at his trial, he maintained that he had

[57] *Novoe vremya*, 23 July (5 August) 1909 (P. A. Kulakovsky, 'Slavyanskie sezdy i polsky vopros', 1).   [58] *Ibid.*, 29 April (12 May) 1909.
[59] *Slovanský přehled*, edited by A. Černý, who had earlier been critical of the right wing orientation of many of the Russians involved in the Neo-Slav movement (A. Černý, 'Slovanské sjezdy r. 1908', p. 12), published the following comment on the St Petersburg Conference of Slavonic Societies by the Pole H. Boczkowski: 'Whilst there remain active in the ranks of the Neo-Slavs such "Slavs" as Messrs Bashmakov, Kulakovsky, Vergun, Filevich and others – it will not only be impossible to expect a solution of the Polish–Russian dispute, but any positive Slav effort whatsoever.' *Slovanský přehled*, XI (1909), p. 441.
[60] Archive of the Czech National Council, Slav Congress file (letter dated 16 April 1909), cited by Herman, 'Novoslovanství a česká buržoasie', p. 294.

attended the discussions largely in order to oppose the attempt by the right wing to dominate the Russian section of the movement. In addition, he claimed, he had wished to contribute towards improving relations between Russia and Austria–Hungary.[61] From various accounts of the proceedings, it appears that, although the gathering was ostensibly a meeting of the Executive Committee, it was attended by more than the twelve members who had been elected onto this body at the Neo-Slav Congress the previous year. A correspondent of *Novoe vremya* estimated the number of participants at about sixty. In addition to the Neo-Slav delegates themselves, the meetings were also attended by representatives of the Slavonic Benevolent Society and the Society for Slav Culture.[62] From the Czech side Kramář was accompanied by Preiss, Klofáč, Scheiner, B. Pavlů, and Dürrich. Among the Russians who participated in the discussions were Krasovsky, Bobrinsky, Vergun, Lvov, and Maklakov. Most of the other Slavs who had been represented at the Prague Congress also sent delegates to the St Petersburg meeting. Prominent amongst these were Dmowski; the Bulgarian, Bobchev; the Croat, Tresić-Pavičić; and the Serb, R. Koshutich.[63] The only exception was the Austrian Poles who did not attend as they considered that Neo-Slavism was doing little to aid the Polish cause. During the first session of the meetings, Dmowski explained the absence of his compatriots from the Habsburg Empire on the grounds that they did not believe that Russia could detach itself from German influence and meet the Polish wishes for guarantees of their nationality.[64]

During the five days of talks discussion ranged over the same variety of topics that had been covered at the Neo-Slav Congress the previous year, and the St Petersburg deliberations can, in fact, be considered as an extension of those held in Prague. As far as the future of the movement was concerned, by far the most significant were the two political issues raised; that of Russo-Polish relations, and that of the annexation of Bosnia and Herzegovina

---

[61] *Proces dra. Kramáře*, II, pp. 67, 74–5, 113.

[62] *Novoe vremya*, 13 (26) May 1909. J. Preiss estimated the number of participants at about 50. *Proces dra. Kramáře*, III, part 1, p. 78.

[63] H.H.St.A., PA, XL 219, *Panslav Bewegung* 4, Bienerth to Aehrenthal, 18, Moscow, 10 June 1909; *Rech'*, 12 (25)–17 (30) May 1909; *Novoe vremya*, 13 (26), 14 (27), 16 (29), 17 (30) May 1909.

[64] *Novoe vremya*, 13 (26) May 1909. Kramář, in 'Po petrohradských konferencích', pp. 578–80, was, not unexpectedly, highly critical of the unco-operative attitude adopted by the Galician Poles.

together with the associated wider Balkan problems. The aims of the Czech representatives, and those of Kramář in particular, were clear and precise. They wanted to see the Russian authorities make some concessions to the Poles in the spirit of the Prague resolution and, secondly, to prevent the Serbs from including anti-Austro-Hungarian demands in the Neo-Slav programme, on the grounds that these were of a political nature and, therefore, outside the scope of the movement. The struggle within the Committee, as Kramář himself later admitted, was not an easy one.[65]

The considerable importance which Kramář attached to the Polish issue is evident from the emphasis he placed on this problem in his public utterances during the Neo-Slav meetings. In an interview with a correspondent of *Novoe vremya*, given by the Czech leader on his arrival in St Petersburg, Kramář dwelt extensively on the subject of Russo-Polish relations, criticising the attitude of the Russian government as 'somewhat unsound' but, despite his evident pessimism, expressing confidence that the Russian authorities would reconsider their attitude towards the Poles.[66] In speeches delivered on various occasions during the Neo-Slav deliberations in the Russian capital Kramář repeatedly returned to this theme, often linking it with the wider issue of the balance of power in Eastern Europe. He argued that, in order to counteract the growing dependence of the Austro-Hungarian Empire on Germany, it was imperative for the Slavs within the Dual Monarchy to achieve unity, which could not come about without a prior Russo-Polish reconciliation. This view was endorsed by the Polish and liberal Russian representatives but, predictably, rejected by the more conservative Russians present. The right wing Russian point of view was outlined, after the St Petersburg talks, by Kulakovsky, who expressed great objection to the pre-eminent position given by the Neo-Slavs to the Russo-Polish dispute. In a series of articles, which appeared in *Novoe vremya*, he argued that many Slavs considered the question of Russo-Polish relations 'to be not only an internal Russian matter, which was of no concern to other Slavs, but also to be of secondary importance. Indeed, would it not be of greater significance for the Slavs if Croats and Serbs were to fully unite, or if a total

---

[65] *Proces dra. Kramáře*, II, pp. 79–80; Kramář, 'Předmluva', *Slovanstvo*, p. VII.
[66] *Novoe vremya*, 12 (25) May 1909.

cessation of discord between Bulgarians and Serbs were to come about?'[67]

In the bitter debate on Russian Poland, Dmowski and his associates accused the Russian government of undermining the Neo-Slav movement by refusing to create a more favourable climate for the development of better relations between Russians and Poles. The Polish representatives were particularly hostile towards the recently announced proposals of the Russian government to form a new Russian province of Kholm (Chełm) which would incorporate the Polish provinces of Lublin and Siedlce, and thus reduce the territory of the Russian division of Poland.[68] The Russian authorities maintained that the areas involved were predominantly inhabited by Ukrainians, whom they regarded as Russians and, therefore, of little concern to the Poles. This official Russian attitude was echoed by the right wing Russians present at the Neo-Slav discussions, Vergun, Filevich and others, who not only maintained that the Poles were not receiving unfair treatment but that it was essential for the Neo-Slavs to get their priorities right and to concentrate on the danger to which Slavdom was exposed in the Balkan Peninsula.[69]

In addition to the Russo-Polish conflict, a further inter-Slav dispute received some consideration at the Neo-Slav discussions. It was raised by the Russophil Ukrainian Glebovitsky who protested about the Polish oppression of the Ukrainian population of Galicia, whom he referred to as 'Galician Russians'. This issue was also taken up by Krasovsky who expressed the hope that the conflict in Galicia, which was damaging to all the Slavs, would soon cease and that 'that section of the Russian nation' inhabiting Galicia would soon enjoy the right of free cultural development.[70] The problem of Galicia, however, does not appear to have received major attention at the St Petersburg meetings although it was of considerable concern to many of the more conservative members of the Russian Neo-Slav movement. This concern had been

[67] *Ibid.*, 25 July (7 August) 1909 (Kulakovsky, 'Slavyanskie sezdy i polsky vopros', II).
[68] Reddaway and others eds., *The Cambridge History of Poland*, II, pp. 405–6; Chmielewski, *The Polish Question*, pp. 111–37.
[69] *Novoe vremya*, 13 (26), 14 (27), 16 (29), 17 (30) May 1909; S. S. Bobchev, 'Maiskite slavyanski săveshtaniya v Petersburg i Moskva', *Bălgarska sbirka*, XVI (1909), pp. 407–9, 416.
[70] *Novoe vremya*, 13 (26), 17 (30) May 1909; *Proces dra. Kramáře*, III, part 1, p. 78; Bobchev, 'Maiskite slavyanski săveshtaniya', p. 408.

demonstrated earlier when, following the conclusion of the Prague Congress, a group of Russian delegates, headed by Bobrinsky and accompanied by Glebovitsky, departed for an extensive tour of Galicia and Bukovina in order to ascertain how the Ukrainian population was being treated. After the visit the Russians were highly critical of the Austro-Hungarian administration of these territories for countenancing Polish oppression of the Ukrainians.[71] The same right wing section of the Russian Neo-Slav movement objected vigorously when two members of the liberal Moscow Society for Slav Culture, A. L. Pogodin and M. A. Slovinsky, attempted to speak out in defence of the cultural rights of the Ukrainian and White Russian peoples within the Russian Empire.[72]

During discussions on the Balkan question the Czech Neo-Slav leadership was subjected to severe attacks over their refusal to oppose the annexation of Bosnia and Herzegovina. Kramář justified his policy, and that of his associates, over the annexation issue, by arguing that as Russia was unwilling to go to war no other action was possible, and he pledged himself to defend the interests of the Slav inhabitants of Bosnia and Herzegovina and to demand autonomy for the areas concerned. He was attacked not only by the conservative Russians and the Serbs, but also by his domestic political rival, Klofáč. Klofáč, claiming to speak for the mass of the Czech working people, castigated the Austrian Slav deputies who supported the annexation, accusing them of 'cowardice', and was also critical of what he termed as the 'declamatory' attitude of the Russian intelligentsia over Slav affairs. The Serbs also directed their criticism at the Russians for not taking a firmer line against Austria–Hungary, and against those Croats, such as Tresić-Pavičić, who favoured the annexation because the incorporation of the Balkan provinces strengthened the South Slav element within the Habsburg Empire.[73] The basic Serbian point of view was outlined in a statement by Koshutich who affirmed Serbian support for the principles of Neo-Slavism but was resolutely opposed to Austro-Slavism which, in his opinion, had

[71] For details of the visit see G. V. Komarov, *Po slavyanskim zemlyam. Posle prazhskogo sezda* (2nd edn, St Petersburg, 1909), and Bobrinsky, *Prazhsky sezd*, pp. 44–105. The Russian party consisted of V. A. Bobrinsky, G. V. Komarov, V. M. Volodimirov, A. S. Gizhitsky, and E. M. Dementev.
[72] *Novoe vremya*, 17 (30) August 1909 (Kulakovsky, 'Slavyanskie sezdy i polsky vopros', IV); Bobchev, 'Maiskite slavyanski săveshtaniya', p. 409.
[73] *Novoe vremya*, 13 (26), 16 (29), 17 (30) May 1909.

recently contaminated the Neo-Slav movement. The Serbs maintained the dictum that 'he who wished to be a true Slav, cannot be
an Austro-Slav'. The major problem confronting the Slavs, in
the view of Koshutich, was the desperate Serbian situation in the
wake of the recent annexation of Bosnia and Herzegovina. The
Serbs considered Austria–Hungary to be acting as the vanguard of
Germany, and felt themselves to be in mortal danger from German
expansion into the Balkans. *Rapprochement* with the Habsburg
Empire, which had been suggested as the only 'realistic' course
of action available to the Serbs, was therefore out of the question.
The only 'realistic' policy envisaged by Koshutich was the formation of an alliance between Bulgaria, Serbia, and Montenegro
under the leadership of Russia.[74] The outlook for collaboration
between Serbia and Bulgaria, however, was not propitious. This
became evident when, during the course of the discussions, yet
another inter-Slav dispute came to the surface: the Serbs and
Bulgarians present clashed over plans for the future of Macedonia,
a territory which, though at the time under Turkish control, was
coveted by both nations.[75]

Despite the friction evident during the Neo-Slav talks Kramář
was able to convince the majority of those present, thanks to the
support of liberal Russians such as Lvov, Maklakov, and Volodimirov, over the Polish issue, and with the aid of the Poles and
Bulgarians in the dispute over the annexation, that the acceptance
of his formula was essential for the survival of the movement.[76]
This is evident from the following extracts from the resolution
issued at the conclusion of the St Petersburg meetings. Referring
to the Russo-Polish dispute, the resolution stated that:

Following the consideration, at the meeting of the Executive Committee,
of all aspects of Russo-Polish relations, the Executive Committee
recognises that the realisation of a Russo-Polish settlement, both within
Russia and outside, can be achieved only through the unaltered acceptance of the principles of the Prague Congress; namely, only if recognition is given to the full equality of both nations, [discriminatory]
emergency legislation avoided, and recognition given to the rights of

[74] *Ibid.*, 30 May (12 June) 1909. The idea of a Balkan alliance, outlined by
Koshutich, foreshadowed the emergence of the Balkan League in 1912. The
Balkan League, which also included Greece was, however, directed primarily
at Turkey.
[75] PRO, FO, 371/728, Nicolson to Grey, 21140, St Petersburg, 30 May 1909.
[76] *Proces dra. Kramáře*, II, p. 80.

both nations to their mother tongue, schools, and institutions guaranteeing national development.

Regarding the situation in the Balkans, it was declared that:

After hearing the views of the Serbian members of the Committee during consideration of the question of the annexation of Bosnia and Herzegovina, an event which stirred the entire Slav world, the Slav Executive Committee has reached the view that the purely political aspects [of the annexation] which were introduced do not fall within the Committee's terms of reference. Nevertheless, the Committee turns to all Slav members of the Austro-Hungarian Parliament with the request that every effort be made to ensure the introduction, in Bosnia and Herzegovina, of autonomous administration on the broadest possible basis which would assure the political, national, cultural, and economic development of these lands. Simultaneously, it appeals to all representatives of the independent Slav nations to turn their attention towards the cultivation of cultural links with their brethren in Bosnia and Herzegovina.[77]

The struggle within the Neo-Slav movement, however, was far from over. Shortly after Kramář and others who had participated in the St Petersburg talks had left the Russian capital for a visit to Moscow, *Novoe vremya* published a declaration by the Serbian representatives at the meetings which, the newspaper claimed, had motivated the official resolution approved by the Executive Committee. The Serbian statement read as follows:

1. A concerted effort must be directed towards the creation of a political and economic association of independent Balkan Slav nations under Russian leadership.
2. The independent sections of the Serbian nation support the Austro-Hungarian Slav peoples in their struggles which, up to the annexation of Bosnia and Herzegovina, had been directed towards achieving independent cultural development and the greatest possible

[77] H.H.St.A., PA, XL 219, *Panslav Bewegung* 4, Berchtold to Aethrenthal, 21E, St Petersburg, 3 June/21 May 1909; *Novoe vremya*, 17 (30) May 1909. The resolutions were drawn up by a committee consisting of the following: M. V. Krasovsky, V. A. Maklakov, V. A. Bobrinsky, and N. N. Lvov (Russians); V. Dudykevich, and M. Glebovitsky (Russophil Ukrainians); R. Dmowski, and L. Dymsza (Poles); K. Kramář, J. Scheiner, and J. Preiss (Czechs); A. Tresić-Pavičić (Croat); M. Drashkovich, and R. Koshutich (Serbs); S. S. Bobchev, and A. Lyudskanov (Bulgarians). Kramář was in the chair. Also invited to attend were N. A. Khomyakov and J. Olizar.

Neo-Slavism in decline, 1908–1910

political and national rights within the boundaries of the Austro-Hungarian Monarchy. The southwards expansion of Austria-Hungary over the Save and the Danube [rivers], together with the incorporation of the Serbian population, cannot be reconciled with Slav interests and consequently all Slavs, both within Austria–Hungary and outside it, will consider any support of Austria–Hungary as constituting an anti-Slav activity.

3. Bosnia and Herzegovina, being Serbian territories, fall within the sphere of the state interests of the Serbian nation as an independent entity. It is, therefore, essential that the [entire] Slav world should assist the political, cultural, and economic development of the population of Bosnia and Herzegovina.[78]

The publication of this document greatly angered Kramář and his allies, and caused the Czech leader considerable embarrassment. The Poles Dmowski and Olizar warned Kramář, who was then in Moscow, by telegraph of the impending publication of the Serbian document. Kramář, in turn, cabled his protest to St Petersburg. He vigorously denied that the views expressed in the document had motivated the resolution issued at the conclusion of the talks and maintained that the Serbian proposals had, in fact, been re-jected by the Executive Committee.[79] The action of the Serbian Neo-Slav delegates clearly indicated that the dissensions within the movement remained unresolved and that the cracks had not even been successfully papered over.

During the time spent in the Russian capital the Czech leaders, in addition to attending the deliberations of the Neo-Slav Execu-tive Committee, held discussions with highly placed Russian political figures. Kramář had meetings with, among others, the Prime Minister, P. A. Stolypin, and Charykov and S. D. Sazonov from the Foreign Office, but not with the Minister of Foreign

[78] H.H.St.A., PA, XL 219, Panslav Bewegung 4, Berchtold to Aehrenthal, 21E, St Petersburg, 3 June/21 May 1909; Novoe vremya, 17 (30) May 1909. A German diplomatic report from Vienna refers to a further document alleged to have originated from the Executive Committee of a Slav conference held in St Petersburg, presumably the Neo-Slav meeting. The programme of Slav action, outlined in this secret circular, was of such an extreme nature that it was most unlikely to have received Kramář's approval. Die Grosse Politik der Europäischen Kabinette, 1871–1914. Sammlung der Diplomatischen Akten des Auswärtigen Amtes (40 vols., Berlin, 1922–7), XXVI, part 2, pp. 844–5, no. 9563, Brockdorff-Rantzau to Bethmann Hollweg, Vienna, 25 July 1909.
[79] Proces dra. Kramáře, II, pp. 82, 85. Preiss also claimed that the Serbian resolution had been defeated. Ibid., part I, p. 78.

Affairs, Izvolsky, who was away from St Petersburg at the time.[80]
Although the attitude of the Russian government towards the
Neo-Slav talks was described by one observer as 'sympathetic',[81]
the private discussions between the Czech and Russian leaders were
not entirely amicable. During the course of the interview given on
his arrival in St Petersburg to a correspondent of *Novoe vremya*,
Kramář attacked Izvolsky for having failed to keep the undertaking made at Buchlau. Stolypin, at a subsequent meeting,
rebuked the Czech politician for his criticism of the Foreign
Minister.[82]

During the conversations with Russian leaders, Kramář attempted to explain to his hosts the motives behind his approval of
the annexation of Bosnia and Herzegovina, pointing out the
advantages to be gained from the increase in size of the Slav
population of the Habsburg Empire. It appears, however, that
economic questions formed the main topics of the discussions.
Significantly, Preiss, a prominent Czech banker, who had outlined
the proposals for the creation of a Slav bank at the Prague Congress, was included in the talks, and himself held discussions on
economic matters with both the Prime Minister and the Minister
of Finance, Kokovtsov.[83]

The two, from the Czech point of view, most significant
economic issues discussed in the private conversations with
Russian leaders, the establishment of a Slav bank and the staging
of a Slav exhibition, also came up for consideration at the Neo-
Slav meetings.[84] The Czech Neo-Slavs, impatient with the lack of
progress made by the committees elected to draw up detailed

[80] *Ibid.*, I, p. 38; II, pp. 77, 86, 113. Sazonov was at the time preparing to
succeed Charykov as deputy Minister of Foreign Affairs. Charykov was about
to take up the post of ambassador in Constantinople.
[81] PRO, FO, 371/731, Nicolson to Grey, 21133, St Petersburg, 28 May 1909.
[82] *Proces dra. Kramáře*, II, p. 86; Kramář, *Pět přednášek*, p. 32. Kramář's
criticism of Izvolsky does not appear in the published version of the interview
in *Novoe vremya*, 12 (25) May 1909.
[83] *Proces dra. Kramáře*, II, pp. 113–14; III, part 1, p. 80. Preiss created a very
favourable impression on his Russian hosts, in particular on A. A. Stolypin
the brother of the Prime Minister, who suggested that the Czech financier be
seconded to the Russians for a period of five years. In a letter to his wife,
Kramář commented magnanimously: 'I would not wish to lose him for us,
but ultimately, the strengthening of Russia would be of even greater significance.' *Ibid.*, I, p. 40.
[84] H.H.St.A., PA, XL 219, *Panslav Bewegung* 4, Berchtold to Aehrenthal, 21F,
St Petersburg, 3 June/21 May 1909; *Novoe vremya*, 14 (27) May 1909; Bobchev, 'Maiskite slavyanski săveshtaniya', pp. 411–13.

proposals for both these schemes, had prepared their own plans which they presented to the Executive Committee in St Petersburg and to the appropriate Russian authorities. The proposals for the Slav bank were summarised, in a pamphlet on the subject, as follows: 'For commercial purposes...[it is proposed] to establish in Prague a bank, under the name of the Slav Bank of Prague, with a capital of 10 million crowns. This capital will be raised by Slav financial institutions, which will also be represented in the management [of the bank].'[85] The revised scheme was for a venture considerably more modest in size than originally planned. At the outset, during the Prague Congress, the projected Slav bank had been envisaged as having a working capital of 100 million crowns, ten times the amount now proposed.

The lack of enthusiasm shown for the proposals from the Russian side had brought about the realisation that the Slav bank, if it were ever to come into being, would have to be founded outside Russia. As it was the Czech business community which was principally interested in the scheme, the Bohemian capital was the obvious alternative choice for situating the projected bank. The Czech Neo-Slavs, however, did not entirely abandon the hope of having a Russian based financial institution supplying credit to Russian customers with the object of financing the purchase of products of Czech owned industry. The second point contained in the new proposals was directed towards achieving this aim:

For the purposes of providing credit (for municipal and railway improvements), [it is proposed] to establish a banking institution in Russia, which would be provided with all the [necessary] legal requirements by the Russian authorities. This institution will also be known as the Slav Bank, with a possible additional title, in order to distinguish it from the Slav Bank of Prague.[86]

This proposal to establish a second bank inside Russia, working within the Russian financial system, was also a device for circumventing the outdated and restrictive Russian financial legislation, which discriminated against foreign capital.

Great emphasis was placed on the need for a close association between the two proposed Slav financial institutions and it was

[85] *Slovanská banka. Zpráva a návrhy českého výboru slovanského komitétu* (Prague, 1909), p. 15. The pamphlet was prepared by Kramář and Preiss.
[86] *Ibid.*

envisaged that the two banks, in co-ordination, would provide most of the services that were expected of the originally projected larger Slav bank. The Czech proposal continued:

Both these Slav institutions will act in very close co-operation in order that, by their joint activities, they may strive towards the realisation of the ultimate aims of a Slav bank; the facilitation of large financial transactions for the benefit of Slav states, and the placing of bonds issued by Slav owned public companies on the large western [stock-]markets.

The promoters of the Slav bank had also not completely abandoned the idea of operating entirely inside Russia, and concluded their revised proposals with the following hopeful words: 'The Czech committee is of the opinion that it may be possible, at some later stage when the activities of the Slav Bank of Prague have developed to the required extent, to transfer the Bank to Russia and thus arrange even closer ties between the two institutions.'[87]

Evidently the problems surrounding the establishment of a comprehensive Slav bank inside Russia, as originally envisaged, had proved insurmountable and compromise proposals had been prepared. Opposition to the original scheme had come, not only from the Russian authorities, but also from certain Czech financial circles. Some Czech financiers considered Preiss' first project, delivered at the Prague Congress, to be too ambitious and were only prepared to participate in a more modest venture.[88] French financial circles, on whose assistance the Czech Neo-Slavs were relying, were also not interested in the plan as first outlined.[89]

Even the revised, less ambitious, plans for a Slav bank which Preiss outlined during the meetings in St Petersburg in May 1909, met with little enthusiasm from the assembled Neo-Slavs. The Czech financier received unqualified support for his proposals from only one other person present, the Slovene Hribar, who pledged financial participation in the venture under discussion by South Slav banks. A representative of the Russian Poles, J. Montwiłł, agreed in principle with the concept of a Slav bank, but was

---

[87] *Ibid.*
[88] Archive of the Czech National Council, Slav Congress file, report of Kramář's speech at the inaugural meeting of the Journalistic and Informational Section of the Slav Committee, 2 March 1909, cited in Herman, 'Novoslovanství a česká buržoasie', p. 295.
[89] Negotiations had taken place, through Russian and Polish financiers, with a leading French statesman, M. Rouvier, who besides being a politician was also a partner in a large French bank. *Ibid.*, pp. 295–6.

unhappy about some of the details of the Czech proposal. The opposition of the Russian Neo-Slavs was voiced by Krasovsky, who argued that Preiss' plan was incompatible with Russian financial legislation and that, besides, Russia was short of capital. Krasovsky outlined an alternative proposal which envisaged the establishment of two banking institutions; a Slav commercial and industrial bank based in Prague, and a consortium of Russian banks with an agency in the same city. Doubts about the Czech proposals were also voiced by Fedorov, a former Minister of Finance in the Russian Government, who proposed the establishment of a special committee, which would attempt to reconcile the Czech banking proposals with Russian financial legislation and would also ascertain the views of the Russian authorities and of commercial and trading interests. This proposal was accepted by the Neo-Slav gathering and a committee was established, which included in its membership Fedorov and Krasovsky.[90]

The revised proposals for a Slav bank presented by the Czechs in 1909 also proved unacceptable to the Russian authorities and financial circles, neither of which were prepared to support the encroachment of foreign, though Slav, banking institutions into Russian financial affairs. Despite this, *Novoe vremya* was not opposed to the Slav bank in principle. In an editorial article on the subject, advocating greater economic co-operation amongst the Slav peoples and citing the successful example of the German *Zollverein*, it stressed that 'only economic mortar can unite the Slavs so firmly that they will be able to resist the German *Drang nach Osten*'.[91] This view, however, was not widely shared. Particularly in Moscow, as Kramář later explained, where, as a result of an economic recession, 'the atmosphere was very subdued', the industrialists and businessmen regarded the Neo-Slav movement as 'dangerous, fearing a conflict with Germany, and consequently adopted a negative attitude towards both the Slav bank and the exhibition'.[92] The Russian Ministry of Finance proposed, as an alternative to the Czech financial plans, that an already existing

---

[90] *Novoe vremya*, 14 (27) May 1909; *Čas*, 3 October 1909 (B. Pavlů, 'Slovanská banka').   [91] *Novoe vremya*, 11 (24) May 1909.
[92] Kramář, 'Po petrohradských konferencích', pp. 577–8. Kramář continued: 'Nevertheless, they were unable to resist the magic of the declared aims of the Neo-Slav movement, and during consultations with us resolutely favoured the suggestion that the impending Russian exhibition...should also be all-Slavonic [in character].'

Russian bank be renamed the Slav Bank, and instructed to perform some of the tasks required of the originally projected institution. This suggestion was regarded by the Czechs as being totally unsatisfactory and was, consequently, rejected.[93] The general Russian disinterest in the Czech inspired proposals for the formation of a Slav bank appears to have dissipated much of the enthusiasm for the idea. The efforts by the special committee, founded on the suggestion of Fedorov during the Neo-Slav talks of 1909 to prepare the ground in Russia for the foundation of such a bank, met with little success. Giving evidence at Kramář's trial, Preiss expressed the opinion that the Slav bank project died a lingering death at the St Petersburg meetings. The conversations had, he claimed, been inconclusive, and even the basic decision about where to situate the proposed bank, whether in St Petersburg, Moscow or Prague, had not been taken.[94]

The other project enthusiastically promoted by the Czech Neo-Slavs – the Slav exhibition – received rather less attention during the talks. The detailed proposals drawn up by the Czechs envisaged a large scale exhibition to be held either in St Petersburg or Moscow between 1913 and 1915. The exhibition was to be divided into eleven sections, each concerned with one of the following areas; fine arts, ethnography, literature, military and naval matters, industry, agriculture, social organisation, cultural aspirations, history and archaeology, engineering and architecture, and finance and trade. The entire venture was to be financed by the states, regions and municipalities participating in the exhibition.[95] Although very little information about the discussions emerged at the time, it was subsequently revealed by Preiss that during the talks held in connection with the Neo-Slav Executive Committee meeting with the Russian authorities, Moscow was selected as the site for the exhibition and the Russian government stated its willingness to make a substantial financial contribution to the project.[96] Despite this, however, it appears that no definite decisions concerning the proposed Slav exhibition were taken. The reasons for this inaction, as indicated by Kramář in connection

[93] *Proces dra. Kramáře*, III, part 1, p. 78.
[94] *Ibid.*
[95] *Proekt programy obscheslavyanskoi vystavki v Rossii* (Prague 1909). The pamphlet was prepared by Kramář and Preiss. See also *Rech'*, 15 (28) May, 1909.
[96] Preiss, 'Anketa o slovanské výstavě', p. 1.

with the proposed Slav bank, were the business recession and the fear of foreign competition.[97]

In common with most other Neo-Slav assemblies, the St Petersburg meetings in the spring of 1909 produced few concrete results. In the words of one Russian observer, the meetings passed 'with a gale of words and an endless torrent of speeches and toasts'.[98] The orators portrayed the optimism customary on these occasions. In one of the multitudinous speeches the President of the Duma, Khomyakov, referred to the figurative complaint made earlier by Kramář, that the young blossom of Neo-Slavism had been beset by the frost of recent political developments. The view expressed did not cause Khomyakov concern. He commented: 'The spring is indeed cold, but an experienced person does not despair. He knows that the loss of a few flowers will not destroy the tree, for sometimes he himself picks off the flowers in order to promote root formation and to help the tree gain strength. The fruit will develop in time.'[99] The optimism expressed in the horticultural analogy by the President of the Duma was, however, belied by reality. In another speech the same speaker approached rather closer to the truth when he observed that the Slavs had progressed from quarrelling to arguing and, very likely, would eventually reach agreement and achieve unity.[100] Leaving aside the expressed hope for the future, the achievement attained so far, which the speaker indicated, was very modest indeed. The one definite decision taken at the Neo-Slav meetings, on the suggestion of the Bulgarian delegation, was to hold a second Neo-Slav Congress the following year in the Bulgarian capital, Sofia.[101] The pious hope reported to have been expressed by the Russian delegates at the conclusion of the Prague gathering the previous year – 'May the Lord grant that the following Pan-Slav Congress takes place in Russia!'[102] – had gone unheard. Despite the fact that the intention of the leaders of the Neo-Slav movement had been to hold a further congress in Russia, conditions in that country evidently militated against this.

[97] *Ibid.*, p. 2.   [98] *Novoe vremya*, 25 May (7 June) 1909.
[99] *Ibid.*, 17 (30) May 1909.   [100] *Ibid.*, 16 (29) May 1909.
[101] *Ibid.*, 17 (30) May 1909; *Proces dra. Kramáře*, II, p. 88; S. S. Bobchev, 'Vůdce neoslavismu', *Dr. Karel Kramář. Život, dílo, práce*, ed. V. Sís, II, p. 201. Kramář stated that the suggestion to hold the next congress in Sofia came from G. Kalinkov, but Bobchev claimed that the idea was his.
[102] Bobrinsky, *Prazhsky sezd*, p. 42.

The slender achievements of the Neo-Slav gathering in St Petersburg prompted one neutral observer, Nicolson, to remark that: 'It seems to me that these reunions though they may bring scattered members of the race together to interchange ideas are not likely for the present to lead to any practical results. The whole proceedings appear to be somewhat academic and vague.' He added, as an afterthought: 'Still, the movement for a closer union among the Slav races may develop and though its initial stages cannot be said to have been particularly hopeful or brilliant, it is desirable to note and watch it.'[103]

Commenting on the St Petersburg conference, Beneš pointed out that: 'Both contentious questions [the Russo-Polish dispute and the aftermath of the annexation of Bosnia and Herzegovina] appeared in their full magnitude and the first internal crisis of the movement became evident.'[104] Although, for the moment, Neo-Slavism had survived, no solutions had been found to these pressing problems which were threatening the very existence of the movement. The proceedings of the Executive Committee meeting could by no means be described as having been successful, for even the myth of unanimity behind the final official statement had been exploded by the publication of the Serbian resolution. The private talks between the Czech representatives and leading Russian statesmen also yielded little of lasting value.

Summarising the outcome of the Neo-Slav conferences Nicolson reported that he had been informed, by an unnamed person who attended the meetings, that the Bulgarians were in 'exuberant and exultant spirits' while the Serbs and Poles were 'depressed'.[105] No indication was given of the attitude of the Czechs present. It appears, however, that Kramář arrived in St Petersburg with considerable apprehension, for he was fully aware of the formidable difficulties which confronted, not only him personally, but the entire Neo-Slav movement. The tone of the interview given to *Novoe vremya* on his arrival in the Russian capital was decidedly pessimistic and he spoke of 'many problems which required solution'.[106]

[103] PRO, FO, 371/731, Nicolson to Grey, 21133, St Petersburg, 28 May 1909.
[104] Beneš, *Úvahy o slovanství*, p. 163.
[105] PRO, FO, 371/731, Nicolson to Grey, 21133, St Petersburg, 28 May 1909.
[106] *Novoe vremya*, 12 (25) May 1909. See also *Rech'*, 15 (28) May 1909. A correspondent of that newspaper observed that Kramář 'no longer shines with his earlier cheerfulness; he has evidently tired and lost faith in the enterprise he initiated'.

The gravity of the situation was also evident from the fact that he gave serious consideration to resigning from the Executive Committee if his views were not adopted.[107] Nevertheless, he later commented bravely on the meetings of 1909 that: 'Somehow I succeeded in piecing together the Slav Committee and we accepted the invitation of the Bulgarians to hold the Second Congress in Sofia the following year. I confess that I left St Petersburg, and later Moscow, with a certain satisfaction that matters had not turned out worse.'[108] Admittedly, it appeared at the time that the instigator of Neo-Slavism had succeeded in preventing the complete disintegration of the movement. He recorded with satisfaction that 'Neo-Slavism has survived the serious crisis caused by the annexation of Bosnia and Herzegovina, and also has not been crushed by the anti-Polish policies of the Russian government', but added a warning about the 'heavy trials' and 'bitter disappointments' which would inevitably precede 'the realisation of the dreams of the previous July'.[109] An unfortunately apt choice of words with which to describe the ideals of the Prague Congress.

It was subsequently to become evident that the St Petersburg meetings had achieved nothing more than a temporary arrest in the decline of the movement. No significant concessions had been won from the Russian authorities on behalf of the Poles, and a reconciliation between the Czechs and the Serbs was as far removed as ever. As regards Kramář's professed intention of preventing the Russian political right wing from dominating the movement, future events were to show the extent of the failure to achieve this. Neo-Slavism had indeed, just as the Executive Committee, been 'pieced together', but as no solutions had been found to the many problems bedevilling the movement, the fragments could not remain together for long.

This point was noted at the time by *Rech'*, the organ of the Kadet Party, whose full participation in the Neo-Slav movement Kramář was most anxious to secure. Despite the fact that prominent members of the Kadet Party had participated in the Neo-Slav discussions, *Rech'* expressed strong reservations about the movement. It was particularly concerned about the dichotomy within

---

[107] *Proces dra. Kramáře*, II, pp. 12, 77. Kramář mentioned the possibility of resignation in a letter to his wife.
[108] Kramář, *Pět přednášek*, pp. 32–3.
[109] Kramář, 'Po petrohradských konferencích', p. 577.

the Russian branch of the movement, arguing that Russian Neo-Slavism contained 'opposing and mutually hostile tendencies'. Referring to the differences between conservatives and liberals, which had become evident during the meetings of the Russian Slavonic societies in April 1909 and again at the Neo-Slav talks themselves the following month, *Rech'* pointed out that unless this diversity of opinion was resolved, Neo-Slavism would achieve nothing.[110] The Kadets were evidently unhappy about the role played by the Russian right wing in the movement and intended to maintain their distance from it whilst this situation continued. This clearly indicated the lack of success Kramář had in attempting to attract Russian liberals into the movement in order to prevent it from falling increasingly under right wing domination.

Judged on a purely personal basis, Kramář's visit to St Petersburg and Moscow in 1909 was no more successful, and was in marked contrast with the triumphant journey made in the spring of the previous year. During the time spent in Russia, he failed to dispel the atmosphere of distrust with which he was regarded as a result of his failure to oppose the annexation of Bosnia and Herzegovina. His lack of action during the annexation crisis had alienated many Russians both inside and outside the Neo-Slav movement, and he observed that the climate of opinion in the Russian capital was hostile towards him.[111] The criticism of his policies, voiced mainly in *Novoe vremya*, continued during the St Petersburg meetings. One correspondent observed that those Slavs from the Habsburg Empire who had supported the annexation in the Reichsrat were 'somewhat uncomfortable' when speaking of Slav unity.[112] In another article it was claimed that for Kramář the events of the last year resulted in 'the ruin of all his policies'.[113] Later, during the summer of 1909 *Novoe vremya* also published a series of five articles by Kulakovsky entitled 'The Slav Congresses and the Polish Question' in which Kramář was severely castigated for his interference in Russo-Polish relations and for

[110] *Rech'*, 15 (28) May, 19 May (1 June) 1909.
[111] Kramář, *Pět přednášek*, p. 32. Personal relations between the Czech leader and some other participants in the Neo-Slav gathering, the Serbs in particular, were also strained. At a public meeting in Moscow, following the actual Neo-Slav talks, Kramář had a violent argument with the Serb Koshutich, who attacked the Czech leader on his record during the annexation crisis. On the return journey from Russia, Kramář also had a heated argument with another Serb, Kumanudi. *Proces dra. Kramáře*, II, p. 85; III, part 1, p. 78.
[112] *Novoe vremya*, 25 May (7 June) 1909.   [113] *Ibid.*, 15 (28) May 1909.

countenancing the annexation of Bosnia and Herzegovina. In contrast, Klofáč, a more radical nationalist and less questioning Russophil than Kramář, was praised by the author for his opposition to the annexation and, in addition, for supporting the Serbian point of view during the Neo-Slav talks in St Petersburg.[114] At these meetings attempts had been made to remove Kramář from the leading position in the Neo-Slav movement. To the bitter disappointment of the instigator of Neo-Slavism, Vergun and his associates hailed Klofáč as a true Slav, implying that he was more suited to lead the movement than Kramář. This was not only due to the fact that Klofáč had appeared less acquiescent over the annexation, but also because he had been more outspoken during the visit to the Russian capital than his rival.[115]

Writing about the Neo-Slav consultations on his return to Prague Kramář, nevertheless, painted the following, characteristically optimistic, picture of the attitude adopted towards the movement in Russia.

The St Petersburg meetings provided clear and conclusive evidence that the new movement has rooted itself firmly, and that it is now impossible for anyone to stop it. It is particularly pleasing to see how Russian society, initially so cool and indifferent towards any Slav initiative, is now beginning to recognise that Slavdom can no longer be ignored and that a stand, either for or against, has to be taken. With the exception of the reactionary circles which are, naturally, aware of the fact that Neo-Slavism entails the revival of Russia, a new Russia in which there will be no trace of the old absolutism or of the senseless and futile oppression of the Poles, everyone else is adopting a friendly attitude towards Slavdom. [116]

The reality was, however, very different. Despite the optimistic public assessment of the situation in Russia, the St Petersburg visit, in the spring of 1909, left Kramář a bitterly disillusioned man.

[114] *Ibid.*, 23 July (5 August), 25 July (7 August), 14 (27), 17 (30) August, 21 August (3 September) 1909 (P.A. Kulakovsky, 'Slavyanskie sezdy i polsky vopros', I–v).
[115] Šantrůček, *Václac Klofáč*, pp. 121–2; *Obžalovací spis proti V. Klofáčovi*, p. 17. Kramář complained in a letter to his wife that even the Prime Minister, P. A. Stolypin, insisted on meeting Klofáč. Scheiner, the Czech Sokol leader, was omitted from the list of persons invited to attend a private function at the residence of A. A. Stolypin, the brother of the Prime Minister, in order that Klofáč could attend. *Proces dra. Kramáře*, III, part 2, p. 131.
[116] Kramář, 'Po petrohradských konferencích', p. 577.

A letter sent from Russia, at the time, to his wife, betrayed his disappointment not only with the current proceedings but with the entire Neo-Slav movement. He wrote: 'We had a great idea, but it was premature. Russia is not yet ready for it.'[117]

[117] H.H.St.A., *Polizei Direktion Wien*, Pr.Z. 21636K/54, 27 March 1916.

6

The 1910 Sofia Neo-Slav Congress

A further meeting of the Neo-Slav Executive Committee was called to St Petersburg early in 1910. In the months intervening between this and the previous session of the Committee several events had taken place which produced significant effects on the Neo-Slav movement. The influences exerted were both encouraging and discouraging, though the latter by far outweighed the former.

During the autumn of 1909, while Kramář was residing at his villa in the Crimea, he received a visit from Izvolsky. This was the first occasion on which the Czech leader and the Russian Minister of Foreign Affairs had met since the international crisis precipitated by the Austro-Hungarian annexation of Bosnia and Herzegovina. Izvolsky had taken objection to Kramář's assertion, made in an interview with a correspondent of *Novoe vremya* earlier that year, that he, Izvolsky, had not adhered to the agreement reached with his Austro-Hungarian counterpart at the Buchlau meeting of 1908. The Russian Foreign Minister took the opportunity of refuting this accusation and gave Kramář his account of the Buchlau proceedings, which differed significantly from Count Aehrenthal's version. During the course of the discussion Izvolsky succeded in convincing the Czech leader that it was Aehrenthal who had failed to keep his word. He maintained that the Austro-Hungarian Minister of Foreign Affairs, contrary to what had been agreed, failed to give the Russian Foreign Ministry prior warning of the annexation and, in addition, refused to place the issue of Bosnia and Herzegovina before a congress of the European powers as arranged. Izvolsky claimed that, during the Buchlau meeting, discussion about the proposed European congress reached such an advanced stage that even the venue was considered. In addition to the problem of the Balkan provinces occupied by Austria–Hungary under the Treaty of Berlin the congress was also to be concerned with the question of obtaining the right of free passage for Russian warships through the Straits

of Constantinople and with making arrangements for granting
Serbia access to the sea.[1] The proposed European congress never
materialised. Izvolsky, angered by what he alleged was Aehrenthal's
duplicity, summed up his feelings about his Austro-Hungarian
counterpart in the words: 'Although the Emperor may make
Aehrenthal a Count, he will never make him a gentleman.'[2]
Izvolsky's revelations had a profound effect on Kramář. He
accepted the Russian Minister's account of the Buchlau meeting
without question, and indicated his disapproval of Aehrenthal's
conduct by breaking off all personal contacts with him. Kramář
claimed that he did not so much as exchange a single word with the
Austro-Hungarian Foreign Minister up to his death in 1912.[3]
Regarding relations between Russia and Austria–Hungary, Kramář
came to believe that they had deteriorated beyond repair. At his
trial he stated that after the conversation with Izvolsky:

I saw that the abyss between the two leading statesmen could never be
bridged, and that the chasm dividing the two states was extremely deep.
My long term policy, directed consistently towards improving Austro-
Russian relations since I saw in this a guarantee of absolute freedom of
action for our [i.e. Austro-Hungarian] foreign policy, together with a
means of preventing Germany from ever exercising any influence on
our internal affairs, was, for the foreseeable future, unless the unexpected
were to occur, destroyed.[4]

Despite this gloomy prognostication, the climate of relations
between Russia and Austria–Hungary improved slightly during
the early months of 1910, when exploratory negotiations, concerned
largely with Balkan problems, took place between the two governments. Little progress was made, however, and although normal
diplomatic relations between Vienna and St Petersburg were
restored, the more cordial atmosphere proved to be of a short

---

[1] Kramář, *Na obranu*, p. 26; Kramář, *Pět přednášek*, p. 33; *Proces dra. Kramáře*
II, p. 114. A concise account of the Buchlau proceedings, by Izvolsky himself
is contained in *British Documents*, v, pp. 382–4, no. 292, 'Memorandum
communicated by M. Izvolsky to Sir F. Bertie', enclosed in Bertie to Grey,
Paris, 4 October 1908. This approximately coincides with the version given
to Kramář, though it is less specific on certain issues. No mention is made, for
instance, of a discussion concerning the venue for a congress of European
powers.
[2] Kramář, *Na obranu*, p. 26; Kramář, *Pět přednášek*, p. 34.
[3] Kramář, *Na obranu*, p. 26; Kramář, *Pět přednášek*, p. 34.
[4] *Proces dra. Kramáře*, II, p. 115.

duration.[5] Kramář and his Neo-Slav associates obviously welcomed this development and he made a statement to that effect.[6] The Neo-Slavs fully realised that their movement was unlikely to achieve its economic and other aims while tension remained high between Russia and Austria–Hungary. Indeed, the very survival of the movement was wholly dependent on the maintenance of friendly relations between the two powers. This was clearly indicated by the fact that the deterioration of relations between the Habsburg Empire and Russia, which followed the annexation of Bosnia and Herzegovina, marked the end of the Austro-Hungarian government's benevolent attitude towards the Neo-Slavs. In June 1909 Aehrenthal informed Count Berchtold, the Austro-Hungarian ambassador in St Petersburg, that 'stricter control' would have to be exercised over the contacts between Czech and Russian politicians.[7] A campaign, critical of the Neo-Slav movement, was launched simultaneously in the semi-official Vienna press.[8]

It appears that, immediately following the St Peterburg Neo-Slav meetings of May 1909, Kramář had abandoned hope of Russia and Austria–Hungary ever reconciling their differences. In a speech in the Reichsrat, made shortly after his return to Vienna, he declared that it now appeared that the Slavs of the Habsburg Empire had no part to play in determining the foreign policy of their state, which was controlled by Germany. He therefor concluded that it was a 'naivety' to think that a *rapprochement* with Russia was still possible.[9] However, the slight improvement in relations between Russia and Austria–Hungary, temporary though it proved to be, evidently exerted an encouraging influence on Kramář and his associates. His energetic participation at the 1910 St Petersburg Neo-Slav meetings certainly did not appear to be the action of a person who had abandoned all hope of achieving his objectives.

The early part of 1910 brought a further definite gain for the Czechs. In the spring of that year the long awaited Russian

[5] A. F. Pribram, *Austrian Foreign Policy, 1908–1918* (London, 1923), p. 33.
[6] *The Times*, 10 February 1910.
[7] *Österreich-Ungarns Aussenpolitik von der bosnischen Krise bis zum Kriegsausbruch 1914: Diplomatische Aktenstüke des Österreichisch-Ungarischen Ministeriums des Äussern*, ed. L. Bittner and H. Uebersberger (8 vols., Vienna, 1930), II, pp. 360–1, no. 1644, message to St Petersburg, Vienna, 10 June 1909.   [8] *Neue Freie Presse*, 2, 4, 11, 16 July 1909.
[9] *Stenographische Protokolle des Hauses der Abgeordneten, XIX. Session* (Vienna, 1909), I, pp. 1208–15.

consulate was opened in Prague.[10] The Czechs had been cam-
paigning for a Russian consulate in the Bohemian capital for some
considerable time, largely because they believed that, in addition
to acting as a moral support, Russian representation would be of
great advantage in furthering commercial relations between Russia
and the Czech lands. Previously, opposition to the frequently repeated Czech request came not only from Vienna, as might have
been expected, but also from the Russian side. The Russian
government's reluctance to open consular offices in Prague had
been due, partially, to a lack of interest but principally to the fear
of antagonising the Austrian authorities, who were likely to regard
the existence of the consulate as stimulating the growth of Czech
Russophil tendencies.[11]

Although the opening of a Russian consulate in the Czech
capital was not part of the official Neo-Slav programme, the Czech
leaders of the movement had played an important role in achieving
this aim. Kramář had raised this issue in discussions with Russian
government representatives during his visit to St Petersburg in
1908,[12] and it appears that this met with a favourable response
from the Russians. The international crisis over the annexation of
Bosnia and Herzegovina delayed the implementation of the project, and it was not until the Neo-Slav Executive Committee
meeting in St Petersburg in 1909 that it became known that plans
for opening a Russian consulate in Prague were in an advanced
stage and that a consul had been selected – Prince G. N. Trubetskoy. The choice of the young liberal aristocrat, known for his
sympathetic attitude towards the Slavs in the Habsburg Empire
did not, however, meet with the approval of the Austro-Hungarian
authorities. The Russian government gave way and selected instead for the Prague post an unknown and uncontroversial member
of the Russian consular service, V. G. Zhukovsky.[13]

Much less encouraging, but of far greater significance for the
future of the Neo-Slav movement, was the continuing deterioration of Russo-Polish relations. Shortly after the conclusion of the

[10] W. Leppmann, 'Ruský konsulát v Praze. Kapitola k politice v Čechách před
světovou válkou', *Naše revoluce*, XIII (1937), p. 6.
[11] *Ibid.*, pp. 3–4; Consulates of the other leading powers, Britain, France,
Germany, and the United States, had been in existence in Prague for some years.
[12] H.H.St.A., PA, XL 219, *Panslav Bewegung* 2, Berchtold to Aehrenthal,
27B, St Petersburg, 2 June/20 May 1908; *Novoe vremya*, 17 (30) May 1908.
[13] Leppmann, 'Ruský konsulát v Praze', pp. 6–8.

Neo-Slav meetings in the spring of 1909 the British ambassador in St Petersburg was informed, by an unnamed Russian Pole, that few practical results were expected from the discussions. Nicolson reported that his visitor: 'Deeply regretted the policy of the Russian government towards their Polish subjects and attributed it in part to the strong nationalist feeling which of late had made itself so conspicuous in Russia and partly, if not chiefly, to pressure from Berlin.' The ambassador's Polish informant, 'did not regard the future of his compatriots in Russia with any optimism'.[14] This unhappy forecast was soon to be realised.

In the spring of 1909 the Russian government made public its plans for the creation of a new Russian province of Kholm, incorporating parts of Russian Poland. Although the Kholm province did not come into being until 1912, the plan served as a clear indication that the attitude of the Russian government towards the Poles had not altered for the better. The proposal for the creation of the Kholm province greatly disturbed all sections of the Polish nation, and was regarded by some as being tantamount to the fourth division of Poland.[15] A further proposed Russian measure which added to Polish disquiet was the plan to introduce zemstvo institutions (a form of representative local government) into the western provinces of the Russian Empire. This measure, though appearing on the surface to be a democratic reform, was devised by P. A. Stolypin in order to reduce the influence of the Polish and other non-Russian elements in the population of the areas concerned. The electoral system was so constructed as to favour those sections of the population which were largely of Russian origin, at the expense of the predominantly Polish landowners. This scheme, after provoking a constitutional crisis in Russia, eventually came into force in 1911.[16]

[14] PRO, FO, 371/728, Nicolson to Grey, 21140, St Petersburg, 30 May 1909.
[15] Reddaway and others eds., *The Cambridge History of Poland*, II, pp. 405–6; A. Černý, 'Otázka Cholmská', *Slovanský přehled*, XIV (1912), pp. 153–8, 213–21. A. Černý was strongly critical of the Russian action, and concluded the article by stating that, in his view, 'the detachment of the Kholm area, now being carried out, is a coercive act [prompted] by Russian reactionary forces'. Kramář's critical attitude to the scheme was expressed in an article in *Národní listy*, 18 February 1910 ('Zasedání slovanského výkonného výboru v Petrohradě').
[16] For details see G. A. Hosking, *The Russian Constitutional Experiment: Government and Duma, 1907–1914* (Cambridge, 1973), pp. 116–46, and Chmielewski, *The Polish Question*, pp. 82–110.

Most Poles reacted indignantly to the measures proposed by the Russian authorities. From the Neo-Slav point of view the attitude adopted by Dmowski and his allies, who were associated with the movement, was of the greatest significance. Dmowski, though no longer the leader of the Polish deputies in the Duma, but nevertheless retaining a prominent position on the Polish political scene, was extremely dissatisfied with conditions in Russian Poland. During a conversation with the British ambassador in St Petersburg the Polish leader 'took a gloomy view of Polish prospects in Russia and said that during his life-time the situation of his compatriots had never been so disheartening'. He expressed concern that the Russian government's 'apparent intention to suppress the cultural and educational development of the Poles except on strictly Russian lines would greatly lower the standard of Polish civilisation'. Dmowski failed to understand why the Russian authorities continued their oppression of the Polish nation, a policy which was producing considerable hostility against Russia within the Empire's vulnerable western borders.[17]

The growing Polish dissatisfaction with their Russian rulers was accompanied by an increasing disillusionment with the Neo-Slav movement. Dmowski and his associates had, initially, been attracted to the movement largely because they believed it would contribute towards improving conditions in Russian Poland. They calculated that the combined pressure exerted by the small Slav nations on the Russian authorities might be sufficient to induce a change in the Russian attitude towards the Poles. During the course of 1909 it became increasingly evident that Neo-Slavism had failed to achieve this aim and, in consequence, the interest of the Russian Poles in the movement declined. The Austrian Poles had discontinued their support of the Neo-Slav movement earlier, before the commencement of the Executive Committee meeting in May 1909.

The dissatisfaction of the Russian Poles with the Neo-Slav movement reached such an extent that, early in 1910, they made known their intention of boycotting the Neo-Slav Congress, due to take place in Sofia in the summer of that year. Dmowski explained to the British ambassador, during the above-mentioned conversation, that: 'In view of the recent manifestation by leading

---

[17] PRO, FO, 371/937, Nicolson to Grey, 6906, St Petersburg, 15 February 1910.

Russians in the Duma against the Poles it would be impossible for the latter to take part in the forthcoming Neo-Slav Congress in Sophia.'[18] This was a reference to an acrimonious debate which had taken place in the Duma on the very eve of the Neo-Slav meetings and in the presence of Kramář, concerning the transformation of a church in the Kholm area from the Roman Catholic to the Orthodox faith. During the course of this debate Count Bobrinsky was particularly hostile to the Poles and an angry exchange took place between him and another prominent member of the Neo-Slav movement, the Pole Dymsza.[19]

Nicolson continued the report of his conversation with Dmowski as follows:

It was clear that the Russian Neo-Slavs were Russian nationalists first and Neo-Slavs on occasions only. The two characters were incompatible. The attitude of the Russian Government towards their Polish subjects was hampering the development of the Neo-Slav movement towards a combination of all Slavs, Czechs, Poles, and so forth. M. Kramarz, the Czech leader, felt deeply the difficulties which, unconsciously perhaps, the Russian Government were raising against a union between Czechs and Poles in the Austro-Hungarian Monarchy. The Austrian Poles, with the treatment of their compatriots by Germany and Russia before them, were perforce led to be supporters of the Austrian Government, and could not risk their position by uniting with the Czechs against the German influences. If Russia were but to modify her policy towards her Polish subjects, the Poles both in Austria and Germany would be encouraged to coalesce with their Slav brethren. As matters stood the Poles were discouraged, and Russia was allowing a most favourable opportunity to slip by of putting herself at the head of a great Slav combination.[20]

It was against this background, of what had amounted to a threatened withdrawal of the Russian Poles from the movement, that the Neo-Slav Executive Committee met, for the second time since its creation, in St Petersburg, between 10 February (29

[18] *Ibid.*

[19] *Gosudarstvennaya duma, stenograficheskie otchety, tretiy sozyv, sessiya III* (St Petersburg, 1910), part II, cols. 434–43; *Novoe vremya*, 29 January (11 February) 1910. Kramář later claimed that he had persuaded Bobrinsky, an implacable enemy of the Poles, to make a conciliatory speech in the Duma. The Russian, however, did not comply, and in the heat of the debate delivered instead an aggressive address. Kramář, *Na obranu*, p. 27.

[20] PRO, FO, 371/978, Nicolson to Grey, 6906, St Petersburg, 15 February 1910.

January) and 15 (2) February 1910.[21] In contrast with the meetings held in the Russian capital the previous year, the gathering of 1910 was a subdued affair. The deliberations were held in private and attendance was limited to members of the Neo-Slav Executive Committee, though even that was not fully represented. Also in sharp contrast with the meetings of the previous spring, the discussions were not accompanied by extravagant banquets and speeches. Only one evening was devoted to the public presentation of papers on the contemporary conditions of the Western and Southern Slavs, given, respectively, by Kramář and the Bulgarian representatives.[22] The general lack of enthusiasm shown by the Neo-Slavs in St Petersburg did not escape the attention of File-vich who, writing in *Novoe vremya* after the events, rather optimistically ascribed this to the fact that 'Slav gatherings have become everyday affairs and Slav questions have become closely and indissolubly interwoven in the issues not only of our foreign policy, but also of our internal life'.[23] Elsewhere, however, *Novoe vremya* was much less sanguine about the outlook for the Neo-Slav movement and referred to 'submerged rocks' which would have to be avoided before the projected Sofia Congress could become a reality.[24] The hazards confronting the Neo-Slavs, far from being beneath the surface, were, in fact, clearly evident to anyone. Although, ostensibly, the chief object of the discussions was the preparation of a programme for the forthcoming Congress, the debate centred round the issue of whether the Congress should, in fact, take place. At the root of the problem, of course, lay the vexed question of Russo-Polish relations, which dominated the proceedings and a considerable amount of time was devoted to the discussion of the proposal to form the new Russian province of Kholm and the plan to introduce zemstvos in the western provinces of the Russian Empire.[25]

Although the strained state of Russo-Polish relations had cast doubts on the participation of the Russian Poles in the Neo-Slav talks, their representatives did take part in the discussions.

---

[21] *Novoe vremya*, 29 January (11 February) – 3 (16) February 1910; *Rech'*, 31 January (13 February), 4 (17) February, 1910; *Národní listy*, 18 February 1910.
[22] *Novoe vremya*, 31 January (13 February) 1910.
[23] *Ibid.*, 3 (16) February 1910.   [24] *Ibid.*, 27 January (9 February) 1910.
[25] *Národní listy*, 18 February 1910 (Kramář, 'Zasedání slovanského výkonného výboru').

Dmowski, Straszewicz and Olizar were, in fact, the only Poles present, for as had been the case at the previous meeting of the Neo-Slav Executive Committee, the Austrian Poles declined to attend. The Russian Neo-Slavs were represented by Krasovsky, Lvov, Maklakov, Khomyakov and Bobrinsky. In contrast with the strong Russian attendance, only one Czech was present at the meetings, Kramář, the chairman of the Executive Committee. The only other Slav nationality represented at the discussions were the Bulgarians, who sent two representatives, A. Lyudskanov and G. Kalinkov. Bobchev, the most prominent figure in the Bulgarian Neo-Slav movement, was unable to attend due to illness.[26]

Predictably, it was the Bulgarian representatives at the talks who spoke out most strongly against any attempts to delay the projected Sofia Congress, arguing that the decision had already been taken at the 1909 Executive Committee meeting and that preparations for the gathering in the Bulgarian capital were already under way. A Polish request for the postponement of the Congress, until Russo-Polish relations improved sufficiently to permit the Poles to attend, was rejected at the insistence of the Bulgarians, despite the fact that Kramář himself favoured such a delay.[27] The Neo-Slav Executive Committee decided to proceed as planned with the arrangements for the Second Congress due to be held in Sofia later that year, and a programme was duly drafted.[28]

In a statement issued at the conclusion of the Neo-Slav talks, by a majority of the participants, it was agreed that, although the Executive Committee 'fully recognised the importance of the reasons impelling the Poles to insist on a postponement of the Congress', it would be 'impossible' to do so. This was due to the fact that consideration had to be given to 'the effects which a

[26] *Novoe vremya*, 27 January (9 February), 29 January (11 February), 3 (16) February 1910.

[27] *Ibid.*, 3 (16) February 1910; *Národní listy*, 18 February, 13 July 1910; S. S. Bobchev, 'Slavyanskiyat săbor v Sofiya', *Bălgarska sbirka*, XVII (1910), pp. 141–2.

[28] The topics to be discussed at the Sofia Congress were: the contemporary conditions of the South Slav lands, cultural co-operation, a report on the activities of the Association of Slav Journalists, economic co-operation (including the questions of a Slav bank and a Slav exhibition), the foundation of a union of Slav tourist organisations, and general organisational work on Slav co-operation. *Vtori podgotovitelen Slavyansky săbor v Sofiya* (Sofia, 1911; hereafter cited as *Slavyanski săbor v Sofiya*), p. 4; H.H.St.A., PA, XL 219, *Panslav Bewegung* 5, Mittag to Aehrenthal, 50B, Sofia, 2 July 1910; PRO, FO, 371/834, Findlay to Grey, 24892, Sofia, 6 July 1910.

postponement of the Congress would have amongst the Slav peoples of the Balkan peninsula'.[29] The Polish representatives, who were described as regarding the Congress to be 'inopportune' in the present circumstances, dissented from the majority report and issued a statement of their own. In this, they argued that the ideals of the Prague Congress had not been truly realised, and the conditions of the Polish people in the Russian Empire allowed to deteriorate with the connivance of persons who professed to adhere to the principles of Neo-Slavism. In view of these developments the Poles concluded that 'at the present time...we do not consider it possible to reach a decision concerning our participation at the forthcoming congresses'.[30]

Despite the strenuous efforts made at the St Petersburg meetings to induce the Poles to attend the projected Sofia Congress, they refused to give a definite affirmative undertaking. Kramář was very active, personally, in attempting to mediate between the Russians and the Poles on the Neo-Slav Executive Committee, and appealed for moderation from both sides.[31] His endeavour did not meet with total failure and agreement was reached that one final attempt would be made to heal the breach between the Russians and the Poles. On his initiative, a small Russo-Polish Commission was established with the purpose of solving, 'in the spirit of the Prague resolutions', the various problems which were responsible for aggravating relations between the two Slav nations.[32] It was hoped that the results of the Commission's work would enable the Poles to be present at the coming Congress.

The problems of the Russian Poles, important though they were to the Neo-Slav movement, were now allowed to dominate the

[29] *Novoe vremya*, 3 (16) February 1910; *Národní listy*, 18 February 1910. The majority report was signed by K. Kramář, M. V. Krasovsky, N. N. Lvov, V. A. Maklakov, N. A. Khomyakov, A. Lyudskanov and G. Kalinkov. V. A. Bobrinsky had left St Petersburg during the meetings, and did not participate in their final stages.

[30] *Novoe vremya*, 3 (16) February 1910; *Národní listy*, 18 February 1910. This minority report was signed by R. Dmowski, L. Straszewicz and J. Olizar.

[31] *Proces dra. Kramáře*, II, p. 98.

[32] *Národní listy*, 18 February 1910 (Kramář, 'Zasedání slovanského výkonného výboru'); *Novoe vremya*, 3 (16) Feburary 1910; *Proces dra. Kramáře*, IV, part I, pp. 56–7. This Commission consisted of M. V. Krasovsky, V. A. Bobrinsky, N. N. Lvov, V. A. Maklakov, and N. A. Khomyakov on the Russian side, and the Poles, R. Dmowski, L. Straszewicz, L. Dymsza, J. Olizar, and J. Swieżyński. The Russian, V. M. Volodimirov was elected as secretary.

Executive Committee meetings. The Balkan situation was examined in detail,[33] and considerable time was also devoted to the discussion of the recurrent issue of the creation of a Slav bank. During the interval since the previous Neo-Slav deliberations, further developments had taken place concerning the proposed bank. In the autumn of 1909, *Novoe vremya* announced that the Slav bank was soon to become a reality. M. V. Kozarovitsky, whose proposal for a Russo-Slavonic Chamber of Commerce had been rejected by the Neo-Slavs earlier in the year,[34] was reported to have reached an agreement with the Russian Minister of Finance, Kokovtsov, regarding the establishment of a Slav bank. Kozarovitsky's proposal, as outlined in *Novoe vremya*, was intended not only to promote commerce between the Slav nations, but also to assist them in decreasing their dependence on German banking institutions. It was also envisaged that the Slav bank would act as a barrier to German and Austro-Hungarian economic penetration of the Balkans and the Near East, areas considered as being of vital importance to Slav interest. Such a bank, reported the correspondent of *Novoe vremya*, would have to be located in Russia and not in Austria–Hungary, a country considered by Russian financial circles to be an 'enemy of the Slavs'.[35]

These proposals caused considerable consternation in Czech business circles, for it was evident that Kozarovitsky's plan would, inevitably, have damaging consequences on Czech industry and commerce.[36] The organ of the Czech Realist Party, *Čas*, commented, with alarm, that:

The Russians are naturally turning their attention to the German [economic] yoke in the Balkans, making no distinction for Austria, because Austrian policy in that area is identical with Germanism. They

---

[33] *Proces dra. Kramáře*, IV, part 1, p. 57.
[34] Kozarovitsky had put forward this scheme during the Neo-Slav discussion in St Petersburg in May 1909. The plan was rejected by the Executive Committee of the movement as the proposer's character was considered to be 'unreliable'. *Čas*, 3 October 1909 (B. Pavlů, 'Slovanská banka'). Nevertheless, a Russo-Slavonic Chamber of Commerce did come into existence in 1909, though it appears to have had no direct connections with the Neo-Slav movement. *Novoe vremya*, 31 August (13 September) 1909.
[35] *Novoe vremya*, 13 (26) September 1909.
[36] Herman, in 'Novoslovanství a česká buržoasie', p. 298, cites an unsigned letter in the Archive of the Czech National Council addressed to V. Černý, in which it is stressed that 'Kozarovitsky's absolutely unacceptable plan' for a Slav bank must be prevented from becoming a reality.

are, however, forgetting that Austrian industry includes also Czech industry, and furthermore, that the greatest part of Austrian industry is based in Bohemia. And, despite the participation of Bohemian Germans in the industrial production of the goods exported to the Balkans from the Czech lands, we Czechs are nevertheless involved far more deeply, either as factory owners and businessmen or as workers. Neo-Slavism, *Čas* demanded, must not lend its name to what was, for the Czechs, a potentially harmful project.[37]

The indignant words of the Czech Realist newspaper prompted a reply from the Neo-Slavs. Pavlů, on behalf of the movement, disassociated Neo-Slavism from the banking proposals outlined by Kozarovitsky stressing that this project had no connection whatsoever with the Neo-Slav plan for the creation of a Slav bank. In addition, Pavlů gave voice to the disillusionment with the Russian government felt amongst the Czech Neo-Slavs. He wrote:

The Neo-Slavs were fully aware of all the difficulties which would be placed in their path, by both the relatively underdeveloped state of Slav economic activity and the well known disinclination of the Russian government to support acts of Slav self-help. It is precisely this un-willingness which is further proof of the fact that the Neo-Slav movement cannot be equated with tendencies to be of service to the Russian government.[38]

The Czechs, represented by Kramář, persisted in their opposition to Kozarovitsky's plan at the 1910 St Petersburg meetings where, largely thanks to the efforts of Fedorov who had been active in Russia preparing the ground on their behalf, they succeeded in gaining some support for their own banking schemes. Present at the meeting of the Executive Committee on the proposed Slav bank were the Russian Minister of Finance, Kokovtsov; the President of the Duma, Khomyakov; and representatives of several Russian banks. A unanimous decision was taken in favour of establishing a Slav bank during the current year. This agreement appears to have been made in principle only, for no specific details of the scheme were announced. The question of the participation of Czech capital in the venture was left until Preiss visited St Petersburg for detailed negotiations, at some future date.[39]

During the course of the discussions several Russian objections to the Slav bank proposal came to light. The Russian Minister of

[37] *Čas*, 2 October 1909.   [38] *Čas*, 3 October 1909 (Pavlů 'Slovanská banka').
[39] *Novoe vremya*, 30 January (12 February), 31 January (13 February) 1910; *Národní listy*, 16 February 1910.

Finance, Kokovtsov, expressed the fear that the projected bank would result in diverting Russian funds outside the Russian Empire and, in addition, stated that the proposed initial capital of five million roubles was insufficient. In the opinion of *Národní listy*, however, it became obvious at these consultations that the real obstacle preventing the creation of a Slav bank was the fact 'that Russian banks had close ties with those in Berlin, which were exerting pressure on the Russians to ensure that the Slav bank project came to nothing'. The Young Czech Party newspaper reported optimistically that at the discussions it was, nevertheless, generally believed that Russian capital was now sufficiently strong to stand on its own and need no longer take its orders from Berlin. There was, therefore, in the view of the correspondent of *Národní listy* an excellent chance that a Slav bank would soon become a reality.[40] Czech financial circles were, however, less enthusiastic. At a subsequent meeting of the Slav Bank Subcommittee of the Czech National Council, held in Prague in May 1910, the latest banking proposals were rejected, despite Kramář's energetic support for the scheme.[41]

Although the developments concerning the Slav bank were regarded by some Czech Neo-Slavs as promising they were, nevertheless, far from overjoyed at the outcome of the Executive Committee discussions. Kramář described the meetings as 'unhappy', and stressed that 'a critical moment had arrived for the future of the Neo-Slav movement'.[42] The expectations of a brighter future for the Slav nations, expressed at the Prague Congress, remained unfulfilled, largely due to the continuing Russo-Polish dispute, which had, in the intervening period, deteriorated even

[40] *Národnílisty*, 16 February 1910.
[41] Archive of the Czech National Council, minutes of the meeting of the Slav Bank Subcommittee of the Slav Committee on 2 May 1910, cited in Herman, 'Novoslovanství a česká buržoasie', pp. 297–8. Preiss had by this time, presumably, abandoned hope of ever seeing the realisation of his proposal for a Slav bank. He was not present at the 1910 St Petersburg discussions, nor at the Slav Bank Subcommittee meeting in Prague. The *Živnostenská banka*, meanwhile, on the recommendation of Preiss, who was one of the directors, turned its attention towards obtaining direct access into the Russian financial system. For this purpose it established, early in 1911, the Warsaw Industrial Bank (*Warszawski Bank Przemysłowy*). Shortly afterwards, this bank opened branches in several towns in Russian Poland. J. Horejsek, 'Neúspěšný obchod Živnobanky v Polsku', *Slovanský přehled*, LVII (1971), pp. 139–40.
[42] *Národní listy*, 18 February 1910 (Kramář, 'Zasedání slovanského výkonného výboru').

further. And although Kramář himself fervently hoped that the results of the work carried out by the Russo-Polish Commission would enable the Poles to attend the Sofia Congress, he was aware that 'the hopes for a successful outcome of the conciliatory Commission were mixed with considerable pessimism'.[43] Kramář was not alone in his pessimism. Dmowski also expected little from the Russo-Polish Commission, and did not expect the Poles to attend the forthcoming Sofia Congress.[44]

Pessimism was also expressed in *Rech'*. A correspondent of that newspaper considered the Neo-Slav movement to have 'come abruptly to an end' with the withdrawal of the Poles. Responsibility for this was placed on the anti-Polish policies pursued by the Russian government and on the attitude of the Russian right wing, represented by persons such as Bobrinsky and Filevich, active within the Neo-Slav movement itself.[45]

Although it was premature to write off completely the Neo-Slav movement, the feeling of despondency concerning Russo-Polish relations was soon shown to have been fully justified. The Russo-Polish Commission, formed as a last desperate effort to reconcile the two Slav nations, and thus maintain the unity of the Neo-Slav movement, failed completely. The Commission met in private on six occasions during May, at which matters concerning education, religious freedom, and the proposed zemstvo legislation were discussed. The work of the Commission was suddenly halted, however, due to the withdrawal of two of its Russian members. Lvov ceased to participate because of ill health, and Bobrinsky departed following disagreements amongst the Russian participants.[46] The reason for Bobrinsky's withdrawal appears to be linked with his insistence that the Commission should be concerned with Russo-Polish relations not only inside the Russian Empire, but also outside the frontiers of Russia – in Galicia.[47] In a statement issued by

[43] *Ibid.*   [44] *Rech'*, 4 (17) February 1910.   [45] *Ibid.*
[46] *Novoe vremya*, 6 (19), 7 (20), 14 (27), May 1910; *Rech'*, 5 (18), 6 (19), 7 (20) 9 (22), 11 (24) May 1910; *Národní listy*, 31 May 1910. Bobrinsky's departure was precipitated by Lvov's reference to the proposed western provinces zemstvo legislation as a 'vile bill'.
[47] *Novoe vremya*, 6 (19) May 1910. When the Commission was originally formed during the Neo-Slav Executive Committee meetings early in 1910, its membership was to include four representatives from Galicia: the Russophil Ukrainians, V. Dudykevich and M. Glebovitsky; and the Poles, M. Zdziechowski and A. Doboszyński. *Ibid.*, 3 (16) February 1910. These persons, however, did not participate in the work of the Commission.

the reduced Commission following the departure of two of its Russian members it was explained that, although 'it was possible to establish certain principles which would guide the relations of the two nations wherever they came into contact', the Commission consisted entirely of representatives from the Russian Empire and, therefore, could concern itself in detail only with conditions inside Russia.[48]

But, whatever the reasons for the disintegration of the Commission, the outcome was clear-cut. No further meetings ever took place. The Polish side of the Commission explained the situation in a letter to Kramář, and concluded with the words:

Having failed for reasons beyond our control...to achieve the desired results in the Commission established by the Executive Committee and, furthermore, taking into consideration developments in conditions since the last sitting of the Committee, the conviction expressed by us at the February meetings has been confirmed. [As we then stated] the Pan-Slav Congress due to be held in Sofia in July will, if it takes place, not continue in the spirit of the Prague Congress, and will be unable to give the required emphasis to the principles of Neo-Slavism. The Poles, who only on the basis of these principles see any hope of true Slav unity, will consequently be unable to attend.[49]

The Russian Poles had, in effect, formally withdrawn from the Neo-Slav movement. This move was a serious blow to the hopes of the Czech Neo-Slavs who, throughout the existence of the movement, had given the highest priority to the question of Polish participation in it. In the view of the instigators of the movement, the greatest obstacle preventing an improvement in relations between the Slav nations, in particular between Russia and the Western Slavs, was the oppressive policy carried out by the Russian government in the Russian division of Poland. The antagonism between the Russian and Polish nations, engendered by the activities of the Russian authorities, also prevented the formation of a united Slav front within the Austro-Hungarian Empire. The achievement of a Russo-Polish understanding was,

---

[48] *Národní listy*, 31 May 1910. Bobrinsky subsequently criticised the statement issued after his departure by the Commission on the grounds that it gave the false impression that Galician issues were not discussed. He maintained that they had been included in the talks. *Novoe vremya*, 14 (27) May 1910.

[49] *Národní listy*, 1 June 1910. The signatories of the letter were: R. Dmowski, L. Straszewicz, L. Dymsza, J. Olizar, and J. Swieżyński.

therefore, regarded by the Neo-Slavs as being of primary importance. Consequently, if the movement was to have any future
whatsoever, it had to succeed in the self-imposed task of mediating
between the two estranged Slav nations. The departure of the
Poles served as an explicit indication that this aim was unlikely to
be realised. Kramář, who vigorously supported all attempts at
settling this grievous inter-Slav dispute, began to believe that the
situation had deteriorated almost beyond repair. His pessimism
was clearly expressed in the following comment, made during the
summer of 1910: '[Russo-Polish relations] are, at the present
time, desperate, perhaps worse than ever before, because of an
additional factor, which is making the situation even more hopeless
for the Poles. Previously, they hated the Russian government and
bureaucracy, but believed in the Russian people. Today, the Poles
are losing even this hope.'[50]

Kramář's dismay at the withdrawal of the Poles from the
Neo-Slav movement was not shared by the Russian right wing.
Bobrinsky virtually welcomed the Polish decision not to attend
the Sofia Congress by remarking that 'the absent are always in
the wrong'.[51] *Novoe vremya*, however, did express regret over the
Polish decision but remained convinced that the non-participation
of the Poles in the Sofia Congress 'would not have a harmful
effect' on the development of Slav unity.[52] In a later editorial
article, prompted by recent clashes between Poles and Russophil
Ukrainians in the Galician city of Lvov, it declared more resolutely
that 'Slav questions will have to be resolved without the Poles'.[53]

Despite the announced Polish boycott, preparations for the Sofia
Congress were continued, supported by the right wing of the
Russian Neo-Slav movement. The Bulgarian Neo-Slavs made a
strenuous effort to encourage attendance at the Congress. Bobchev,
the leader of the Bulgarian branch of the movement, undertook an
extensive tour of the Slav countries for this purpose.[54] These
efforts were rewarded by a considerable measure of success. During
the summer months of 1910, Sofia played host to a series of Slav
meetings and other events. The Neo-Slav Congress itself was
accompanied by gatherings of, amongst others, Slav journalists,

[50] *Ibid.*, 12 June 1910.   [51] *Slovanský přehled*, XII (1910), pp. 387–8.
[52] *Novoe vremya*, 31 May (13 June) 1910.   [53] *Ibid.*, 23 June (6 July) 1910.
[54] J. Polívka, 'Slovanský sjezd sofijský v červenci 1910', *Slovanský přehled*, XII
(1911), p. 22; Bobchev, 'Vůdce neoslavismu', pp. 201–2.

physicians, and apiarists, and by an exhibition of Russian books.[55] This exhibition, consisting of 50000 volumes published in the Russian Empire, demonstrated, in the words of the British diplomatic representative in Bulgaria, 'the intellectual hegemony of Russia'.[56] A large international Sokol gymnastic display, in which, from Bohemia alone, over seven hundered gymnasts took part, was also held in the Bulgarian capital. In addition to the large contingent of Bulgarian gymnasts, other participants came from Russia, Serbia, and Croatia. In total, over 4000 persons participated in the ceremonies.[57] The British representative in Sofia, comparing favourably the gymnastic display with the other Slav meetings, described the former as a 'real success', not on account of any important practical outcome, but because of the strong emotional impact produced by this harmonious mass meeting of Slav youth.[58]

Potentially more significant, though less spectacular, was another of the secondary meetings, the Congress of Slav Journalists. This gathering, termed the Ninth Congress of Slav Journalists and the First Congress of the Pan-Slav Union of Journalists, was held in the Bulgarian capital between 4 July (21 June) and 6 July (23 June) 1910.[59] Though not directly linked with the Neo-Slav movement, the journalistic association shared many of its aims and ideals. These aims were outlined by Hrubý, a member of the editorial board of *Národní listy*, as being to promote the organisation of Slav journalism, to guarantee the true and accurate reporting of news, and to encourage the growth of Slav reciprocity. The Slav journalists also claimed some credit for the formation of the Neo-Slav movement by having 'prepared the ground' for this during

[55] *Slavyanski sŭbor v Sofiya*, pp. 192–8; *Národní listy*, 4 July 1910. A Congress of Slav socialists followed, though this was in no way connected with the Neo-Slav movement. *Čas*, 29 July 1910.

[56] PRO, FO, 371/834, Findlay to Grey, 26733, Sofia, 19 July 1910. Findlay, pointing out that the cost of this and of a further exhibition of Russian household crafts 'must have been considerable [and] can hardly have been defrayed from private funds', suggested that the 'Russian Government had a considerable interest in the congress'.

[57] H.H.St.A., PA, xl 219, *Panslav Bewegung* 5, Mittag to Aehrenthal, 50D, Sofia, 2 July 1910, and 58B, Sofia, 12 July 1910; *Slavyanski sŭbor v Sofiya*, p. 193; *Národní listy*, 6 July 1910.

[58] PRO, FO, 371/834, Findlay to Grey, 26733, Sofia, 19 July 1910.

[59] For the programme of the Congress of Slav Journalists see H.H.St.A., PA, xl 219, *Panslav Bewegung* 5, Mittag to Aehrenthal, 50C, Sofia, 2 July 1910; and PRO, FO, 371/834, Findlay to Grey, 24892, Sofia, 6 July 1910.

the course of their previous meetings. The first gathering of Slav journalists, restricted to those from within the Austro-Hungarian Empire, had been held in Prague in 1898, during the celebrations of the centenary of the birth of Palacký. Further meetings were held the following year in Cracow; in Dubrovnik in 1901; in Ljubljana and Plzeň (Pilsen), respectively, during the succeeding two years; in Opatija in 1905; in Uherské Hradiště in 1906; and again in Ljubljana in 1908.[60] The Sofia Congress was the first to be attended by Slav journalists from outside the Dual Monarchy. Representatives of Slav journalists from Austria–Hungary were joined by delegates from Russia, Serbia, and Bulgaria.[61]

The issues debated at these meetings altered very little from year to year. Although various subjects such as the freedom of the press or Russo-Polish relations[62] were referred to at different times, the main preoccupation of the Slav journalists was with the proposed creation of a Slav news agency. The decision to establish such an agency had first been taken as early as 1898.[63] Five years later, a Czech delegate reported to the Congress of Journalists that no progress had been made in this direction due to the lack of interest amongst the other Slavs. Consequently, the Czechs proposed to establish their own press agency hoping that other Slav nations within Austria–Hungary would join later.[64] At the 1905 Congress, the assembled journalists were informed that the project was no nearer fruition; neither the Czech nor the Austro-Hungarian Slav news agencies had come into being. The chief reason for the failure was the lack of financial support. The sum of 13 000 crowns, which had been raised from Czech sources, was totally inadequate to finance the founding of the desired agency. Significantly, it was the increased interest in Russia, following the outbreak of the Russo-Japanese War, that gave an added stimulus to the attempts to establish the agency. As reports from Western sources were considered to lack objectivity, and those from Russia

[60] Hrubý, *Slovanská vzájemnost v časopisech*, pp. 1–5.
[61] PRO, FO, 371/834, Findlay to Grey, 24892, Sofia, 6 July 1910. Despite the resolution passed at the 1908 Prague Neo-Slav Congress in favour of widening the attendance at the Ljubljana meeting of Slav journalists (held later that year) to include representatives from all the Slav nations, no official delegates from outside Austria–Hungary were present in the Slovene capital. *Národní listy*, 7 September 1908.   [62] *Národní listy*, 3 June 1903, 15, 17 May 1905.
[63] Hrubý, *Slovanská vzájemnost v časopisech*, p. 3; *Národní listy*, 9 September 1908.   [64] *Národní listy*, 2 June 1903.

were both inadequate and belated, the embryonic Czech News Agency dispatched a representative to St Petersburg with the task of obtaining objective reports direct from the battlefield. However, due to the reaction following the assassination of the Russian Minister of the Interior, V. K. Pleve, in July 1904, these plans came to nothing.[65] At the 1908 Congress in Ljubljana, again, no progress was reported, lack of capital being the principal reason.[66] The Sofia Congress of Slav Journalists proved to be no exception, and the project once again came up for discussion. Despite all the previous deliberations on the subject, and despite the fact that a resolution had been passed at the Prague Neo-Slav Congress, two years previously, in favour of creating a Slav news agency, this had not yet become a reality. Financial support was still not forthcoming and, in addition, the Austro-Hungarian authorities did not regard the project with great favour.[67] The journalists' meeting in Sofia once again unanimously resolved to create a Slav news agency based in Vienna which, according to the British representative in Sofia, would have the object 'of keeping the other Slav agencies [in Russia, Serbia, and Bulgaria] informed as to the struggle of the Austrian Slavs, in and out of Parliament, and of freeing the Slavs from dependence on German telegraphic agencies of which the tendency was anti-Slav.'[68] The Journalistic Section of the Slav Committee of the Czech National Council submitted a resolution to the same effect to the Sofia Neo-Slav Congress.[69]

The Neo-Slav Congress itself commenced on 7 July (24 June) 1910,[70] the day following the conclusion of the meeting of Slav journalists. This Second Congress of the Neo-Slav movement, like its predecessor, was not representative of the entire Slav world. The absences at the Sofia gathering were even more pronounced than they had been in Prague, two years previously. Most significant was the absence of the Russian Poles, who carried out their intended boycott of the entire proceedings. No official representatives of the Polish nation, from the Russian, Austrian, or

[65] *Ibid.*, 17 May 1905.   [66] *Ibid.*, 9 September 1908.
[67] Hrubý, *Slovanská vzájemnost v časopisech*, p. 6; *Národní listy*, 5 July 1910.
[68] PRO, FO, 371/834, Findlay to Grey, 24892, Sofia, 6 July 1910.
[69] Hrubý, *Slovanská vzájemnost v časopisech*, p. 7.
[70] *Slavyanski săbor v Sofiya*, p. 36. For the agenda of the Neo-Slav Congress see *ibid.*, p. 4; H.H.St.A., PA, XL 219, *Panslav Bewegung* 5, Mittag to Aehrenthal 50B, Sofia, 2 July 1910; and PRO, FO, 371/834, Findlay to Grey, 24892, 6 July 1910.

German divisions, were present at the Congress though several Poles, mainly journalists, attended as guests of honour.[71] On behalf of the entire Polish nation Zdziechowski, a Galician Pole who had been a member of the Polish delegation at the Prague Congress, sent a letter to the Sofia gathering in which he expressed regret that the Poles found it impossible to attend. He explained that:

We Poles are unable to work together with representatives of reactionary, anti-Slav Russia, bent on the Russification and destruction of the Polish nation, such as [A. I.] Guchkov and Bobrinsky, who voted in the Duma in favour of the suppression of the constitution of Finland and openly advocated the destruction of Poland and thus impress on the Slav Congress an anti-Slav, anti-Christian, and anti-humanitarian character.

Zdziechowski concluded his message by sending 'warmest greetings to our Russian friends, [A. A.] Stakhovich and [A. L.] Pogodin, and fraternal wishes for the continued flourishing of the Bulgarian nation'.[72] Similar letters were also received from representatives of the Russian Poles, including Count Potocki, who had also attended the Prague Neo-Slav Congress.[73]

Also absent at Sofia, as at the Prague Congress, were the White Russians, the majority of the Ukrainians, and the Lusatian Sorbs. The Slovaks, on the other hand, were present for the first time at a Neo-Slav gathering. They were officially represented by the poet, author, and journalist, S. Hurban-Vajanský, and several other Slovak journalists attended as guests of honour.[74] Vajanský was the leader of the older generation of Slovak nationalists, grouped in the Slovak National Party, who believed that the best course of action for the Slovak nation was to concentrate on matters of a linguistic and literary nature, and who looked to Russia for political support and eventual liberation. Vajanský and his associates supported, with great enthusiasm, the idea of Slav co-operation, and particularly that of forming closer ties with Russia, but

[71] H.H.St.A., PA, XL 219, *Panslav Bewegung* 5, 'Slavischer Kongress in Sophia 1910'; PRO, FO, 371/834, Findlay to Grey, 26733, Sofia, 19 July 1910; *Slavyanski sŭbor v Sofiya*, p. 26; *Čas*, 14 July 1910.
[72] *Čas*, 15 July 1910; *Proces dra. Kramáře*, I, p. 45.
[73] *Slavyanski sŭbor v Sofiya*, pp. 228–30. *Národní listy*, 13 July 1910; *Čas*, 11 July 1910.
[74] H.H.St.A., PA, XL 219, *Panslav Bewegung* 5, 'Slavischer Kongress in Sophia 1910'; *Slavyanski sŭbor v Sofiya*, pp. 21–6; *Národní listy*, 10 July 1910.

saw this somewhat differently from Kramář and his allies. *Prúdy*, a liberal Slovak periodical, commented after the Sofia Congress that: 'Naturally, we cannot include Vajanský among the orthodox Neo-Slavs when every word pronounced by Kramář in the defence of Neo-Slavism, against the representatives of the old [Pan-Slav] direction who were present, was a thorn in his flesh.'[75] Vajanský's presence was one indication of the dilution of the original Neo-Slav ideas by those who could more accurately be described as Pan-Slav or even Pan-Russian supporters.

At the Sofia Congress, as had been the case in Prague, even those delegations which were present were not wholly representative of their respective nations. A considerable number of political and other groups chose not to be associated with the Neo-Slav movement and sent no representatives to the Congress. The Social Democrats from all the attending Slav nations again, as at the previous Congress, refused to participate for ideological reasons. The Bulgarian Social Democrats doubtlessly echoed the attitudes of many of their Slav comrades when they spoke out, in no uncertain terms, against the Neo-Slav Congress, stigmatising it as 'Stolypin's Congress' and condemning it as an 'enterprise of Russian absolutism', assisted by the Slav bourgeoisie in Russia and Austria–Hungary, aimed at preparing for the economic penetration of the Balkans.[76]

Even after discounting the Social Democrats, the delegation of the host nation, led by Bobchev and Lyudskanov,[77] who had both been present at the Prague meeting, was by no means representative of the entire Bulgarian people. The unbounded enthusiasm for the Congress, shown by the Bulgarian Neo-Slavs, was in sharp contrast with the attitude adopted by the Bulgarian authorities and by opinion in general. The British representative in Sofia reported to London, before the Congress commenced, that

no great sympathy is felt in Bulgaria for the Neo-Slav movement. Slavism in Bulgaria is practically synonymous with Russophilism, i.e. a certain feeling of gratitude for benefits conferred by Russia on Bulgaria in the past and a lively expectation of favour to come. The Bulgarians are,...far from being pure Slavs by race, and the connecting links

[75] Pal'o, 'Poznámky k slovanskému sjazdu', *Prúdy*, I (1909), p. 259.
[76] *Čas*, 10 July 1910; *Novoe vremya*, 6 (19) July 1910.
[77] For the full composition of the Bulgarian and other delegations, see H.H.St.A., PA, XL 219, *Panslav Bewegung* 5, 'Slavischer Kongress in Sophia 1910' and *Slavyanski sŭbor v Sofiya*, pp. 17–26.

between them and the rest of Slavs are rather religion and language than the ties of blood. This perhaps accounts for the small amount of enthusiasm which has hitherto been displayed at the prospect of the congress being held in Sophia, and the choice of the capital does not appear to have been a very happy one from the neo-Slav point of view.[78]

Similar views were expressed by the correspondent of *Čas* covering the Sofia events, who reported that the Bulgarians were not enthusiastic members of the Slav community. Those who were interested in Slav affairs, *Čas* explained, tended to concentrate on relations with Russia, ignoring the other Slav nations; but there were also many who were totally opposed to any Slav policy, as was evident from the criticisms voiced against the Congress. 'We cannot fail to realise', the *Čas* correspondent concluded, 'that here [in Sofia] we are not on our home ground.'[79] In contrast with this, however, *Novoe vremya* reported that amongst the majority of the Bulgarian people enthusiasm for the Congress was 'greater than had been expected.'[80]

The Bulgarian government, despite the fact that the Ministry of Education had contributed a sum equivalent to £3000 towards the Slav Congresses,[81] refused to be further involved in the proceedings and, as far as was possible, refrained from any association with the Neo-Slav guests. In order to avoid meeting the delegates of the Congress King Ferdinand, and leading members of the Bulgarian government, left Sofia for the duration of the Slav gatherings. It appears that the Bulgarian authorities did not wish to seem to be supporting the Neo-Slav movement, out of a desire not to antagonise the government of the Habsburg Empire. The Bulgarian Prime Minister, A. Malinov, travelled to Vienna where he assured the Austro-Hungarian authorities that the Sofia Congress was not intended to be directed against the Dual Monarchy.[82]

The criticism voiced against the Czech delegation at the previous Neo-Slav Congress, that it consisted overwhelmingly of

[78] PRO, FO, 371/834, Findlay to Grey, 24892, Sofia, 6 July 1910.
[79] *Čas*, 14 July 1910. The British representative in Sofia also reported that 'hostile criticism of the Congress' had appeared in the press and that 'meetings were held to protest against its taking place' in the Bulgarian capital. PRO, FO, 371/834, Findlay to Grey, 24892, Sofia, 6 July 1910. See also *Rech'*, 21 June (4 July), 24 June (7 July), 25 June (8 July), 26 June (9 July), 28 June (11 July) 1910.   [80] *Novoe vremya*, 27 June (10 July) 1910.
[81] PRO, FO, 371/834, Findlay to Grey, 14950, Sofia, 26 April 1910.
[82] PRO, FO, 371/834, Findlay to Grey, 26733, Sofia, 19 July 1910; *Novoe vremya*, 6 (19) July 1910.

politicians and that cultural and other aspects of national life were under-represented, was not applicable to the Czechs who attended the Sofia gathering. The delegation contained many represent-atives of the arts and sciences, academics, journalists, economists, and others prominent in public life outside the field of politics. Amongst the Czechs present at the Second Neo-Slav Congress were; the Mayor of Prague, Groš; the editor of *Národní listy*, Holeček; the Sokol leader, Scheiner; the Slavist scholar, Polívka; and Pavlů from the Czech National Council.[83] Surprisingly, Preiss, who had actively participated at most previous Neo-Slav meetings, was not present in the Bulgarian capital, though invited. He did, however, send to the Congress papers concerned with the proposed Slav bank and Slav exhibition, which were read during the proceed-ings.[84] Also absent, despite having been sent invitations, were A. Černý and Masaryk.[85] Masaryk continued to remain apart from the Neo-Slav movement and had made it known that he was not expecting 'any practical results' from the Sofia Congress.[86]

Politically, however, the Czech delegation was less representa-tive than that which attended the previous Congress. Only three political parties sent official delegates to Sofia; the Young Czechs and the National Socialists, represented by Kramář and Klofáč respectively, and the small Progressive State-Rights Party.[87] The strongest Czech political grouping, the Agrarians, declined to attend.[88] This action was indicative of the suspicion with which they regarded all endeavours to promote Slav co-operation. The Agrarians feared that these attempts, if successful, would result in increased agricultural imports into the Dual Monarchy from Russia and the Balkans, which would threaten their sectional economic interests.[89] The boycott of the Sofia meeting by con-siderable sections of Czech political opinion was, to a large extent, also due to reasons not dissimilar from those which were responsible for the distant attitude of the Bulgarian authorities. It was felt by many that the Congress, which was to be primarily concerned

[83] H.H.St.A., PA, XL 219, *Panslav Bewegung* 5, 'Slavischer Kongress in Sofia 1910'; *Slavyanski săbor v Sofiya*, pp. 24–5.
[84] *Slavyanski săbor v Sofiya*, pp. 13, 24–5, 176–7. Preiss had ceased to attend meetings of the Neo-Slav movement earlier in the year, see above p. 176, n. 41.
[85] *Ibid.*, pp. 13–14, 24–5.   [86] *Čas*, 12 April 1910.
[87] *Slavyanski săbor v Sofiya*, pp. 24–5; Polívka, 'Slovanský sjezd sofijský', p. 72.
[88] V. Červinka, 'Druhý přípravný sjezd slovanský v Sofii', *Česká revue*, III (1909–10), p. 706.   [89] Kramář, *Na obranu*, p. 75.

with the problems of the Balkan Slavs, would inevitably result in
exacerbating relations between the Czechs and the Vienna government. The leading Czech Neo-Slavs were fully conscious of this
danger, and during preparatory consultations between the Czech
representatives, Kramář declared with emphasis: 'It is up to us,
Austrian Slavs, to ensure that no unacceptable decisions are taken
[at Sofia]. We must not come into conflict with the state in which
we live.'[90]

In addition, many Czechs, and others, who were generally in
sympathy with the aims of Neo-Slavism as originally outlined,
were embarrassed by the pronounced right-wing colouring acquired
recently by the Russian section of the movement, and were consequently reluctant to attend the Congress in the Company of the
Russians. The large Russian delegation[91] present at the Sofia
meetings fully reflected the transformation of Russian Neo-
Slavism, consisting predominantly of men with strong conservative leanings. Liberal Russians were almost totally absent.[92] Kramář
himself subsequently complained that the Russian delegation was
'one-sidedly, nationalistically Russian and anti-Polish in spirit'.[93]

The majority of the Russians who attended the Second Neo-
Slav Congress were members of the St Petersburg Slavonic
Benevolent Society; men such as Bashmakov, Bobrinsky, G. V.
Komarov, Kulakovsky, and Vergun who, despite their previous
association with the Neo-Slav movement, could nevertheless more
accurately be described as Pan-Slavs than Neo-Slavs. The
strongest political group within the Russian delegation was formed
by the Octobrists, headed by A. I. Guchkov, the President of the
Duma, who was the leader of the entire Russian party. His brother,
N. I. Guchkov, Mayor of Moscow, was also present.[94] Another

[90] Archive of the Czech National Council, minutes of a meeting of the Slav
Committee, held on 2 May 1910, cited in Herman, 'Novoslovanství a česká
buržoasie', p. 300.
[91] *Národní listy*, 6 July 1910, reported that 132 Russians had arrived in Sofia for
the various Slav meetings.
[92] Kramář, *Na obranu*, p. 27; *Národní listy*, 13 July 1910; PRO, FO, 371/834,
Findlay to Grey, 26733, Sofia, 19 July 1910. For details of the composition
of the Russian delegation, see H.H.St.A., PA, XL 219, *Panslav Bewegung* 5,
'Slavischer Kongress in Sophia 1910', and *Slavyanski sǎbor v Sofiya*, pp. 21–3.
[93] *Národní listy*, 10 August 1910. Kramář expressed a similar view in 'Předmluva'
to *Slovanstvo*, ed. Polívka and Bidlo, pp. XII–XIII.
[94] *Slavyanski sǎbor v Sofiya*, pp. 21–2. N. A. Khomyakov resigned from the
Presidency of the Duma early in 1910 and Guchkov was elected as his
successor.

prominent Octobrist, N. A. Khomyakov, who had associated himself with the Neo-Slav movement during the Executive Committee
meetings in St Petersburg in 1909 and 1910, declined to attend,
however, for what he claimed were business reasons.[95] The leader
of the Russian delegation to the 1908 Prague Congress, Krasovsky,
a conservative member of the State Council, was also not present
in Sofia despite being invited. The Kadet Party, which had previously shown slight interest in the Neo-Slav movement, appeared
not to be maintaining this. It was represented at the Congress only
by A. A. Stakhovich and also by A. L. Pogodin, who attended as a
guest of honour. The Kadet leader, Milyukov, declined to attend
although invited, as did another prominent Kadet, Maklakov who,
unlike Milyukov, had been present at the Prague Congress. Another
liberal Russian previously associated with the Neo-Slav movement,
but absent at Sofia, was Lvov. Stakhovich and Pogodin, however,
were not the only Russian liberals present. Moderate Russian
political opinion was also represented by several delegates from
the liberal Society for Slav Unity (*Obschchestvo edinenie Slavyan*)
in Odessa.[96] Also included within the Russian delegation were
A. S. Gizhitsky, chairman of the recently formed Russian Sokol
organisation, and the neuropathologist Bekhterev.[97] Amongst
the guests of honour who accompanied the official Russian delegates were General N. G. Stoletov, commander of the Bulgarian
units in the Russo-Turkish War of 1877–8, and hero of the battles
in the Shipka Pass, and the journalist Svatkovsky.[98] Volodimirov,
one of the persons most directly responsible for instigating the
Neo-Slav movement, was unable to attend due to illness.[99] The
organisers of the Sofia Congress also extended an invitation to the

[95] *Novoe vremya*, 6 (19) July 1910 (letter from N. A. Khomyakov to S. S.
Bobchev). Khomyakov was evidently not entirely happy about the prospects
for the Congress. In his letter to Bobchev he implored him to 'stand by the
resolutions of the Prague Congress and do not permit their revision'.
[96] *Slavyanski săbor v Sofiya*, pp. 5–9, 21–3; *Novoe vremya*, 6 (19) July 1910;
Čas, 14 July 1910. Milyukov had been expected to attend the Congress on
account of his close association with Bulgaria. He spent a period of exile in
Sofia during the 1890s. The Kadet leader made it known, however, that he
did not wish to become associated with the representatives of 'official Russia'
who were attending the Congress. *Novoe vremya*, 27 January (9 February),
2 (15) July 1910.
[97] *Slavyanski săbor v Sofiya*, p. 21; *Proces dra. Kramáře*, IV, part 1, p. 61.
[98] *Slavyanski săbor v Sofiya*, p. 23.
[99] *Ibid.*, p. 218; Červinka, 'Druhý přípravný sjezd slovanský', p. 706. Volodimirov died shortly afterwards.

Russian author, L. N. Tolstoy, who declined to attend on the grounds of old age, but sent a letter outlining his views on Slav unity.[100] The selection of the Russian delegation aroused some criticism amongst the more liberal Russian Neo-Slavs. Even during the Neo-Slav Executive Committee meeting in St Petersburg early in 1910, at which preparations for the Congress were made, friction amongst the Russian members of the movement of differing political persuasions became evident. The Bulgarian representatives at the meeting expressed the desire for the Russian delegation to represent all shades of political opinion in Russia.[101] In other words, they were anxious that the traditional Russian Pan-Slav point of view be represented alongside the more liberal Neo-Slav attitude. This caused displeasure to the liberals, such as Pogodin, who wished to see Russian 'public opinion', and not 'official' Russia, represented in Sofia.[102] Other Russian Neo-Slavs were also unhappy about the way the Congress was shaping. A group of Russian delegates who had attended the 1908 Prague Neo-Slav Congress held a meeting in St Petersburg during May 1910 with the object of 'clarifying the situation concerning the Sofia Congress'. Two of the persons present, Maklakov and Krasovsky,

[100] In his letter to the Congress, which was read out during the proceedings, Tolstoy emphasised the importance of a universal Christian union and warned against the dangers of smaller, exclusive associations. 'It is natural', he conceded, 'for the Slavonic nationalities, experiencing in themselves the evil effect of the union of Austrian, German, Russian and Turkish states, to wish to oppose this evil, to join together into their own association, but this new association, if it takes place, would inevitably be drawn into just such action, not only of conflict with other associations, but even into oppression and exploitation of weaker associations and of separate individuals.' Although Tolstoy admitted that the object of any union, the achievement of strength, was desirable, he believed that this goal could only be attained through a union of 'all humanity'. Limited associations, he maintained, only hindered the progress of mankind and he was, therefore, opposed to their aims. Concluding on a hopeful note, however, Tolstoy wrote: 'I have been particularly stirred to say what I have, by my belief that this principle of universal religious union...will be accepted before all other peoples of the Christian world by precisely the peoples of Slavonic race.' Tolstoy's message was received with enthusiasm by the assembled Slav delegates, and a letter of thanks was drafted immediately. *Slavyanski säbor v Sofiya*, pp. 179–82; 'Count Leo Tolstoy and the Slavonic Congress at Sophia, 1910', *The Slavonic and East European Review*, VIII (1929–30), pp. 246–48; V. Charvát, 'Tolstoy a Slované', *Slovanský přehled*, XIII (1911), pp. 105–6.
[101] *Novoe vremya*, 27 January (9 February), 30 January (12 February) 1910.
[102] *Ibid.*, 3 (16) February 1910.

argued that the forthcoming Slav gathering in Sofia could not be regarded as a successor to the 1908 Prague Congress. In their view, on account of the fact that invitations had been issued to persons who had aided the Bulgarians gain their national independence but who had no links with the Neo-Slav movement, and due to the probable absence of the Poles, the Sofia Congress could not be regarded as the Second Preparatory Slav Congress, as it officially was, but should be considered a festival of Bulgarian independence. Maklakov and Krasovsky therefore suggested that the delegates to the Prague Congress should attend the Sofia gathering only as 'guests of honour'.[103] This advice was not taken, however, and the Russian delegation in Sofia included eight persons who had also attended the Prague Congress but, as mentioned earlier, neither Maklakov nor Krasovsky were present.[104] It was not only individuals who were conspicuous by their absence at the Sofia Congress. The liberal Moscow Society for Slav Culture also refused to participate officially due to the fact that it had been invited to send only one representative to Sofia, whereas other organisations had stronger representation. The protest of the Moscow Society prompted the chief organiser of the Congress, Bobchev, to issue a statement to the press in which he argued that the Moscow Society for Slav Culture was not being discriminated against. He explained that the Congress organisers had invited all societies active in the field of Slav affairs to send one representative each to Sofia but that in addition to this many individuals were invited to attend in their own right, irrespective of their society membership. Thus some societies appeared to have stronger representation than others.[105] Whatever the justice of this particular issue, it was evident that at least some Russian Neo-Slavs were profoundly unhappy about the ascendancy of the Russian right wing over the movement and were unwilling to become associated with the Sofia Congress. This attitude was fully endorsed by the Kadet newspaper *Rech'*.[106]

---

[103] *Ibid.*, 17 (30) May 1910.   [104] *Slavyanski săbor v Sofiya*, pp. 5, 21–2.
[105] *Novoe vremya*, 3 (16), 4 (17) July 1910; *Čas*, 2 July 1910. Bobchev's assertion appears to be contradicted in the official record of the Congress, which lists up to five persons as representatives of certain societies. On the other hand, included amongst the persons individually invited are four members of the Moscow Society for Slav Culture; M. M. Kovalevsky, P. N. Milyukov, A. L. Pogodin and A. A. Stakhovich. *Slavyanski săbor v Sofiya*, pp. 5–9, 21–3.
[106] *Rech'*, 22 June (5 July) 1910.

During the course of the Congress itself, disharmony also became apparent amongst the Russian representatives. This was precipitated by the formal inclusion within the Russian delegation of the Russophil Ukrainians from Galicia. Amongst these were Markov, who had been responsible for calling the meeting of Slav deputies in Vienna in 1907 for the first discussion of the proposal to organise a Slav congress, and Glebovitsky, who had accompanied Kramář on his visit to Russia the following year.[107] The adhesion of the Russophil Ukrainians to the Russian delegation resulted in two of its more liberal members severing their links with the official Russian representatives as a gesture of protest. The two dissenting Russians, Pogodin, and I. M. Lutsenko, a member of the Odessa Society for Slav Unity, argued that the Ukrainians should be represented by a separate delegation. The dispute was further intensified by Lutsenko's assertion that some of the Russian delegates were 'wolves in sheep's clothing'. He singled out three in particular, Bobrinsky, Vergun, and a professor at the University of Kiev, T. D. Florinsky, as enemies of the Ukrainians, and accused Markov of betraying the Ukrainian nation. During a private meeting of the Russian delegation in Sofia another moderate Russian, Stakhovich, who defended the stand taken by Pogodin and Lutsenko, clashed angrily with Bobrinsky. The attitude of the liberal Russians provoked one of their compatriots, A. V. Vasil'ev, a representative of the city of St Petersburg, to accuse them of attempting to disrupt the Congress. Harmony was eventually restored by the leader of the delegation, A. I. Guchkov, who argued that the attitude towards the Ukrainians was a matter for individual discretion. It was significant, however, that Vasil'ev referred to the targets of his criticism as 'Neo-Slavs' and castigated them for their only recently aroused interest in Slav affairs, whereas the 'Slavophils' had been working for the realisation of the Slav idea for some considerable time.[108] Evidently, some of the Russian representatives at the Sofia Congress did not identify themselves with the Neo-Slav movement.

The remaining participants at the Congress, those of the South Slav nations, the Croats, Serbs, and Slovenes, who formed one delegation, were also far from being representative of their respective peoples. This was most marked in the case of the Croats.

---

[107] *Slavyanski săbor v Sofiya*, p. 22; *Proces dra. Kramáře*, IV, part 1, p. 61.
[108] *Novoe vremya*, 1 (14) July 1910; *Rech'*, 3 (16) July 1910.

No delegates from Croatia-Slavonia, a part of the Hungarian
section of the Habsburg Empire, attended; both the Croatian
Nationalists and the Serbo-Croatian Coalition declined to be
present. The Nationalists, who were dreaming of the creation of
a Greater Croatia, hopefully with the aid of the Austrian authorities, had little in common with the Neo-Slavs. The absence of the
Coalition it was claimed was, however, not due to any conflict with
the aims of Neo-Slavism but because they did not expect the
Congress to achieve concrete results. A more credible explanation
was provided by the fact that, prior to expected negotiations with
the Hungarian government, the Serbo-Croatian Coalition had no
desire to create difficulties for itself by participating in what the
Hungarian authorities regarded as being, by definition, an anti-
Hungarian Congress.[109] The only official Croatian delegate present
was Tresić-Pavičić from Dalmatia.[110] The Slovenes were represented by Gabršček of the Liberal Party. As had been the case at
the previous Congress, no members of the Slovene Clerical Party
attended. The reason behind their absence, as it had been in
Prague, was not lack of sympathy for the Neo-Slav cause, but
simply the fact that their internal political rivals, the Liberals,
were already closely involved in the movement.[111] Hribar, the
Slovene member of the Austrian-Slav trio which visited St Petersburg in 1908, was unable to attend, due to indisposition.[112] The
third South Slav group, the Serbs, were substantially represented at the Congress, despite the fact that Neo-Slavism was
no more popular in Serbia in 1910 than it had been two years previously.[113] The Serbian delegation, which was under the leadership of K. Stoyanovich, the President of the Serbian National
Assembly (the Skupshtina) also included a representative from
Montenegro.[114]

[109] *Národní listy*, 13 July 1910; *Novoe vremya*, 6 (19) July 1910.
[110] *Slavyanski sŭbor v Sofiya*, pp. 23, 38; *Čas*, 14 July 1910.
[111] *Národní listy*, 13 July 1910; *Čas*, 14 July 1910. Although Gabršček is not
listed amongst the delegates in *Slavyanski sŭbor v Sofiya*, he is, nevertheless,
mentioned on pp. 168–72.
[112] Červinka, 'Druhý přípravný sjezd slovanský', p. 706.
[113] Forgach to Aethrenthal, 30B, Belgrade, 17 July 1910, cited in Beneš, *Úvahy
o slovanství*, pp. 189–90. Forgach reported that the noted geographer, Professor J. Cvijich, had been invited to head the Serbian delegation, but declined to do so on the grounds that such congresses were unrealistic and of
little value to Serbia. The Austro-Hungarian ambassador in Belgrade added
that: 'Mr Cvijich's deductions concur with local Serbian opinion.'
[114] *Slavyanski sŭbor v Sofiya*, pp. 23–4; *Čas*, 14 July 1910.

It is evident that Kramář did not travel to Sofia with high expectations. In an article, published in *Národní listy* before his
departure, he issued the following warning:

The atmosphere [at the Sofia Congress] will be far from happy. However, Slav Congresses cannot be expected to be one long succession of
joyful ceremonies. The condition of Slav affairs will not permit this.
In our case, at least, the promotion of the Slav idea has not been exhausted by ceremonial banquets and enthusiastic toasts. For us it has
involved hard work, endless patience and persistence, bitter disappointments, and an indomitable belief in the ultimate victory of the idea of
true brotherhood between the Slavs.[115]

In a further article, written after the event, he pointed to the difficulties of holding the Congress in the Balkans: problems which
were not only caused by the 'deep distrust between the Serbs and
the Bulgarians over Macedonia', but also by the 'traditionally
misdirected policies' of Austria–Hungary in that area.[116] Sub-
sequentially, at his trial, he stated that he had been aware, before
the Congress had commenced, that during its course 'the collapse
of Neo-Slavism would become apparent'.[117] But whatever he
subsequently claimed to have believed before the Congress began,
his performance during the proceedings betrayed few signs of
anxiety, and he appeared as confident and energetic as ever.

During the first session of the Congress, held in the Sofia National
Theatre on 7 July (24 June) 1910, the organiser, Bobchev, was
elected to the chair and Kramář chosen as honorary chairman.[118]
Loyal greetings were sent to King Ferdinand. Then followed a
series of over two dozen short introductory speeches delivered by
representatives of the participant delegations and various Slav
cultural and other organisations.[119] In his opening address, again
as at the previous gathering delivered in a collection of Slavonic
languages, the Czech leader, after praising the Slav consciousness
of the Bulgarian nation, emphasised the importance of the
movement remaining faithful to the ideals of the Prague Congress.
The principles of freedom, equality, and brotherhood in Slav
relations, he maintained, had to be upheld.[120] In this, and in

[115] *Národní listy*, 12 June 1910.
[116] *Ibid.*, 10 August 1910 (K. Kramář, 'Po sofijském sjezdu', 1).
[117] *Proces dra. Kramáře*, 11, p. 89.
[118] *Slavyanski săbor v Sofiya*, pp. 36–7; *Čas*, 14 July 1910; *Národní listy*,
10 July 1910.   [119] *Slavyanski săbor v Sofiya*, pp. 39–56.
[120] *Ibid.*, p. 52; Červinka, 'Druhý přípravný sjezd slovanský', p. 707.

other speeches, Kramář reiterated that Neo-Slavism was concerned purely with cultural and economic matters and that it had
no interest in politics, and warned that the movement must do
nothing to exacerbate relations between the Slav nations and the
states in which they lived. Any involvement in politics would,
inevitably, result in the destruction of all hopes of progress in the
fields of economics and culture.[121] Kramář proceeded, in the words
of the correspondent of *Národní listy*, to give a 'pragmatic descrip-
tion' of the progress made by the movement during the two years
since the Prague Congress.[122] Then, turning his attention to the
absent Poles, the Czech leader expressed regret that they had felt
it necessary to boycott the Congress, but he also gave an assurance
that their justified complaints were fully understood by the Neo-
Slavs, whose principle was: 'Those who oppress other Slav
peoples cannot themselves be considered Slavs.'[123] These words,
obviously aimed at the Russian authorities and those who supported their policies, were enthusiastically received by the two
most prominent liberal Russians present, Stakhovich and Pogodin.[124] The statement was indicative of the vigorous attempt
made by Kramář to combat the right-wing colouring given to
the Congress by the majority of the Russian delegates, and to
maintain the Neo-Slav movement within the bounds he had
originally envisaged.[125]

During the following two days, the Congress met several times
in full session to hear a collection of papers concerned with the
main points on the agenda, the cultural and economic situation of
the Balkan Slavs.[126] The majority of the work, however, was carried
out subsequently during simultaneous sittings of sections of the

---

[121] *Slavyanski săbor v Sofiya*, p. 53; *Čas* 10, July 1910.

[122] *Národní listy*, 13 July 1910.

[123] *Slavyanski săbor v Sofiya*, p. 52. Kramář had used these brave words previously. A similar phrase was contained in a telegram sent from the Crimea
to a group of Czechs visiting Warsaw in 1909. J. S. Hevera, 'Novoslovanství',
in M. Sísová and others, *Karel Kramář. K padesátým narozeninám jeho*, p. 136.

[124] *Čas*, 14 July 1910.

[125] Kramář claimed that his address had been approved in advance by the leaders
of all the national delegations, including A. I. Guchkov. He also insisted that
'during the entire course of the Congress no one had the courage to make the
slightest objection against the decisions taken in Prague [at the previous
Neo-Slav Congress]'. *Národní listy*, 10 August 1910 (Kramář, 'Po sofijském
sjezdu', 1); Kramář, *Na obranu*, p. 27.

[126] *Slavyanski săbor v Sofiya*, pp. 60–113; *Čas*, 16 July 1910 (B. Pavlů, 'Slovanský sjezd v Soffi').

Congress, chosen for the discussion of various subjects.[127] Originally, three separate sections had been created to deal with economic, cultural, and Slavistic matters respectively, but during the course of the Congress, on the suggestion of Kramář, the last two were amalgamated, due to the fact that it was difficult to distinguish between the two subjects and also that there were few Slavistic scholars present.[128]

The economic section concerned itself with the issues ever present at Neo-Slav meetings – the proposals for the creation of a Slav bank and the organisation of a Slav exhibition. There appears, however, to have been a significant lack of enthusiasm for both these subjects, and the sessions of the economic section were reported to have been marked by a general apathy.[129] Papers on both these subjects had been prepared by Preiss but, due to his absence, were read out by other persons. In the revised proposals concerning the Slav bank, which were approved by the Congress, Preiss noted, with premature satisfaction, that the Russian authorities had at last agreed to participate in such a St Petersburg based institution. Banking circles in other Slav countries were urged to assist the venture and a decision was taken to call a meeting of the Slav Bank Committee, as established at the Prague Congress but supplemented by a few additional delegates, to St Petersburg in the near future.[130] This meeting, however, never took place and, as stated by one of the delegates, Pavlů, the Sofia Congress, in general, maintained 'a determined silence over the Slav bank issue'.[131]

Somewhat greater attention was paid to the second topic, the proposed Slav exhibition. In his paper on this subject Preiss referred to the programme for a Slav exhibition which had been prepared the previous year by the Czechs on behalf of the Exhibition Committee, in accordance with the resolution of the Prague Congress, and presented to the Neo-Slav Executive Committee meeting in St Petersburg in the spring of 1909.[132] These detailed

---

[127] *Slavyanski săbor v Sofiya*, pp. 114–78; Polívka, 'Slovanský sjezd sofijský', p. 114.
[128] *Slavyanski săbor v Sofiya*, pp. 85–6; Polívka, 'Slovanský sjezd sofijský', p. 114; *Čas*, 16 July 1910 (Pavlů, 'Slovanský sjezd v Sofii').
[129] *Čas*, 23 July 1910 (B. Pavlů, 'Po slovanském sjezdě'). The proceedings of the economic section received comparatively little attention in the officially published record of the Congress, *Slavyanski săbor v Sofiya*, pp. 176–8.
[130] *Ibid.*, p. 176; Polívka, 'Slovanský sjezd sofijský', p. 114.
[131] *Čas*, 23 July 1910 (Pavlů, 'Po slovanském sjezdě').
[132] Polívka, 'Slovanský sjezd sofijský', p. 114.

plans for an exhibition, to be staged either in St Petersburg or Moscow between 1913 and 1915, envisaged a comprehensive display, ranging from the arts, through trade and commerce, to military and naval matters. Discussions were held with the Russian authorities, and Moscow was chosen as the exhibition site. The Russian government, Preiss also claimed, had agreed to make a financial contribution to the venture. Despite this promising beginning, little further progress was made with the arrangements. In an article on the subject, published almost a year later, Preiss offered the following explanation:

From the very outset of the discussions the only obstacles were the objections of both Russian and Polish industry which showed no great interest in the exhibition due to the fact that, as business was in recession, they were in no mood to incur additional expenses. Later it become apparent that, as a whole range of political and economic factors were militating against the holding of a general Slav exhibition in 1913 in accordance with the original decision of the Slav Committee, it would have to be postponed to a substantially later date. [133]

Both the Russian authorities and Russian industry were, evidently, unwilling to open their domestic markets to competition from smaller Slav nations, of which the Czechs were industrially and commercially the most highly developed and, therefore, the most dangerous. In addition, the strained international relations between Russia and Austria–Hungary did not make the realisation of the project any easier. The difficulties seemed insurmountable and, as Preiss continued: 'Consequently, the idea came about to progress in stages towards the goal of holding a general Slav exhibition by attempting first to organise exhibitions in fields which were simpler and less demanding in preparatory work.'[134]

The Slav delegates assembled in Sofia decided in favour of a more modest exhibition, to be staged in Prague in 1913. The plan, proposed by Kramář, and termed by him 'the most important decision of the Sofia Congress', envisaged an exhibition limited to the fields of arts and crafts, and ethnography, which, he maintained would 'show us and the world the unique characteristics of Slavism' and, if successful, 'would be a real demonstration of Slav spiritual unity and cultural solidarity'.[135] With economic interests

---

[133] Preiss, 'Anketa o slovanské výstavě', p. 2.   [134] *Ibid.*
[135] *Národní listy*, 14 August 1910 (Kramář, 'Po sofijském sjezdu', IV). See also *Slavyanski sŭbor v Sofiya*, pp. 177–8; *Proces dra. Kramáře*, II, p. 96; Preiss, 'Anketa o slovanské výstavě', pp. 2–3.

ever close to his heart, he indicated that in addition such an exhibition could be of considerable value also from this point of view, by introducing foreign buyers to the products of Slav craft industries. Kramář's proposals were supplemented by A. I. Guchkov's suggestion to include a festival of Slav music.[136]

The Neo-Slavs did not, however, completely abandon hope of holding the originally envisaged comprehensive exhibition, and the Congress declared that it was imperative that final arrangements be made, and the date and venue settled. Although the view persisted that every effort should be made to stage the proposed exhibition in Russia hopes were evidently not very high, as alternative plans were made. If it proved impossible to hold the general exhibition in Moscow or St Petersburg, it was to be held in Prague in 1915 in accordance with the programme prepared earlier.[137] Kramář himself seemed to have little hope of the exhibition ever taking place in Russia. Shortly after the conclusion of the Sofia Congress, he wrote:

Frankly, [the organisation of] a Slav economic exhibition is a task of utmost difficulty. In the first instance, naturally, we have nothing originally Slavonic to offer in the fields of industry and commerce (yarns, cardboard, and machines have few national characteristics). Secondly, competitive conditions between Russian and non-Russian Slavs, together with those within Russia itself, are exerting a somewhat unfavourable influence on the idea of an industrial exhibition. The Moscow industrial circles have no interest in an exhibition, they do not wish to see anything that would increase the competitive position of other industrial centres, and an economic exhibition in Prague would be, almost exclusively, a Czech affair.[138]

This pessimistic assessment proved to be well founded. The great Slav exhibition never materialised, neither in Russia nor elsewhere. The plan for a less ambitious exhibition, restricted to cultural and allied subjects, approved by the Sofia Congress, met the same fate. Although a considerable amount of preparatory work had been

[136] *Slavyanski săbor v Sofiya*, pp. 177–8; *Čas*, 16 July 1910 (Pavlů, 'Slovanský sjezd v Sofii'); *Národní listy*, 14 August 1910 (Kramář, 'Po sofijském sjezdu', IV).
[137] Polívka, 'Slovanský sjezd sofijský', p. 114; *Čas* 16 July 1910 (Pavlů, 'Slovanský sjezd v Sofii').
[138] *Národní listy*, 14 August 1910 (Kramář, 'Po sofijském sjezdu', IV).

carried out by Kramář and Preiss,[139] the project was abandoned in compliance with the wishes of the Austro-Hungarian authorities. The government's displeasure concerning the proposed exhibition was communicated to Kramář directly by the Prime Minister, Count Stürgkh, and the Governor of Bohemia, Count Thun.[140]

The meetings of the cultural section of the Sofia Congress also centred round the discussion of familiar topics, but the proceedings there were described by Polívka, who was in the chair, as being 'richer and more comprehensive' than in the economic section.[141] The subjects debated and approved included proposals for establishing a common Slav terminology in the fields of science, technology, and commerce; the creation of a Slav lexicon; and for a further expansion of the exchange of Slav books. Closer co-operation was urged between Slav universities, theatres, and other cultural and scientific bodies, together with the implementation of plans, previously outlined, regarding the creation of a Slav news agency, and the organisation of Slav tourism.[142]

Although theoretically, as indicated by Pavlů, it was precisely in the fields of cultural relations 'where, despite political differences, the most useful work could be carried out',[143] the proceedings of the cultural section of the Congress were enlivened by political controversy. At one of the meetings the Russian liberal, Stakhovich, proposed a composite resolution reaffirming the adherence to the principles of freedom, equality, and brotherhood, as outlined by Kramář; demanding an open discussion of Russo-

---

[139] *Máj*, IX (1911), p. 194. During the course of 1911, the literary periodical *Máj*, which five years previously had been responsible for conducting a survey of opinion regarding a Slav Congress, now turned its attention to the subject of the proposed cultural exhibition. A survey of opinion was launched, accompanied by an editorial article on the projected Slav exhibition by J. Preiss, 'Anketa o slovanské výstavě v Praze r. 1913', *Máj*, IX (1911), pp. 1–4, 21–3. The results of the survey were never published. The Slav Committee of the Czech National Council held several meetings to discuss the exhibition arrangements, and some preliminary proposals were announced. Herman, 'Novoslovanství a česká buržoasie', p. 301.
[140] *Proces dra. Kramáře*, II, p. 100. See also Heinz, 'Der Neoslawismus', pp. 110–14.
[141] Polívka, 'Slovanský sjezd sofijský, p. 114. Another participant, B. Pavlů, shared this view. See *Čas*, 23 July 1910 (Pavlů, 'Po slovanském sjezdě').
[142] *Slavyanski săbor v Sofiya*, pp. 114–76; *Národní listy*, 11 July 1910; *Čas*, 11 July 1910; *Novoe vremya*, 4 (17) July 1910.
[143] *Čas*, 23 July 1910 (Pavlů, 'Po slovanském sjezdě').

Polish problems, and the solution of all inter-Slav disputes; and protesting against the views of Bobrinsky, which Stakhovich regarded as being alien to the Neo-Slav concept. These proposals were, however, ruled out of order by the chairman. Stakhovich repeated his attempted protest at a sitting of the economic section, where he clashed with A. I. Guchkov, but his intervention was again ruled out of order on the grounds of its political nature.[144] Another Russian with moderate political views present at the Sofia Congress, Pogodin, was subjected to an acrimonious attack from the Russophil Ukrainians within the Russian delegation, after raising an objection to a point made by Tresić-Pavičić during a debate in the cultural section. The Croatian representative, while reporting on the progress made towards a literary union of the Serbs and Croats, likened the relations between the two South Slav nations to those between the Ukrainians and the Great Russians.[145] As he had earlier indicated, Pogodin believed strongly that Russia should adopt a more tolerant attitude towards the Ukrainian nationalists, in order that they may become 'as true friends as the Czechs or the Slovenes'.[146]

In accordance with Kramář's forecast, the Sofia meetings did not consist entirely of joyful ceremonies, though banquets and other festivities featured prominently on the programme of events. At some of these, the atmosphere was rather strained and the mood far from convivial. During one dinner given in honour of the Slav guests, Pogodin again irritated the right wing Russians present by proposing a toast to the absent Poles and Ukrainians. Bobrinsky responded by drinking to those who were not traitors of Slavdom.[147] In addition to attempting to maintain peace between the conflicting sections of the Russian delegation Kramář, and the other Czechs present in Sofia, experienced considerable difficulties in ensuring that nothing was said or done in public that could be construed by the Austro-Hungarian authorities as being disloyal or hostile. He frequently repeated his, now familiar, assertion that the Neo-Slav

[144] *Čas*, 16 July 1910 (Pavlů, 'Slovanský sjezd v Sofii').
[145] Polívka, 'Slovanský sjezd sofijský', p. 115.
[146] A. L. Pogodin, 'Rusko a rakouští Slované', *Moravsko-slezská revue*, VI (1910), p. 64.
[147] *Čas*, 9, 16, 23 July 1910; PRO, FO, 371/834, Findlay to Grey, 26733, Sofia, 19 July 1910. The balance was redressed somewhat by another incident, when one of the Polish guests from the German division of Poland drank to the unity of the Russian nation and embraced V. A. Bobrinsky. *Novoe vremya*, 6 (19) July 1910.

movement must not be concerned with politics or undertake any steps that would bring members of the movement into conflict with their own states,[148] and strenuous efforts were made by the Czechs to adhere to this. An attempt made by the Serbian delegate, Koshutich, during the opening session of the Congress, to condemn the recent actions of the Austro-Hungarian government and to proclaim the unity of the Bulgarian and Serbian nations against this common enemy,[149] was rebuffed by Kramář, who later emphasised that the Congress must not be regarded as a demonstration of the Austrian Slavs against the Habsburg Empire.[150] In another incident, Kramář was reported to have complained to Bobchev that, during an Orthodox religious ceremony, prayers had not been offered for the Emperor of Austria though other sovereigns of Slav nations had been mentioned.[151]

The disputes were not restricted to the field of politics, and even occurred over what might be considered the less contentious question of language. A suggestion made by certain members of the Russian delegation, for Russian to be adopted as the general Slav language, met with considerable opposition, and failed to gain the approval of the Congress. The Russian proposal was described by Pavlů as an attempt at an 'unnecessary imposition'.[152] In its place the Congress approved a compromise resolution which advocated the teaching of the Cyrillic alphabet in the schools of those Slav lands where the Latin alphabet was in use.[153]

Disagreements and disputes, of one form or another, were a prominent feature of the Neo-Slav Congress proceedings, and prompted the British representative in Sofia to report: 'It was with the greatest difficulty that even a superficial harmony was

[148] *Slavyanski sŭbor v Sofiya*, p. 53; *Čas*, 10 August 1910; *Národní listy*, 10 August 1910 (Kramář, 'Po sofijském sjezdu', 1).
[149] *Proces dra. Kramáře*, IV, part 1, pp. 63–4.
[150] *Čas*, 16 July 1910 (*Pavlů*, 'Slovanský sjezd v Sofii').
[151] PRO, FO, 371/834, Findlay to Grey, 26737, Sofia, 19 July 1910.
[152] *Čas*, 23 July 1910 (Pavlů, 'Po slovanském sjezdě'). Polívka, the Czech chairman of the cultural section, conceded that Russian was the only possible common Slav language, but maintained it was unacceptable as such until modernised. For the time being, he urged the various Slav nations to practise the suggestion, made by Kollár, of learning other Slav languages. Polívka, 'Slovanský sjezd sofijský', p. 119. Pavlů was also prepared to admit the 'prevalence' of the Russian language, but was opposed to any formal ruling on the issue. *Čas*, 23 July 1910 (Pavlů, 'Po slovanském sjezdě').
[153] *Slavyanski sŭbor v Sofiya*, pp. 166–8.

preserved.'[154] In addition, the Congress left much to be desired from an organisational point of view. Access to, participation in, and even voting in all proceedings were open to anyone, which not surprisingly tended to create considerable confusion. Although a detailed programme had been prepared for the Congress by the Neo-Slav Executive Committee, this was frequently ignored, and the discussion of unscheduled subjects often ousted more important items from the agenda.[155] Furthermore, a thorough assessment of the proceedings was made difficult by the organisers' omission to circulate, to both the participants and the press, printed versions of the papers delivered.[156]

Despite all these difficulties, the leading figures present at the Congress concluded the event, as was customary on these occasions, with a public demonstration of confidence and satisfaction. The leader of the Russian delegation, A. I. Guchkov, praised Kramář for ensuring that the Congress had 'not become a spectacle of inter-Slav disputes, as our enemies were forecasting but, on the contrary...a festival of Slav reciprocity'.[157] Bobchev, the organiser and chairman of the Congress, even after an interval of several years still maintained that the Sofia gathering had been 'most inspiring'.[158] In his closing address Bobchev declared that 'we are now all working together for the realisation of the programme, drawn up decades previously by the famous patriarch of Slavophilism, Kollár, a programme of spiritual and cultural intercourse, revived in Prague and consolidated in Sofia'. Bobchev also made the optimistic assertion that 'the path has been prepared for the third [Neo-Slav] Congress' which would meet within a year at a time and place to be determined by the Executive Committee.[159]

---

[154] PRO, FO, 371/834, Findlay to Grey, 26737, Sofia, 19 July 1910.
[155] *Čas*, 16 July 1910 (Pavlů, 'Slovanský sjezd v Sofii'); Polívka, 'Slovanský sjezd sofijský', p. 24.
[156] *Čas*, 16 July 1910 (Pavlů, 'Slovanský sjezd v Sofii').
[157] *Slavyanski săbor v Sofiya*, p. 186.
[158] S. S. Bobchev, 'The Slavs after the War', *The Slavonic and East European Review*, VI (1927–8), p. 292.
[159] *Slavyanski săbor v Sofiya*, pp. 188–91. Although neither the venue nor the date of the next congress had been decided, the sizes of the respective delegations had been determined as follows: 65 Russians, 25 Poles, 22 Czechs, 6 Slovenes, 10 Croats, 15 Serbs, and 15 Bulgarians. The delegates were to be drawn from academic, commercial and political circles. Kramář in an article in *Národní listy*, 14 August 1910 ('Po sofijském sjezdu', IV), offered the unlikely explanation that: 'The time and place of the future Congress was

Kramář, in an apparently ebullient mood, stated in his concluding words that the Congress had succeeded in reinforcing the basic tenets of the Neo-Slav movement. He admitted, however, when congratulating Bobchev on his successful chairmanship of the gathering that there had been 'discord' during the Congress, brought about by 'misunderstandings'. Kramář ascribed these misunderstandings to 'the notorious distrustfulness of the Slavs'.[160] Referring to the decision, taken in principle, to hold a further Congress at an unspecified date and place, he declared: 'Our work has been successfully completed, and the hopes of our enemies, that the Sofia Congress would be the last, are proved to have been in vain. We have witnessed, not the funeral, but the greatest strengthening of the Slav idea, we shall joyfully call a third, fourth, fifth, and further Slav Congresses.'[161] It appears, however, that this flamboyant display of unbounded confidence and optimism was not a true reflection of Kramář's inner feelings. During his trial in 1916, the Czech leader confessed that: 'The Sofia Congress marked the end of the Neo-Slav movement, its ceremonial burial. A Russo-Polish reconciliation...was out of the question, external conditions were so desolate – there therefore remained no alternative but to bid farewell to the beautiful, idealistic dreams.'[162] When the prosecution drew the attention of the defendant to the discrepancy between the two above quoted remarks, Kramář replied that at the conclusion of the Sofia Congress he had, naturally, been unable to state openly that the Neo-Slav movement had reached its end. His insistence that the principles of the movement had been strengthened was, he maintained, not an untruth. Neo-Slavism had successfully resisted contamination by the right-wing ideas held by many of the Russian delegates. Nevertheless, in his mind, Kramář claimed, he had been aware that nothing could be achieved against Russian nationalism.[163]

These assertions are to some extent substantiated by, what was in effect, a lengthy post-mortem examination of the Sofia Congress

---

deliberately not specified, in order not to prejudice the chances of its speedy convention.' Červinka, in 'Druhý přípravný sjezd slovanský', p. 709, stated that the next Congress would 'probably' take place in Prague, in 1911.

[160] *Slavyanski sŭbor v Sofiya*, pp. 184–5.   [161] *Národní listy*, 11 July 1910.

[162] *Proces dra. Kramáře*, II, p. 97. Even allowing for the fact that at his trial Kramář was intent on proving that the Neo-Slav movement, regarded by the prosecution as subversive, had ceased to exist after 1910 he was, undoubtedly, supported by the facts.

[163] H.H.St.A., *Polizei Direktion Wien*, Pr.Z. 21636K/71, 15 April 1916; *Proces dra. Kramáře*, III, part 2, p. 186.

in particular, and the Neo-Slav movement in general, conducted by Kramář in four instalments in the pages of *Národní listy* during August 1910. Although these articles contained the expected optimistic references to the successful nature of the Sofia Congress,[164] and emphasised that 'Neo-Slavism had survived the crisis of infancy, and that there was no reason for concern about its future', it was clearly evident, from his words, that the future of the movement was very much in jeopardy. He repeated his regret at the absence of the Poles and, though he granted that most Neo-Slavs understood the difficulties confronting their Polish colleagues, he nevertheless believed more could have been achieved for the Polish cause had their representatives attended the meetings.[165] As for the absence of Russian liberals Kramář declared, with considerable bitterness, that 'they have a gift for always doing things directly contrary to the dictates of common sense'. Had their representatives been present in Sofia, he argued, 'the results of the Congress would have been more positive'.[166] Turning to the cultural aspects of the Congress, Kramář claimed that significant progress had been made. However, in order for the decisions taken to be implemented, a strong executive was required. The lack of such a body, he complained, was 'the most painful aspect of Neo-Slavism. Hitherto, the greater part of the work has been carried out in Prague.' After remarking, somewhat dismally, that 'we departed from Sofia with a feeling of satisfaction, that not all that had filled our hearts with such great happiness two years previously in Prague had been lost', Kramář expressed the hope that the entire Slav world would again come together at the cultural exhibition due to be staged in Prague in 1913. There, he believed, 'we shall all sincerely and heartily shake hands, despite the fact that the policies of states and governments prevent the realisation of all that we desire in the interest of peace and love between the Slav nations'.[167]

The editorial staff of *Národní listy* were also rather cautious in assessing the outcome of the second Neo-Slav Congress, although they viewed the future with some optimism. The Sofia proceedings

[164] In the first article of the series Kramář wrote: 'Despite all the difficulties, the Sofia Congress was a far greater success than had geen anticipated.' *Národní listy*, 10 August 1910 (Kramář, 'Po sofijském sjezdu', I).
[165] *Ibid.*, 11 August 1910 (Kramář, 'Po sofijském sjezdu', II).
[166] *Ibid.*, 12 August 1910 (Kramář, 'Po sofijském sjezdu', III).
[167] *Ibid.*, 14 August 1910 (Kramář, 'Po sofijském sjezdu', IV).

were described as 'incomplete' but having, nevertheless, carried out some 'honest work, which would not disappear without trace'.[168] Writing in the Realist organ, *Čas*, Pavlů painted a similar picture. Commenting that 'the Neo-Slav movement had not disintegrated, but neither had it been strengthened', he recorded, with relief, that the conflict between the rival forces represented in Sofia had not occurred, but regretted that the principles of the movement had not been further elaborated.[169] Another prominent Czech participant, Polívka, confirmed that the Sofia meetings lacked the aura of the previous Prague Congress, but nevertheless maintained that the second Congress had been a useful working session.[170] A more critical appraisal came from the pen of Beneš who, with the various instances of discord uppermost in his mind and together with the benefit of hindsight, wrote in 1925: 'Despite the external manifestations of the Congress, the entire atmosphere [of the proceedings] clearly indicated the state of the Neo-Slav movement.'[171]

Russian reaction to the Congress was mixed. Writing in *Novoe vremya* one of the Russian participants, Vergun, declared the Congress to have been, in general, a success and compared it favourably with the earlier Neo-Slav gathering in Prague. Vergun explained that: 'The sincerity of the speeches and the warmth and conviction of the speakers distinguished the Sofia Congress from the stilted atmosphere experienced during the Congress in Prague.' He also noted, with satisfaction, that the 'troublesome ideologues' of Austro-Slavism had been absent from the Congress.[172] This last point was also taken up in an editorial article in the same newspaper entitled 'A Defeat for Austro-Slavism'. *Novoe vremya* expressed considerable delight that the Sofia Congress had clearly indicated that 'Neo-Slavism was not identical with Austro-Slavism'.[173] The conservative Russian newspaper was evidently satisfied that the Russian point of view had carried the day at the second Neo-Slav Congress.

Earlier, however, a correspondent of *Novoe vremya* had been rather less pleased with the outcome of the Congress. It was pointed out, with considerable bitterness, that although the object

---

[168] *Ibid.*, 13 August 1910.
[169] *Čas*, 23 July 1910 (Pavlů, 'Po slovanském sjezdě').
[170] Polívka, 'Slovanský sjezd sofijský', p. 22.
[171] Beneš, *Úvahy o slovanství*, p. 166.   [172] *Novoe vremya*, 9 (22) July 1910.
[173] *Ibid.*, 28 July (10 August) 1910.

of the Sofia gathering had been the strengthening of Slav unity, particularly between the Russians and the other Slav peoples, the entire world had in fact witnessed disunity amongst the Russians themselves. Responsibility for this spectacle was placed on the Russian liberals, whose 'childish behaviour' indicated a 'lack of patriotism'. The article concluded with the cry: 'God deliver Slavdom from such treacherous friends and it will, sooner or later, be able to handle its enemies alone.'[174] The activities of the handful of Russian liberals present at the Congress had clearly antagonised conservative Russian opinion, and marred what it otherwise regarded as a not unsuccessful demonstration of Russian leadership of the Slav world.

The Russian liberals themselves, as their scant representation at the Congress indicated, paid relatively little attention to the events in Sofia. *Rech'* in an editorial article dismissed the Congress as 'a series of pompous demonstrations accompanied by much customary window-dressing'. In the opinion of that newspaper the Sofia Congress had, in fact, little connection with Neo-Slavism as it had been originally conceived. True adherents to the movement, *Rech'* maintained, were to be found 'not so much amongst the participants at the Congress as amongst those who refused to attend'.[175] The same newspaper had complained, shortly before the commencement of the event, of the 'intrusion of ideology' into the Sofia Congress. The ideology it had in mind was, of course, that of the Russian right wing, which constituted one of the two opposing forces within the Neo-Slav movement. *Rech'* argued that the 'deep fissure which had been present in the movement from its inception, had now developed into an unbridgeable chasm'. The idealistic Neo-Slavism of the Prague Congress of 1908, it argued, had nothing in common with the chauvinism of the right wing dominated Third Duma, whose representatives were playing leading roles at the Sofia gathering. Although *Rech'* wished the Sofia Congress well it considered it unwise to term it 'the second Neo-Slav Congress', for that invited the rejoinder 'second and last'.[176] This prophesy was to be borne out by events.

From the point of view of Kramář and his allies at the time, however, the Sofia Congress, though not an overwhelming success, was certainly far from the widely expected disaster. Despite the

[174] *Ibid.*, 2 (15) July 1910.   [175] *Rech'*, 30 (13 July) 1910.
[176] *Ibid.*, 22 June (5 July) 1910.

numerical superiority of the right-wing Russian delegates, the more liberal Neo-Slavs present succeeded in preventing the former from publicly imposing their reactionary ideology on the Congress. In the eyes of many, the mere association of the Russian conservative forces with the Neo-Slav movement was sufficient evil, but a complete identification with the view held by the Russian right wing would have been an even greater misfortune. Much of the credit for this achievement was due to Kramář and the Czech delegation who, as Pavlů commented, 'were the greatest barrier against the [representatives of] old Slavophilism and avoided association with such right-wing Russians as Bobrinsky'.[177] A more independent view, that of the British representative in Sofia, confirms this observation. M. C. Findlay wrote that: 'The Neo-Slavs, under the guiding influence of Dr Kramarz, may be said to have been so far successful that they prevented the Pan-Slavists from capturing the congress.'[178] Reports, published by Bashmakov and certain other members of the Russian delegation, claiming that the two streams of thought, Slavophilism and Neo-Slavism, had coalesced at the Congress, were denied by other participants.[179] A Polish journalist, T. S. Grabowski, who was present as a guest of honour at the Sofia gatherings, also denied reports that Kramář had been uncritical of the reactionary Russian delegates. Grabowski stated that the contrary was true – he himself had witnessed both Kramář and Bobchev make 'very energetic and even desperate attempts' to contain the Russian right wing. Furthermore, he claimed, that 'they constantly defended the Polish cause, and during the exploits of Pogodin and Stakhovich they took a stand very favourable to us [i.e. the Poles] which resulted in a sharp clash between Kramář and Bobrinsky'.[180]

Some nationalistic members of the Russian delegation were certainly not elated by what had taken place at Sofia. Kulakovsky, a close associate of Bobrinsky, made a highly critical attack on Kramář for his public defence of the Poles, and his assertion that those who oppressed another Slav nation could not be considered true Slavs. Kulakovsky observed that Kramář was

---

[177] *Čas*, 23 July 1910 (Pavlů, 'Po slovanském sjezdě').
[178] PRO, FO, 371/834, Findlay to Grey, 26737, Sofia, 19 July 1910.
[179] Polívka, 'Slovanský sjezd sofijský', p. 25.
[180] T. S. Grabowski, 'Ještě novoslovanský sjezd v Sofii', *Slovanský přehled*, XIV (1912), p. 79.

powerless to deprive Russia of her Slavonic character, even if the Russians had Russified and absorbed all the Poles. And besides, frankly, by Russifying the Poles, the Russian nation would become more Slavonic, despite the strictures of Mr Kramář and all the principles of Neo-Slavism, which have now become 'Pogodin–Stakhovich rubbish' having sought refuge in the Moscow based Kadet Society for Slav Culture. Thus, after a little reflection, the beautiful sounding phrases are shown to be senseless, and the arrow, aimed at Russia from Austria, has missed its target.[181]

Vergun, on the other hand, was not displeased with Kramář's behaviour, claiming that the Czech leader 'conducted himself in a manner appropriate to a true Slav statesman', and adding that although Kramář prevented any unnecessary attacks on Austria–Hungary or Turkey, he nevertheless 'behaved with generous Slav tolerance towards those of a different mind'.[182]

In one respect, however, Kramář undoubtedly did please the Russian right wing. During the course of the Sofia meetings, Bobrinsky publicly expressed his gratitude to the Czech leader for having supported the Russophil Ukrainians, who maintained that they were, what the Russian nationalists considered them to be, an integral part of the Russian nation.[183]

The mere fact that the valuable, though nevertheless negative, achievement of preventing the domination of the Russian right wing was generally considered the outstanding success of the Sofia Congress, indicated how little the gathering had actually achieved. Indeed, the scepticism of some observers regarding the Neo-Slav movement was such that they considered the very existence of the Congress as a success.[184] As had been the case at the Prague Congress the tone of the speeches made in Sofia had been enthusiastic, though perhaps a little more muted. In contrast with the previous Neo-Slav assembly, the Sofia Congress made few significant new decisions, and its achievements were largely limited to rather irresolute appeals for the realisation of proposals for Slav co-operation, produced during the initial stages of the movement. Little or no progress had been made with any of these schemes during the intervening two years. A Slav bank had not been

[181] P. A. Kulakovsky, 'Slavyanski sezd v Sofii', cited in *Proces dra. Kramáře*, II, pp. 94, 96.   [182] *Novoe vremya*, 9 (22) July 1910.
[183] *Proces dra. Kramáře*, I, p. 46.
[184] PRO, FO, 371/834, Findlay to Grey, 26737, Sofia, 19 July 1910.

established, a Slav news agency did not exist, and preparations for the great Slav exhibition due, originally, to have been held in Moscow the following year, had not even commenced. The enthusiasm for these and other projects seems to have waned, as it became increasingly evident that the chances of implementation were slight. The British representative in Sofia accurately summarised the outcome of the Congress in the following words: 'The results do not seem to be very great, nor do the various proposals... appear likely to have much practical effect.'[185]

In addition, the Sofia Congress failed to make any progress towards eradicating the two principal inter-Slav disputes which were poisoning the atmosphere of the Slav world: the protracted, acrimonious Russo-Polish conflict; and the more localised, though no less bitter, disagreement between Bulgaria and Serbia over Macedonia. A proposal, by a member of the Russian delegation, to establish a Slav Conciliation Commission, to be responsible for solving the various disputes dividing the Slav nations, received scant attention.[186] Although a memorandum on the situation in Macedonia, appealing for the resolution of the dispute between the two Balkan Slav states concerned, was submitted to the Congress by Macedonian *émigrés*, the document was, without discussion, simply referred to the Neo-Slav Executive Committee.[187] The Russo-Polish dispute, ever in the forefront of Neo-Slav minds, was raised at the meetings, due largely to the insistence of Kramář, despite the absence of the Polish delegates.[188] Nevertheless, as might have been expected, the Congress did not achieve the slightest improvement in Russo-Polish relations, as he himself admitted. Moreover, it became increasingly evident that the dispute was insoluble within the existing Russian state.[189] The knowledge that the Neo-Slav movement was, in this vital respect, impotent, did

---

[185] *Ibid.*

[186] Červinka, 'Druhý přípravný sjezd slovanský', p. 714.

[187] *Novoe vremya*, 4 (17) July 1910. Regarding relations between Serbia and Bulgaria, it was later maintained by the Austro-Hungarian authorities that the foundations of the Balkan League, an alliance of which both Serbia and Bulgaria became members, had been laid during the Sofia Congress. *Proces dra. Kramáře*, I, p. 49; II, p. 99. This is unlikely to have been the case, as neither government was represented at the Neo-Slav gathering.

[188] Grabowski, 'Ještě novoslovanský sjezd v Sofii', p. 80. Kramář himself wrote, in *Národní listy*, 11 August 1910 ('Po sofijském sjezdu', II): 'The Poles were not present in Sofia, but the Russo-Polish question was.'

[189] Kramář, *Na obranu*, p. 27; *Proces dra. Kramáře*, II, p. 97.

nothing to increase the confidence of its members or to ensure its survival as a coherent force. From the point of view of Czech–Russian relations the Sofia Congress also produced few, if any, positive results. During the course of the proceedings the Czech delegation succeeded in antagonising still further the right-wing Russians, represented by Bobrinsky and his associates from the St Petersburg Slavonic Benevolent Society. This, together with the espousal of the Polish cause, did not enhance the standing of the Czechs in the eyes of the Russian government. As regards the Russian liberals, with whom many of the Czech Neo-Slavs were most eager to associate, the fact that they were barely represented at the Congress served to indicate their lack of interest in achieving closer ties with Kramář and his allies. The absence of representatives from the moderate centre of the Russian political spectrum was a considerable disappointment to him, and he complained bitterly that the liberal Russians 'simply do not understand us Western Slavs – or perhaps they are incapable of understanding us, as they fail to comprehend our nationalism... They see only the chauvinistic nationalism of hatred, which is so fashionable in Russia today'.[190]

The most significant long term outcome of the Sofia Congress was the fact that the movement failed to survive. The Congress itself was not directly responsible for the demise of the movement, which was caused primarily by unfavourable international political conditions, but it failed to give sufficient inspiration or sense of purpose to ensure the continued existence of Neo-Slavism. Although several subsequent events, such as the Congress of Slav Journalists held in Belgrade in 1911 and the celebrations, including a Sokol festival, which accompanied the unveiling of the memorial to Palacký in Prague the following year, did have Neo-Slav overtones, nevertheless, the movement officially never met again. The Neo-Slav Executive Committee held no further meetings, and after the death of Krasovsky in 1911, his place as leader of the Russian branch of the movement remained unfilled.[191] Despite Kramář's assertion to the contrary at Sofia, the passage of time has shown, conclusively, that the second Congress was, in reality, the funeral ceremony of the Neo-Slav movement.

[190] *Národní listy*, 12 August 1910 (Kramář, 'Po sofijském sjezdu', III).
[191] *Proces dra. Kramáře*, IV, part 2, p. 32.

7

The end of a dream, 1910–1914

The atmosphere of unease, which prevailed in European international relations as a consequence of the Austro-Hungarian action in the Balkans in 1908, persisted and, during the next few years, conditions deteriorated even further, culminating in the general conflagration of the First World War. Throughout this period attention was focused mainly on the explosive situation in the Balkan Peninsula where a series of local wars contributed greatly to maintaining the tension. Following the humiliation sustained at the hands of Austria–Hungary and Germany over the annexation of Bosnia and Herzegovina, Russia concentrated intensely on strengthening its position in that strategically important area. The principal aim of Russian foreign policy, the direction of which had passed in 1910 into the control of Sazonov, was to form closer ties with the independent Balkan states with the object of creating an alliance directed against the Habsburg Empire. These endeavours met with success and an alliance known as the Balkan League, involving Serbia, Bulgaria, Greece and Montenegro, came into being in 1912 though it was directed more against Turkey than against Russia's main rival, the Dual Monarchy.[1]

Austria–Hungary, together with its ally Germany, although at the time having no definite knowledge of the secret negotiations between the Balkan states encouraged by Russia, viewed the developments leading up to the formation of the Balkan League with understandable apprehension. Although Vienna had no quarrel with one of the principal partners in the Balkan alliance, Bulgaria, and vice versa, relations with the other main participant, Serbia, were very different. The Habsburg authorities regarded the Empire's independent, small, but volatile, Slav neighbour as

For details see E. C. Thaden, *Russia and the Balkan Alliance of 1910* (Pennsylvania, 1965); E. C. Helmreich, *The Diplomacy of the Balkan Wars, 1912–1913* (Harvard, 1938), pp. 3–89; and also S. D. Sazonov, *Vospominaniya* (Paris–Berlin, 1927), pp. 58–63.

a constant source of danger. This enmity was partly due to the fact that Serbia, by its very existence, encouraged the irredentist tendencies of the Serbs and other South Slavs resident within the Dual Monarchy, and partly because the independent South Slav state, enjoying Russian patronage, formed a considerable barrier to the eastwards expansion of both the Austro-Hungarian and German Empires. The Serbs, in turn, viewed the Habsburg Monarchy with undisguised hostility, and regarded the government in Vienna as constituting an even greater menace to their freedom than that in Constantinople. The annexation of Bosnia and Herzegovina, combined with the oppression of the South Slav inhabitants of Croatia and the annexed provinces and followed by the infamous Agram High Treason Trial and the Friedjung Trial, only served to further reinforce this attitude.[2]

The persisting tension in relations between the Habsburg Monarchy and neighbouring Serbia, together with the fear of growing Russian involvement in the area, resulted in increasing the Austro-Hungarian authorities' suspicion of Slav intentions. The Vienna government, consequently, adopted a more cautious attitude towards attempts to foster any form of co-operation between the Slav nations, both inside and outside the Dual Monarchy.

[2] The protracted High Treason Trial conducted in Agram (Zagreb), the capital of Croatia, during the course of 1909 was intended by the Hungarian authorities to prove the existence of a conspiracy aiming to detach the South Slav territories from the Habsburg Empire and to create a Greater Serbia. Of the fifty or so Serbs who were placed on trial over thirty were found guilty and sentenced to lengthy terms of imprisonment though no conclusive evidence of their guilt was produced. Masaryk, then a member of the Austrian Parliament, raised the subject of the Agram Trial in the Reichsrat, condemning the actions of the Hungarian authorities and drawing attention to the ineptitude of the court. Those found guilty at Agram subsequently appealed to a higher court, which acquitted them of the original charges. The second trial, a libel case brought by several prominent Austro-Hungarian South Slavs who had been accused in an article by the Austrian historian H. Friedjung of conspiracies similar to those in the Agram Trial, took place in Vienna towards the end of 1909, intervening between the two hearings of the Treason Trial. During the course of the libel proceedings it became evident that the material on which Friedjung based his allegations, purporting to have been obtained from Serbia and supplied to him by the Austro-Hungarian Ministry of Foreign Affairs, was forged. Masaryk, who appeared as a witness during the trial, later succeeded in proving that the documents concerned had been fabricated at the Austro-Hungarian legation in Belgrade. Although the Habsburg Ministry of Foreign Affairs never admitted any complicity in the forging of the documents, both these cases resulted in further discrediting the Balkan policies of the Vienna government. See R. W. Seton-Watson, *The Southern Slav Question*, pp. 179–92, 200–87, 307–28.

The above-mentioned Agram Trial was one example of this new policy, and the less tolerant view taken by the authorities towards the Neo-Slav movement in the summer of 1909 was another. Even when, following the strains of 1908 and 1909, relations between Vienna and St Petersburg returned to normal, and became for a short period almost cordial, the Austro-Hungarian authorities, nevertheless, maintained a close observation of the activities of the Slavs within the Dual Monarchy who were suspected of being sympathetic towards Russia. Amongst those subjected to scrutiny were, predictably, the Neo-Slavs.[3] Conditions were not improved by the persistence of racial strife within the Habsburg Empire. The electoral reform of 1907, introduced largely in order to eradicate these conflicts, had manifestly failed to do so. In Bohemia in particular, hostility between the Czech and German elements of the population increased in severity, as was reflected by the obstructive tactics employed by the German deputies in the Bohemian Diet and, in turn, by the Czech obstruction of the Vienna Parliament. The Austrian government, though anxious in the interest of harmony to maintain a balance between the warring nationalities, tended, inevitably, to act in favour of the German population, being itself predominantly German in character. The growing internal problems in Bohemia and elsewhere resulted in heightening further the suspicions of the authorities about the potentially hostile activities of the Czechs and their Slav associates. It was due largely to these reasons of domestic and international politics combined with the fact that the movement had, up to that time, achieved none of its basic aims that Neo-Slavism, as a coherent political force, practically faded out of existence after the Sofia Congress and few serious attempts were made to revive it.

Although a Congress of Slav Journalists, conducted in the spirit of Neo-Slavism, took place in Belgrade during the summer of 1911,[4] no steps were taken at the occasion to instil new life into the movement. This Congress, the tenth in the series, was attended mainly by journalists from the Slav peoples of the Habsburg Empire, although in addition to the Serbian hosts, Russian and

---

[3] This is evident from the multitude of reports from various sources collected together in the H.H.St.A., PA, XL 219, 220, *Panslav Bewegung* 1–17. Criticism of the Neo-Slav movement was also voiced in the Delegations by Count Aehrenthal and others. *Národní listy*, 15, 16 October 1910.

[4] H.H.St.A., PA, XL 220, *Panslav Bewegung* 11, Ugron to Aehrenthal, 42B, Belgrade, 29 June 1911, and 53D, Belgrade, 15 July 1911.

Bulgarian journalists were also present. The main subject under discussion at the gathering concerned, yet again, the creation of a Slav news agency. Despite the fact that the Russian St Petersburg Telegraph Agency was planning to extend its network of correspondents in Slav centres, the assembled journalists, much to the disappointment of their Russian colleagues, insisted on persevering in their efforts to form a separate Slav news agency.[5] In other respects also, the meeting of Slav journalists did not prove to be a particularly auspicious manifestation of Slav solidarity. During one of the accompanying banquets the orchestra, whilst playing the national anthems of the participants, omitted to play the Russian anthem, though it included the Polish one. One of the Polish journalists present then added insult to injury by expressing gratitude that the 'offensive tune' had not been played. The Russian delegates protested vigorously and, led by Vergun, withdrew from the banquet.[6] Although the incident itself was trivial, the attitude of the Russians, such as Vergun, was significant. Writing later in *Novoe vremya*, he described the Belgrade Journalists' Congress as a demonstration of 'concealed Austro-Slavism'. He alleged that although the supporters of Austro-Slavism had made appearances at both the Prague and Sofia Neo-Slav Congresses, the 'good sense' of the other participants triumphed over the 'petty intrigues' of those who advocated 'a great Slav Austria'. At the recent meeting in Belgrade, however, the Austro-Slavs were unrestrained and this gave rise to a 'considerable scandal'. The major objective of the Austro-Slavs was, in his opinion, to reduce the Russian delegates to a secondary position whilst giving precedence to the Polish and Czech representatives.[7]

A further opportunity for the revival of Neo-Slavism occurred in 1912, during the Slav gathering in Prague in connection with the unveiling of the monument to Palacký. Again, no attempt was made to resuscitate the movement although, as was evident from the speech delivered at the unveiling ceremony, Kramář had not abandoned his views on Slav co-operation. Quoting Palacký's famous words, written in 1865, warning against the dangerous consequences of introducing the proposed dualistic reconstruction of the Empire,

[5] *Novoe vremya*, 13 (26) June, 29 June (12 July), 7 (20) July 1911.
[6] *Ibid.*, 2 (15), 7 (20) July 1911; *Proces dra. Kramáře*, III, part 1, p. 74; *Slovanský přehled*, XIV (1912), p. 45.
[7] *Novoe vremya*, 7 (20) July 1911 (D. N. Vergun, 'Zamaskyrovanny avstro-slavism').

'We existed before Austria, and we shall exist also after it', Kramář exhorted the nation to remain faithful to the ideals of the great Czech historian and national leader. Palacký's ideas of national autonomy for the Czech nation within a Habsburg Empire which was just to all its component nationalities were, the speaker maintained, as relevant in 1912 as they had been during the lifetime of their originator. Turning from the position of the Czech nation within the Dual Monarchy to the wider issue of inter-Slav relations, Kramář reminded his audience that the guiding principles of the Neo-Slav Congress of 1908 had also been the principles of Palacký. He continued:

We do not desire the forcible creation of new state units, our aim is not the construction of a great Pan-Slav empire; that is contrary to both Palacký's ideas and ours. We wish to see a new spirit of Slavism; the spirit of justice for all, that is, justice from all the Slav nations, from the largest to the smallest, towards every other fraternal Slav people with whom they are neighbours; we wish to see the absolute exclusion of all use of force against others.[8]

Familiar words which, despite their frequent repetition, were still no nearer to realisation.

The unveiling of the Palacký monument was the highlight of a week of intensive activities, during the course of which a Sokol festival and a Congress of Slav Journalists, the last to be held, also took place. No Russian representatives attended the Journalists' Congress,[9] presumably as a result of the disagreements at the meeting the previous year, although a considerable number of Russians were present at the Sokol festival. Over eight hundred Russian Sokols arrived for the celebrations, led by their chairman, Gizhitsky, who had participated in both the Prague and Sofia Neo-Slav Congresses. The Russian delegation included two other former Neo-Slavs, the academics Bekhterev and Francev. Also present in Prague was an official from the Russian Ministry of Education, V. T. Shevyakov. Guests from most other Slav nations, and from Britain, France and the United States, also attended. The Slav guests included the Slovene, Hribar; the Russophil Ukrainian, Glebovitsky; and the Pole, Straszewicz, all earlier active in the Neo-Slav movement.[10]

[8] *Národní listy*, 1 July 1912 (evening edition); *Proces dra. Kramáře*, II, p. 104. Palacký's words first appeared in *Idea státu rakouského* (Prague, 1865), p. 67.
[9] *Slovanský přehled*, XIV (1912), p. 397; *Proces dra. Kramáře*, III, part 1, p. 74.
[10] *Památník šestého sletu všesokolského*, pp. 225–8; *Národní listy*, 30 June, 1, 2 July 1912.

The Sixth Sokol Congress took place between 29 June and 1 July. Over 35 000 gymnasts participated in mass displays, staged before a quarter of a million visitors to Prague. The gymnastic performances were, by all accounts, executed with the utmost precision and constituted an impressive spectacle. The British journalist, Steed, who was present at the festivities, recalled that, during the gymnastic demonstrations, he remarked to Kramář: 'These are not gymnasts, they are an army.' The Czech leader replied in the affirmative, adding 'with proper weapons they would count in a European war'.[11] Masaryk's more pacific outlook is evident from a conversation with Steed which took place the following day when, as the British journalist reported, at an open air meeting in the centre of Prague the assembled Sokols

spontaneously sang the 'Hei Slovane' – a stirring air which had become a kind of inter-Slav hymn...Turning to Professor Masaryk who was by my side, I expressed amazement. He replied, characteristically, 'Yes, it is stupendous, but I wish our Czechs would sing words less jingo. The Poles sing "Poland is not yet lost" to the same air and the other Slav peoples sing other words, but our people sing, as you know, "Thunder and lightning, thunder and lightning, the Russians are with us and those who withstand them the French will sweep away". That is not quite the right spirit for a national revival.'[12]

Despite the militant potential of the Sokols, the presence in Prague of a substantial number of Russian guests did not give rise to any significant pro-Russian demonstrations. Although the Russian delegation was enthusiastically welcomed on its arrival in the Czech capital the Sokol festivities were, in general, devoid of Russophil fervour. It is likely that the approval given by the Russian Duma, on the eve of the Prague celebrations, to the proposals for the creation of the Kholm province, thus detaching territory from Russian Poland, did little to enhance the popularity of Russia in the eyes of many Czechs.[13] The absence of pro-Russian feeling did not escape the attention of *Novoe vremya* which reported, with some disappointment, that the Sokol movement had

[11] Steed, *Through Thirty Years*, I, p. 359. Steed was not the only person to be impressed by the military potential of the Sokols. A Russian representative, V. D. Kuzmin-Karavayev wrote, after witnessing the performances: 'If all that the Sokols lack are weapons, all that the Czechs lack is national independence.' *Proces dra. Kramáře*, I, p. 49.
[12] Steed, *Through Thirty Years*, I, pp. 359–60.
[13] *Slovanský přehled*, XIV (1912), p. 397.

come under the influence of the Austro-Hungarian government, adding that it was evident that 'the earlier enthusiasm of the Czechs for the Slav idea has significantly weakened'.[14]

Although the Palacký celebrations of 1912 were undoubtedly an important demonstration of Czech nationalist feelings, indicating the strength and purpose of the Sokol organisation, and despite the fact that the festivities were conducted in the spirit of what were known as Neo-Slav ideas, nevertheless, no definite effort was made to revive the movement. Kramář did not even attempt to convene a meeting of the Neo-Slav Executive Committee, although representatives of most of the Slav nations involved, some of whom had been personally associated with the movement, were present in the Czech capital.[15] *Slovanský přehled*, in an editorial article on the Prague gatherings, drew attention to the similarities between the current events and the celebrations surrounding the laying of the foundation stone of the Palacký monument in 1898 which were, in effect, responsible for the subsequent birth of the Neo-Slav movement. Pointing to the lack of achievement during the intervening fourteen years the writer, A. Černý, remarked that 'the only positive result has been the appearance of the monument itself (although that has taken long enough)'. Černý continued:

How negligible are the achievements of Neo-Slavism the seeds of which had then been sown, germinating during the subsequent visit of the Austro-Slav trio [Kramář, Hribar, and Glebovitsky] to St Petersburg, and which so rapidly withered and degenerated that it is difficult to ascertain whether the movement has perished or whether it still survives.[16]

Although it is impossible to state with any certainty why the opportunity was not seized to stage a concerted effort at reviving the Neo-Slav movement, an explanation may be found in the internal political conditions in the Czech lands and Austria-Hungary in general. Kramář had launched the Neo-Slav movement four years previously, motivated, partly, by the desire to maintain his position as leader of the Czech nation, despite the losses suffered by his party at the general election of 1907. At the time of the 1912 Palacký celebrations he no longer required a device to achieve this for although, as indicated by the results of the parliamentary elections of 1911, the Young Czech Party

[14] *Novoe vremya*, 16 (29) June 1912.   [15] *Proces dra. Kramáře*, II, p. 100.
[16] *Slovanský přehled*, XIV (1912), p. 397.

continued to decline, largely to the advantage of the Agrarians and National Socialists, Kramář, nevertheless, remained acknowledged as one of the principal leaders of the nation. The Young Czech Party's share of the total votes cast for Czech political parties in the first ballot in 1911 fell from 7.31 per cent in 1907 to 5.18 per cent, whereas the Agrarians increased their share from 19.22 per cent to 23.56 per cent, and the National Socialists from 6.98 per cent to 8.77 per cent. In terms of parliamentary representation the Young Czechs suffered a loss of one seat, their total being reduced to fourteen. The Agrarians, however, gained a further ten seats, securing a total of thirty-seven; and the National Socialists increased their parliamentary strength from six to thirteen, with their Progressive State-Rights Party allies gaining one further seat, giving them a total of four. The Czech Social Democrats, now split into Autonomist and Centralist factions, suffered a slight decline in their proportion of total votes gained but increased their parliamentary strength to twenty-six, a gain of two seats. The Clericals, on the other hand, increased their share of the total vote but saw their representation in the Reichsrat reduced from seventeen members to seven.[17] However, despite the decline in popularity of the party of which he was leader, Kramář remained a prominent figure on the Czech political scene. Other factors militating against an attempted Neo-Slav revival were, undoubtedly, the movement's lack of achievement so far, the uncooperative attitude of the Russian government over the treatment of Poland, and also the desire to do nothing to antagonise the Austrian authorities, or the Bohemian Germans, with whom the Czechs were, at the time, attempting to negotiate a settlement.

Although the Neo-Slav movement did not show signs of life during the summer of 1912, the events of the autumn and winter did, for a short while, stimulate hopes of a revival. The secret formation of the Balkan League during the course of 1912 was followed in October by the declaration of war on Turkey by the

[17] Figures adapted from K. K. Statistische Central-Commission, *Österreichische Statistik*, VII, part 1, 'Die Ergebnisse der Reichratswahlen im Jahre 1911', pp. 6, 10–11; Bosl ed., *Handbuch der Geschichte der böhmischen Länder*, pp. 460–1; Jenks, *Austrian Electoral Reform*, p. 215. The number of votes cast in the first ballot for the five major Czech parties were as follows: Social Democrats, 376 608; Agrarians, 257 717; Clericals, 211 180; National Socialists, 95 901; Young Czechs, 56 673.

four Balkan partners. By the end of November most of the Turkish forces in the Balkans had been defeated, the Bulgarians were threatening Constantinople, and the Serbs were advancing towards the Adriatic coast. An armistice was signed early in December though this was interrupted for a period during February and March 1913 when Turkey recommenced hostilities only to suffer further defeats.[18]

The spectacular successes of the armies of the Balkan allies caused considerable excitement throughout the Slav world, where the war was seen largely in terms of a conflict between the Slavs and the Ottoman Empire. In Russia, news of the allied victories was received with great jubilation. Although the government maintained a cautious and correct attitude towards events in the Balkans, Pan-Slav opinion was elated. The various Slavonic associations intensified their activities, holding public meetings and organising collections to finance the provisions of medical personnel and supplies to their embattled brethren.[19] Slavonic banquets were held attended by leading public figures in addition to ardent Pan-Slavs such as Bobrinsky and his followers, during the course of which, in the words of one uninvolved observer, 'patriotic songs were sung and fiery speeches were made'.[20] The Russian government, though maintaining its support of the Balkan League, did not participate in these enthusiastic public manifestations and, largely out of a desire to avoid offence to Austria–Hungary, popularly regarded as an enemy of the Balkan Slavs, it attempted to cool the excessive fervour of Pan-Slav opinion. Although several Pan-Slav demonstrations were held in St Petersburg and Moscow, these were later prohibited by the authorities, as were the Slavonic banquets.[21] This new-found enthusiasm

[18] Helmreich, *The Diplomacy of the Balkan Wars*, pp. 193–203, 281–314.
[19] 'Russia and the War in the Balkans', *The Russian Review*, I, no. 4 (1912), pp. 150–1; *Národní listy*, 1 January 1913.
[20] PRO, FO, 371/1743, Buchanan to Grey, 6225, St Petersburg, 6 February 1913, and 7143, St Petersburg, 10 February 1913. See also *Novoe vremya*, 19 January (1 February), 28 January (10 February), 22 March (4 April), 29 March (11 April) 1913.
[21] PRO, FO, 371/1743, Buchanan to Grey, 6225, St Petersburg, 6 February 1913. Buchanan reported that the authorities had forbidden the holding of a Slavonic banquet and were 'continuing their policy of keeping under strict control and of suppressing as far as possible any public manifestations of Slav sympathy'. Although this particular banquet did later take place, the authorities subsequently literally silenced the banquets by permitting them to be held only if no speeches were made. The organisers found this stipulation

among certain sections of Russian opinion for the Slav cause, reminiscent of the atmosphere in Russia at the time of the Russo-Turkish War of 1877–8,[22] was, however, restricted largely to sympathy for the Orthodox South Slavs. The Western Slavs, including the Czechs, gained little benefit from it.[23]

The Balkan War also attracted a considerable amount of interest within the Czech lands. Nationalist opinion enthusiastically supported the cause of the Balkan allies, and opposition to the possibility of Austro-Hungarian intervention in the war was widespread. Monetary collections were made in aid of the Balkan League, and medical supplies and personnel were dispatched to the scenes of the fighting. Nationalist newspapers and periodicals provided extensive coverage of the campaigns, and leading Czech poets gave additional moral support to their South Slav brethren through the composition of rousing verses. The outbreak of the Balkan War, accompanied by the Austro-Hungarian government's evident displeasure at the widespread victories of the Balkan League, placed many prominent Czech political figures in a quandary, similar to that brought about by the annexation crisis four years earlier. Their sympathies were again with a cause to which their state, the Habsburg Empire, was opposed. The majority of Czech deputies in the Vienna Parliament resolved this dilemma by expressing in public their support for the Balkan Slavs, yet simultaneously approving military preparations taken by the Austro-Hungarian government against Serbia and Russia.[24] Kramář justified this course of action on the grounds that, 'we have to show...that we are not enemies of the Empire'.[25]

Relations between the Habsburg Monarchy and Russia had, as a result of the Balkan conflict, once again seriously deteriorated. Late in 1912 the danger of war between the two Empires was

unacceptable and cancelled the arrangements. *Novoe vremya*, 21 January (3 February), 26 January (8 February), 29 April (12 May) 1913. See also 'Russia and the Balkan Crisis', *The Russian Review*, II, no. 2 (1913), pp. 181–2.
[22] 'Russia and the War in the Balkans', p. 151.
[23] In the first edition of the then revived journal of the St Petersburg Slavonic Benevolent Society, *Slavyanskiya izvestiya*, the editor, V. N. Korablev, was critical of the Czechs for priding themselves on their Western outlook and accused them of regarding Russians with disdain. *Národní listy*, 1 January 1913.
[24] D. Šlaisová, 'Ohlas první války balkánské 1912–1913 v českém prostředí', *Slovanské historické studie*, I (1955), pp. 244–61; M. Paulová, *Balkánské války 1912–1913 a český lid* (Prague, 1963), pp. 47–50, 69.
[25] *Národní listy*, 13 October 1912.

acute, with both sides massing troops in adjacent areas. The military successes of the Balkan allies gave rise to several political issues of substantial interest to the Habsburg Empire, the most significant of these being the Serbian demand for access to the Adriatic. The Austro-Hungarian government was totally opposed to Serbia gaining such facilities and insisted that Serbian forces be withdrawn from Durazzo (Durres), where they had reached the coast. Russia, not wishing to provoke a war with Austria–Hungary, withdrew from supporting Serbia on this point and the great powers consequently agreed in principle to the formation of an Albanian state, thus depriving Serbia of direct access to the sea. The remaining territorial disputes being gradually settled, in principle at least, by the major powers, the war itself was formally concluded by the Treaty of London, signed by the belligerent states towards the end of May 1913.[26]

At the height of the Balkan crisis several unsuccessful attempts were made at mediation between the Dual Monarchy and Serbia over the issue of access to the Adriatic. Amongst those endeavouring to achieve this aim were two leading Czech political figures. Masaryk, who visited Belgrade towards the end of 1912, acted on the instigation of the Serbian government as an intermediary in an attempt to find a compromise solution acceptable to both parties. The Austro-Hungarian Foreign Minister, Count Berchtold, who had succeeded Count Aehrenthal in 1912, however, rejected the overtures.[27] Kramář, likewise, attempted to mediate in the crisis, bringing considerable pressure to bear on the Austro-Hungarian government to permit Serbia to retain the occupied Albanian territory thus gaining access to the sea. He argued, in the Delegations and elsewhere, that Serbian preoccupation with Albania would ensure the easing of tension in Bosnia and would, therefore, be beneficial to the Habsburg Empire. In addition to making these energetic persuasive attempts he travelled secretly to Belgrade where, with the knowledge of Count Berchtold and of the Prime Minister Count Stürgkh, he consulted with members of the Serbian government. The Serbs assured their visitor that they desired friendly relations with the Habsburg Empire but emphasised the economic necessity of an Adriatic port. On his return to Vienna, however, Kramář's

[26] Helmreich, *The Diplomacy of the Balkan Wars*, pp. 206–26, 326–40.
[27] T. G. Masaryk, *Světová revoluce za války a ve válce* (Prague, 1925), p. 14.

peace-making endeavours met with a similar response from the authorities as did those of Masaryk. The Austro-Hungarian government refused to yield.[28] The principal motives behind the Czech interventions were, undoubtedly, those of self interest. War between the Habsburg Empire and Serbia would have had disastrous repercussions on the standing of the Czech nation within the Dual Monarchy. The reluctance of Czech military personnel to be transported to border areas during the height of the crisis was indicative of the unwillingness of the Czechs to be involved in a war against the South Slavs.[29] The resulting conflict with the Austro-Hungarian government would, inevitably, have provoked repressive action from the Habsburg authorities and further exacerbated the already strained racial situation in Bohemia and the other Czech lands. Economic reasons formed a further factor supporting the desire for improving relations with the neighbouring South Slav state. In retaliation against what they regarded as the hostile Balkan policies of Austria–Hungary the Serbs, following the annexation of Bosnia and Herzegovina, instituted a boycott of all goods originating from the Dual Monarchy, with no exceptions for the products of Czech owned industries. The industry and commerce of the German Empire, not included in the boycott, were reaping the benefits of the Serbian protest action – a state of affairs which the Czech industrial middle class found particularly painful.[30] Finally, it was believed that improved relations between the Habsburg Empire and Serbia would result in an improvement in relations with Russia,

[28] *Proces dra. Kramáře*, II, pp. 125–7; III, part I, pp. 71–2; Kramář, *Na obranu*, p. 28.
[29] Šlaisová, 'Ohlas první války balkánské', pp. 250–1; Paulová, *Balkánské války*, pp. 64–7, 69–73.
[30] *Proces dra. Kramáře*, II, p. 126; Masaryk, *Rakouská zahraniční politika a diplomacie*, p. 74. The following statistics on Serbian imports from Austria–Hungary and Germany are cited in *Naše doba*, xx (1913), p. 375:

Year	Total value of Serbian imports in thousands of francs	Imported from Austria–Hungary		Imported from Germany	
		Value in thousands of francs	(%)	Value in thousands of francs	(%)
1908	75 635	32 272	42.67	21 368	28.24
1909	73 535	17 967	24.43	28 852	39.24

an aim constantly in the forefront of the minds of many Czech political leaders, particularly of those who had been involved in the Neo-Slav movement.

Kramář and his political associates were also of the opinion that the victories of the independent Balkan states would exercise a favourable effect on relations between Russia and the Dual Monarchy. He maintained that if the dictum 'The Balkans to the Balkan nations' were fully applied Russian and Austro-Hungarian interests in that area would no longer come into conflict, and a *rapprochement* between the two Empires would follow.[31] A significant consequence of the Balkan conflict, from the Czech point of view, was the fact that Serbia and Bulgaria, fortified by defeating Turkey, would, hopefully, form a barrier against the eastwards expansion of Germany. With Germany thus excluded, the division of the Balkan Peninsula into Russian and Austro-Hungarian spheres of influence would, the Czechs believed, bring tranquillity to the area, particularly if they succeeded in their objective of making the government of the Dual Monarchy more responsive to internal Slav pressures.[32]

The rapid succession of decisive victories won by the predominantly Slav Balkan allies produced a considerable psychological influence on the Czech nation and not least on those who still placed some hope in the Neo-Slav movement. In a leading article published in *Národní listy* on New Year's Day 1913, Kramář was at his most lyrical. Referring to the uniting of the South Slav delegations which had taken place at the 1908 Prague Congress, he declared that no one then imagined how spectacular the consequences of this move would be in future years. The entire Slav world, he maintained, could rightly be proud of the achievements of their Balkan brethren. Pointing to the moral, he continued:

The Slavs have at last become aware of what can be achieved if internal dissensions are overcome and their brotherhood recognised. Undoubtedly, all true Slavs now share the feeling – if only the splendid example of the Serbs and Bulgarians would infect the other Slavs by the magic of success! There are many unnecessary disputes in our midst, harmful to us all; moreover, there is one particular dispute between two Slav nations, which is catastrophically destroying the

[31] *Národní listy*, 5 February 1913 (K. Kramář, 'Poslání kn. Hohenloha'); *Proces dra. Kramáře*, II, pp. 124–5.
[32] K. Kramář, *Problémy české politiky. Dvě řeči* (Prague, 1913), pp. 20–1.

concept of ideal Slav unity. Words have been ineffectual, perhaps the example will carry force. If, even today, it is not realised in Russia that the Russo-Polish dispute is for the Russian nation simply suicidal, then one must indeed despair over the foresight of Russian statesmen. If only the brilliant example of Slav unity in the Balkans, which has achieved miracles, would illuminate the hearts and minds of the two greatest Slav nations, the Russians and the Poles![33]

This heartfelt cry, however, went unheard. The Russian government continued on its anti-Polish course, introducing still further injustices in Russian Poland.[34] Prominent among these acts, in addition to the western provinces zemstvo legislation and the creation of the Kholm province was the acquisition by the government of the Polish owned Warsaw–Vienna Railway. This was a severe blow to Polish economic life, as Polish employees were rapidly replaced by Russian staff.[35] The intensified Russian oppression of the Finns also did nothing to enhance the standing of the Russian authorities in Czech estimation.[36]

These unfavourable features partially explain why a potentially suitable occasion for the demonstration of Czech Russophil feelings passed relatively unnoticed early in March 1913. The event was the celebration of the tercentenary of the accession of the Romanov dynasty to the Russian throne. A service of commemoration held in the Russian Orthodox Church in Prague on 6 March was attended by, amongst others, the Prague Chief of Police, representatives of the consular corps and of the Prague municipal authorities, and by the Governor of Bohemia, Count Thun. As was evident from the persons present, the celebrations were dynastic in character and lacked any Pan-Slav overtones. The official nature of the ceremony no doubt militated against any popular demonstrations of pro-Russian feeling, and none were

[33] *Národní listy*, 1 January 1913 (K. Kramář, 'Slovanstvo').
[34] *Ibid.*, 12 January 1913. Czech sympathies were, however, not entirely with the Poles as was evident from a leading article in *Národní listy* published on the fiftieth anniversary of the outbreak of the Polish uprising of 1863. In this it was asserted that the entire Slav world had suffered as a result of the Polish action. Therefore, the editorial argued: 'We have little reason for a joyous celebration of the event. It is only to be regretted, and we entreat our heavily tried Polish brethren, never again to be led into taking such a foolhardy step, as they did fifty years previously.' *Ibid.*, 22 January 1913.
[35] Reddaway and others eds., *The Cambridge History of Poland*, II, p. 406.
[36] *Národní listy*, 9 May 1913. The Russification of Finland recommenced in 1907 and increased in severity over the following years.

reported.[37] The Romanov celebrations did, however, provide an occasion for Czech publicists to restate their criticism of alleged German influence in Russian court circles and to express the hope that, as the importance of the court declined, the Russian authorities would adopt a more understanding policy towards the other Slav nations, in particular towards the Poles.[38] Kramář, in an article on the same subject, drew attention to the fact that the Romanov tercentenary coincided with the achievement of liberation by the South Slav nations. With characteristic optimism he forecast that the period of 'traditional Russian policy towards the Slavs' was now over and that a period of new, 'broader and greater' policies had arrived.[39] These hopes for a brighter future were, evidently, not being realised at the time. The negative attitude, adopted by the Russian authorities towards the manifestations of enthusiasm for the South Slavs, prompted *Národní listy* to comment that, 'of Russian diplomacy it could never be said that it possessed a Slav heart, unfortunately, it does not even possess a Slav head'. Solace was found, however, in the Russian nation, and the article continued with the happy disclosure that 'the Slav heart of the Russian people' had come to life.[40]

The elation within the Czech nation caused by the success of the Balkan alliance was accompanied by renewed hopes of reviving the Neo-Slav movement. In a further editorial article in *Národní listy* Kramář again lamented the Russian oppression of the Poles but concluded on a hopeful note, claiming that the despair of the Polish nation was unjustified and that he himself was 'unwilling and incapable of despairing'. Kramář continued: 'Neo-Slavism has passed through severe trials, but it has not perished. In the Balkans it formed the ideological foundation for the fraternal union of the Serbs and Bulgarians, and even in Russia it had rooted itself deeper than we imagined, when we observed how coldly it was received by many.'[41] This optimistic assertion was based on an editorial article concerned with the attitude of the Habsburg Empire towards the Balkan Peninsula published in the Russian newspaper *Novoe vremya*, in which the claim was made that:

[37] *Národní listy*, 7 March 1913. Leppman, in 'Ruský konsulát v Praze', p. 10, suggests that Zhukovsky deliberately chose to make the celebrations official in character in order to avoid any pro-Russian demonstrations.
[38] *Ibid.*, 5 March 1913 (leading article by J. Hrubý).
[39] *Ibid.*, 6 March 1913 (K. Kramář, 'Jubileum Romanových').
[40] *Ibid.*, 6 May 1913.   [41] *Ibid.*, 23 February 1913 (K. Kramář, 'Slovanské věci').

'The old Slavophilism is dead. Now we can speak only of that Slav formula, which does not restrict others, but gives all the opportunity of independent development.'[42] This, Kramář maintained, was a complete restatement of the principles of Neo-Slavism, and he argued that:

The ideas of the Prague Congress are the only ones capable of giving Slav reciprocity the moral foundation of right and justice demanded by the new era, when each nation wishes to lead its own life, but all desire an ideal, spiritual unity with related nations. For these reasons Neo-Slav ideas are victorious; for these reasons they have become the creed of all true Slavs, and will lead to the solution of the most difficult Slav problem, the Russo-Polish dispute, thereby founding the spiritual unity of all Slavdom, which is the most ardent desire of us all.[43]

These fervently expressed hopes were, however, soon to be shattered by the outbreak of another war in the Balkans. A dispute between the Balkan allies over the spoils of the war against Turkey, primarily over the possession of Macedonia, led to the disintegration of the Balkan League. Despite several attempts at mediation, hostilities erupted again at the end of June between Bulgarian forces on the one hand and Serbian and Greek forces on the other. Rumania also declared war on its southern neighbour and in a little over a month Bulgaria was defeated and a new peace conference had convened in Bucharest. Under the treaty signed the following month Bulgaria not only surrendered conquests of the First Balkan War to its former allies but also ceded territory to Rumania. Meanwhile, Turkey had also rejoined the fray and succeeded in regaining some areas lost during the earlier fighting.[44]

Amongst the attempts to mediate between the two conflicting parties, at least two were made by the Czechs. The first was made by Kramář during a visit to Paris in the spring of 1913 where he had inconclusive meetings with, amongst others, the diplomatic representatives of Russia and some of the Balkan states concerned. The other attempt was undertaken by Klofáč who travelled to the Balkans during May 1913 where he attempted, also without success, to mediate between Serbia and Bulgaria.[45]

[42] *Novoe vremya*, 6 (19) February 1913.
[43] *Národní listy*, 23 February 1913 (Kramář, 'Slovanské věci').
[44] Helmreich, *The Diplomacy of the Balkan Wars*, pp. 380–406.
[45] M. Paulová, *Dějiny Maffie. Odboj Čechů a Jihoslovanů za světové války, 1914–1918* (2 vols., Prague, 1937), I, pp. 29–32; Sís, ed., *Dr. Karel Kramář. Život, dílo práce*, I, pp. 92, 94.

The fratricidal Second Balkan War caused utter ruin to all hopes of reviving the Neo-Slav movement. The development of the Balkan League and particularly the *rapprochement* between Serbia and Bulgaria, regarded by promoters of the movement as a successful and encouraging example of Slav co-operation, proved to be of short duration. Surveying the events of what he termed the 'difficult year' 1913, Kramář generously distributed responsibility for the discord between the Balkan Slavs to the entire Slav world. Attributing the Serbo-Bulgarian conflict directly to the frustration of Serbia's desire for an Adriatic port, the Czech leader placed the responsibility for this firmly on the shoulders of Russia. In response to the rhetorical question: 'What action did Russia undertake in order that Serbia, whose victorious standards had reached the Adriatic, did not have to retreat from there?' he replied, decisively: 'None'. With evident disenchantment, Kramář offered the following explanation for the failure of his dream:

The great idea of Slav brotherhood is still, unfortunately, no more than a ceremonial congress slogan, affecting us all only during festive occasions, but which has not yet become the guiding star in the harsh, everyday struggle. It has not attracted anyone by its concrete contents of a clear picture of a better Slav future, for which it would be worth while sacrificing immediate advantages and granting generous concessions to other Slav nations. The Slav idea has never been more than an emotional concept. It satisfied the need to dream of something greater and more idealistic, but was insufficiently strong to overcome the national egotism of the Slav nations.[46]

The Second Balkan War, combined with the deteriorating situation in Russian Poland following the creation of the Kholm province, convinced Kramář that for the time being at least there was little point in persevering with Neo-Slav activities.[47] Once the instigator and the most ardent promoter of the movement had given up the struggle, the end became inevitable. Neo-Slavism, which had ceased to exist as a coherent organisation following the Sofia Congress in 1910, now faded into oblivion and was, with one small exception, never heard of again. Summarising the situation in a single sentence, Beneš wrote: 'Neo-Slavism, which had come into being with high expectations following the Russian revolution

---

[46] *Národní listy*, 1 January 1914 (K. Kramář, 'Slovanství na prahu nového roku').   [47] Kramář, *Na obranu*, p. 28.

perished, after a troubled six year existence, in the clatter of weapons of the First World War.'[48]

Despite the failure of the Neo-Slav movement, due to a combination of unrealistic aims, internal divisions, and unfavourable international political conditions, some of the needs which it was designed to satisfy remained. Foremost among these, in addition to the requirement for some form of moral assistance in the struggle against German expansion, was the desire of Czech owned industry and commerce to exploit the almost unlimited potential of the internal Russian market, besides gaining easier access to the markets of the Balkan Slav states. By 1913, when it had become patently obvious that Neo-Slavism had failed to achieve what had been expected of it, the need of Czech industry for wider markets was more urgent than it had been at the time of the founding of the movement in 1908. The rapid and substantial growth made in the economic life of the Czech nation during the preceding decades, was appreciably slowing down. The deteriorating general economic situation within Austria–Hungary resulted in considerable unemployment in the Czech lands, which formed the industrial centre of the Dual Monarchy. The situation was further exacerbated by the deadlock in the Bohemian Diet, a consequence of the racial strife in the province, resulting in the refusal of the central government to sanction an increase in local taxation, which brought the provincial administration close to bankruptcy.[49] The highly developed, though relatively small, Czech industries were experiencing difficulties competing with the large German industrial undertakings on the home market, and their continuing survival depended, to a large extent, on maintaining and increasing exports. The Serbian boycott of Austro-Hungarian goods did not improve the situation as, formerly, Czech industry had exported a significant proportion of its products to the Balkan area. All attempts at achieving concerted Slav action in the economic field having failed – notably the Slav bank and Slav exhibition projects – direct approaches to the other Slavs, particularly the Russians, were then initiated from the Czech side. Towards the end of 1913, the task of co-ordinating the attempts to promote the expansion of Czech

---

[48] Beneš, *Úvahy o slovanství*, p. 168.
[49] The Vienna government attempted, unsuccessfully, to cajole the warring nationalities into reaching a settlement by withholding authorisation to increase local excise duty on beer until a Czech–German understanding had been reached.

industry and commerce into other Slav lands were entrusted to the Economic Section of the Czech National Council. Present at the preparatory meetings of this body, amongst persons prominent in the economic life of the nation, were Kramář and Masaryk.[50] Masaryk had previously demonstrated a considerable interest in maintaining and strengthening economic links between the Czechs and the Balkan Slavs. Early in 1911 in a speech to the Delegations critical of Austro-Hungarian Balkan policies he held the Vienna government responsible for the loss of the Balkan markets to Germany, declaring: 'We Czechs cannot calmly observe how the policies of Count Aehrenthal are damaging Czech industrial interests in the Balkans.'[51] The same criticism applied also to the policies of Aehrenthal's successor, Count Berchtold. In a further speech, made in the spring of 1913, Masaryk drew attention to Russian economic rivalry in the Balkans and attacked the Austro-Hungarian authorities for failing to take effective measures to counter this threat. He explained that:

Naturally, Russia has been and is opposed to Austria and [equally] naturally we have to reckon with this adversary, but the Russian danger cannot be removed by abuse alone...Russian businessmen are, at this moment, considering how to utilise the Danube for Russian exports to the Balkans,...and Russian products are already being sold there... We [in Austria–Hungary, however,] pursue a policy which is economically sterile, and which succeeds only to irritate our opponent, but is of no benefit to anyone.[52]

Other Czechs, mainly those who had been active in the Neo-Slav movement, were more concerned with increasing trade with Russia, though they did not neglect the Balkans. Preiss was again very active in the field, and made several journeys to Russia in order to promote the export of Czech-made agricultural machinery and tram-cars. One of the visits to the Russian capital was made early in 1913, on this occasion in connection with the proposed import of Russian iron-ore for the steelworks at Vítkovice in

---

[50] Archive of the Czech National Council, minutes of meetings of the Economic Section of the Council, held on 25 September and 8 October 1913, cited in Herman, 'Novoslovanství a česká buržoasie', p. 304.

[51] *Stenographische Protokolle der Delegation, 43. Session*, pp. 59–65. See also Masaryk, *Rakouská zahraniční politika*, p. 74.

[52] *Národní listy*, 27 May 1913.

Moravia, when the Czech banker had a meeting with Sazonov, the Foreign Minister. However, despite the fact that Sazonov was reported to be in favour of increasing trade with Austria–Hungary, Preiss failed to negotiate the iron-ore purchase, as the Russian authorities were opposed to exporting through the Polish borders.[53]

Further attempts were also made to achieve some form of Slav co-operation in the field of banking. During the course of 1913, Klofáč, in his correspondence with Vergun, repeatedly urged the acceptance of a proposal to found a joint Czech–Russian bank under the direction of the Sokol leader, Scheiner.[54] These appeals went unheard. Another unsuccessful attempt to establish a Slav bank was made the following year, although on this occasion the Czechs played no more than a peripheral role. Hribar, who had been closely associated with previous endeavours to establish a Slav bank within the Neo-Slav movement, turned his attention to the formation of a joint banking institution to be active predominantly in the Balkan area. Although the Slovene banker and politician succeeded in arousing the interest of several important personages in Russia, thanks largely to the intercession of the Serbian Prime Minister, N. Pashich, the project failed to materialise, due mainly to the lack of interest in French financial circles whose co-operation was considered essential. Following the failure of these negotiations, held in St Petersburg and Paris, Hribar travelled to Prague, where he reported to Preiss.[55]

The problems confronting the Czechs, in the years immediately preceding the outbreak of the First World War, were not exclusively of an economic nature. Politically, the situation was no more favourable. Despite the fact that the Czechs had attained what could be described as a degree of negative autonomy through their obstructive tactics, they were far from satisfied with their political achievements. Racial strife between the Czech and German populations of Bohemia and the other Czech lands persisted, though in Moravia, where a settlement had been reached in 1905, the problem was less acute. The high rate of unemployment, which accompanied the financial difficulties in Bohemia and the economic stagnation of the Habsburg Empire towards the close of the first decade of

[53] *Proces dra. Kramáře*, III, part 1, p. 80.
[54] Arkhiv Ministerstva Innostrannykh Del, Moscow, 'Posolstvo v Vene', 604, p. 51, cited in Křížek, 'Česká buržoasní politika a "česká otázka"', p. 656.
[55] Hribar, *Moji spomini*, II, pp. 63–6, 73–93.

the century contributed further to the heightening of tension, and the situation progressively deteriorated. Nevertheless, frequent attempts were made to find solutions to the various aspects of the complex crisis, one of the most contentious points of which was the question of the official administrative language, which epitomised the other social, political, and economic disputes outstanding. Although, legally, the situation in Bohemia had remained unchanged since the failure of the Badeni language ordinances in 1899, with German remaining as the official internal language of the civil service and provincial authorities, the Czech language was, nevertheless, making considerable inroads into previously predominantly German areas. This progress was due to a large extent to the energetic activities of the Czech Schools Association (*Ústřední matice školská*) which assiduously established private Czech language schools wherever possible and subsequently, as soon as the statutory provisions were met, compelled the state educational authorities to assume responsibility for their maintenance.[56]

The Habsburg authorities, disturbed and embarrassed by the internecine conflict in Bohemia, persevered in their efforts to mediate between the Czech and German nationalities. In 1909, the Austrian government under the direction of Baron Bienerth outlined a plan, similar to that proposed earlier by Körber, for a tripartite administrative division of Bohemia. The proposal was to subdivide the province, for the purposes of local government, into twenty administrative districts – ten of which were to be predominantly Czech, with Czech as the official language; six districts were to be German, in which the German language would predominate; and the remaining four districts were to be mixed. Similar linguistic divisions were proposed for the civil service and the judiciary. However, the combined opposition of the more extreme elements of both the Czech and German nationalities, neither of which was prepared to concede anything to the other side, led to the breakdown of these and other negotiations staged during the course of the following year. A further attempt to reach a settlement was made early in 1911 when, following a general

[56] F. Bělehrádek, 'Školství menšinové a ústřední matice skolská', in *Česká politika*, ed. Tobolka, v, p. 416. When a private school achieved an attendance of over forty local children, the state was obliged to assume responsibility for the running of the school.

election, Baron Gautsch again became the Austro-Hungarian Prime Minister. Shortly before his fall, Gautsch's predecessor, Bienerth, had appointed Count Thun as Governor of Bohemia, entrusting him with the task of conciliating the belligerent nationalities. Several meetings were held under Thun's auspices, but they failed to produce any results. By the summer of 1913, under yet another Premier, Count Stürgkh, it had become apparent that peace negotiations had little chance of success and, as, in addition, the Bohemian administration had become insolvent, the paralysed Bohemian Diet was dissolved by the Emperor on 26 July and replaced by an Imperial Administrative Commission. The attempts at a negotiated settlement between the Czechs and Germans in Bohemia finally broke down early in 1914. Although further meetings were due to take place later that year, they were preceded by the outbreak of war.

The Slovaks in northern Hungary were in an even worse predicament than the Czechs. Although, even there, some little progress had been made in the areas of political, cultural, and educational development, the process of Magyarisation to which they were being subjected showed no signs of abatement. The intensified oppression, which followed the modest successes of the non-Magyar nationalities in the general election of 1906, culminated on 27 October 1907, with the killing of fifteen Slovaks, and the wounding of many others, by Hungarian troops at the village of Černová, near Ružomberok. The bloodshed occurred when the villagers attempted to prevent the consecration of their church by any person other than A. Hlinka, the local priest and a leading figure in the Slovak nationalist movement, who was at the time under suspension by the Hungarian authorities for political activities and, therefore, prevented from performing his religious functions.[57] The Černová massacre, and the ensuing trial of over fifty villagers on charges of violent behaviour, for which they received heavy prison sentences, resulted in attracting the attention of European opinion to the plight of the Slovaks and the other non-Magyar nationalities in Hungary. Nevertheless, the situation in Slovakia did not significantly improve. The new legislation enacted by the Minister of Education, Count Apponyi, during 1907, resulted in more intensified persecution of Slovak and other non-Magyar education. Economic development of the

[57] R. W. Seton-Watson, *Racial Problems in Hungary*, pp. 339–51.

Hungarian component of the Dual Monarchy remained very retarded, and the ensuing suffering again fell most heavily on the minority nationalities. The large-scale emigration from Hungary, mostly to North America, indicated the extent of dissatisfaction, and the high proportion of Slovaks among the emigrants was a clear pointer to the particularly unfavourable conditions in the Slovak counties. The non-Magyar nationalities of Hungary suffered a further political reversal in the general election of 1910 when, due to the discriminatory electoral system and to Magyar intimidation of the electorate, their parliamentary representation was reduced to eight seats, three of these being held by Slovaks. Throughout this period, the basic dichotomy within the Slovak nationalist movement remained, with the leadership of the Slovak National Party retaining its faith in autocratic Russia, and the Hlasists, who still did not form a distinct political organisation, striving for closer ties with the Czechs.[58]

In addition to the deteriorating domestic situation in the Czech lands and in the Slovak parts of Hungary it was becoming apparent, especially after the annexation crisis of 1908, that the Habsburg Empire was growing increasingly dependent on German support in the field of international relations. The Czech political leaders, together with their Slav allies in the Dual Monarchy, gradually became aware of the impossibility of diverting Austria–Hungary away from Germany and the Triple Alliance, which had been one of the chief objectives of their 'foreign policy' since its inception. The hopes, which many Slav politicians had placed in the introduction of universal suffrage, believing that it would lead to the transformation of, at least, the Austrian part of the Habsburg Empire into a Slav-ruled state, remained unfulfilled. The political unity of the Austrian Slavs, an essential prerequisite of this plan, proved to be an unattainable dream, despite all the energetic attempts made by those involved in the leadership of the Neo-Slav movement, which had as one of its principal aims the achievement of this unity. Although the nucleus of a united organisation of Slav deputies in the Vienna Reichsrat, the Slav Union (*Slovanská jednota*), had been established in February 1909,

[58] Lettrich, *History of Modern Slovakia*, pp. 36–42; Tobolka, *Politické dějiny československého národa*, III, part 2, pp. 597–602; V. Borodovčák, 'Myšlenka slovanské vzájemnosti na Slovensku v letech 1900–1914', *Slovanství v národním životě Čechů a Slováků*, ed. V. Šťastný and others (Prague, 1968), pp. 328–36.

it did not succeed in uniting the Slavs and never included representatives of all the Slav nationalities from the Austrian part of the Dual Monarchy. The large group of conservative Polish deputies refused to align itself with the Slav Union in the Reichsrat and repeatedly combined with the German members against the Slavs. The Ukrainian Nationalists also remained outside this parliamentary grouping. Furthermore, shortly after it came into being the Slav Union foundered over the military provisions bill. The more radical Czech parties, the National Socialists in particular, refused to comply with the decision of the Slav Union to support the government measures, and left the Union. Later, other dissensions appeared in the Slav ranks, and the parliamentary alliance was not reconstituted in the new Reichsrat which followed the 1911 general election. In that parliament effective co-operation also proved impossible for the Czech political parties which had formed a Czech Union (*Jednotný český klub*). This disintegrated in June 1912, again over military provisions, when the National Socialists refused to vote for the measure, despite the decision of the majority of the Czech deputies to support the government.[59]

One of the main reasons for the lack of solidarity amongst the Habsburg Slavs during this period was the Czech apprehension that an agreement would be reached between the South Slavs and the Habsburg authorities creating a third, South Slav, component of the Austro-Hungarian Empire, equal in status with the existing two sections. The Czech political leaders feared that this arrangement, favoured particularly by the Croats, would reduce the probability of achieving a federal reconstruction of the Monarchy, and would result in isolating the Czechs in the Austrian part of the Empire.[60] During the course of 1912, further difficulties arose when the Slovene Clericals, together with the Ukrainian Nationalists, refused to support the Czech demand for financial provision for the improvement of navigation on Bohemian waterways, and Kramář threatened retaliatory action in Parliament against his

[59] The Slav Union, which at the time of its foundation formed the largest parliamentary grouping (it had 123 members, mostly Czech and South Slav deputies), developed from another group, the Slav Centre (*Slovanské centrum*), which had come into being a few months previously. The only Czechs present in the earlier formed organisation were the Clericals.
[60] Kramář, *Na obranu*, p. 25; Kramář, *Problémy české politiky*, p. 11, text of a speech 'O politické situaci' delivered on 19 January 1913. The Young Czech leader stated categorically: 'At no cost shall we permit the ripening South Slav question to be solved in the sense of trialism.'

unco-operative allies.[61] As a consequence of these disagreements it became increasingly evident that any form of effective Slav political co-operation within the Austro-Hungarian Empire was unlikely to materialise. The failure of traditional Czech policies to achieve their desired results led, inevitably, to a complete reappraisal of the situation. Leading Czech political figures gradually became aware of the fact that, within the framework of Austria–Hungary, no satisfactory solutions could be found to the problems confronting the Czech and Slovak nations and, as a result, thoughts began to turn towards the drastic measure of dissolving the Empire. This was a significant departure from previous Czech political thinking for, earlier, few responsible Czech politicians would have even considered a national existence outside the Dual Monarchy, let alone the formation of a fully independent Czech or Czechoslovak state. The objective of the majority of politically active Czechs had been the achievement of national autonomy within a reformed Austro-Hungarian Empire.[62]

In a speech, delivered early in 1913 Kramář expressed this conviction in the following words:

[The creation of] an independent Czech state in the centre of Europe in the direct line of German political and economic expansion is considered in Bohemia to be out of the question, except by immature political infants. Due to its geographical position and its economic importance, the Kingdom of Bohemia is predestined to form the foundation stone of a great power, either indigenous or alien. The former proved untenable. It is because our nation has the greatest opportunity to achieve undisturbed, independent development in such a heterogeneous Empire, where no other nation forms the overwhelming majority, and

[61] Kramář, *Problémy české politiky*, pp. 43–9, 'O politické situaci'.
[62] Z. V. Tobolka, 'Československé politické strany doby předválečné o konečných cílech svého národa', in *Idea československého státu*, ed. J. Kapras, B. Němec, and F. Soukup, (2 vols., Prague, 1936), I, pp. 114–26. S. H. Thomson in *Czechoslovakia in European History* (2nd edn, Princeton, 1953), p. 231, claims that censorship and fear of the Austro-Hungarian authorities prevented demands for independence being voiced, and that the published Czech political programmes created a misleading impression. Although undoubtedly, there is some truth in this assertion, nevertheless, the extremists who advocated the breaking-up of the Habsburg Empire followed by full independence for the Czech and Slovak nations were few in number. Only the relatively insignificant Progressive State-Rights Party publicly favoured such a radical solution. A manifesto, published on the occasion of the Party Congress in May 1914, openly demanded the establishment of an independent Czech state.

because in such an Empire it can entertain hopes that through its own cultural and economic strength and its political potential it can exert an influence on the internal and external policies of the state, that it is entirely natural that Czech policy has always been, and still is, to reckon with one thing – with Austria. Albeit in a different, better form than Austria is today, with its historical German policies, exacerbated further by Magyar violence against the Slavs during the last forty-five years.[63]

Later, in the autumn of that year, following the Second Balkan War, Kramář reiterated these views, stating that: 'If there are people in Bohemia who believe that now, after the Peace of Bucharest, the time has come for a European solution of the Czech question, it only indicates that there is a shortage of lunatic asylums in Bohemia.'[64] Although these statements were pronounced primarily in defence of Young Czech policies, which were under attack from the more radical elements for their conciliatory attitude towards the Bohemian Germans with whom the Young Czechs advocated a negotiated settlement,[65] the views expressed were, nevertheless, widely accepted.

Even as late as the summer of 1914, after the assassination of the Archduke Francis Ferdinand and his wife at Sarajevo on 28 June, but before the outbreak of war, Kramář's public stand remained unaltered. In a speech delivered early in July, in which he condemned the assassination but placed the responsibility for it on the shoulders of the Austro-Hungarian government for failing to adopt an understanding policy towards the South Slavs, he also referred to the Slav policies of his party, reiterating that there would be no withdrawal from association with the Slav world. Declaring resolutely that 'A Czech is a Slav!', Kramář continued:

But...we protest in the most determined manner to those who believe that through our sincere Slavism we wish to harm the Empire. This is not and never has been our aim. We have no desire to leave the Empire. The Empire has no reason whatsoever to fear out intentions. At all times and on all occasions, even in the most distressing situations, even following the occupation of Bosnia (which created a very grave situation for the other Slavs), we stood resolutely on the fact that we must not pursue a policy against the Monarchy. We remain true Slavs, but our

[63] Kramář, *Problémy české politiky*, pp. 4–5, text of a speech delivered in Prague on 11 January 1913.
[64] K. Kramář, *In memoriam* (Prague, 1913), p. 39.
[65] Kramář, *Problémy české politiky*, pp. 49–50; Kramář, *In memoriam*, p. 43.

Slav feelings do not necessitate the pursuit of any policies involving the disruption of the state or of redrawing the frontiers of Europe.[66]

Proposals for just such a reshaping of frontiers were, however, at the time in the forefront of the speaker's mind. A few weeks before making this last public declaration of faith in the continued existence of the Habsburg Empire, Kramář had been developing other ideas. Although remaining consistent in his beliefs that a fully independent Czech or Czechoslovak state was not a viable proposition, and that national autonomy could only be achieved and preserved within a federal framework, the Czech leader no longer envisaged the sovereign power being that of Austria–Hungary. During May 1914, shortly before the outbreak of the First World War, Kramář prepared a secret plan for the formation of a large federal Slav state – a Slav empire – exchanging Austro-Hungarian hegemony for that of Russia.[67]

Such a far-reaching transformation of the map of Central Europe presupposed a considerable alteration in the power situation there – as could be produced only by a major war. It is precisely this fact that provides an explanation for the change in Kramář's political thinking regarding the future existence of the Czech nation. So long as the eastern half of Europe remained in a state of greater or lesser stability, with the power divided between Russia, Germany, and Austria–Hungary, there was little likelihood of any significant changes taking place. The only hope for a brighter future for the Czechs and other Slavs within the Habsburg Empire, lay in the internal reform of the state. Gradually, however, the international balance of power in the area altered. It became increasingly evident that war between Russia, on the one hand, and Austria–Hungary and Germany, on the other, was not beyond the bounds of possibility. Together with this awareness grew the realisation that out of this conflict, should it take place and if it resulted in the defeat of Austria–Hungary, there could arise alternative solutions to the Czech and Slovak questions, within a politically very different Europe. Speaking shortly after the outbreak of the First World War, Kramář stated that 'at the conclusion of this terrible war, the map of Europe will be

[66] *Národní listy*, 5 July 1914 (K. Kramář, 'O současném stavu politickém'). See also, J. Werstadt, 'K úloze Karla Kramáře v našem odboji; soubor dokumentů a projevů', *Naše revoluce*, XVI (1938), pp. 3–11.
[67] See below, pp. 238–9.

unrecognisable'.[68] Later, he explained that, 'on the day war was declared on Russia I said farewell to Austria for ever, whatever the outcome of the conflict. It was clear to me that if the Central Powers were victorious, Austria would become a vassal of Germany; if they lost, Austria would be dissolved.'[69] Despite the fact that Kramář subsequently stated that, at the time he drew up his proposals for a Slav empire, that is before the assassinations at Sarajevo, it, in his own words, 'never occurred to me that there might be a war',[70] nevertheless, the Czech leader was obviously aware of just such an eventuality.[71] Kramář, it appears, had become convinced of the long term probability of war between Russia and the Habsburg Empire following the annexation of Bosnia and Herzegovina in 1908, and this awareness was further reinforced by the Balkan upheavals in subsequent years. In a draft of a letter to Count Thun, the Governor of Bohemia, written towards the end of 1914, after the outbreak of war, Kramář stated:

I became firmly convinced of the inevitability of this war following Aehrenthal's annexation. When my final pleas and efforts (as you are aware, I travelled incognito to Belgrade with the knowledge of Berchtold) to lesson the likelihood of war for some time to come, by satisfying Serbian demands for access to the sea, were shown to be futile, I awaited fatalistically the moment when the inevitable would occur.[72]

---

[68] *Národní listy*, 2 August 1914 (K. Kramář, 'Světová válka'). See also Werstadt, 'K úloze Karla Kramáře v našem odboji', p. 14.

[69] Werstadt, 'K úloze Karla Kramáře v našem odboji', p. 58, citing from a series of articles by Kramář, published in *Národní listy*, 23, 25, 26 March 1924.

[70] Kramář, *Pět přednášek*, pp. 56–7. The historian, J. Papoušek, pointing to the contradiction between Kramář's public declarations at the time (confirmed by his later assertion that he was not anticipating a war) and the project for a Slav empire (which was precisely the type of policy for which he was castigating his Czech political opponents and which presupposed a major war), described the Czech leader's behaviour as a 'psychological enigma' which could only be explained by the fact that Kramář was keeping 'two irons [in the fire]'. *Národní osvobození*, 24 June, 1, 5 July 1934 (J. Papoušek, 'Před dvaceti lety'). Another Czechoslovak historian, M. Paulová, argued that Kramář was sincere in his policy of preserving and reforming the Habsburg Empire 'whilst the existence of Austria-Hungary corresponded with Russian interests'. The project for a Slav empire was regarded by Paulová as a contingency plan for use in the event of a war, when all other policies had failed. Paulová, *Dějiny Maffie*, I, pp. 62–6.

[71] Sís, ed. *Dr. Karel Kramář. Život, dílo, práce*, I, pp. 93–5.

[72] *Proces dra. Kramáře*, II, pp. 196–200; III, part I, pp. 137–9. The passage cited is from a copy of a letter which, the prosecution alleged, had been found in the

Partial corroboration of this assertion, in so far as he regarded the annexation crisis as a watershed in the history of Europe, can be found in Kramář's earlier statements. Despite the fact that at the time, he had sanctioned the incorporation of Bosnia and Herzegovina into the Dual Monarchy, and despite the fact that he continued to proclaim publicly his belief in the necessity of the continued existence of the Habsburg Empire, in his later utterances on foreign policy the Czech leader frequently alluded to the damaging effect the annexation had produced on his political plans. Thus, for example, in a speech delivered in November 1910, Kramář declared that: 'The annexation had a catastrophic effect on my life's work. I attempted to do all that lay within my limited powers to render assistance to my nation to become happy and great in a free and powerful Austria respected by all. My policies are now in ruin. Berlin will conduct the affairs of Austria, not us.'[73]

Kramář's proposal for the political reorganisation of Eastern Europe involved the creation of a vast federal Slav empire, headed by the Russian Tsar, and comprising all the Slav nations, the European territory of which would extend from the Baltic to the Adriatic, and from Bohemia eastwards. European and Asiatic Russia, Poland, the Czech lands, Bulgaria, Serbia, and Montenegro were to be united into one state, with a common legislature, army, and customs tariff. Although the originator of the scheme envisaged that the component parts of the empire would enjoy a certain measure of autonomy, consistent with the Neo-Slav principle of the equality of each Slav nation, nevertheless, the political predominance of Russia was inevitable. The Czechoslovak component of the Slav state was to consist not only of the Czechs and Slovaks, but also of the Lusatian Sorbs, in addition to the non-Slav populations of the areas concerned. Territorially, besides the Czech Crownlands, it was to include Lusatia and Slovakia, extended through Hungary down to an equally enlarged Serbia.[74]

possession of the accused, the original of which had been sent by him to Thun on the occasion of the New Year 1915. Kramář did not contradict this, but when Thun himself later gave evidence he denied having received that particular letter citing as evidence the archival record of the correspondence. Kramář then offered the explanation that the document quoted by the prosecution was an earlier draft of a letter to Thun, which was never sent. Nevertheless, he did not repudiate the ideas expressed in it.

[73] *Národní listy*, 11 November 1910.
[74] The relevant documents from the Russian archives were first published by

It appears that Kramář first mentioned these, as he termed them, 'theoretical ideas' in May 1914 in conversation with the Russian journalist Svatkovsky, with whom he had previously closely co-operated within the Neo-Slav movement. On Svatkovsky's suggestion Kramář committed his proposals to paper in the form of a memorandum, which was conveyed to the Russian Minister of Foreign Affairs, Sazonov, during his visit to Rumania in the summer of that year.[75] Sazonov's reaction to the plan is not known, but the Russian ambassador in Vienna, N. N. Shebeko, when forwarding a copy of the project to the Russian Minister of Foreign Affairs, described it as being of a 'rather fantastic nature'.[76] This attitude was probably shared by the Russian Government which appears to have showed no interest whatsoever in the Czech leader's proposals.

Kramář was not alone in preparing contingency plans for the collapse of the Habsburg Monarchy. Almost simultaneously, Klofáč informed the Russian ambassador in Vienna of his views on the dismemberment of Austria–Hungary, in the event of the Empire being defeated in a war with Russia.[77] Although little is known about these proposals, it is believed that Klofáč favoured the creation of an independent Czechoslovak monarchical state, comprising the Czech lands and Slovakia, with the throne occupied

J. Papoušek in *Národní osvobození*, 24 June, 5 July 1934 ('Kramářova ústava slovanské říše z června 1914'). The documents, sent from the Russian embassy in Vienna to Sazonov in St Petersburg on 19 (2) June 1914, consist of a covering letter from the embassy and three enclosures. These are some explanatory notes from V. P. Svatkovsky, and two memoranda; the first entitled 'The Constitution of the Slav Empire (based on the *Deutsche Bundesakte*)', and the second 'The Slav Empire and its Neighbours'. In the covering letter and the accompanying notes from Svatkovsky it is explained that the draft constitution had been drawn up by Kramář, whereas the second memorandum had been prepared by Svatkovsky after conversations with Kramář and leaders of the South Slavs. See also Paulová, *Dějiny Maffie*, I, pp. 635–40 (appendixes I and II). T. G. Masaryk, in *Světová revoluce*, p. 25, likened Kramář's proposal to the solar system, 'in which the planets, the Slavonic peoples, were to revolve round the Russian sun'.

[75] *Národní osvobození*, 24 June, 1, 5 July 1934 (Papoušek, 'Před dvaceti lety'); Kramář, *Na obranu*, pp. 61–2. When the documents were made public by Papoušek in 1934, Kramář denied his authorship of the draft constitution. In his earlier writings, however, he himself had referred to it.

[76] *Národní osvobození*, 24 June 1934 ('Kramářova ústava slovanské říše').

[77] Šantrůček, *Václav Klofáč*, p. 144. It was also reported that Klofáč held discussions with the Russian Minister of Foreign Affairs about the positioning of the frontiers of the future Czechoslovak state. B. Pares, *My Russian Memoirs* (London, 1931), p. 286.

by a member of the Russian royal family. In addition, Klofáč persisted in his endeavours to promote closer ties with Russia by offering the services of his political followers to assist the Russian cause should war break out between the two Empires. During a visit to St Petersburg in January 1914 he held discussions with Sazonov and the Chief of the General Staff, J. G. Zhilinsky, regarding the nature and organisation of this proposed assistance, which would include espionage and sabotage activities. The Russian officials were reported to have reacted with indifference to these ideas.[78] Later, in April of that year, Klofáč sent to St Petersburg, via the Russian consul in Prague, Zhukovsky, detailed plans for the establishment of an intelligence network in eastern Moravia and Silesia, to be run by his political organisation. Klofáč proposed that, in the areas concerned, the National Socialist Party leadership would 'prepare a number of reliable persons...on whom, in the event of an advance by Russian forces through Silesia into eastern Moravia, the Russians could utterly depend'.[79]

However, despite all these Czech endeavours, the Russian authorities continued to show very little concern about the fate of the Czech nation. This is clearly illustrated by the fact that the Russian ambassador in Vienna, Shebeko, became somewhat alarmed on hearing of Klofáč's plans, and instructed his consul in Prague to exercise caution when dealing with opposition forces in Bohemia, in order not to endanger relations with the Habsburg Empire.[80] The Russian consul, Zhukovsky, responded by complaining to his superior, that: 'Ever since my arrival in Prague, I have had to behave most circumspectly towards the extremely tactless endeavours of the Czechs to entice me into opposition to the Austrian goverment.' Despite the attempts by Czech political figures to use his office for these purposes, Zhukovsky claimed that he had 'made contacts with purely Austrian groups and carefully

---

[78] A. Popov, 'Chekhoslovatsky vopros i tsarskaya diplomatiya v 1914–1918 gg.', *Krasny arkhiv*, XXXIII (1929), p. 5. See also Šantrůček, *Václav Klofáč*, pp. 124–5.

[79] *Mezhdunarodnye otnosheniya v epokhu imperializma. Dokumenty iz arkhivov tsarskogo i vremennogo pravitel'stv, 1878–1917 gg.*, ed. M. N. Pokrovsky and others, Series III (1914–1917) (10 vols., Moscow–Leningrad, 1931–9), II, pp. 381–4, no. 292, Zhukovsky to Sazonov, 12, Prague, 25/12 April 1914. Klofáč's memorandum is appended to Zhukovsky's dispatch. See also Popov, 'Chekhoslovatsky vopros', p. 5.

[80] *Mezhdunarodnye otnosheniya*, II, p. 473, no. 305, Shebeko to Sazonov, Vienna, 6 May/23 April 1914.

maintained these connections'. The consul denied having any
'official relations' with the Czech National Council, and claimed
that he had informed the leaders of the National Socialist Party to
take their subversive plans directly to St Petersburg.[81]
The reasons for this lack of interest were largely traditional.
Russia had never been greatly concerned about the Western branch
of the Slav family of nations, particularly about the Czechs, who
were not of the Orthodox faith, and were considered by the Russian
authorities to have dangerously enlightened political ideas. Indeed,
Masaryk had explained earlier, in 1895, that in the unlikely event
of the disintegration of the Austro-Hungarian Empire, he foresaw
no desire by Russia to incorporate '6 or 10 million [Czech and
Slovak] Catholics, for the Russians are well aware that our people
would align themselves with the Poles'.[82] During a visit to
St Petersburg in February 1914, Scheiner heard the expression
of this Russian attitude directly from the lips of the Minister of
Foreign Affairs. Sazonov stated bluntly that: 'On account of your
[nation's] geographical situation, cultural heritage, character, and
feeeling, you are too far removed from our nation, and we have
no special interest...in your political aspirations.'[83] Later that
year, the Russian consul in Prague informed his superiors that
Kramář, together with his associates, 'viewed Russia's role in the
Slav world from a very one-sided viewpoint, failing to take into
consideration its historic and religious institutions, and was interested only in the economic penetration of Russia'.[84]

[81] *Ibid.*, II, p. 382, n. 1, dispatch no. 17 from Zhukovsky, Prague, 18/5 May
1914. Reference is made to this dispatch in an editor's footnote to no. 292,
Zhukovsky to Sazonov, 12, Prague 25/12 April 1914; Popov, 'Chekhoslovatsky
vopros', p. 5.
[82] T. G. Masaryk, *Naše nynější krise. Pád strany staročeské a počátkové směrů
nových* (6th edn, Prague, 1948), p. 283. The work was first published in
1895.
[83] Tobolka, *Politické dějiny československého národa*, III, part 2, p. 632. In
apparent contradiction to this statement is Pavlů's claim, made in a report to
Kramář from Russia in December 1912, that: 'The Russians want us to stage
an uprising, which is pure romanticism, we have only one goal – which is
cultural.' *Proces dra. Kramáře*, III, part 2, p. 192. This discrepancy can,
perhaps, be explained by the fact that Pavlů had been in contact with some of
the more enthusiastic members of the Slavonic Societies in Russia rather than
the Russian authorities.
[84] *Mezhdunarodnye otnosheniya*, II, p. 382, n. 1, dispatch from Zhukovsky, 17,
Prague, 18/5 May 1914. The Russian consul stated that although he 'avoided'
the Young Czechs, he considered the Czech National Socialists, who were
'not associated with Neo-Slavism' as 'significant' from the Russian point of view.

In direct contradiction of this evidence, not all of which was available at the time, Kramář stated, in defence of his policies, that: 'I know...from personal discussions with Minister Sazonov before the war, that he was interested in us [Czechs]. In addition, Svatkovsky transmitted very detailed information about our activities and intentions to the Ministry of Foreign Affairs, because it was very interested in this.'[85] There is, undoubtedly, an element of truth in Kramář's assertion. A slight change had occurred in the attitude of the Russian government in the years immediately preceding the outbreak of the First World War. Although, at the time, Russia did not desire a European conflict as it was not yet prepared for war, without which, most observers believed, there was little likelihood of alterations to the political structure of the continent, nevertheless, those in power in St Petersburg no longer considered the dissolution of Austria–Hungary as being beyond the bounds of possibility. The intensification of the disputes between the nationalities in the Dual Monarchy gave rise to the belief that disintegration could come about as a consequence of internal pressures.[86] Sir G. Buchanan, who was British ambassador in St Petersburg at the time, recollected that during an audience with the Tsar, in April 1913, Nicholas II 'expressed the opinion that the disintegration of the Austrian Empire was merely a question of time, and that the day was not far distant when we would see a kingdom of Hungary and a kingdom of Bohemia. The South Slavs would probably be absorbed by Serbia, the Roumanians of Transylvania by Roumania, and the German provinces of Austria incorporated in Germany.'[87] The motivation for this new Russian interest in the Habsburg lands was, however, that of power politics and not fraternal concern for the well-being of the Czech, or other Slav, subjects of the Dual Monarchy. The possible dissolution of Austria–Hungary concerned the Russian authorities because they were aware that the repercussions of such an upheaval would inevitably affect Russian interests in the Balkans and the Near East.

Russian interest in the Czech, and other Habsburg Slavs

[85] Kramář, *Na obranu*, p. 62.
[86] J. Papoušek, *Carské Rusko a naše osvobození* (Prague, 1927), pp. 22–3.
[87] Sir G. Buchanan, *My Mission to Russia and Other Diplomatic Memories* (2 vols., London, 1923), I, p. 182. Buchanan added that: 'I ventured to observe that such a recasting of the map of Europe could hardly be effected without a general war.'

increased still further with the growing awareness of the inexorably approaching war. In a report made to the Ministry of Foreign Affairs several months after hostilities had commenced, Zhukovsky, the former consul in Prague, stated that the Czechs had been making secret preparations for the event of a war. Despite the fact that he had earlier denied having such dealings with any Czech political figures, he disclosed that, while in the Bohemian capital, he had requested Czech leaders to prepare a manifesto outlining the Czech orientation towards the *Entente* powers. Zhukovsky recorded with satisfaction that the Austro-Slav aspirations, voiced by Kramář at the 1908 Prague Neo-Slav Congress, were no longer of any relevance, and that in the Czech lands 'attention was [now] principally devoted to the problem of the final liberation of the Slav nations in the Dual Empire, and to the governmental structure of the possible future Slav Union, under the protectorate of Russia, within which the Slavs would be unified'.[88]

During his period of activity in Prague the Russian consul, though careful not to offend the susceptibilities of the Austro-Hungarian authorities, had in fact been assiduously endeavouring to promote Russian interests. One of the consul's most cherished projects was the proposed establishment of a Russian Association (*Ruský klub*) in Prague. His objective, in addition to generally stimulating Czech interest in Russia, was to counter the influence of various Russian groups already illegally in existence in the Bohemian capital which, following the 1905 Russian Revolution, had come under the control of radical *émigrés*. Detailed plans for the project, and for an associated Russian Centre were prepared during 1913 by Zhukovsky and his assistants in conjunction with V. Černý, Scheiner, and Klofáč from the Czech side. A site was selected for the construction of a building to house the Centre. In addition to the proposed Russian Association itself, the projected building was to contain the Russian consulate, the local offices of the Russian Orthodox Church, and also provide accommodation for Russian visitors to Prague. Despite the fact that in April 1913 *Novoe vremya* announced, with considerable satisfaction, that a Russian Association was being founded in

---

[88] Popov, 'Chekhoslovatsky vopros', pp. 5–6, Zhukovsky to Shilling, 23/10 October 1914 (report entitled 'The Renewal of the Independent Kingdom of Bohemia').

Prague the project never reached fruition, thanks to the unco-operative attitude of the Austro-Hungarian government.[89] As Zhukovsky reported to his superiors in the Vienna embassy in January 1914, the Habsburg authorities were not prepared to sanction the existence of the proposed Association on the grounds that it might constitute 'a danger to the interests of the state'. The Russian consul added that Kramář had been informed by the Austrian Minister of the Interior that the heir to the throne, the Archduke Francis Ferdinand, was strongly opposed to the project.[90] The Czechs associated with this proposed venture, all earlier active in the Neo-Slav movement, were clearly perse-vering in their Russophil activities, despite the failure of Neo-Slavism.

A little later that year, the final postscript was added to the Neo-Slav movement. An unofficial attempt was made from the Russian side to revive the movement and thus, presumably, to strengthen relations with the Czechs and other Slav peoples. In April 1914 the St Petersburg Society for Slav Reciprocity issued invitations to twenty-four persons prominent in the Slav world, many of whom had been active in the Neo-Slav movement, to attend a private meeting in the Russian capital. The letter of invitation pointed out that although the vicissitudes of the fratri-cidal Second Balkan War and the continuing Russo-Polish conflict were 'insufficiently powerful to shake the great Slav idea', they nevertheless exerted an unfavourable influence on its development and implementation. Slav organisations dedicated to carrying out the ideas of the Prague and Sofia congresses, it was argued, were finding it not only impossible to extend their activities but also to preserve the steps already taken. The letter continued: 'In these circumstances it appears essential that attention be turned to the immediate Slav tasks and to marking out the path for the near future. Although the calling of a third Slav congress in the present circumstances appears difficult, it would be fully possible to organise meetings of prominent representatives of the various Slav nations.' The first such gathering, the invitation suggested, should be held in St Petersburg during May 1914. It was envisaged

---

[89] Leppmann, 'Ruský konsulát v Praze', pp. 10–12. See also *Novoe vremya*, 5 (18) April 1913.
[90] *Mezhdunarodnye otnosheniya*, I, pp. 106–7, no. 100, Zhukovsky to Kudashev, 6, Prague, 25/12 January 1914.

that the agenda would include the following items: ' 1, the creation
of a Slav bank; 2, the teaching of Slavistics in schools; 3, Slav
participation in the projected all-Russian exhibition, and; 4, railway communication between the Slav lands.' The Russian consul
in Prague, when informing St Petersburg of this development,
added that he believed that the Czechs concerned – they included
Kramář, Klofáč, Scheiner and Preiss – had accepted the invitation,
but that it was unlikely that the meeting would take place on the
dates suggested, as these coincided with the meetings of the
Austro-Hungarian Delegations.[91] Kramář later confirmed that he
had received the invitation, which had been extended to him by
A. A. Stolypin, the brother of the former Prime Minister. Kramář
stated, however, that he had declined to attend and the proposed
meeting had never taken place.[92]

Despite this belated increase in interest in the Czechs, the indication which Sazonov had conveyed to Scheiner was much closer
to the truth than Kramář's very different assessment of the
situation. This is evident from the fact that, even during the war,
Russia had no definite aims as far as the Czechs and Slovaks were
concerned. The Russian government then appeared to vacillate
between desiring the preservation of the Habsburg Empire, with
a tri-partite structure in which the Kingdom of Bohemia would
be equal in status with the Austrian and Hungarian components
of the state, on the one hand, and the dissolution of Austria–
Hungary and the creation of an independent Czech or Czechoslovak state, on the other.[93]

The plans and hopes of the Czech Russophils were, however,
not the only ones expressed at the time. In complete contrast with
Kramář's project for a Slav Empire under Russian control were
the ideas of Masaryk. Up until the commencement of hostilities,
Masaryk remained opposed to the dissolution of the Dual Monarchy, although, as he himself stated, his conviction had gradually
weakened as the war approached. He explained that:

Unlike Palacký, I had already reached and expressed the conclusion
that, if democratic and social movements should gain strength in

---

[91] *Ibid.*, II, pp. 379–81, no. 291, Zhukovsky to Sazonov, 11, Prague 25/12 April
1914.　　[92] *Proces dra. Kramáře*, IV, part 2, p. 33.
[93] See Papoušek, *Carské Rusko a naše osvobození*, and M. Abrash, 'War Aims
towards Austria-Hungary: The Czechoslovak Pivot', *Russian Diplomacy and
Eastern Europe, 1914–1917* (New York, 1963), pp. 78–123.

Europe, we might hope to win independence. In later years, especially after 1907, the better I got to know Austria and the Habsburg dynasty, the more I was driven into opposition. This dynasty, which in Vienna and in Austria seemed so powerful, was morally and physically degenerate.[94]

Shortly after the outbreak of the First World War, at a secret meeting in Rotterdam, Masaryk outlined his plans for the future of the Czech and Slovak nations to R. W. Seton-Watson. In a memorandum to the London Foreign Office about this clandestine meeting, Seton-Watson described the Czech Realist leader's maximum programme, to be realised only if Germany were completely defeated. In that event, Masaryk envisaged the creation of an independent state consisting of Bohemia, Moravia, Silesia, and Slovakia. Seton-Watson continued that, in his informant's opinion:

The new state could only be a kingdom, not a republic; a decided majority of the nation would favour this. In the interest of its future and above all in the interest of the future of Russo-Czech relations – this he strongly emphasised – it would be wiser not to place a Russian Grand Duke on the throne, but rather a western prince, preferably a Dane or a Belgian. He is of the opinion that in that event the intimacy with Russia is more likely to subsist – paradoxical as it may seem at first sight – than in the event of a direct Russian sovereignty which would tend merely to bring out the differences of outlook.[95]

Masaryk later conceded that, as Scheiner had indicated to him, a Russian ruler on the Bohemian throne would, nevertheless, have been a popular choice.[96]

On 28 July 1914, a few months prior to the meeting in Rotterdam, Austria-Hungary, as a consequence of the Sarajevo assassinations, declared war on Serbia, and Europe plunged into the cataclysm of the First World War. This war was to have far-reaching consequences on the political structure of Europe. In the eastern half of the European continent there were no victors at the conclusion of

---

[94] Masaryk, *Světová revoluce*, p. 35. Masaryk returned to the Vienna Parliament in 1907.
[95] PRO, FO, 371/1900, 67456, Memorandum of Conversation between Prof. Masaryk and Mr Seton-Watson, at Rotterdam, on 24–25 October 1914; R. W. Seton-Watson, *Masaryk in England* (Cambridge, 1943), pp. 40–7. Masaryk further pointed out that the German minority in Bohemia would accept a Danish ruler, but never a Russian.
[96] Masaryk, *Světová revoluce*, pp. 23–4. Masaryk also added that he himself favoured a republic, but believed that the majority of the people would prefer a monarchy.

the conflict. The three local major powers involved all suffered defeats; Germany capitulated, Russia was racked by revolution, and Austria–Hungary ceased to exist. Out of this unique situation arose a series of new independent states – amongst them Czechoslovakia.

Conclusion

The Neo-Slav movement was, undoubtedly, the most significant, and most interesting, development in the field of relations between the Czech and Slovak nations and Russia in the years immediately preceding the outbreak of the First World War. Despite its limited two year existence and almost total lack of lasting success, the movement exerted a considerable influence on general inter-Slav relations at that time.

Neo-Slavism was essentially a Czech creation. It came into being as the consequence of a Czech initiative and during its short life span was sustained largely by Czech enthusiasm, though representatives of other Slav peoples, from both inside and outside the Habsburg Empire, did also adhere to the movement. Judging by its objectives, both declared and undeclared, Neo-Slavism was the final manifestation of Czech Austro-Slavism. This interpretation, made by Beneš,[1] was, however, challenged by Kramář, the person most closely associated with the movement, who asserted that he was opposed to the principles of Austro-Slavism.[2] The disagreement appears to be a matter of interpretation. The principal aim of the Neo-Slav movement, to be achieved through the promotion of greater understanding between the Slav nationalities, was to prepare the ground for united Slav action within the Dual Monarchy, by eliminating existing inter-Slav conflicts which, though in some cases originating outside the Habsburg Empire, nevertheless had repercussions within it. It was believed that if the Slav majority within Austria–Hungary could form a united political force, then the predominant nationalities of the Dual Monarchy, the Germans and Magyars, would no longer be able to control the political life of the state. The internal structure of the Habsburg Empire could then be remodelled on a federal basis, and its foreign policy diverted from the existing close alliance with Germany and replaced by a *rapprochement* with Russia. These objectives are

[1] Beneš, *Úvahy o slovanství*, p. 61.   [2] Kramář, *Na obranu*, p. 14.

almost identical with those which Beneš distinguished as being characteristic of Austro-Slavism, the only exception being the desire for an alliance with Russia,[3] which is precisely the point at issue with Kramář. Kramář repudiated Austro-Slavism because he believed it to be potentially divisive of the Slav world. The creation of a second Slav power would, in his opinion, be the cause of new conflicts, as it would inevitably become the rival of Russia.[4] If, however, the element of traditional Czech Russophilism is also taken into consideration, it becomes apparent that any Czech conception of a Slavicised Habsburg Empire would almost certainly gravitate towards Russia, and the Neo-Slav movement then fits into the pattern of Czech Austro-Slav aspirations.

The timing of the Neo-Slav initiative is also revealing of its character. The movement came into being during 1908 due to a combination of recently altered circumstances, which produced the need for its creation and also gave rise to expectations of the desired objectives being successfully accomplished. The long cherished Czech hope of achieving united action amongst the diverse Slav peoples of the Dual Monarchy became increasingly important after 1906 when full manhood suffrage was introduced in the Austrian lands of the Empire, and the national composition of the Vienna Parliament predetermined in such a form that the Slavs theoretically outnumbered the other ethnic groups by a slender margin. Slav unity within the Habsburg Empire, therefore, acquired an immediate practical political significance it had previously lacked. Theoretically, at least, the Slavs could now have a decisive voice in the government of the Austrian lands and in the foreign policy of the entire Dual Monarchy. The electoral reform measures were also responsible, less directly, for adding a personal factor to the motivation of the Neo-Slav movement. The first general election under the reformed franchise, which took place in 1907, radically altered the composition of the legislature, and included amongst those political organisations which lost support, was the Young Czech Party led by Kramář. Kramář's enthusiastic

[3] Beneš defined the following four factors as being characteristic of Austro-Slav thinking: (1) the Slav peoples formed a numerical majority in Austria-Hungary and believed, therefore, that (2) the introduction of greater democracy into the political life of the Empire would improve their position. (3) They did not desire the dissolution of the Dual Monarchy, but (4) wished to see it transformed into a federation of autonomous states. Beneš, *Úvahy o slovanství*, pp. 57–9.   [4] Kramář, *Na obranu*, p. 22.

espousal of the Neo-Slav movement, of which he was virtually the sole instigator, can be at least partially ascribed to his wish to restore his own power and prestige after the electoral failure of the Young Czechs.

These factors alone, however, would not have been sufficient to give rise to the Neo-Slav movement for, although they increased the need for such an initiative, they did not in themselves hold out promise of success. It was certain political developments outside Austria–Hungary which provided the required basis for optimism. Almost any move towards Slav unity involved, directly or indirectly, the establishment of closer relations with Russia. This aspect of inter-Slav relations was regarded with some ambivalence by many Western Slavs, the Czechs in particular, who wished to avoid too close an association with Russian absolutism. The revolutionary events of 1905 in Russia appeared to remove this obstacle, as it was widely believed at the time that constitutional rule was replacing the autocratic government of that country. These developments not only gave rise to the hope that a Russian government more responsive to public opinion would show greater understanding for the problems of the small Slav peoples, but also increased the attraction of inter-Slav co-operation in the eyes of those who had previously been inhibited by the autocratic character of Russia. In addition, thanks to the recent changes in Russia, the claim could be made, with at least some degree of credibility, that inter-Slav relations would now enter an entirely new phase and be based on the liberal principles of liberty, equality and brotherhood. In actual fact, by the time the Neo-Slav movement was launched in 1908 Russian constitutionalism was on the retreat and the autocracy was re-asserting its power, which reduced the likelihood of changes in Russian government policy and, therefore, in no way enhanced the prospects of the movement's success. As Beneš pointed out, the post-revolutionary developments inside Russia deprived Neo-Slavism of its 'ideological basis'.[5] These realities, however, did not reduce the enthusiasm or the optimism of those responsible for the formulation of Neo-Slavism.

In addition to these short term factors giving rise to the Neo-Slav movement, which determined the time of its emergence, there were also longer term reasons for the creation of the movement. One of these is indicated by the fact that Neo-Slavism came

---

[5] Beneš, *Úvahy o slovanství*, p. 193.

into existence largely as a result of Young Czech sponsorship. At the time the Young Czech Party was a prominent, albeit recently weakened, nationalistic force in the Czech lands, but it was also the main political organisation of the Czech industrial and commercial middle class. It was, therefore, primarily dedicated to furthering the social, political and economic interests of this group in Czech society. Due to the intense national rivalry between the Czech and German inhabitants of the Czech lands the Czech middle class had established, towards the end of the nineteenth century, its own economic basis in direct competition with the Bohemian Germans. By the turn of the century the Czechs had achieved considerable successes in certain spheres of commerce and manufacturing, but prospects of further economic expansion were restricted by the limited size of the Czech home market, and by the severe competition with German enterprises within the predominantly German areas of the Dual Monarchy. As a result of these pressures, Czech industry and commerce became increasingly export orientated and became conscious of the considerable openings for trade offered in the relatively underdeveloped Slav lands, both inside and outside the Habsburg Empire. The vast dimension of the Russian Empire and the almost unlimited commercial opportunities there, coupled with the belief that the Russians were a friendly and related people, led the Czech middle class to make strenuous efforts to achieve closer trading links with that country. One of the purposes of the Neo-Slav movement was to assist in attaining this objective – as is evident from the time and energy expended by the Czech leaders of the movement on the abortive attempts to create a Slav bank and to organise a Slav trade and industrial exhibition. Economic considerations were not, however, the sole motivation for the Neo-Slav initiative; other long term causes were equally significant.

Amongst these contributory factors was the tradition of Czech Russophilism. Despite its bourgeois nature and origins the Neo-Slav movement did, for a limited period, enjoy considerable popular support. This can be accounted for by the fact that Czech national consciousness transcended social stratifications. Most Czechs, irrespective of their socio-economic standing, regarded the Bohemian Germans as their chief political and economic rivals and almost instinctively turned to the other Slav nationalities including Russia, for support in their domestic struggle, though still retaining considerable suspicion of Russian political institutions. This attitude was even shared by a substantial section of the Czech Social Democratic Party.

Although general Czech Russophilism undoubtedly did play a role in the Neo-Slav movement, more important still were the related political objectives of Czech 'foreign policy'. The external political aims of the Czech national leadership, though in a sense Russophil, stopped far short of the ultimate expression of this attitude, namely, the wish for incorporation within the Russian state. Obviously during the period concerned, the public declaration of such an objective within the Habsburg Empire was not possible, even if it had been desired. There is, however, no evidence to indicate that such a policy was seriously contemplated. The plans drawn up for the inclusion of the Czech nation within the Russian Empire were not produced until the period of international tension immediately preceding the outbreak of the First World War, and mark a radical departure from previous political thinking on this issue. During most of the period under study the Czech political leadership continued to favour the preservation of the Austro-Hungarian Empire, though in a modified federalised form. It was due to the failure to achieve the desired internal transformation of the Dual Monarchy that, at the turn of the century, the Czech national leadership began actively to seek support for their endeavours outside the Habsburg Empire. This initiative was made in two directions, towards Western Europe and also towards Russia. The approach to Russia appeared somewhat later than that made to the West, and manifested itself largely in the form of Neo-Slavism. But despite the undeniable attraction of Russia, the Czech Neo-Slavs could truthfully claim that they did not desire to change international frontiers. No such changes were included amongst the objectives of Czech 'foreign policy'. Almost the entire political leadership of the Czech nation of whatever political persuasion was, at the time, opposed to the dissolution of the Austro-Hungarian Empire, for it was believed that in no other state system could the national existence of the Czech people be as secure. A fully independent political existence, interposed between the major powers of Germany and Russia, was not regarded as a feasible proposition, nor was the likely outcome of such an experiment, the incorporation into either of the two large states, regarded as desirable. The principal aims of the Czech leadership were twofold. They wished to achieve a reconstruction of the Dual Monarchy on a federal basis, which would enable each component nationality of the Empire to enjoy full cultural and limited political autonomy. In addition, they desired to see the introduction of such a political system in the Habsburg Empire that would enable the Slav peoples to take full advantage of their numerical superiority within the state, and to play a role in the Imperial government at least equal to that of the non-Slav nationalities. It was for these reasons that the majority of the Czech nation actively supported demands for extending the franchise in the Dual Monarchy.

However, even when electoral reform had been accomplished in the Austrian lands of the Habsburg Empire and the Slavs had gained a small theoretical majority in the Vienna Parliament, problems remained. The Slav nationalities within Austria were divided amongst themselves, and appeared unlikely to take advantage of their newfound parliamentary strength. A measure of agreement on political objectives became, therefore, vitally important, and the Neo-Slav movement was designed to facilitate such an understanding between the Austrian Slavs. The major obstacle preventing Slav unity within the Dual Monarchy was the attitude of the Austrian Poles. The Polish ruling class in Galicia, the Austrian division of Poland, in exchange for limited autonomy of the province, had become strong supporters of the Austrian German dominated central authorities in Vienna. A radical realignment of the Poles was, therefore, essential if the objectives of Czech policy were to be achieved. It was widely believed, by the Czechs and others that this would only become possible after Russian oppression of the Polish nation in the Russian division of Poland had ceased, as this fact was considered the main reason for the attachment of the Austrian Poles to the Habsburg authorities. The Czech Neo-Slavs, dedicated to achieving Slav unity, paid great attention to obtaining the support of the Poles, and the achievement of a Russo-Polish understanding in Russian Poland became, therefore, the prime immediate concern of the movement. Although the Austrian Poles never became deeply involved with the Neo-Slav movement, a substantial section of Polish opinion inside Russia led by Dmowski did, for a time, adhere to it. But, despite intense concentration on the problem, the Neo-Slavs failed to improve the situation in the Russian division of Poland, and the

Russian Poles withdrew from the movement. Responsibility for the failure to achieve an understanding between the Russians and the Poles rested entirely with the Russian authorities. The Russian government showed no comprehension whatsoever of Neo-Slav aspirations and its continuing repressive activities in Russian Poland condemned the movement to failure.

Russian officialdom was not alone in adopting a position of total disinterest in the Neo-Slav movement; other sections of Russian society reacted likewise. Included amongst these were persons of liberal outlook, contained mostly within the Kadet Party, situated near the centre of the Russian political spectrum, who had achieved increased prominence in Russian political life following the 1905 Revolution. It was this group that the Czech Neo-Slavs were particularly anxious to interest in the movement, partly in order to enhance the credibility of the movement's claim to enlightenment and liberalism, and partly because it was believed that only these new political forces in Russia could achieve the much desired understanding with the Poles. Although several prominent Russian liberals did show an interest in the movement during its initial stages and were present at the Prague Congress in 1908, they later turned completely away from Neo-Slavism. In general, the Russian liberals avoided association with a movement which based its appeal on the close ethnic relationship between the Slav peoples, in order to avoid the danger of becoming tainted by Pan-Slavism and its reactionary connotations. Doubtless also relevant is the fact that, after 1907, Russian liberalism was struggling to preserve its own political position in a climate of increasing reaction and had little time for pursuing external interests, even had these been desirable.

The lack of interest shown by moderate Russian political opinion in the Neo-Slav movement left the field open to the adherents of traditional Russian Pan-Slavism, characterised by its uncritical admiration of Russian autocracy and its dedication to the Russian Orthodox faith. When the Second Neo-Slav Congress met in Sofia in 1910 the Russian branch of the movement was almost entirely dominated by persons possessing such conservative political attitudes. This development caused considerable displeasure to the Czech instigators of the movement, who were anxious to avoid becoming associated with what they regarded as the discredited traditional form of Russian Pan-Slavism. The

Czech Neo-Slavs wished not to be connected with Russian con-
servatism, in order to increase the popular appeal of the movement amongst the non-Russian Slav peoples and in addition were
aware of the fact that the principal interests of Russian Pan-
Slavism tended to be concentrated on the Orthodox Slavs of the
Balkans at the expense of the religiously distinct Western Slavs.
Despite evident similarities of outlook the Russian Pan-Slavs
recieved little support from their government, although the Tsarist
authorities did utilise Pan-Slavism whenever it suited the requirements of their foreign policy. Neither was the Russian government
interested in the Neo-Slavs though subsequently, in the years
immediately preceding the outbreak of the First World War, it
did pay somewhat increased attention to the affairs of the Slavs
within the Dual Monarchy, including those of the Czechs and
Slovaks. This development did not occur until the Russian authorities became aware of the likelihood of military conflict with the
Habsburg Empire, by which time the Neo-Slav movement had
faded into oblivion. Prior to the deterioration of relations between
Russia and Austria–Hungary, when the Russian government still
maintained hopes of coming to terms with the Dual Monarchy, it,
naturally, attempted to achieve an understanding with the Habsburg authorities and not with the powerless Austrian Slavs.

The Austrian government, predominantly German in character,
also had little use for Neo-Slavism, though it did tolerate its
existence. For a brief period, in fact, it hoped that the movement
could be exploited to achieve a closer relationship with the Russian
Empire. Sharing a common dynastic tradition with Russia, the
Habsburg authorities contemplated the formation of an alliance
between the two powers and including the German Empire as a
third member. The power interests of Austria–Hungary, however,
took precedence over monarchical solidarity and relations between
Russia and the Dual Monarchy grew progressively more strained
after the annexation of Bosnia and Herzegovina in 1908. The
deterioration in relations between the two powers was due chiefly
to the fact that, following the reverse sustained at the hands of the
Japanese in the Far East, the Russian government transferred the
focus of its foreign policy to the Balkan area where Russian
interests came into conflict with those of the Habsburg Empire.

The absence of a lasting understanding between the governments
of Austria–Hungary and Russia sealed the fate of the Neo-Slav

Conclusion

movement, and simultaneously proved conclusively its ineffective-
ness. It became evident that the Neo-Slavs possessed insufficient
power to influence the policies of the governments concerned even
to maintain favourable conditions for the movement's continuing
development, let alone to achieve their ultimate objectives. An
essential precondition for the successful existence of the movement
was the continuation of an atmosphere of cordiality between the
two major powers concerned. As soon as it had become evident
to the Vienna authorities that their interests and those of Russia
could not be reconciled, Neo-Slavism lost its potential usefulness
and was treated with increasing suspicion. Without the benevolent
neutrality of the Habsburg authorities, the Czech founders of the
Neo-Slav movement could not persevere in their thankless quest for
greater Slav understanding. Similarly, nothing could be achieved
without at least the tacit consent of the Russian authorities.

Kramář, however, disputed this explanation of the failure of
Neo-Slavism offered by Beneš, in his critique of the movement.[6]
The movement's founder argued that it was the inability of the
Russians and the Poles to come to terms that caused the extinction
of the movement, and that relations between Russia and Austria–
Hungary were of no relevance.[7] His reasoning was based on the
belief that a Russo-Polish understanding was the vital prerequisite
for Slav co-operation in Austria–Hungary, which would enable the
Habsburg Slavs to play a more effective political role within their
state, and ultimately bring about a firm alliance with Russia.
Beneš, however, had fewer illusions about the capabilities of Neo-
Slavism and analysed the movement against the conditions in
which it existed rather than against its ambitions.

The demise of Neo-Slavism was not, however, entirely due to
external factors but also to the internal contradictions and in-
adequacies of the movement. The Neo-Slavs persistently attempted
to avoid potentially embarrassing domestic and international
complications by ostensible non-involvement in matters of a
political nature. Nevertheless, inescapably, despite all protestation
to the contrary, the movement did have political objectives, as
Kramář himself subsequently admitted.[8] These, however, could
not be expressed openly at the time, as neither the existing internal

---

[6] *Ibid.*, p. 156.   [7] Kramář, *Na obranu*, pp. 27–8.
[8] *Proces dra. Kramáře*, II, pp. 331–3. At his trial Kramář stated: 'Naturally
with the Neo-Slav movement I also followed political objectives.'

conditions within the Dual Monarchy, nor the current climate of relations between Austria–Hungary and Russia, would permit this. In the absence of an overtly defined political programme, the Neo-Slavs were compelled to restrict their appeal for Slav co-operation to cultural and economic matters which, although attractive in themselves, were insufficiently rewarding to acquire adequate lasting support. The Neo-Slavs were in fact confronted with an insoluble dilemma. Without a definite political programme the movement had little chance of achieving its aims, yet if its full political objectives had been enunciated its very existence would have immediately been placed in jeopardy. In launching the Neo-Slav movement Kramář and his colleagues were, in fact, attempting to achieve the impossible.

Bibliography

UNPUBLISHED SOURCES

Haus-, Hof- und Staatsarchiv, Vienna – Politisches Archiv.
Public Record Office, London – Foreign Office.
Heinz, O. 'Der Neoslawismus'. Unpublished doctoral dissertation for
the University of Vienna, 1963.

PUBLISHED SOURCES

DOCUMENTS

British Documents on the Origins of the War, 1898–1914, ed. G. P. Gooch
and H. Temperley. 11 vols. London, 1926–38.
Dotaz německých poslanců o chování se českého národa za války, ed.
Z. V. Tobolka. 2 vols. Prague, 1918.
Foreign Office Peace Handbooks, vol. I, no. 1, 'Austria–Hungary'; no. 2,
'Bohemia and Moravia'; no. 3, 'Slovakia'; no. 4, 'Austrian Silesia'.
London, 1920.
Gosudarstvennaya duma, stenograficheskie otchety. St Petersburg, 1906–14.
*Die Grosse Politik der Europäischen Kabinette 1871–1914. Sammlung der
Diplomatischen Akten des Auswärtigen Amtes*, ed. J. Lepsius, A. M.
Bartholdy, and F. Thimme. 40 vols. Berlin, 1922–7.
Jednání I. přípravného slovanského sjezdu v Praze 1908. Prague, 1910.
K.K. Statistische Central-Commission. *Österreichische Statistik*, vol. VII,
part 1, 'Die Ergebnisse der Reichratswahlen im Jahre 1911'.
Vienna, 1912.
Österreichisches Statistisches Handbuch, 1901. Vienna, 1902.
*Léta 1906–1907. Prameny k revolučnímu hnutí a ohlasu první ruské
revoluce v českých zemích v letech 1905–1907*, ed. O. Kodedová and
others. Prague, 1962.
*Mezhdunarodnye otnosheniya v epokhu imperializma. Dokumenty iz
arkhivov tsarskogo i vremennogo pravitel'stv 1878–1917 gg.*, ed.
M. N. Pokrovsky and others. Series II (1900–13) 20 vols; series III
(1914–17) 10 vols. Moscow–Leningrad, 1931–9.
Obžalovací spis proti Václavu Klofáčovi a Rudolfu Giuniovi, ed. Z. V.
Tobolka. Prague, 1919.

L'Office Central de Statistique du Royaume de Hongrie. *Annuaire statistique hongrois, 1901.* Budapest, 1903.

Österreich-Ungarns Aussenpolitik von der bosnischen Krise bis zum Kriegsausbruch 1914: Diplomatische Aktenstüke des Österreichisch-Ungarischen Ministeriums des Äussern, compiled by L. Bittner; A. F. Pribram; H. Srbik; and H. Uebersberger, ed. L. Bittner and H. Uebersberger. 8 vols. Vienna, 1930.

Památník šestého sletu všesokolského v Praze 1912. Prague, 1912.

Pátý slet všesokolský v Praze ve dnech 28.–30. června a 1. července 1907, ed. J. Scheiner. Prague, 1907.

Proces dra. Kramáře a jeho přátel, ed. Z. V. Tobolka. 5 vols. Prague, 1918–20.

Proekt programy obscheslavyanskoi vystavki v Rossii. Prague, 1909.

Rok 1905. Prameny k revolučnímu hnutí a ohlasu první ruské revoluce v českých zemích v letech 1905–1907, ed. O. Kodedová and others. Prague, 1959.

Slovanská banka. Zpráva a návrhy českého výboru slovanského komitétu. Prague, 1909.

Stenographische Protokolle über die Sitzungen des Hauses der Abgeordneten des österreichische Reichstrates. Vienna, 1898–1914.

Stenographische Sitzungs-Protokolle der Delegation des Reichsrates. Vienna, 1898–1914.

Vtori podgotovitelen Slavyanski săbor v Sofiya. Sofia, 1911.

IV. Slet všesokolský pořádaný v Praze, ed. J. Scheiner. Prague, 1901.

NEWSPAPERS

Čas	*Neue Freie Presse*
České slovo	*Novoe vremya*
Den	*Právo lidu*
Lidové noviny	*Rech'*
Národní listy	*The Times*

BOOKS

(Symposia containing several relevant articles are listed below, but the individual contributions are also listed as articles.)

Allen, W. E. D. *The Ukraine: A History.* Cambridge, 1940.

Aksakov, N. P. *Vseslovyanstvo,* preface by S. T. Sharapov. Moscow, 1910.

Albertini, L. *The Origins of the War of 1914,* trans. and ed. I. M. Massey. 3 vols. London, 1952–7.

Albrecht-Carrié, R. *A Diplomatic History of Europe Since the Congress of Vienna.* London, 1958.

Beneš, E. *La Problème autrichien et la question tchèque. Étude sur les luttes politiques des nationalités slaves en Autriche.* Paris, 1908.
Úvahy o slovanství. Hlavní problémy slovanské politiky, 2nd edn. Prague, 1947.
Beuer, G. *New Czechoslovakia and her Historical Background.* London, 1947.
Bidlo, J. *Dějiny slovanstva,* vol. 1 of *Slované: Kulturní obraz slovanského světa,* ed. M. Weingart. Prague, 1927.
Bidlo, J. and Polívka, J., eds. *Slovanstvo. Obraz jeho minulosti a přítomnosti.* Prague, 1912.
Bobrinsky, V. A. *Prazhsky sezd. Chekhiya i Prikarpatskaya Rus'.* St Petersburg, 1909.
Boghitschewitsch, M. *Die auswärtige Politik Serbiens, 1903–1914.* 3 vols. Berlin, 1928–31.
Bosl, K. ed. *Handbuch der Geschichte der böhmischen Länder.* 4 vols. Stuttgart, 1967–70.
Bretholz, B. *Geshichte Böhmens und Mährens.* 4 vols. Reichenberg, 1922–4.
Buchanan, Sir G. *My Mission to Russia and Other Diplomatic Memories.* 2 vols. London, 1923.
Butvín, J. and Havránek, J. *Dějiny Československa,* vol. III, *1781–1918.* Prague, 1968.
Čapek, K. *Hovory s T.G. Masarykem.* London, 1941.
Čapek, T. *The Slovaks of Hungary; Slavs and Panslavism.* New York, 1906.
Carlgren, W. M. *Iswolsky und Aehrenthal vor der bosnischen Annexionskrise. Russische und osterreichisch-ungarische Balkanpolitik 1906–1908.* Uppsala, 1955.
Čejchan, V., ed. *Dějiny česko-ruských vztahů 1770–1917,* vol. 1 of *Dějiny československo-sovětských vztahů nové a nejnovější doby.* Prague, 1967.
Černý, A. *K otázce shody rusko-polské* (Reprinted from *Slovanský přehled,* II, 1900). Prague, 1900.
Masaryk a Slovanstvo. Prague, 1921.
Československá akademie věd. *Přehled československých dějin.* 3 vols. Prague, 1958–60.
Charmatz, R. *Österreichs äussere und innere politik von 1895 bis 1914.* Leipzig–Belin, 1918.
Chmielewski, E. *The Polish Question in the Russian State Duma.* Knoxville, 1970.
Clementis, V. *'Panslavism', Past and Present,* trans. P. Selver, London, 1943.
Slováci a Slovanstvo, intro. J. David. London, 1943.
Czech National Alliance in Great Britain . *Austrian Terrorism in Bohemia,* intro. T. G. Masaryk. London, 1916.

Dmowski, R. *Niemcy, Rosya i kwestya polska*. Lvov, 1908.

Dolanský, J. *Masaryk a Rusko předrevoluční*. Prague, 1959.

Doležal, J. and Beránek, J. *Ohlas první ruské revoluce v českých zemích*. Prague, 1954.

Dr. Karel Kramář: K šedesátým narozeninám jeho. Prague, 1920.

Drage, G. *Austria–Hungary*. London, 1909.

Russian Affairs. London, 1904.

Efremov, P. N. *Vneshnaya politika Rossii, 1907–1914 gg*. Moscow, 1961.

Eliot, Sir C. *Turkey in Europe*, 2nd edn. London, 1965.

Erickson, J. *Panslavism*. London, 1964.

Fadner, F. *Seventy Years of Pan-Slavism in Russia; Karazin to Danilevskii, 1800–1870*. Georgetown, 1962.

Fay, S. B. *The Origins of the World War*, 2nd edn. 2 vols. London, 1936.

Fischel, A. *Der Panslavismus bis zum Weltkrieg*. Stuttgart–Berlin, 1919.

Florinsky, M. T. *Russia: A History and an Interpretation*. 2 vols. New York, 1960.

Gooch, G. P. *Before the War: Studies in Diplomacy*. 2 vols. London 1936–8.

History of Modern Europe, 1878–1919. London, 1923.

Recent Revelations of European Diplomacy, 4th edn. London, 1940.

Grabowski, T. S. *S.S. Bobczew, historyk, publicysta i słowianofil bułgarski*, vol. 1 of *Poprzez Słowiańszczyzne*. Cracow, 1910.

Gueshoff, I. E. *The Balkan League*, trans. C. C. Mincoff. London, 1915.

Halecki, O. *A History of Poland*. London, 1955.

Hejret, J. *Češi a Slovanstvo*. London, 1943.

Helmreich, E. C. *The Diplomacy of the Balkan Wars 1912–1913*. Cambridge, Mass., 1938.

Hermann, A. H. *A History of the Czechs*. London, 1975.

Hodža, M. *Federation in Central Europe: Reflections and Reminiscences*. London, 1942.

Hölzle, E. *Der Osten in ersten Weltkrieg*. Leipzig, 1944.

Hosking, G. A. *The Russian Constitutional Experiment: Government and Duma, 1907–1914*. Cambridge, 1973.

Hribar, I. *Moji spominy*. 4 vols. Ljubljana, 1928–33.

Hrubý J. *Slovanská vzájemnost v časopisech*. Prague, 1910.

Hrushevsky, M. *A History of Ukraine*, ed. O. J. Frederiksen, preface G. Vernadsky. New Haven, 1941.

Izvolsky, A. P. *The Memoirs of Alexander Iswolsky*, ed. and trans. C. L. Seeger. London, 1920.

Jaszi, O. *The Dissolution of the Habsburg Monarchy*, 2nd edn. Chicago, 1961.

Jenks, W. A. *The Austrian Electoral Reform of 1907*. New York, 1950.

Jirásek, J. *Rusko a my. Dějiny vztahů československo-ruských od nej-staršich dob do roku 1914*, 2nd edn. 4 vols. Prague, 1945–6.

Kaizl, J. *Z mého života*, arranged Z. V. Tobolka. 3 vols. Prague, 1909–14.

Kann, R. A. *The Multinational Empire: Nationalism and National Refcrm in the Habsburg Monarchy, 1848–1918.* 2 vols. New York, 1950.

Kohn, H. *Pan-Slavism: Its History and Ideology.* Notre Dame, 1953. Also 2nd revised edn. New York, 1960.

Kokovtsov, V. N. *Iz moego proshlago. Vospominaniya 1903–1919 gg* 2 vols. Paris, 1933.

Komarov, G. V. *Po slavyanskim zemlyami. Posle prazhskogo sezda,* 2nd edn. St Petersburg, 1909.

Korablev, V. N. *Slavyansky sezd v Prage 1908 goda* (Reprinted from *Slavyanskiya izvestiya.*). St Petersburg, 1908.

Kosch, W. *Die Deutschen in Österreich und ihr Ausgleich mit den Tschechen.* Leipzig, 1909.

Kovařík, F. *Zážitky a dojmy ruského Čecha za carství.* Prague, 1932.

Kramář, K. *In memoriam.* Prague, 1913.

Na obranu slovanské politiky. Prague, 1926.

Paměti Dr. Karla Kramáře, arranged K. Hoch. Prague, 1938.

Pět přednášek o zahraniční politice. Prague, 1922.

Poznámky o české politice. Prague, 1906.

Problémy české politiky. Dvě řeči. Prague, 1913.

Křížek, J. *T. G. Masaryk a naše dělnická třída.* Prague, 1955.

Krofta, K., ed. *Dějiny československé.* Prague, 1946.

Politická postava Karla Kramáře. Prague, 1930.

Leger, L. P. M. *Le Panslavisme et l'intérêt français.* Paris, 1917.

Lettrich, J. *History of Modern Slovakia.* London, 1956.

Lützow, F. *Bohemia: An Historical Sketch.* London, 1910.

Macartney, C. A. *The Habsburg Empire, 1790–1918.* London, 1968.

Macůrek, J. *ČSR a SSSR. Pohled na dějinné styky československo-ruské.* Brno, 1947.

ed. *Slovanství v českém národním životě.* Brno, 1947.

Maklakov, V. A. *Vlast' i obshchestvennost' na zakate staroi Rossii. Vospo-minaniya.* 3 vols. Paris, 1936.

Masaryk, T. G. *Der Agramer Hochverratsprozess und die Annexion von Bosnien und Herzegowina,* 2nd edn. Vienna, 1909.

Naše nynější krise. Pád strany staročeské a počátkové směrů nových, 6th edn. Prague, 1948.

Politická situace. Poznámky ku poznámkám. Prague, 1906.

Rakouská zahraniční politika a diplomacie. Prague, 1911.

The Slavs among the Nations (reprinted from *La Nation Tchèque* of 15 March 1916). London, 1916.

The Spirit of Russia: Studies in History, Literature, and Philosophy, trans. E. and C. Paul. 2 vols. London, 1919, 3rd vol., trans. R. Bass, London, 1967.

Světová revoluce za války a ve válce. Prague, 1925.

Matuš, K. *Paměti.* Prague, 1921.

Maurice, C. E. *Bohemia, from the Earliest Times to the Foundation of the Czecho-Slovak Republic in 1918,* 2nd edn. London, 1922.

May, A. J. *The Hapsburg Monarchy, 1867–1914.* Cambridge, Mass., 1951.

Miller, W. *The Ottoman Empire and its Successors, 1801–1927,* 3rd edn. London, 1966.

Milyukov, P. N. *Vospominaniya, 1859–1917,* ed. M. M. Karpovich and B. I. Elkin. 2 vols. New York, 1955.

Monroe, W. S. *Bohemia and the Čechs.* London, 1910.

Mousset, A. *The World of the Slavs,* trans. A. M. Lavenu. London, 1950.

Namier, L. B. (Sir L.) *Germany and Eastern Europe,* intro. H. A. L. Fisher. London, 1915.

Vanished Supremacies: Essays on European History 1812–1918. London, 1958.

Nejedlý, Z. *Boje o nové Rusko,* 3rd edn. Prague, 1953.

Dr. Kramář: Rozbor politického zjevu. Prague, 1920.

Nicolson, H. *Sir Arthur Nicolson, Bart., First Lord Carnock: A Study of the Old Diplomacy.* London, 1930.

Niederle, L. *Slovanský svět. Zeměpisný a statistický obraz současného Slovanstva.* Prague, 1909.

Nosek, V. *Independent Bohemia: An Account of the Czech-Slovak Struggle for Liberty.* London, 1918.

The Spirit of Bohemia. London, 1926.

Papoušek, J. *Carské Rusko a naše osvobození.* Prague, 1927.

Masaryk a naše revoluční hnutí v Rusku. Prague, 1925.

Pares, Sir B. *A History of Russia,* 4th edn. London, 1955.

My Russian Memoirs. London, 1931.

Paulová, M. *Balkánské války 1912–1913 a český lid.* Prague, 1963.

Dějiny Maffie. Odboj Čechů a Jihoslovanů za světové války 1914–1918. 2 vols. Prague, 1937.

Perman, D. *The Shaping of the Czechoslovak State: Diplomatic History of the Boundaries of Czechoslovakia, 1914–1920.* Leiden, 1962.

Petrovich, M. B. *The Emergence of Russian Panslavism 1856–1870.* New York, 1956.

Pfaff, I. and Závodský, V. *Tradice česko-ruských vztahů v dějinách. Projevy a doklady.* Prague, 1957.

Pogodin, A. L. *Slavyanski mir: Politicheskoe i ekonomicheskoe polozhenie slavyanskikh narodov pered voinoy 1914 goda.* Moscow, 1915.

Portal, R. *The Slavs,* trans. P. Evans. London, 1969.

Pribram, A. F. *Austrian Foreign Policy 1908–1918,* foreword G. P. Gooch. London, 1923.

The Secret Treaties of Austria–Hungary, 1879–1914, English ed. A. C. Colridge. 2 vols. Cambridge, Mass., 1920–1.

Puškarev, S. G. and Šapilovský, V. P., eds. *Karel Kramář a Slovanstvo.* Prague, 1937.

Radić, S. *Slovanská politika v habsburské monarchii.* Prague, 1902.

Reddaway, W. F., Penson, J. H., Halecki, O., and Dyboski, R., eds. *The Cambridge History of Poland.* 2 vols. London, 1941–50.

Riasanovsky, N. V. *A History of Russia*, 2nd edn. Oxford, 1969.

Riha, T. *A Russian European: Paul Miliukov in Russian Politics.* Notre Dame, 1969.

Šantrůček, B. *Václav Klofáč: (1868–1928). Pohledy do života a díla.* Prague, 1928.

Sazonov, S. D. *Vospominaniya.* Paris–Berlin, 1927.

Schlesinger, R. *Central European Democracy and its Background: Economic and Political Group Organization.* London, 1953.

Federalism in Central and Eastern Europe. London, 1945.

Schmitt, B. E. *The Annexation of Bosnia, 1908–1909.* Cambridge, 1937.

The Coming of the War, 1914. 2 vols. New York, 1930.

Selver, P. *Masaryk*, intro. J. Masaryk. London, 1940.

Seton-Watson, H. *The Decline of Imperial Russia, 1855–1914.* London, 1952.

The Russian Empire, 1801–1917. Oxford, 1967.

Seton-Watson, R. W. *The Balkans, Italy and the Adriatic.* London, 1915.

Europe in the Melting Pot. London, 1919.

(*Scotus Viator*). *The Future of Austria–Hungary and the Attitude of the Great Powers.* London, 1907.

German, Slav and Magyar: A Study in the Origins of the Great War. London, 1916.

A History of the Czechs and Slovaks. London, 1943.

Masaryk in England. Cambridge, 1943.

The New Slovakia. Prague, 1924.

(*Scotus Viator*). *Racial Problems in Hungary.* London, 1908.

The Rise of Nationality in the Balkans. London, 1917.

The Role of Bosnia in International Politics, 1875–1914. London, 1931.

The Southern Slav Question and the Habsburg Monarchy. London, 1911.

Seton-Watson, R. W. and others. *Slovakia Then and Now: A Political Survey*, arranged R. W. Seton-Watson. London, 1931.

Seton-Watson, R. W., Wilson, J. D., Zimmern, A. E., and Greenwood, A. *The War and Democracy.* London, 1914.

Sirotinin, A. N. *Rossiya i Slavyane.* St Petersburg, 1913.

Sís, V. ed. *Dr. Karel. Kramář. Život, dílo, práce vůdce národa.* 2 vols. Prague, 1936–7

Karel Kramář. Život a dílo. Prague, 1930.
ed. *Odkaz a pravda Dr. Karla Kramáře.* Prague, 1939.
Sísová, M., and others. *Karel Kramář. K padesátým narozeninám jeho.* Prague, 1910.
Smith, C. J. *The Russian Struggle for Power, 1914–1917.* New York, 1956.
Šolle, Z. *České země v období rozmachu kapitalismu a nástupu imperialismu.* Prague, 1956.
Srb, A. *Politické dějiny národa českého od počátku doby konstituční,* 2 vols. Prague, 1926.
Šťastný, V. and others, eds. *Slovanství v národním životě Čechů a Slováků.* Prague, 1968.
Stavrianos, L. S. *The Balkans since 1453.* New York, 1965.
Steed, H. W. *The Hapsburg Monarchy,* 2nd edn. London, 1914.
Through Thirty Years, 1892–1922: A Personal Narrative. 2 vols. London, 1924.
Sumner, B. H. *Russia and the Balkans, 1870–1880.* Oxford, 1937.
Survey of Russian History. London, 1944.
Tsardom and Imperialism in the Far East and Middle East, 1880–1914. London, 1940.
Taylor, A. J. P. *The Habsburg Monarchy, 1809–1918. A History of the Austrian Empire and Austria–Hungary,* 2nd edn. London, 1948.
The Struggle for Mastery in Europe, 1848–1918. Oxford, 1957.
Tcharykow, N. V. *Glimpses of High Politics: Through War and Peace, 1855–1929.* London, 1931.
Temperley, H. W. V. *History of Serbia.* London 1917.
Thaden, E. C. *Russia and the Balkan Alliance of 1910.* Pennsylvania, 1965.
Thomson, S. H. *Czechoslovakia in European History,* 2nd edn. Princeton, 1953.
Tobolka, Z. V., ed. *Česká politika.* 5 vols. Prague, 1906–13.
Politické dějiny československého národa od r. 1848 az do dnešní doby. 3 vols. Prague, 1932–6.
Trubetzkoi, G. N. *Russland als Grossmacht,* 2nd edn. Stuttgart, 1917.
Vakar, N. P. *Belorussia: The Making of a Nation.* Cambridge, Mass., 1956.
Valiani, L. *The End of Austria–Hungary.* London, 1973.
Vávra, J. ed. *Z bojů za svobodu a socialismus.* Prague, 1961.
Vernadsky, G. *A History of Russia,* 4th edn. New Haven, 1954.
Vucinich, W. S. *Serbia between East and West: The Events of 1903–1908.* Stanford, 1954.
Wanklyn, H. G. *Czechoslovakia.* London, 1954.
Wedel, O. H. *Austro-German Diplomatic Relations, 1908–1914.* Stanford, 1932.

Weingart, M. *Slovanská vzájemnost; úvahy o jejích základech a osudech.* Bratislava, 1926.

Wichtl, F. *Dr. Karl Kramarsch, der Anstifter des Weltkrieges,* 3rd edn. Munich–Vienna, 1918.

Winter, E. *Der Panslawismus nach den Berichten der österreichisch-ungarischen Botschafter in St Petersburg.* Prague, 1944.

Wiskemann, E. *Czechs and Germans: A Study of the Struggle in the Historic Provinces of Bohemia and Moravia.* London, 1938.

Wolff, R. L. *The Balkans in Our Time.* Cambridge, Mass., 1956.

Young, E. P. *Czechoslovakia: Keystone of Peace and Democracy.* London, 1938.

Zeman, Z. A. B. *The Break-up of the Habsburg Empire 1914–1918. A Study in National and Social Revolution.* London, 1961.

ARTICLES

Abrash, M. 'War Aims toward Austria–Hungary: The Czechoslovak Pivot.' *Russian Diplomacy and Eastern Europe, 1914–1917.* New York, 1963; 78–123.

Bělehrádek, F. 'Školství menšinové a ústřední matice školská.' *Česká politika,* ed. Z. V. Tobolka. 5 vols. Prague, 1906–13; v (1913), 335–430.

Bobchev, S. S. 'Maiskite slavyanski săveshtaniya v Peterburg i Moskva.' *Bălgarska sbirka,* XVI (1909), 404–17.

'Minulata slavyanska godina.' *Bălgarska sbirka,* XVI (1909), 89–93.

'The Slavs after the War.' *The Slavonic and East European Review,* VI (1927–8), 291–301.

'Slavyanskiyat săbor v Sofiya.' *Bălgarska sbirka,* XVII (1910), 141–6.

'Vůdce neoslavismu'. *Dr. Karel Kramář. Život, dílo, práce vůdce národa,* ed. V. Sís. 2 vols. Prague, 1936–7; II, 199–203.

'Za predstoyashtiya slavyanski săbor v Praga.' *Bălgarska sbirka,* XV (1908), 452–64.

'Za slavyanskiya săbor v Praga.' *Bălgarska sbirka,* XV (1908), 557–62.

'Zásluhy Dra. Karla Kramáře o Slovanstvo.' *Karel Kramář a Slovanstvo,* ed. S. G. Puškarev and V. P. Šapilovský. Prague, 1937; 56–61.

Boczkowski, H. 'Dr. Kramář proti Ukrajincům.' *Slovanský přehled,* XIV (1912), 133–5.

'Letošní slovanské sjezdy.' *Moravsko-slezská revue,* VII (1910–11), 38–42.

Borodovčák, V. 'Myšlenka slovanské vzájemnosti na Slovensku v letech 1900–1914.' *Slovanství v národním životě Čechů a Slováků,* ed. V. Šťastný and others. Prague, 1968; 327–43.

'Myšlenka slovanské vzájemnosti v slovenské národní ideologii v letech dualismu 1867–1900.' *Slovanství v národním životě Čechů a Slováků*, ed. V. Šťastný and others. Prague, 1968; 284–300.

Borodovčák, V., Gondor, F., Hrozienčik, J., and Panovová, E. 'K characteru slovensko-ruských vztahů v druhé polovině devatenáctého století.' *Z bojů za svobodu a socialismus*, ed. J. Vávra. Prague, 1961; 96–111.

Bradley, J. F. N. 'Czech Nationalism and Socialism in 1905.' *The Slavic Review*, XIX (1960), 74–84.
'Czech Nationalism in the light of French Diplomatic Reports, 1876–1914.' *The Slavonic and East European Review*, XLII (1963–4), 38–53.
'Czech Pan-Slavism Before the First World War.' *The Slavonic and East European Review*, XL (1961–2), 184–205.
'The Old Catholics and Pan-Slavism in Bohemia in 1904.' *The Slavonic and East European Review*, XXXIX (1960–1), 512–16.

Brož, R. 'Slovanská konference v Praze.' *Pokroková revue*, IV (1907–8), 632–6.

Černý, A. 'Běloruské snahy národní a literární v l. 1909–1910.' *Slovanský přehled*, XIII (1911), 217–23, 401–16.
'Na prahu velké doby. K současným událostem v Rusku.' *Slovanský přehled*, VII (1905), 433–45.
'Nejnovější úvahy o slovanské otázce.' *Slovanský přehled*, X (1908), 113–16, 168–74, 257–61, 300–7.
'Nová kniha o Slovanstvě.' *Slovanský přehled*, XIV (1912), 226–30, 276–9.
'O slovanské vzájemnosti v době přítomné.' *Naše doba*, XIII (1906), 650–8, 735–40, 807–13.
'Odpověd'' na otevřený list L. Pantělějeva.' *Slovanský přehled*, VIII (1906), 12–15.
'Otázka autonomie království polského.' *Slovanský přehled*, VIII (1906), 101–17.
'Otázka cholmská.' *Slovanský přehled*, XIV (1912), 153–8, 213–21.
'Po slovanských dnech v Petrohradě a ve Varšavě.' *Slovanský přehled*, X (1908), 437–46.
'Slovanské sjezdy r. 1908.' *Slovanský přehled*, XI (1909), 7–15, 61–9.

Červinka, V. 'Druhý přípravný sjezd slovanský v Sofii.' *Česká revue*, III (1909–10), 705–15.
'Slovanství na Rusi. Drobný příspěvek k historii posledních let.' *Půl století Národních Listů: Almanach 1860–1910*. Prague, 1910; 83–7.

Charvát, V. 'Tolstoy a Slované.' *Slovanský přehled*, XIII (1911), 105–6.
'Count Leo Tolstoy and the Slavonic Congress at Sofia, 1910.' *The Slavonic and East European Review*, VIII (1929–30), 246–8.

'Diplomaticheskaya podgotovka balkanskoy voiny 1912 g.' *Krasny arkhiv*, VIII (1925), 2–48, IX (1925), 1–131.

Dolanský, J. 'Masaryk a slavjanofilství I. V. Kiřějevského.' *Československá rusistika. Časopis pro slovanské jazyky, literaturu a dějiny SSSR*, I (1956), 230–59.

Faissler, M. A. 'Austria–Hungary and the Disruption of the Balkan League.' *The Slavonic and East European Review*, XIX (1939–40), 141–57.

Grabbe (Count). 'Karel Petrovič Kramář v Petrohradě r. 1908.' *Dr. Karel Kramář. Život, dílo, práce vůdce národa*, ed. V. Sís, 2 vols. Prague, 1936–7; II, 222–5.

Grabowski, T. S. 'Ještě novoslovanský sjezd v Sofii.' *Slovanský přehled*, XIV (1912), 27–32, 78–82, 119–23.

Grobelný, A. 'Ohlas první ruské revoluce na Ostravsku.' *Slovanské historické studie*, I (1955), 181–226.

Hantsch, H. 'Pan-Slavism, Austro-Slavism, Neo-Slavism: The All-Slav Congresses and the Nationality Problems of Austria–Hungary.' *Austrian History Yearbook*, I (1965), 23–37.

Herman, K. 'Česká buržoasie a Rusko v letech 1908–1914.' *Dějiny česko-ruských vztahů 1770–1917*, ed. V. Čejchan. Prague, 1967; 322–30.

'Hlavní rysy česko-ruských vztahů v letech 1870–1917.' *Z bojů za svobodu a socialismus*, ed. J. Vávra. Prague, 1961; 81–95.

'K vývoji českého kapitálu.' *Otázky vývoje kapitalismu v českých zemích a v Rakousku-Uhersku do roku 1918.* Prague, 1957; 76–88.

'Novoslovanství a česká buržoasie.' *Kapitoly z dějin vzájemných vztahů národů ČSR a SSSR.* Prague, 1958; 236–310.

'Slovanství v českém životě v době nástupu imperialismu.' *Slovanství v národním životě Čechů a Slováků*, ed. V. Šťastný and others. Prague, 1968; 301–26.

Herman, K. and Sládek, Z. 'Karel Kramář a jeho slovanství.' *Slovanský přehled*, LVI (1970), 321–36.

'Slovanská politika Karla Kramáře.' *Rozpravy československé akademie věd. Řada společenských věd*, LXXXI, no. 2 (1971).

Hevera, J. S. 'Novoslovanství.' M. Sísova and others, *Karel Kramář. K padesátým narozeninám jeho*. Prague, 1910; 130–47.

Hoch, K. 'Politická koncepce.' M. Sísova and others, *Karel Kramář. K padesátým narozeninám jeho*. Prague, 1910; 49–79.

Horejsek, J. 'Neúspěšný obchod Živnobanky v Polsku.' *Slovanský přehled*, LVII (1971), 139–45.

Hribar, I. 'Několik vzpomínek.' *Dr. Karel Kramář: K šedesátým narozeninam jejo.* Prague, 1920; 31–4.

'Slovanský postup.' *Máj*, IX (1911), 617–19, 629–30.

'Slovutnému jubilantu pozdrav.' *Dr. Karel Kramář. Život, dílo, práce vůdce národa*, ed. V. Sís. 2 vols. Prague, 1936–7; II, 207–8.

Bibliography 269

Janda, M. 'Několik poznámek ke stykům V. I. Lenina s Česko-
slovanskou stranou sociálně demokratickou.' *Z bojů za svobodu a
socialismus*, ed. J. Vávra. Prague, 1961; 124–5.
Kerner, R. J. 'The Czechoslovaks from the Battle of White Mountain
to the World War.' *Czechoslovakia: Twenty Years of Independence*,
ed. R. J. Kerner. Los Angeles, 1940; 29–50.
Kieniewicz, S. and Wereszycki H. 'Poland under Foreign Rule,
1795–1918'. *History of Poland*. Warsaw, 1968; 399–633.
Kodedová, O. 'Národnostní otázka v letech 1905–1907.' *Československý
časopis historický*, III (1955), 192–222.
Kohn, H. 'The Impact of Pan-Slavism on Central Europe.' *The Review
of Politics*, XXIII (1961), 321–33.
'The Viability of the Habsburg Monarchy.' *The Slavic Review*, XXII
(1963), 37–42.
Kolejka, J. 'Moravský pakt z roku 1905.' *Československý časopis
historický*, IV (1956), 590–615.
Konirsh, S. G. 'Constitutional Aspects of the Struggle between
Germans and Czechs in the Austro-Hungarian Monarchy.' *The
Journal of Modern History*, XXVII (1955), 231–61.
Kořálka, J. 'The Czech Question in International Relations at the
Beginning of the 20th Century.' *The Slavonic and East European
Review*, XLVIII (1969–70), 248–60.
Kovalevsky, E. P. 'Representative man.' *Dr. Karel Kramář. Život, dílo,
práce vůdce národa*, ed. V. Sís. 2 vols. Prague, 1936–7; II, 227–30.
Kozicki, S. 'Roman Dmowski, 1864–1939.' *The Slavonic and
East European Review*, XVIII (1939), 118–28.
Kramář, K. 'L'Avenir de l'Autriche.' *Revue de Paris*, VI, part I,
(January–February 1899), 577–600.
'Dojmy z Ruska.' *Čas*, V (1891), 5–6, 22–4, 52–5, 69–72, 84–5.
'Europe and the Bohemian Question.' *The National Review*, XL
(September 1902–February 1903), 183–205.
'M. Kramář et la politique slave.' *Le Monde Slave* (new series),
III, no. 11 (1926), 283–303.
'Po petrohradských konferencích.' *Česká revue*, II (1908–9), 577–82.
'Předmluva.' *Slovanstvo. Obraz jeho minulosti a přítomnosti*, ed.
J. Polívka and J. Bidlo. Prague, 1912; VI–XIV.
'Rakouská zahraniční politika v XIX. stol.' *Česká politika*, ed. Z. V.
Tobolka. 5 vols. Prague, 1906–13; I (1906), 49–181.
'Ruské problémy. *Nová česká revue*, II (1904–5), 241–54.
'Die Slawenkonferenz in Prag.' *Österreichische Rundschau*, XVI
(July–September, 1908), 213–19.
'Za vedení národní strany svobodomyslné.' *Česká politika*, ed. Z. V.
Tobolka. 5 vols. Prague, 1906–13; III (1909), 525–795.
Krejčí, F. V. 'Nové slovanství.' *Akademie*, XII (1908), 439–45.

370 Bibliography

Křížek, J. 'Annexion de la Bosnie et Herzegovine.' *Historica*, IX (1964),
135–203.
'Česká buržoasní politika a "česká otázka" v letech 1900–1914.'
Československý časopis historický, VI (1958), 621–61.
'"Česká otázka" v buržoasní politice na počátku první světové
imperialisticke války.' *Československý časopis historický*, VII (1959),
625–43.
'Slovanské národy a konec habsburské monarchie.' *Slovanský
přehled*, LIV (1968), 353–60, 441–7; LV (1969), 11–19, 186–91.
Landa, M. J. 'Bohemia and the War.' *The Contemporary Review*, CVIII
(July–December 1915), 100–4.
Lappo, J. 'Dr. Karel Kramář a slovanská myšlenka.' *Karel Kramář a
Slovanstvo*, ed. S. G. Puškarev and V. P. Šapilovský. Prague
1937; 18–27.
Laptěva, L. P. 'Vývoj ideje slovanství v Rusku v XIX. a na počátku
XX. století.' *Slovanský přehled*, LIV (1968), 304–9.
Lebedev, V. I. 'Chekhoslovatskaya politika tsarskogo pravitel'stva.'
Volya Rossii, II, no. 8–9 (1924), 209–26.
Lednicki, W. 'Panslavism.' *European Ideologies. A Survey of 20th
Century Political Ideas*, ed. F. Gross. New York, 1948; 808–912.
'Poland and the Slavophil Idea.' *The Slavonic and East European
Review*, VII (1928–9), 128–40.
Leppmann, W. 'Ruský konsulát v Praze. Kapitola k carské politice v
Čechách před světovou válkou.' *Naše revoluce*, XIII (1937), 1–20.
'Russland und die tschechischen Autonomie-bestrebungen vor dem
Weltkriege.' *Berliner Monatschefte*, XII (1934), 1008–22.
Levine, L. 'Pan-Slavism and European Politics.' *Political Science
Quarterly*, XXIX (1914), 664–86.
Macháček, F. 'The Sokol Movement: Its Contribution to Gymnastics.'
The Slavonic and East European Review, XVIII (1938–9), 73–90.
Maklakov, V. A. 'Proti germanismu slovanství.' *Dr. Karel Kramář.
Život, dílo, práce vůdce národa*, ed. V. Sís. 2 vols. Prague, 1936–7;
II, 231–6.
'T. G. Masaryk: Selections from Writings and Speeches,' trans.
R. Selver. *The Slavonic and East European Review*, XIII (1934–5),
522–30.
May, A. J. 'The Novibazar Railway Project.' *The Journal of Modern
History*, X (1938), 496–527.
Miller, H. A. 'Nationalism in Bohemia and Poland.' *The North
American Review*, CC (1914), 879–83.
Milyukov, P. N. 'A New Slavonic Policy.' *The Slavonic and East
European Review*, VI (1927–8), 481–95.
'Slovanstvo a demokracie.' *Slovanský přehled*, XVIII (1926), 17–21.

'The World War and Slavonic Policy.' *The Slavonic and East European Review*, VI (1927–8), 268–90.

Novikov, N. N. 'Panslavismus a osvobozenecké hnutí v Rusku.' *Slovanský přehled*, X (1908), 147–52, 218–23.

Odložilík, O. 'Components of the Czechoslovak Tradition.' *The Slavonic and East European Review*, XXIII (1945), 97–106.

'Russia and Czech National Aspirations.' *Journal of Central European Affairs*, XXII (1963), 407–39.

Pal'o. 'Poznámky k slovanskému sjazdu.' *Průdy*, I (1909), 258–62.

Panther. 'Poles, Czechs and Jugoslavs.' *The New Europe*, III, no. 34 (1917), 219–31.

Papoušek, J. 'Masaryk i Slavyanstvo.' *Volya Rossii*, VIII (1930), 277–94.

'Předpoklady politických vztahů Ruska k Československu v letech 1907–1927.' *Od pravěka k dnešku. Sborník prací z dějin československých*. 2 vols. Prague, 1930; II, 469–99.

Pátek, J. 'Okolo "slovanské banky".' *Pokroková revue*, IV (1907–8), 591–4.

Pogodin, A. L. 'Nemocný Neoslavismus.' *Moravsko-slezská revue*, VI (1910), 438–9.

'Rusko a rakouští Slované.' *Moravsko-slezská revue*, VI (1910), 62–4.

'Ze života Slovanů.' *Moravsko-slezská revue*, VI (1910), 107–9.

Polívka, J. 'Rusko a lux ex Oriente.' *Česká revue*, XII (1918–19), 321–35, 377–84, 433–43, 489–504, 545–53.

'Slovanský sjezd sofijský v červenci 1910.' *Slovanský přehled*, XIII (1911), 22–5, 72–6, 114–21.

Pollák, P. 'Slovanská myšlenka v slovensko-ruských vztazích v době první světové války.' *Slovanství v národním životě Čechů a Slováků*, ed. V. Šťastný and others. Prague, 1968; 359–65.

Popov, A. 'Chekhoslovatsky vopros i tsarskaya diplomatiya v 1914–1917 gg.' *Krasny arkhiv*, XXXIII (1929), 3–33, XXXIV (1929), 3–38.

Prazak, A. 'The Slovak Sources of Kollar's Pan-Slavism.' *The Slavonic and East European Review*, VI (1927–8), 579–92.

Preiss, J. 'Anketa o slovanské výstavě v Praze r. 1913.' *Máj*, IX (1911),1–4 21–3.

Puškarev, S. G. 'Kramář a Rusko.' *Karel Kramář a Slovanstvo*, ed. S. G. Puškarev and V. P. Šapilovský. Prague, 1937; 36–48.

Říha, O. 'O národním hnutí a národnostní otázce 1848–1918.' *Československý časopis historický*, II (1954), 47–68.

'Roman Dmowski o polsko-ruské otázce.' *Česká revue*, I (1907–8), 577–84, 674–81.

Rozvoda, J. 'Přípravný slovanský sjezd v Praze.' *Česká revue*, I (1907–8), 641–6.

'Russia and the Balkan Crisis.' *The Russian Review*, II, no. 2 (1913), 181–2.

272   Bibliography

'Russia and the War in the Balkans.' The Russian Review, I, no. 4 (1912), 150–2.
Samorukov, N. I. 'České a slovenské národní hnutí a národnostní otázka v období kapitalismu a imperialismu.' Československý časopis historický, II (1954), 69–77.
Scheiner, J. 'Sokolstvo.' Slovanstvo. Obraz jeho minulosti a přítomnosti, ed. J. Polívka and J. Bidlo. Prague, 1912; 693–722.
Seton-Watson, R. W. 'Karel Kramář.' The Slavonic and East European Review, XVI (1937–8), 183–9.
'Pan-Slavism.' The Contemporary Review, CX (July–December 1916), 419–28.
Sís, V. 'Dr. Karel Kramář a Slovanstvo.' Karel Kramář a Slovanstvo, ed. S. G. Puškarev and V. P. Šapilovský. Prague, 1937; 27–36.
Sísová, M. 'Život.' M. Sísová and others, Karel Kramář. K padesátým narozeninám jeho. Prague, 1910; 10–48.
Šlaisová, D. 'Ohlas první války balkánské 1912–1913 v českém prostředí.' Slovanské historické studie, I (1955), 227–63.
Slavík, J. 'O slovanskou politiku.' Slovanský přehled, XIX (1927), 90–4.
'Slovanství Karla Kramáře.' Slovanský přehled, XXIX (1937), 185–90.
'Slovanský postup. Anketa Máje.' Máj, IV (1905–6), 414, 433–5, 449–51, 465–8, 481–3, 497–9, 529–32, 545–8, 561–3, 577–9, 593–5, 609–11, 625–7, 641–3, 657–8.
'Slovo úvodní.' Slovanský přehled, I (1899), 1.
Šťastný, V. 'Polemika v Čase roku 1891 o polsko-ruské otázce.' Slovanské historické studie, V (1963), 85–116.
'Slovanství v období českého buržoasního loajalismu a nástupu dělnické třídy.' Slovanství v národním životě Čechů a Slováků, ed. V. Šťastný and others. Prague, 1968; 265–83.
Stronski, S. 'Polský hlas.' Dr. Karel Kramář. Život, dílo, práce vůdce národa, ed. V. Sís. 2 vols. Prague, 1936–7; II, 215–17.
Struve, P. B. 'A Great Russia.' The Russian Review, II, no. 4 (1913), 11–30.
Švihovský, V. 'Slovanské sjezdy.' Naše doba, XVI (1909), 26–31, 98–103.
Thomson, S. H. 'A Century of a Phantom: Panslavism and the Western Slavs.' Journal of Central European Affairs, XI (1951), 57–77.
Tobolka, Z. V. 'Československé politické strany doby predválečné o konečných cílech svého národa.' Idea československého státu, ed. J. Kapras, B. Němec and F. Soukup. 2 vols. Prague, 1936; I, 114–26.
Tresić-Pavičić, A. 'Dr. Kramář – náš přítel.' Dr. Karel Kramář. Život, dílo, práce vůdce národa, ed. V. Sís. 2 vols. Prague, 1936–7; II, 209.
Tůma, K. 'Padesát let boje a práce.' Půl století Národních Listů: Almanach 1860–1910. Prague, 1910; 9–35.

Werstadt, J. 'K úloze Karla Kramáře v našem odboji. Soubor doku-
mentů a projevů.' *Naše revoluce*, XIV (1938), 1–58.
'Masaryk a Seton-Watson. První projekt samostatnosti české z roku
1914.' *Naše revoluce*, IV (1926), 245–66.
Willy. 'S slavyanskogo sezda v Prage.' V. N. Korablev, *Slavyanski
sezd v Prage 1908 goda*. St Petersburg, 1908; 33–44.
Winters, S. B. 'The Young Czech Party (1874–1914): An Appraisal.'
The Slavic Review, XXVIII (1969), 426–44.

Index

For EU product safety concerns, contact us at Calle de José Abascal, 56–1°,
28003 Madrid, Spain or eugpsr@cambridge.org.

www.ingramcontent.com/pod-product-compliance
Ingram Content Group UK Ltd.
Pitfield, Milton Keynes, MK11 3LW, UK
UKHW010348140625
459647UK00010B/910